1943-1975

BRONTE

WATER POLO CLUB

THE SPIRIT OF BRONTE

A History Of
Bronte Amateur Water Polo Club
1943 - 1975

By
Tracy Rockwell

PEGASUS PUBLISHING

The Spirit Of Bronte

A History of Bronte Amateur Water Polo Club
1943 - 1975

by
Tracy Rockwell (1955)

First Published in Australia in 2020
by Pegasus Publishing
PO Box 980, Edgecliff, NSW, 2027

Orders: pegasuspublishing@iinet.net.au
www.pegasuspublishing.com.au

ISBN: 978-1-925909-03-6

Copyright © Pegasus Publishing
An Ashnong Pty Ltd Company

Cover Image:
The legendary Hungarian Olympian 'Kalman Markovits', became the poster boy for Bronte Amateur Water Polo Club, and for the NSW Amateur Water Polo Association and with this impressive image from the 1950's (from 'Water Polo' by Bela Rajki, Museum Press, 1958).

THE SPIRIT OF BRONTE

A History Of
Bronte Amateur Water Polo Club
1943 - 1975

By
Tracy Rockwell

PEGASUS PUBLISHING

CONTENTS

A water polo game underway at Drummoyne Baths, Sydney, circa 1968.

Foreword

Following his masterpiece, "Water Warriors: Chronicle of Australian Water Polo", as well as a number of other books on and off the topic of sport, Dr Tracy Rockwell has been affirmed as the 'Historian' of Australian Water Polo. Therefore, it was a natural choice to have Tracy, himself an outstanding player with Bronte and the Universities Club, put together the history of this once great, but sadly no longer with us, Bronte Water Polo Club, before it was all forgotten.

Assembling all this information, was an enormous and seemingly never ending task, involving many, many hours of research online, at the Mitchell, Waverley Libraries and AWPI offices, as well as through contacting an endless stream of old club members. The 'Bronte Old Boys' network (and it is a great pity that there are no Bronte Young Boys these days), had lit this flame of interest some time ago with the creation of this publication being spoken about for some time,

However, it took Tracy's know-how, his attention to detail and his experience in researching, compiling, editing and publishing, to say nothing of his authorship, to finally bring it all together and produce this great and very worthwhile memorial to a truly great water polo club.

Roland Flesch (Rolly)
Bronte Water Polo Club: 1963-1974

Acknowledgements

While many people contributed in different ways to the production of this book... the following were particularly helpful:

Ted Baldock	*Rolly Flesch*	*Graeme Samuel*
Phil Bower	*Peter Folden*	*Don Sarkies*
Virginia Bower	*Tom Folden*	*Carol Scandrett (Bunton)*
Dave Bullock	*Richard Grills*	*Chris Simpson*
Terry Clark	*Jon Kirkwood*	*Dick Thornett*
Karen Trewhella (Copas)	*Ernie Kritzler*	*John Thornett*
Bob Cope	*Bill McCarthy*	*Robbie Vadas*
John Cotterill	*Peter Montgomery*	*Margaret Wilby*
Lindsay Cotterill	*Dennis Morgon*	*Graeme Wulf*
Oscar Csuvic	*Peter O'Hara*	*... amongst many others*
Brian Ellison	*Peter Primo*	

Introduction

Australians are a modest people, we're not good at remembering important things... we lack the elaborate statues of Europe, the pageantry of England and the flamboyance of the United States. But keeping a record of great events, and of achievements is important. Whereas the arts (paintings, literature, film) aren't normally that significant at the time of their creation, the better ones tend to mature with age, and over time can become incredibly valuable. But sport works in the exact opposite way, in that it's value is immediate, and often after years of hard work, the reward is lifting that coveted trophy. The incredible sacrifice and effort that athletes make to rise at a particular time and capture a championship is ephemeral... and diminishes rapidly after victory. This interesting phenomena is exactly the reason why recording the great deeds of athletes is so very important, and particularly so for the less well documented sports.

Water polo is a widely played participant sport, particularly at schools, but it deserves far greater recognition. As players learn to enjoy the game and become competent, they sometimes progress to playing for one of the many water polo clubs across the country. But it is an honour indeed to become a member of one of the top water polo clubs in Sydney and in NSW, as being champions in that arena is a true mark of distinction! This history is dedicated to the skills, fitness and commitment of the members of Bronte Amateur Water Polo Club, who were indeed champions.

It's not easy making something out of nothing, and although they didn't leave much material to work with, thats exactly how Bronte began. Bronte Club records were scant, never systematically kept and often non-existant, with only results from the NSWAWPA Annual Reports and newspaper cuttings giving an indication of their annual performances. But this history doesn't only feature the Bronte club... it can't! The nature of competition requires a competitor, and it is the victories over difficult competitors that make success all the more sweet... so this history also includes the feats and achievements of many other players and teams from other clubs.

I felt an overwhelming sense of responsibility to publish this book as accurately and as as quickly as possible especially for those unwell, infirm and aging ex-members of the great Bronte Club. I am particularly indebted to Dennis Morgan and Rolly Flesch who over weeks, painstakingly proofed the manuscript, so they deserve special acknowledgement and sincere thanks.

Some 45 years have now passed since the demise of the Bronte Club, but its mark on the history of our great game has not diminished. In closing, it has been my great honour, not only to play for, but to be called upon to write this history of Bronte Amateur Water Polo Club. What follows is a chronological account, indeed a 'family history' of the personalities and heroic performances of a truly great water polo club.

Tracy Rockwell (Rocko)
Bronte Water Polo Club: 1971-1975

BRONTE BEACH &
THE BATHS
(Before 1943)

Men and boys, swim and play in canoes at Bronte beach rock pool. Photo - Sam Hood (1937)

Early Days at Bronte

"Located around 10km from Sydney's CBD and 2km south of Bondi Beach, Bronte is one of the most popular and loved beaches in the entire eastern suburbs. While the beach is relatively small at around 250m in length, what Bronte lacks in size is certainly made up by the charm and character of its surroundings. The sand and rock-lined beach is set against a backdrop of steep cliffs, where today multi-million dollar houses sit perched overlooking Bronte Park, a lovely 10ha valley covered with trees and expansive grasslands that sits behind the beach.

The area around Bronte was originally owned by Mortimer Lewis in the 1830s, who was the Colonial Architect at the time. Mr Lewis sold his 42 acre holding of land to Robert Lowe (Viscount Sherbrooke), who built his home in 1845 and named it Bronte House in honour of Lord Nelson who was the Duke of Bronte in Sicily. The heritage listed bungalow still stands today on what is now Bronte Road and is leased to private tenants by Waverley Council."[1]

▼ *Sydney's Eastern Suburbs was served by a number of different swimming clubs (The Australian Star, 10 April 1908). BELOW: The tramway can be seen in this 1921 photograph of Bronte Beach, as well as the Baths to the left.*

SWIMMING

East Sydney Club—220 yards general handicap, and a 50 yards consolation handicap. Rushcutters Bay Baths.

Waverley Club—66 yards handicap, Bronte Baths.

Eastern Suburbs Club—Members' carnival, Bronte Baths.

BRONTE NEAR SYDNEY.

Bronte Baths

Surf swimming was a dangerous activity with many deaths, but swimming during the long hot Sydney summer came to personify leisure and entertainment for a population that was starved of both. Bronte developed as a picnic location in a secluded area, where you could also swim, but in very unsafe conditions. Local Councils eventually resolved to build baths at Bronte, Bondi and Coogee.

In Waverley, the population in 1887 was relatively small at approximately 2,000 and the area was remote, as most people lived closer to Old South Head Road around Bondi Junction. But a development boom in the 1880's saw a population explosion and families began moving closer to the beaches.

The idea for a pool first began in 1883 when Waverley Council set aside 150 pounds to build sea baths at Bronte. Before the baths there was an existing swimming spot that was protected by natural rocks in the same location, known then as 'the bogey hole at South Nelson Bay.' Construction of Bronte Baths commenced in 1887 under the supervision of A. Williams, an engineer with the NSW Department of Public Works, Harbours and Rivers Branch, and it opened the very same year. At the same time Williams was supervising the building of the Bondi Baths.[2]

BATHING FATALITY AT BRONTE.
PLUCKY ATTEMPTS AT RESCUE.

Considerable excitement was caused amongst the large gathering of holiday seekers at Bronte yesterday afternoon by a bathing fatality. A man named William Fox, married and residing at No 18 Bourke-street, Woolloomooloo, was bathing in the surf, off the beach, about 4pm, when he was carried out by the undertow. As soon us his dangerous position was observed every effort was made to rescue him. A rope having been procured, Mr Lapthorne a member of the Eastern Suburbs Swimming Club, went out to sea as far as the rope would allow, in an attempt to rescue the unfortunate man and although he succeeded in getting in close proximity, the under current was too strong, and frustrated the effort. Two other plucky attempts were made, but unfortunately they were of no avail.

Sydney Morning Herald, 27th Dec 1902

▼ *Surrounded by bathers, a photograph of Bronte Baths on a rough summer day, taken about 1912.*

Bronte Beach, Sydney.

Kerry (Copyright) Sydney.

SURF BRIGADES

Minutes of a meeting of the executive officers of the Surf and Life Saving Clubs held at the Sports Club on Friday 18th October, 1907.

F. Donovan occupied the Chair.

The following Clubs were represented: Manly Surf Club (F.W. Donovan, M.A. Roberts J.J.K. Taylor, S. Ferris, W. Tonge, A.W. Ralph); Bondi Surf Bathers Life Saving Club (E.P. Love, G.H. Henriques, S. Dennis, L. Ormsby); Coogee L.S. Brigade (Claude Daley); Bronte Surf Brigade (H.J. McLauchlin, A. Kemp); Bondi Surf and Social Club (W. Weeks, Jas Clarke, C. Steedman, E.A. Bourke, C. Martens); Maroubra S.C. (J.A. Thorpe); Maroubra (F. Beardmore, S. Manners E. Bell); Royal Life Saving Society (A.J. Hendry-Hon Sec, W.W. Hill); N.S.W.A.S.A. (C. Fitzgerald, A. Male); United Wanderers S.C. (F. Mason); Woollahra Surf Club.

Minutes of Association of Surf and Life Saving Clubs, Waverley Library

---

NSW Amateur Swimming Association

After many efforts on the part of the swimmers, who had to deal with issues like scheduling, lack of co-ordination, the professional swimmers movement and even gambling, the clubs finally succeeded in forming an organisation known as the New South Wales Amateur Swimming Association (NSWASA) on the 22nd February 1892. From that point forward, all amateur aquatic competition regarding swimming, water polo and diving was administered by the NSWASA, with which clubs were thereafter required to affiliate.

Bronte Swimming Clubs

After opening in 1887 the Council initially leased the baths out to private operators. The first manager was Frank Lloyd, followed by Harry Wylie, G. Rowles, the Bond family for almost 50 years, with the final lessee Andrew Cleland, operating the baths well into the 1960s, before Council resumed control over the operation.

▲TOP: A postcard of Bronte Beach, taken in the late 1800's. MID: The new life saving brigades along the Eastern Suburbs held their inaugural meeting on the 18th October 1907. ABOVE: A Bronte surf boat makes a break through the waves.

The formation of swimming clubs soon followed the opening of the baths, and also provided a social focus for the community. Between 1887 and 1894 an abundance of events took place at Bronte, which evolved from a site for 'skinny dipping' into a place with active swimming clubs and organized 'carnivals' that provided local entertainment.

In November 1890 the Waverley Swimming Club held their first tournament at the baths. Four years later the baths scored a coup when the Eastern Suburbs Swimming Club moved its headquarters from the baths at Coogee Aquarium to Bronte.

By 1906 the Waverley Swimming Club and Eastern Suburbs Swimming Club, which were both operating out of Bronte, had merged to form the Eastern Suburbs Swimming Club. In 1941 Eastern Suburbs Swimming Club merged again with Bronte Swimming Club to form the Bronte Amateur Swimming Club, which lasted until 1990.

▼ MID: The Bronte Baths before the installation of handrails. BELOW: Bronte Surf Life Saving Club has been in operation from at least 1907.

BRONTE SURF CLUB

A new surf life-saving club has been formed at Bronte. A meeting was held at the Waverley Council Chambers, and the Mayor of Waverley presided. The following officers were elected: President-Mayor of Waverley (Alderman R.G. Watkins); Hon. Secretary-Mr. E.C. Cohen; Captain-Mr. H. Joseph; Hon. Life Saving Instructor-Mr. J. Bond. The inaugural meeting is to take place on Sunday, 18th October, 1908.

Evening News, 8th October 1908

Bronte Surf Life Saving Club

The history of Bronte Surf Lifesaving Club (SLSC) is somwhat contentious, and complicated. The Surf Life Saving movement did not start with well formed, fully functioning life saving clubs. It began as part of the social and recreational movement of the time. Young people spent the day at the beach with their friends and saving lives was just something that competent people did as a civic duty. The origins of Bronte SLSC are complicated as the main proponents in John Bond, Wylie etc. were also involved in teaching swimming, life saving and physical culture at Bondi, Bronte and Coogee at the same time, and none were based at any particular beach.

▲ TOP: Bronte Baths photographed around 1945. ABOVE: he war came right to Australia's doorstep when three Japanese submarines entered Sydney Harbour and both Sydney and Newcastle were shelled on the 7th and 8th June 1942.

In 1902 a drowning at Bronte was said to result in John Bond forming the first Life Saving Club. Waverley Council had installed single life-lines at Bronte and Bondi and many instances of their use were reported.

In March 1907 members of the Waverley and Eastern Suburbs Swimming Clubs resolved to take up life-saving responsibilities at Bronte. In 1907 Walter Biddel, in association with fellow Waverley Club member H. J. McLaughlin, inaugurated the Bronte Surf Bathing Association. This Association then formed brigades for men, women and juniors who were trained, qualified and put on patrol at Bronte. Biddell also appears to have funded the club.

Surf Life Saving was growing quickly as a movement and by October 1907 an Association of Surf Life Saving Clubs was formed. While Bronte

Brigade was a member, no actual clubhouse existed at that time.

By May 1908, the Royal Life Saving Society was the only body issuing certificates to the surf brigade. Ladies were instructed by Biddell, while male members at Bronte were instructed by Lester Ormsby of the Bondi Surf Bathers Life Saving Club.

▲The crowds flocked back to Bronte Beach at the conclusion of World War II. ▼Water polo began in the late 1860s, but arrived in Australia thanks to Frederick Cavill in 1879.

Bronte SLSC was formed on 8th October 1908, with the instructor being John Bond, while the club president was the Mayor of Waverley. The minutes of the first meeting of the Surf Bathing Association of N.S.W. show the Bronte Surf Brigade as being an inaugural member with H. J. McLauchlin from the swimming clubs as their representative.

The Bronte Brigade under Biddle, and the Surf Life Saving Club co-existed for a few years. Biddle built a club room, provided reels and did most of the patrol activity. But all the evidence shows that he ran his club like a business, wheras what the beach community wanted was a social club, which the surf life saving club provided. After his health failed, Biddle soon left the scene and the surf life savers eventually won out.

Water Polo & Bronte

Water Polo in England & Australia

Water polo as a sport first appeared in England at the Serpentine Club's Gala in 1868. Being initially introduced as a form of entertainment by Mr. Frederick Cavill, the new game spread quickly to Scotland, Wales and Ireland ahead of its introduction to the British colonies, Europe and North America. But it was Cavill, later known as Professor Cavill, who personally introduced the game to Australia, when he and his family emigrated down under in 1879. Australia became the first country outside of Great Britain to adopt the sport.

Although the first water polo matches in Sydney occurred as early as 1881, no organisation evolved to regulate the game, organise competitions or schedule matches until the NSW Amateur Swimming Association was formed in 1892. However, from that point on a Water Polo Committee was established to administer the game in New South Wales, which was followed by a similar arrangement in Victoria a few years later.

NSW Amateur Water Polo Association

Some 25 annual competitions were held under the auspicies of the NSW Amateur Swimming Assocation, but this arrangement came to an end in

▼ An account of when water polo first began (Evening News, 15th Jan 1879). Report of the first water polo match played in Australia - 'Aquatic Polo Match' (The Argus, 8th March 1879, p7).

WATER POLO.

Water polo was first introduced by Mr. Fred. Cavill at the Serpentine Club's gala in 1868. It was then played with a large windball, and the game caused so much excitement that Mr. Cavill organised a team, and toured Great Britain with great success. It is still one of the most popular games in England. Strange to relate, the same gentleman introduced the game in Australia, the first game being played at Hegarty's Baths, Melbourne, 1879, with twelve men a-side.. The first match in Sydney was between the North Shore Club and the old Port Jackson Club, which was played at Woolloomooloo, and ended in a draw. Since then there have been some fine games between the above clubs and Wentworth and Balmain. Since the former three clubs have dropped out of the swimming world the Balmain boys have had very little opposition, though in 1896 the Bondi Club, with its speedy men, threatened them for a time; but the East-enders dropped out after a few struggles, and Balmain has since, without opposition, held the proud distinction of being the champion polo team of Australia.

Two swimming entertainments took place at the Swanston-street Public Baths yesterday in the afternoon and evening. They were for the benefit of Mr. Cavill, and on that account, amongst others, it is to be regretted that the attendance was very poor on each occasion. Mr. Cavill and his two children, and Messrs. Stabback and Strickland, and two or three very good amateurs, performed. Some capital feats were done. One of the most amusing items was an aquatic polo match. In this game a large ball is thrown into the water, and the swimmers are divided into parties. Whichever side can get the ball to the opposite goal wins, as at football.

late 1929. Since water polo had finally re-commenced after the long cessation of competition from 1916 to 1924, there was then a new push to administer the game autonomously.

Owing primarily to the untiring efforts of water polo enthusiasts led by Billy Morris (Pyrmont AWPC), water polo was granted the right of self-determination by the NSWASA parent body on the 25th November 1929. The old Water Polo Committee formed itself into an independent association known as the NSW Amateur Water Polo Association (NSWAWPA).

Bronte Amateur Water Polo Club

The Eastern Suburbs of Sydney traditionally produced a host of swimming talent, but while a number of other clubs including Balmain and Bondi had been formed back in the 19th century, the formation of a Bronte Water Polo Club occurred relatively late. Although evidence shows that water polo was played on and off at Bronte Baths by a number of other Sydney teams, usually as an end to a swimming carnival or an exhibition from the early 1890's, it wasn't until mid way through World War II that a water polo club was actually formed at Bronte. With the war still raging on, the very first Bronte Water Polo Club was formed by a group of young boys that banded together for the 1943/44 summer season.

By 1940 the European war was far away and although many Australians had enlisted, and wartime restrictions were in place, life went on much the same as usual. So... what happened to water polo following the onset of war, when many other sports ceased for the duration.

The NSWAWPA along with a few other sporting organisations made a firm decision to carry on

SWIMMING.

A meeting of the committee of the Waverley Swimming Club was held on Tuesday night at Easy's Hotel, Charing Cross. Mr. F. Petersen, vice-president, presided. Arrangements were made for the opening of the season at Bronte baths on the 14th instant, when a members' handicap race, distance one lap, will be held. A water polo contest and other games will also be included in the afternoon's programme. It was decided to accept the invitation from the Eastern Suburbs Club to play home-and-home polo matches during the season. The club's fifth gala will be held on 9th December. Trophies or donations for the season's operations have been promised by the following honorary members of the club :—Messrs. Geo. Sadler, Thos. Read, Jas. Marks, M.L.A., F. Petersen, Phil'p Rech, and W. M'Leod.

SWIMMING.

The Waverley Swimming Club held the opening meeting of the season, on Saturday afternoon, at the Bronte Baths, lent by Mr. F. W. Lloyd. There was a large attendance, including Mr. James Morgan, M.L.A., Alderman R. J. King, and Mr. Phillip Rech. A scratch water polo contest took place between the qualifying and final heats of the handicap race, the contesting teams representing Waverley and Balmain. The result was in favour of Waverley with 1 goal to nil. This event was an exciting one and attracted considerable attention and amusement.

WATER POLO.

A feature of the Eastern Suburbs A.S.C. carnival at Bronte Baths on Saturday will be a water polo match between Balmain and a combined team selected from the following representative players:—Watkinson, and S. Barrett, Clark (Pyrmont), Weilan (Rose Bay), Waddington (Abbotsford), Coulson, Battershy, ... Hellings (Bondi), and K. Kirkland (Spit). Other events to be decided are the 440 yards championship of eastern district, a first-class handicap, 66yds interclub handicap (seniors), 100yds interclub handicap for juniors, exhibition swims by Moss Christie and Frank Doyle.

▲ Water polo matches were played at Bronte Baths as early as 1893 (SMH, 5th Oct 1893, p.6), (SMH, 17th Oct 1893) & (SMH, 12th Dec 1924).

"May this greatest of all sports continue to progress through the coming year under the guidance of the same men who have not spared themselves in its interest."
Marsden S. Campbell
President NSWAWPA, Sept, 1941

with business as usual, hoping no doubt to avoid the eight year hiatus that water polo suffered after the end of World War I.

1940-41

1940/41 NSWAWPA OFFICIALS: Dr. K. Kirkland (Patron/Chairman); M. Campbell (President); C. E. Chapman (Past President); H. Duker (Registrar); L.S. Carroll (Secretary); H. Doerner (Asst. Secretary); R. Wood & H. McGlinn (Treasurers).

At the NSWAWPA 11th Annual General Meeting on Monday, 16th September 1940, a presentation of Association Life Membership badges, framed and inscribed "Life Member" were presented to Mr. H. Grose and Mr. C. Chapman Sr. for their much valued contributions. A presentation was also made to Mr. Tas King (Pyrmont) in appreciation of his services to the game of water polo.

The Association was also justly proud of its members mentioned in the 'Honour Roll', who were serving their country with the various forces at home and abroad. They used the Annual Report as an opportunity to extend their best wishes to all those who had "rallied to defend Australia's democratic ideals." They also expressed sympathy to the relatives of Bill Butler, Mark Phillips and S.

▼ Bronte Baths about 1966 with Bronte A.S.C. house and a plethora of other structures at left.

Cremer, all of the Bondi Club, who had been reported missing.

For recording purposes, club secretaries were requested to forward the names of all water polo members as they enlisted. A general apology was issued for any names that had inadvertently been omitted from this list.

At the AGM the Annual Report was adopted, and Mr. Campbell moved that "a competition be organised before Christmas."[3]

The Baths & Clubs

Competition matches during this season were played at Balmoral, Drummoyne, Domain, Elkington Park, North Sydney and The Spit Baths. The team entries for the 1940/41 season were drawn from 14 different clubs from across the Sydney Metropolitan area.

The mid-week competitions were conducted along similar lines to the previous seasons with the first four teams in all grades playing off. The number of competing teams dropped from 26 to 21 and the competition began for the first time in many years without the Rose Bay club. The 1st Grade competition consisted of five teams and the 2nd Grade of six teams. The 3rd Grade consisted of ten teams, which played in one division, and four clubs entered teams for the Junior competition.

Permission to make use of Coogee Aquarium for the Sunday night competition was not obtained due to war time lighting restrictions, particularly being on the coast and this led to the abandonment of this competition.

Representatives in NSW Teams

The Regal Cup Series against Victoria was abandoned for an indefinite period at the request

1940/41 Season Statistics N.S.W.A.W.P.A.

Clubs in the Water Polo Competitions.

Clubs	Grades 1	2	3	Total
Balmain	2		●	3
Balmoral			●	1
Bankstown			●	1
Bondi	●	●		2
Drummoyne	●	●	●	3
Enfield			●	1
Manly			●	1
Nth Sydney		●	●	2
Northbridge			●	1
Pyrmont	●		●	2
R'wick/Coogee		●		1
Sydney			●	1
The Spit			●	1
University		●		1
	5	6	10	21

Results of the Water Polo Competitions.

Grade	Premier		Runner-Up
1st	Balmain~5	d.	3~Pyrmont
2nd	Nth Sydney~5	d.	2~Drummoyne
3rd	Pyrmont~6	d.	3~Balmoral
Club Champions			BALMAIN
3 Knockout	Bankstown~6	d.	4~Pyrmont
Juniors	Balmain~5	d.	2~Sydney

"Swimming Clubs were primarily social clubs, and sport was strictly seasonal... you swam in summer and played football in winter. These clubs were also more than just swimming. You swam races, but you also played table tennis in the club room, you surfed together, and playing water polo was a small part of being a member of the club."
Brian Ellison, Apr 2015

NEW SOUTH WALES TEAM
1941 - Runners-Up - Melbourne
Back row (from left): Jack King (c, Pyrmont), Jack Bradbury (North Sydney), Arthur Burge (Drummoyne), Albert Cotter (vc, Balmain), Ben Dalley (g, Balmain), Frank Guthrie (Bankstown), Clem Walsh (Bondi), Eric Johnson (Balmain). Photo - NSWAWPA Archives.

of both Associations and consequently no State representatives were selected. However, despite the international crisis, representative fixtures still went ahead during the 1940/41 season. Some 15 exhibition matches were played throughout this season including notable representative games such as NSW Police v Bondi, a Possibles team defeated Probables (4~3) and a NSW team defeated 'The Rest' (4~0).[3]

The Premierships

Balmain and Bondi had been the form teams just prior to the war, but Bondi was overtaken early in the season by Balmain as competition favourites and Pyrmont also remained a formidable team. After the Association play-offs were completed, Balmain had taken out the 1st Grade premiership for the fourth successive year with an undefeated record. North Sydney annexed the 2nd Grade trophy also being undefeated on the season, while Pyrmont picked up the 3rd Grade premiership with a win over Balmoral. The Club Championship for most consistent club also went to Balmain.[3]

A Junior competition was played this season and featured teams from Balmain, Balmoral, Drummoyne, Manly, Sydney and The Spit, with

"Bronte ASC was a major swimming club with membership well over 300 when I first joined. We swam at State and other major Carnivals and were a significant force. Back in the forties, Clubs had to compete in all events, which included diving. Whilst we had a diving board and a long history of diving at Bronte, nobody could do a proper dive. So we had one rather overweight member enter. He would bounce up and down several times in the correct manner then simply step into space. He never got any points, but the club fulfilled its entry requirements."

Brian Ellison, Apr 2015

Balmain defeating Sydney (5~2) in the grand-final in yet another undefeated display.

A knockout competition was also held for clubs in the 3rd Grade, which featured entries from nine different teams. A determined Bankstown defeated Pyrmont (6~4) in the grand-final of that competition.

Trophies were held by the NSWAWPA for the 1st Grade premiership from 1929/30 to 1940/41 and donated by the Regal Silver Company (not be confused with the Interstate Series of the same name) as well as the Annual Club Championship from 1929/30 to 1940/41.

"Your Executive feels certain that clubs will share the burdens of the Association unflinchingly, for it is a privilege for all of us to carry on the game whilst our comrades are engaged on a more important mission."
NSWAWPA Annual Report 1941/42

1941-42

1941/42 NSWAWPA OFFICIALS: Dr. K. Kirkland (Patron); M. Campbell (President); C. E. Chapman (Past President); Dr. H.K. Porter (Chairman); H. Duker (Registrar); L.S. Carroll & H. Grose (Secretaries); G. Loveridge & F. Carlisle (Asst. Secretaries); B. Erickson (Treasurer).

Although by October 1941 the war in Europe and North Africa had been running for two years, the 1941/42 season commenced during a period of international crisis, which was greatly accentuated after a few rounds of premiership games had been completed. The Japanese had bombed Pearl Harbour in Hawaii in a surprise attack on December 7th 1941, which placed a dark cloud over the country and the continuation of civilian life in general. As a result, a mass call up of young men was initiated, which affected all walks of life and naturally most sports including water polo, were immediately placed in jeopardy.

The NSWAWPA Annual Report for the 1941/42 season began by considering the fact that, while many other sporting bodies had suspended competition due to the hostilities, it was amazing that water polo was still functioning. Of course, at the same time the Association remained supremely aware and respectful of international events.

▼ Sydney was fortunate in erecting a number of swimming baths within the harbour like... the Rose Bay Baths, which also happened to be the site of Sydney's first international airport.

MOTION TO ABANDON THE SPORT OF WATER POLO

Under The National Emergency

Minutes of the NSWAWPA
Monday 5th January 1942

Mr. Campbell (chairman) invited frank and open discussion on the matter, and pointed out the serious effect of allowing the game to die out in the last war, after which it took many years to revive. He stressed the need to carry on when other Associations showed signs of falling by the wayside, and indicated the possibilities of booming the game when others ceased to function. Mr. Todd moved, Mr. Bruce seconded, that the grade competitions be continued, games to be played on two nights weekly. Mr. Duker vigorously opposed the motion, pointing out that the games would produce no gate revenue thus becoming too much of a burden on the Association finances. Mr. Lynch moved, Mr. Erickson seconded, an amendment that the grade games be suspended during this time of national emergency. Various delegates spoke on the matter, and Mr. Cotter asserted that the 1st Grade competition had definitely been 'killed' by the latest military call-up, and thereupon foreshadowed another amendment. Mr. Forbes Carlisle supported Mr. Cotter's remarks, but pleaded for a continuance of the competitions, as did Mr. Grey, the latter suggesting a competition on a handicap basis. Mr. Grose urged a continuance of games but doubted the possibility of playing games after sunset [due to lighting restrictions]. The Chairman put Mr. Lynch's amendment to the vote and it was carried. Mr. Cotter then moved the amendment he had foreshadowed, "That the senior competitions be carried on in some form." Mr. Grey seconded. On being put to the vote, Mr. Cotter's amendment was carried. Mr. Grose then gave notice of motion: 'That the grade competitions as at present constituted be suspended.' Mr. Grey seconded. Mr. Grose further moved: "That a Special Council meeting be called as soon as possible, and that such meeting be empowered to consider the playing of new competitions, and that Secretaries of clubs be contacted requesting them to submit possible entries and personnel". Mr. Grey seconded. Carried.

"Gentlemen, your Executive, in submitting for your consideration the 13th Annual Report and Balance Sheet covering the 1941/42 season, feel that it is not necessary to remind you that operations during the year under review were carried out under conditions unprecedented in the history of the game."
NSWAWPA Annual Report 1941/42

The Association extended their heartiest congratulations to those members who had returned from overseas, and to those members who were still overseas at various battle stations, and wished them a speedy return to civil life. They also offered to the relatives of all those who were on missing lists the deep sympathies of the Association in the hope that "the time was not very distant when their dear ones would be restored to them."

Sincere sympathies were tended to the relatives of all "those who had passed to the great beyond" during the previous twelve months and particularly to the relatives of Wally Magee, Bill Pearce (Bondi), Wally Pont, and L. Holt (Balmain), all of whom had performed excellent work on behalf of the Association.

Of special mention was Wally Pont, who was probably one of the most versatile competitors ever to represent Balmain and New South Wales. He won the NSW Diving Championship in both Springboard and High Platform Diving and was selected as Captain of the NSW Diving Troupe. He also won swimming titles at Breastroke, Backstroke, Freestyle (100, 220 and 440 yards) and played for NSW in Water Polo in 1931. Wally enlisted in the Armed Services in 1940, but sadly died in action on Australia Day 1942, in Malaya.

Due to the cessation of the premiership games the various Councils and baths' proprietors were not prepared to continue the usual share for share arrangement in regard to gate receipts, and the loss of this revenue was responsible for a loss on the entire year's operations. The Association was still financially viable, but it was obvious that during the coming season expenditure had to be cut drastically, and the clubs had to pay greatly increased entrance fees etc., if the Association was to carry on without further loss.

All in all however, the Executive Committee were happy in the fact that unlike World War I when competition was cancelled and the sport took a decade to recover, games were still being organised for those able to play, and thanked both players and referees for their continued loyalty to the sport.[4]

The Baths & Clubs

After just four rounds had been played, the competitions had to be abandoned due to the general military call-up, in response to the Japanese attack on Pearl Harbour on the 7th December 1941. Consequently, an urgent Council meeting of the NSWAWPA was arranged for Monday, 5th January 1942 at which a heated discussion transpired.

In view of the extraordinary conditions under which the NSWAWPA carried on, the result was a triumph for the game in a time of national emergency. Entries were initially received in each of three grades, but after a temporary delay and with the advent of daylight saving, a revised general handicap competition was inaugurated. Despite the difficulties, eight entries were received and many interesting and well contested games took place.

Representatives in NSW Teams

The Regal Cup Series against Victoria was abandoned for an indefinite period at the request of both Associations and consequently no State representatives were selected.

The Premierships

The decimated but still functioning handicap competition in New South Wales saw Balmain defeat The Spit (5~2) in the final, with the Pyrmont and Sydney clubs being the other semi-finalists.

Five entries were received for the Junior competition from Balmain, Drummoyne, Manly, Sydney and The Spit, with the standard of play being reportedly very good. The Spit were an excellent combination and went on to win the competition, but they had strong opposition from the sturdy Sydney team.[4]

1941/42 Season Statistics
N.S.W.A.W.P.A.

Clubs in the Water Polo Competitions.

Clubs	Hcap
Balmain	1
Drummoyne	1
Northbridge	1
Pyrmont	2
Sydney	1
The Spit	2
	8

Results of the Water Polo Competitions.

Grade	Premier	Runner-Up
Handicap	Balmain~5 d.	2~The Spit A
Juniors	The Spit d.	Sydney

▲ Logo of the New South Wales Amateur Water Polo Association, which was inaugurated on the 22nd Nov, 1929.

1942-43

1942/43 NSWAWPA OFFICIALS: Dr. K. Kirkland (Patron); M. Campbell (President); C. E. Chapman (Past President); Dr. H.K. Porter (Chairman); H. Peebles (Registrar); P. Grattan-Smith (Secretary); F. Carlisle (Asst. Secretary); B. Erickson (Treasurer).

"Water polo is the finest of all sports and justifies our best efforts, particularly in times such as these when physical fitness is of such vital national importance."

Marsden S. Campbell,
President NSWAWPA Sept, 1942

The Association regretfully recorded the death of Mr. T. J. Williams, ex-referee and Councillor of the Association, and that of Mr. W. Lynch also of Drummoyne Club who was an Executive member of the Association during the previous season.

The Association was proud to welcome home members and extended greetings with a wish for the safe return of all its members from active service, and also sent best wishes to those who were still away with the forces.

The Executive was pleased to report that as a result of playing most games at Drummoyne Baths, thus enabling the Association to share gate proceeds with Drummoyne Council, very necessary revenue was secured. Assisting the bottom line were players and clubs who responded enthusiastically to a number of appeals, which was responsible for a big increase in revenue.[5]

The Baths & Clubs

Premiership games were again cancelled, but the Water Polo Association decided to conduct a Senior Handicap competition as had been inaugurated in the previous year. The handicapping proved to be very efficient and as a result, interest was maintained at all times.

Representatives in NSW Teams

The Regal Cup Series with Victoria remained an abandoned competition at the request of both Associations.

The Premierships

The competition leaders and minor premiers Pyrmont A, succumbed to Balmain in the semi-finals and exercised their right to challenge Bondi in the

---

1942/43 Season Statistics
N.S.W.A.W.P.A.

Clubs in the Water Polo Competitions.

Clubs	Hcap
Balmain	1
Bankstown	1
Bondi	1
Drummoyne	1
Nth Sydney	1
Pyrmont	2
The Spit	1
University	1
	9

Results of the Water Polo Competitions.

Grade	Premier		Runner-Up
Handicap	Bondi	d.	Pyrmont A
Juniors	The Spit B	d.	Manly

grand-final, but they unfortunately lost.

Four clubs were represented in the Junior competition and although two teams withdrew, the contests were still of a high competitive standard. Junior teams were fielded by Manly, Northbridge, Sydney and The Spit who entered three teams in this competition. The Spit B team who were Junior minor premiers surprisingly lost their final to Manly, but by exercising their right of challenge, came back well to defeat Manly in the grand-final.

▲ For a day at the beach, most visitors caught the Bronte tram, which ran down through the Bronte cutting and remains today a favourite part of the Bronte to Coogee coastal walk.

On the night of the water polo finals, a number of other interesting events were contested including a 'Ball Throwing Competition' won by Leon Ferguson (Bondi); a 'Swim With The Ball Race' won by M. Campbell (The Spit); and a 'Teams Relay Race' which was also won by The Spit Club. [5]

Chapter 2
THE ORIGINAL BRONTE WATER POLO CLUB
(1944 - 1951)

Swimming races at Bronte Baths during the 1930's.

Over the years a number of successful water polo teams had been formed within Sydney's Eastern Suburbs. These included the great Bondi Club, which won seven premierships between 1892 and 1940, and a club led by Cecil Healy playing out of the Domain called Eastern Suburbs, which claimed three consecutive premierships from 1904 to 1906.

However, it was in this still war restricted environment that a Bronte water polo team first came into existence.

1943-44

1943/44 NSWAWPA OFFICIALS: Dr. K. Kirkland (Patron); Dr. H.K. Porter (President); M. Campbell (Past President); F. Carlisle (Chairman); J. Scott (Registrar); H. Peebles & R. Traynor (Secretaries); R. Traynor & J. Dreelin (Asst. Secretaries); B. Erickson (Treasurer).

Despite the loss of a leg whilst on active service, congratulations were passed to Doug Robertson (Pyrmont A) who had been discharged from the Army owing to war injuries, and played as goalkeeper with the winning team.

Congratulations were also extended to Flying Officers G. Erickson and L. Deveridge of the Balmain Club, who were awarded the Distinguished Flying Cross while serving with the RAAF in England.

James Taylor, C.B.E., F.L.H.

During this season it came as a shock to the sporting world in general, and to swimmers and water polo players in particular, to hear that James Taylor had "taken the last plunge from which no swimmer returns." A life member of his old club Balmain, James Taylor was a member of various Balmain swimming teams, which had won State and Australian Championships.

However, he was almost a legendary figure for his water polo powers amongst his contemporaries, who told of his tremendous throw of the ball with his body "out of the water to the hips." He was a member of the Balmain premiership winning water polo teams of 1896, 1899 and 1900.

President of the NSW Swimming Association and Australian Swimming Union for many years, he was a strong, but kindly personality, patron and supporter of amateur ideals. Sporting circles certainly lost a stalwart and a gentleman.

1943/44 RESULTS

WATER POLO WIN

Bronte, which was conceded four goals, beat Bondi, 8-4, in a water polo senior grade match at Drummoyne baths last night. Champion swimmers, Rod Chapman (4) and Jack Campbell (1), scored for Bronte.

The Sun, 24 Nov 1943

WATER POLO DRAW

Draw for the NSW Water Polo Association's senior grade matches next Tuesday is: University v. The Spit, 6.30 pm, at Drummoyne Baths; Sydney v. Bankstown, 7, at Drummoyne; Bronte v. Pyrmont, 7.30, at Drummoyne; Balmain v. Bondi, 7 at Balmain Baths.

The Sun, 30 Nov, 1943

WATER POLO DRAW

NSW Water Polo Association draw for tonight: Bondi v Pyrmont A, 6.30: Sydney v University, 6.50; Bankstown v. Bronte, 7.5, at Drummoyne Baths; Pyrmont B v. The Spit, 6.50; Balmain v Northbridge, 7.5 at Balmain Baths.

The Sun, 30 Nov, 1943

WATER POLO

AT DRUMMOYNE — Pyrmont 5 (J. Humphries 3, R. Quill and J. King goals) beat Bronte 3 (rec. 2); Northbridge 7 (C. Schmidt 3, J. Dreelin 2, P. Dreelin 2, E. Schmidt) beat Bankstown 3 (rec. 4) (A. George); The Spit 1 (M. Campbell) beat University nil.
AT BALMAIN BATHS — Pyrmont B 4 (O. O'Keefe 3, J. Dolley goals) drew with Sydney (rec. 2); 4 (P. Biran, R. Peebles); Balmain received a forfeit from Bondi.

SMH, 9 Dec 1943

WATER POLO

At Drummoyne: Pyrmont A beat Pyrmont B (rec. 5), 8-7; The Spit beat Northbridge, 3-1; Bondi beat Sydney, 8-5. At Elkington Park, Balmain drew with Bronte, 4 all; Bankstown beat University, 5-3.

SMH, 15 Dec 1943

Bronte beat Pyrmont B (received one goal) by 8 to 2 in NSW Water Polo Association's first grade competition at Balmain Baths last night.

The Sun, 22 Dec 1943

WATER POLO

Results of last night's water polo games are: Bronte 6 (O. Drewett 2, J. Campbell 2, R. Chapman 2, K. Barel, R. Palson), beat Pyrmont (rec. 1), 2 (W. McMahon); Bankstown 4 (P. Guthrie 2) beat Sydney, 2 (J. Stewart 2); The Spit 5 (H. Doerner 4, H. Campbell) beat Bondi (rec. 2) (C. Walsh 2); Pyrmont A 4 (R. Humphries 3, J. King, P. Quill) drew with Balmain (rec. 2), 4 (P. Guthrie 2).

SMH, 22 Dec 1943

His life of achievements included being elected as President of the NSWASA and Chairman of the Australian Swimming Union; Member of the International Olympic Committee and he was awarded the Order of Companion of the British Empire (CBE) for Services to Sport, as well as the 'Chevalier de la Legion d'Honneur.'

A fine lad was killed recently in England, where he was a member of the RAAF. Captain of The Spit Junior Water Polo team, which won the State premiership in 1939, Flight-Sergeant Ian Cormack was also a brilliant swimmer and for some time held the NSW Schoolboys 440 yards record at 5 min. 27 sec. He was loved and respected by all that knew him.

An exhibition match between Pyrmont and 'The Rest', which was staged at the Metropolitan All Schools Carnival and controlled by the NSWASA, was well received. Also, an Army team from the far north, organised by Mr. Arthur Burge, a former Hon. Secretary and NSW representative player, visited Sydney and played an exhibition game. The Army team revealed a good knowledge of the game and contained some players who had previously competed in competitions controlled by the Association.[1]

The Baths & Clubs

During the season, metropolitan matches were played at Balmoral, Bankstown, Coogee Aquarium, Drummoyne, Elkington Park, Manly, Northbridge and The Spit Baths. Once again, regular premiership games were abandoned, however ten entries were received for the Senior Handicap competition. Interest was such that the Association was able to add a Junior Handicap competition. Manly, Northbridge and Sydney clubs

1943/44 Season Statistics
N.S.W.A.W.P.A.

Clubs in the Water Polo Competitions.

| Clubs | Handicaps | | Total |
	Senior	Intermed	
Balmain	●	●	2
Bankstown	●		1
Bondi	●	●	2
Bronte	●		1
Manly		●	1
Northbridge	●		1
Pyrmont	2		2
Sydney	●		1
The Spit	●	2	3
University	●		1
	10	5	15

Results of the Water Polo Competitions.

Grade	Premier		Runner-Up
Snr Handicap	Pyrmont A	def	Balmain
Int Handicap	The Spit A	def	Balmain
Juniors	Manly	def	The Spit A

all re-affiliated after a break, but both Drummoyne and North Sydney lapsed. A feature of this season was the appearance of a brand new water polo club from Bronte, which was comprised mainly of players from various local High Schools, and which performed very creditably.

By December of 1943, Sydney Technical High School were premiers with an undefeated record in the High Schools competition.

Representatives in NSW Teams

The Regal Cup Series with Victoria remained an abandoned competition at the request of both the New South Wales and Victorian Water Polo Associations. However Rod Chapman and Jack Campbell (Bronte) were both selected in 'The Rest' representative team, which was defeated by the premiers Pyrmont (2~4) at North Sydney Olympic Pool at the end of March 1944.

The Premierships

Pyrmont A won the Senior Handicap competition over Balmain, the final being keenly contested. An Intermediate competition was inaugurated in this season, which attracted five entries, but the competition was marred by far too many forfeits. The Spit A team being beaten in the final, exercised its right to challenge by virtue of being minor premiers and after a closely contested match, succeeded in beating Balmain in the grand-final.

The Junior competition had six entries with teams from Balmoral, Bondi, Manly, Sydney and The Spit which fielded two teams. The competition rules for the Juniors were that it was open to boys under the age of 16 years on the 1st of October 1943. The competition was played over two rounds, with two points for a win and one point for a draw. The semi-finals were conducted by playing 1st v 3rd, and 2nd v 4th and the winners advanced to the final. The minor premiers had the right to challenge the winners of the semi-final or final and the matches were played every Sunday morning. Many excellent games were witnessed in this competition with Manly defeating The Spit A in the final, after an outstanding match.[1]

1943/44 RESULTS

BRONTE WINS AGAIN

Swim and surf stars, Rod Chapman, and Jack Campbell, helped in another victory for Bronte, in the NSW water polo first grade competition last night.

Bronte (received one) beat The Spit, three goals to two, Campbell, and Chapman scoring one each.

Bronte, beaten only once this season, has had four wins, and a draw. Other teams it has defeated are Bondi, Bankstown, and Pyrmont "B."

The Sun, 5 Jan 1944

WATER POLO

Sydney, 8 (rec. 6), beat Northbridge, 6; Bondi, 9, beat Pyrmont B, 7; Bronte, 3 (rec. 1), beat The Spit, 1; Balmain received a forfeit from University and Pyrmont A received a forfeit from Bankstown.

The Sun, 5 Jan 1944

WATER POLO RESULT

Bronte and Bondi drew, 2-all, in the NSW water polo competition first-grade series at Drummoyne baths last night.

Rod Chapman and Jack Campbell scored for Bronte, which has lost only one match this season.

The Sun, 12 Jan 1944

WATER POLO

Water polo matches last night resulted:— Pyrmont A, 10 (J. King 4, J. Watkinson 4, A. Humphreys 2), beat Pyrmont B, 8 (rec. 4, J. Daley, R. Cooper one each); Northbridge, 6 (C. Schmidt 2, E. Schmidt 2, T. Dreehan, W. Fisbridge), beat Bronte, 3 (rec. R. Chapman 2); Sydney, 4 (rec. 2, G. Loveridge 2), beat The Spit, (B. Ellison); Balmain, 5 (D. Deveridge 2, E. Johnston, B. Dalley, N. Duker), beat Bondi, 4 (rec. 3, L. Ferguson).

SMH, 9 Feb 1944

WATER POLO

Balmain, 7, beat Northbridge (rec. 1), 3; Pyrmont A, 9, beat Sydney (rec. 7), 7; Pyrmont B, 4, drew with The Spit, 2; Bronte received a forfeit from Bondi. Intermediate grade: Balmain, 4, beat The Spit, 2.

SMH, 23 Feb 1944

WATER POLO

Water-polo matches resulted: Balmain, 5 (rec. 2), beat Pyrmont A, 4; Sydney, 4 (rec. 2), beat Northbridge, 3; Bronte, 1, beat The Spit, nil; Pyrmont B, 1, beat Bondi, nil.

SMH, 1 Mar 1944

An interclub teams championship will be contested by The Spit, Bronte, University, and Sydney Clubs.

An exhibition water polo match will be played by Pyrmont and The Rest. Teams are:

Pyrmont: D. Robinson, T. Watkinson, A. Allen, J. Munce, A. Humphreys, E. Quill, J. King. **The Rest:** C. Phillips, R. Deveridge, C. Schmidt, L. Ferguson, R. Chapman, C. Walsh, L. Holt.

Water Polo Challenge Match.—Pyrmont (State premiers) 4 (goal-scorers J. King 2, F. Humphreys, J. Watkinson) d. The Rest 2 (J. Campbell, L. Holt), at North Sydney Olympic Pool.

Daily Telegraph, 27 Mar 1944

Bronte AWPC

The young, but inspired Bronte team probably would have preferred to enter the Junior contest, but they had to be content with the Senior Handicap competition as most of the boys were already 16 years old. However, they were surprisingly able to inflict defeats upon open teams from Bondi, Bankstown, Pyrmont B, and The Spit, losing only to Pyrmont A and Northbridge. Unfortunately, they didn't manage to qualify for the finals, but the young team had made a very promising start on the metropolitan water polo scene, and for Bronte.

PYRMONT AMATEUR WATER POLO CLUB
1943/44 - NSWAWPA Senior Handicap Premiers
Back row (from left): D. O'Keefe, J. Watkinson (Snr - Life Member), J. Watkinson (Jnr), R. Quill, C. Brady, J. Conlon (Life Member), Tas King (President & Life Member). Middle row - D. Robinson, A. Elm, E. Quill. Front row - J. King (Hon. Sec. & Life Member), A. Humphries (c), J. Munce (vc). Photo - NSWAWPA Archives.

BRONTE AMATEUR WATER POLO TEAM
1943/44 - Senior Handicap Team
Rod Chapman, Jack Campbell, D. Drewett, Ken Baret, Roy Falson, Ken Mills & others possibly including Bronte ASC swimmers: M. Paddison, D. Brinkman, J. Gilmore, J. Foster, J.Paine & P. Frost.

1944-45

1944/45 NSWAWPA OFFICIALS: Dr. K. Kirkland (Patron); Dr. H.K. Porter (President); M. Campbell (Past President); Dr. H.K. Porter (Chairman); J. Dreelin (Registrar); R. Traynor (Secretary); J. Dreelin (Asst. Secretary); B. Erickson (Treasurer).

The 'Baths Lighting Embargo' was still in place in NSW, during this season. Often teams had to travel to far distant venues in order to play their games during daylight hours. However, entries in the various competitions were maintained and the standard of play generally augered well for the post war period.

A new entry from 'HMAS Rushcutter' enlivened interest in the Senior Handicap Competition. Also contests between HMAS Rushcutter and various teams from units of the Royal Navy created great interest and were keenly contested. English water polo referees were viewed in operation for the first time and it was satisfactory to note, that their interpretations were generally in line with the Australian referees.

The Association extended their heartiest congratulations to those members who had returned from active service overseas, and it was sincerely hoped that an early demobilisation would allow many other ex-players to rejoin their respective clubs.

The Water Polo Council sincerely regretted the tragic loss of Don Benson, RAAF member of The Spit ASC, who was killed in air operations.[2]

The Baths & Clubs

During the season, metropolitan matches were played at Balmoral, Bankstown, Coogee Aquarium, Drummoyne, Elkington Park, Manly, Northbridge and The Spit Baths. While Balmoral and 'HMAS Rushcutter' had joined the competition, clubs from Bankstown, Bondi and University all lapsed.

Representatives in NSW Teams

The Regal Cup Series remained an abandoned competition during this season, at the request of both Associations. Negotiations took place however, for the possible visit of an Indian water polo team to Australia during this season. It was hoped that an official invitation from Australia would be quickly accepted by the Indian authorities, but nothing more than correspondence eventuated.

The Premierships

After many interesting and well contested games, Balmain defeated the minor premiers, Pyrmont Icebergs in the grand-final of the Senior Handicap competition. Junior and Intermediate competitions were played on the weekends and the standard of play was uniformly good. The Intermediate competition was won by The Spit by a comfortable margin over Balmoral.

In the Juniors, five teams were fielded by Balmoral, Manly,

1944/45 Season Statistics
N.S.W.A.W.P.A.

Clubs in the Water Polo Competitions.

Clubs	Handicaps		Total
	Senior	Intermed	
Balmain	●		1
Balmoral		●	1
Bronte	●		1
HMAS Rushcutter	●		1
Manly		●	1
Northbridge	●		1
Pyrmont	2		2
Sydney	●		1
The Spit	●	●	2
	8	3	11

Results of the Water Polo Competitions.

Grade	Premier		Runner-Up
Snr Handicap	Balmain	d.	Pyrmont Icebergs
Int Handicap	The Spit	d.	Balmoral
Juniors	Manly	d.	Northbridge

Northbridge, Sydney and The Spit, with the minor premiers, Manly going on to defeat Northbridge in the grand-final.[2]

Bronte AWPC

While Bronte had performed well above expectations during the 1943/44 season, and they were listed on the Association draw at the beginning of the 1944/45 competition, no results have been found to show that they actually played any matches in this season.

1945-46

1945/46 NSWAWPA OFFICIALS: Dr. K. Kirkland (Patron); Dr. H.K. Porter (President); M. Campbell (Past President); H. Grose (Chairman); R. Traynor (Registrar); J. Dreelin (Secretary); H. Peebles (Asst. Secretary); B. Erickson (Treasurer).

Now that hostilities had ceased, it was felt that water polo would make rapid progress, particularly in view of the popularity of the game among different sections of the fighting services. As the ex-servicemen returned to civilian life and resumed sporting activities, many found that competitive swimming didn't hold the same attraction, and as they had played inter-service water polo, competitions in the other states began to develop.

The resumption of premiership competitions was responsible for a revival of pre-war interest and enthusiasm. Despite lighting restrictions, which for a time prevented games being held after sunset, the players and spectators were keener than ever. Many returned servicemen renewed their involvement with the game and the public generally demonstrated greater interest in the various competitions than previously.

The Association congratulated Keith Windon (Randwick/Coogee ASC) for being selected as vice-captain of the Australian Rugby Union team, which toured New Zealand. Arthur Buchan (formerly Bankstown ASC) for also being selected as a member of the Australian Rugby Union team.

POPULARITY OF WATER POLO

The growing popularity of water polo among youthful swimmers was emphasised last night by a decision of the Water Polo Association to extend the scope of the current competitions.

It decided to grant permission for a six weeks' intermediate competition, which will be in addition to the weekly senior and junior matches.

Before the season ends late in March or the first week in April the association hopes to play a match against a British Servicemen's team. If suitable arrangements can be made by the vice-president, Mr. H. Grose, the match will take place during the Western Suburbs championships at Balmain baths on February 24.

Last night's results were:—
Balmain, 10 (E. Johnston 5, O. Amedee 3, J. McJannet 2), beat Sydney (rec. 8), 8, at Drummoyne.

Pyrmont, 6 (J. King 3, E. Quill 2, B. Humphrey), beat Northbridge (rec. 2), 3 (R. Woodbridge), at Northbridge.

The Spit, 4 (E. Rolfe, J. Scott, B. Greenfield, K. Murrell), beat Pyrmont Icebergs (rec. 1), 2 (B. O'Keefe), at Northbridge.

(SMH, 24th Jan, 1945)

▼ *Water polo leaped ahead in the post war years with the number of NSWAWPA affiliated clubs doubling within the first five years. Photo - NSWAWPA Archives.*

1945/46 RESULTS

Water Polo Begins

The Amateur Water Polo Association will hold the first round of this season's competitions at Drummoyne and Balmain baths to-night
In view of the forthcoming visit by an Indian water polo team to Australia, these games should create a great deal of interest.

The draw for to-night's games is—
First Grade: Pyrmont v Northbridge, Drummoyne Baths; 10. The Spit v Bronte, Drummoyne Baths; 9. Balmain v Bondi, Balmain Baths. 8.
Second Grade: Sydney v Pyrmont, Drummoyne Baths; 9. Bondi v Balmain, Balmain Baths. 10. University v Bye.

(SMH, 27th Nov, 1945)

Water Polo

First grade: Bondi, 8. Bronte, 1; Spit, 6. Northbridge, 4. Second grade: University, 8. Sydney, 0. Third grade: Balmain "A," 4. Bankstown, 4; North Ramsgate, 4. Pyrmont, 1; Drummoyne, 7. Bondi, 1; Northbridge, 7. North Sydney, 0; Spit, forfeit from Police Cadets.

(SMH, 9th Jan, 1946)

1945/46 Season Statistics
N.S.W.A.W.P.A.

Clubs in the Water Polo Competitions.

Clubs	Grades 1	2	3N	3S	Total
Balmain	●	●		2	4
Bankstown			●		1
Bondi	●	●	●		3
Bronte	●				1
Drummoyne			●		1
Freshwater		●			1
Manly		●			1
Nth Ramsgate			●		1
Nth Sydney			●		1
Northbridge	●	●			2
Police Cadets		●			1
Pyrmont	●	●	●		3
R'wick/Coogee			●		1
Sydney		●			1
The Spit	●	●			2
University	●				1
	6	5	6	8	25

Results of the Water Polo Competitions.

Grade	Premier		Runner-Up
1st	Balmain~4	d.	3~Bondi
2nd	Balmain~6	d.	2~University
3rd	Manly~4	d.	2~Northbridge
Club Champions	BALMAIN		
Juniors	Northbridge~5	d.	3~Manly

And also Jack Campbell (Bronte ASC), Bruce Bourke (North Ramsgate ASC), Ken Jones and Frank O'Neill (Manly ASC), and Vince Riley (Northbridge ASC), all for being selected by the Australian Swimming Union to undergo special swimming training in preparation for the 1948 Olympic Games in London.

A touring Freshwater Surf Club team, which included the likes of Eric Johnston, defeated a Brisbane water polo side (14~5) in an exhibition match at the Valley Baths, Brisbane at the end of February 1946. [3]

The Baths & Clubs

During this season, metropolitan matches were played at Balmoral, Bankstown, Coogee Aquarium, Drummoyne, Elkington Park, Manly, Northbridge and The Spit Baths.

The end of the war saw many young soldiers returning home and water polo benefitted from a jump in both club and player registrations. Freshwater and the Police Cadets affiliated for the first time, while Bankstown, Bondi, Drummoyne, North Ramsgate, North Sydney, Randwick-Coogee and University all re-affiliated after a lapse of several years. Only Balmoral and HMAS Rushcutter clubs lapsed.

Representatives in NSW Teams

Trial games for selection in the NSW team were played at the Balmain Carnival where 'Possibles' played 'Probables' and at the 'HMS Golden Hind' Carnival, where a NSW I played against NSW II.

The selectors called mostly upon the 'old guard' of players who had been State representatives with experience prior to the war, such as Ben Dalley, Jack King, Jack Turnbull and Hermie Doerner. But there were some new faces aswell in Alan Humphrey (Pyrmont) and Roger Cornforth (University). Cornforth had made a remarkable recovery since arriving back in Sydney after spending much of the war in a Japanese POW camp.

The 14th Regal Cup Series, played in Sydney against Victoria resulted in a three game whitewash for NSW (7~4; 6~5; 11~1).

The Premierships

A decision to play the semi-finals and the finals of the senior competitions as opening games at the NSWASA Swimming Championship Carnivals was well received, and the innovation proved very popular.

After two rounds of the competition, Balmain finished the season as minor premiers in 1st Grade. In the play-offs, Pyrmont trounced The Spit (8~2) in the elimination semi-final, and Bondi defeated Balmain (2~1) in the major semi. Balmain then had to overcome a determined Pyrmont side in the final, which they eventually won (4~2) and advanced to the competition decider. It was always going to be a close grand-final, but ultimately Balmain were able to swing the game their way and defeat Bondi (4~3) to take the 1st Grade premiership.

MANLY AMATEUR SWIMMING CLUB
1945/46 - 2nd Grade Water Polo Team
Back row: Leo Crum, Frank O'Neill, Max Whitehead, Ken McMinn, Bob McCouatt. Front row: John Ashley, Ian McKessar, Don Page. Photo - NSWAWPA Archives.

BALMAIN
1945/46 - NSWAWPA 1st Grade Premiers
Back row (from left): L. Holt, G. Barr, Bob Dalley. Front row: K. Erickson, Eric Johnson, Les Deveridge (c), Gordon Amedee, Ben Dalley (g).

Balmain also took out the 2nd Grade title over University (6~2), while Manly annexed the 3rd Grade title. Although play in the grade competitions did not reach pre-war standards, it revealed a marked improvement over the previous seasons. The 'Club Champions' for overall performance across all grades went to Balmain.

A Junior competition was played over two rounds and featured teams from Balmain, Balmoral, Manly, Northbridge and The Spit. Northbridge defeated Manly (5~3) in the grand-final.[3]

NEW SOUTH WALES TEAM
Regal Cup Champions,
Sydney, 1946

Hermie Doerner (c/Co, Bondi)
Roger Cornforth (University)
Ben Dalley (g, Balmain)
Owen Doerner (Bondi)
A. Humphrey (Pyrmont)
Eric Johnson (vc, Balmain)
Jack King (Pyrmont)
C. Schmidt (Drummoyne)
Jack Turnbull (Bondi)
Clem Walsh (Bondi)
J. Watkinson Jr. (Pyrmont)
Harry Grose (Referee).

WATER POLO REFEREE 'DUCKED'

A water polo match between two undefeated clubs at Balmain Baths last night ended when the referee was pushed into the water 45 seconds before the finish. At the time of the incident Balmain were leading Pyrmont 2-1. Play had become heated when a Pyrmont supporter pushed the referee, Mr. Harry Grose, into the water, who lost his spectacles and declared the game abandoned.

Unreferenced Newspaper,
Eric Johnston's Scrapbook, 1946?

1945/46 RESULTS

WATER POLO RESULTS

First grade: Pyrmont v Bronte, 10-nil; Balmain v Northbridge, 6-2. Second grade: Balmain v Sydney, 5-nil; University v Pyrmont, 4-all. Third grade: Pyrmont v Balmain A, 3-all; North Sydney v Freshwater, 5-2; Northbridge v Police Cadets, 8-1; North Ramsgate v Bondi, 7-3; Balmain v Drummoyne, 4-3.

SMH, 6 Feb 1946

WATER POLO RESULTS

First Grade.—Balmain 7, The Spit 2; North Beach 5 v Bronte 4; Bondi 3 v Pyrmont 3. Second grade: University 5 v Balmain 4; Bondi 6 v Sydney 3. Third grade: North Ramsgate 7 v Randwick-Coogee 7; Bondi 9 v Bankstown 4; Drummoyne 4 v Pyrmont 1. Third grade.—Manly 4, Northbridge 3. The Spit forfeited to North Sydney.

SMH, 20 Feb 1946

1946 GRAND FINALS

WATER POLO RESULTS

Grand Final.—First Grade: Balmain, 4 (G. Anedee 2, L. Holt 1, K. Erllson 1), beat Bondi, 3 (J. Ferguson 1, C. Walsh 1, A. Hart 1). Second Grade: Balmain, 3, drew with Pyrmont N.S.W. Juniors, 5, beat Combined High Schools, 2.

SMH, 27 Mar 1946

▼ *The Coogee Aquarium baths were still being used for water polo matches after the war. Photo - NSWAWPA Archives.*

Bronte AWPC

Despite entering the 1945/46 NSWAWPA competition and being listed on the Association draw at the beginning of the season, there are relatively few results showing that Bronte club actually played any matches. A scant few newspaper notices show that they did compete, but the results revealed that they lost matches to both North Beach (sic. Northbridge) and Pyrmont.

1946-47

1946/47 NSWAWPA OFFICIALS: Dr. K. Kirkland (Patron); Dr. H.K. Porter (President); M. Campbell (Past President), A.P. Hart (Chairman); H. Duker (Registrar); H. Doerner (Secretary); E. Johnstone (Asst. Secretary); G. Ward (Treasurer).

There was much talk again this season about a visit by a water polo team from Bombay, which was being planned by Bill Berge Phillips, but nothing eventuated.

With support from the NSWAWPA water polo was flourishing in the country areas with competitions popping up in Singleton/Maitland, Kyogle, Cootamundra/West Wyalong, Echuca, Kempsey, Lismore, Canberra and a number of other regional locations.

Players from three Sydney water polo clubs visited Young to play exhibition games in the Young Olympic Pool on January 26th 1947. The teams included some of the leading first graders from Balmain, Bondi and Pyrmont clubs. And an Eastern District team won the Associations' Interdistrict competition.[4]

The Baths & Clubs

During the season, metropolitan matches were played at Balmoral, Bankstown, Coogee Aquarium, Drummoyne, Elkington Park, Manly, Northbridge and The Spit Baths. In regard to new clubs, Roseville affiliated for the first time, Balmoral re-affiliated after a one year break, while both North Ramsgate and the Police Cadet club lapsed.

CAPTAINS FIGHT AT WATER POLO

Captains of Bondi-Pyrmont and Balmain water polo teams, Hermie Doerner and Eric Johnson, engaged in an underwater fight during an exhibition match at Young yesterday. Bondi-Pyrmont, winners by 5 goals to 4 is the first team to defeat Balmain this season.

Daily Telegraph, 27th Jan 1947

NEW SOUTH WALES TEAM
Regal Cup Champions, Melbourne, 1947

Hermie Doerner (c/Co, Bondi)
Gordon Amadee (res, Balmain)
Roger Cornforth (University)
Ben Dalley (g, Balmain)
Owen Doerner (Bondi)
Eric Johnson (vc, Balmain)
Jack King (Pyrmont)
Dudley Pont (Balmain)
Clem Walsh (Bondi)
Dr. H.K. Porter (Manager)
Bob Traynor (A/Manager)
Harold Duker (Referee).

1946/47 RESULTS

Water Polo Begins

The Amateur Water Polo Association will hold the first round of this season's competitions at Drummoyne and Balmain baths to-night

In view of the forthcoming visit by an Indian water polo team to Australia, these games should create a great deal of interest.

The sites for to-night's games are:—

First Grade: Pyrmont v Northbridge Drummoyne Baths : 7.30. The Spit v Bronte Drummoyne Baths : Balmain v Bondi Balmain Baths 8.

Second Grade: Sydney v Pyrmont Drummoyne Baths : Bondi v Balmain Balmain Baths : 7.30. University ...

SMH, 18 Nov 1946

WATER POLO

First Grade: Balmain, 2 (E. Johnson 2), beat Bronte, nil: Pyrmont, 4 (D. Hyde, C. Quinn, K. Quill, J. King), beat Bondi, 2 (A. Cook, L. Ferguson). Second Grade: Balmain, 6 (E. Erickson 2, R. Beveridge 2, L. Holt 2), beat Pyrmont, 1 (A. Porter): Manly, 2 (F. O'Neill 2), beat Bronte, nil: Drummoyne, 7 (A. Leonard 3, W. Steel, J. Clothier, W. Sneddon, J. Peters), beat Sydney, 2 (S. Peebles, H. Peebles).

SMH, 22 Nov 1946

WATER POLO

A Grade: Northbridge 2, Bronte 2; Balmain 5, Bondi 1; Pyrmont, University, deferred. B Grade: Pyrmont 2, Bondi 0; Balmain 2, Manly 2; University, Drummoyne, deferred; Sydney, bye.

SMH, 27 Nov 1946

Representatives in NSW Teams

None of Bronte's young players were invited to trial for the NSW team, which was dominated by players from Balmain and Bondi.

Seven NSW representatives were retained from the Regal Cup winning team of 1946, the only new caps in the side being Gordon Amadee and Dudley Pont (Balmain).

The 1947 Regal Cup Series was contested from the 22nd to 26th February 1947, against Victoria over three matches played at Richmond Baths in Melbourne. The three match test series was again won by NSW (7~4; 3~1; 3~5).

The Premierships

By season's end, and with no preliminary final, Balmain ran out victors over Bondi (4~3) to take the 1st Grade premiership. Pyrmont won the 2nd Grade competition over Balmain (5~1), and in the 3rd Grade challenge match between the winners of the north and south divisions, Northbridge narrowly defeated Balmain (6~5). The 'Club Champions' for overall performance across all grades, again went to Balmain.

A Junior Competition was played during the season, but few results were posted, with

BALMAIN
1946/47 - NSWAWPA 1st Grade Premiers
Back row (from left): L. Holt, G. Barr, Bob Dalley. Front row: K. Erickson, Eric Johnson, Les Deveridge (c), Gordon Amedee, Ben Dalley (g). Photo - Balmain AWPC.

1946/47 Season Statistics
N.S.W.A.W.P.A.

Clubs in the Water Polo Competitions.

Clubs	1	2	3N	3S	Total
Balmain	●	●		3	5
Balmoral			●		1
Bankstown				●	1
Bondi	●	●		●	3
Bronte	●	●			2
Drummoyne		●		●	2
Freshwater			●		1
Manly		●	●		2
North Sydney			●		1
Northbridge	●		2		3
Pyrmont	●	●		●	3
Randwick/Coogee				2	2
Roseville			●		1
Sydney		●		●	2
The Spit			2	●	3
University	●	●			2
	6	8	9	11	34

Results of the Water Polo Competitions.

Grade	Premier		Runner-Up
1st	Balmain~4	d.	3~Bondi
2nd	Pyrmont~5	d.	1~Balmain
3rd	Northbridge~6	d.	5~Balmain
Club Champions			BALMAIN
Juniors	Northbridge	d.	Unknown

Northbridge being successful.

The Sunday Night Handicap competition was again conducted at Coogee Aquarium and attracted a small number of teams from Bankstown, Ben Buckler, Birchgrove, Bondi, Randwick/Coogee and The Boot (a subsidiary of Bondi).[4]

Bronte AWPC

Despite entering the 1946/47 NSWAWPA competitions and apparently fielding teams in both 1st and 2nd Grades, for some reason Bronte didn't last long.

Evidence taken from local newspapers shows that both Bronte teams were included in the first round of the Association draw posted on 19th November 1946. They were also included in results posted on the 18th, 22nd and 27th of November, with Bronte 1st Grade being narrowly defeated by Balmain (0~2) in the first round and drawing with Northbridge (2~2) in the second round. In the same set of results, Bronte 2nd Grade were narrowly defeated by Manly (0~2) in the first round, but there was no mention of either team thereafter, not even by way of a forfeit.

So what happened to these two Bronte teams? Perhaps the conflicting commitments of the Bronte Swimming Club, or the Surf Life Saving Club became too onerous for the players. It may have been that the time it took to get to matches and back on trains, trams and ferries at places like Bankstown, The Spit and Manly just took too long.

Most likely might be that the Bronte members were persuaded to join other clubs, as the likes of Jack Campbell, turned up later competing for Pyrmont. In any event, despite their promising results, Bronte apparently dropped out of this competition and didn't field another water polo team for four more years.

1947-48

1947/48 NSWAWPA OFFICIALS: Dr. K. Kirkland (Patron); Dr. H.K. Porter (President); M. Campbell (Past President); A.P. Hart (Chairman); H. Duker (Registrar); H. Doerner (Secretary); E. Johnson (Asst. Secretary); R. Traynor (Treasurer).

The Association extended their sincere sympathy to the relatives of Jock Sinclair (Bondi ASC), who apparently collapsed and passed away during a competition match.

The Baths & Clubs

The mid-week competitions commenced on the 11th November and comprised 35 teams competing across three premiership grades. During the season, metropolitan matches were played at Balmoral, Bondi, Coogee Aquarium, Drummoyne, Elkington Park, Northbridge and The Spit.

Although no new clubs entered the competition this season, it was pleasing to see that no clubs lapsed. The first, second and junior competitions all consisted of seven teams and were played over two rounds, with two semi-finals and a final.

The third grade competition attracted the largest number of entries with 11 in the Northern Zone and 10 in the Southern Zone. The week-end competitions were conducted on Sunday nights and attracted 20 team entries. The Sunday programs often included other events such as the '55 yard swim with the ball' contest, which was won by Asher Hart (Bondi) in 32.2 seconds and the 110 yard championship, which was won by Jack Ferguson (Bondi).[5]

▼ *Bronte Water Polo club man, Ken Mills, in an impressive line-up of Bondi Lifeguards, c.1948. Photo - Shirley Mills.*

NEW SOUTH WALES TEAM
1948 - National Co- Champions - Sydney
From Left: Roger Cornforth (University), Eric Johnson (vc, Balmain), Ben Dalley (g, Balmain), Jack King (Pyrmont), Leon Ferguson (Bondi), Hermie Doerner (c/Coach, Bondi), Jack Ferguson (Bondi). Missing: Owen Doerner (Bondi), Bob Traynor (Manager/Ref), Harold Duker (Referee).

▲ Ken Mills (centre) was an outstanding competitor in Surf Life Saving, but later became a valuable team member for Bronte Water Polo Club. Photo - Shirley Mills.

Representatives in NSW Teams

The representative program for the 1947/48 season was both considerable and important in that it heralded the inaugural Australian Championships. At stake for players selected in the NSW team for the inaugural 1948 Australian Championships was also a chance of being chosen in Australia's first ever Olympic Water Polo Team, that was heading to London later in the year.

Ex-Hungarian water polo player Thea Murany coached a squad of Sydney hopefuls in the lead up to the 1948 State team trials. However, the NSW selectors again went for experience with Hermie Doerner, Ben Dalley, Eric Johnson and Jack King accounting for 39 State team caps between them. There were however, two new talented brothers in Jack and Leon Ferguson from the Bondi club, who impressed sufficiently enough to be included.

The strong NSW team finished the 1st National Championships in Sydney, as co-champions with Victoria with Queensland in third place.

The 1948 Olympic Team

The Australian Olympic team was selected after

these championships, and despite winning the national title, only three Victorians were included compared to seven players from NSW. The Aussies played through a European tour, and five matches at the London Olympics, where they placed 18th, but lost only ten of their 23 matches on tour.

The Premierships

By season's end, Bondi had dominated their opposition and finished as minor premiers. In the play-offs, Balmain ended the University's hopes (8~1) and Bondi eliminated Pyrmont (5~1). With no preliminary final both winners progressed straight to the grand-final where Bondi ran out victors over Balmain (6~4) to crown an undefeated season with their first 1st Grade premiership since 1937. Balmain won the 2nd Grade competition, and in the 3rd Grade, Bankstown won the South and North Sydney the North, both being undefeated. The playoff between these two teams lasted over 90 minutes, North Sydney eventually winning (7~5) after two periods of extra-time had been played. So close was the competition between the two dominant clubs that the 'Club Champions' for overall performance across all grades, was shared this season between Balmain and Bondi.

BONDI
1947/48 - NSWAWPA 1st Grade Premiers
Hermie Doerner (c/Coach), Leon Ferguson, Jack Ferguson, Ray Smee, Clem Walsh, Owen Doerner (g), Asher Hart, A. Kirkman.

A Junior competition was played over two rounds and featured teams from Balmain, Balmoral, Bondi, Drummoyne, Manly, Northbridge, North Sydney and The Spit. Northbridge were again too good and made it three in a row by defeating North Sydney (2~1) in the grand-final.

The Sunday Night Handicap competition was conducted at Coogee Aquarium and attracted a large number of teams from Balmain, Ben Buckler, Birchgrove, Bondi, Maroubra, Northbridge, Randwick/ Coogee, Rozelle, Sydney, The Boot

1947/48 Season Statistics N.S.W.A.W.P.A.

Clubs in the Water Polo Competitions.

Clubs	Grades				Total
	1	2	3N	3S	
Balmain	●	●	2		3
Balmoral		2			2
Bankstown				●	1
Bondi	●	●		●	3
Drummoyne		●		●	2
East Sydney				●	1
Freshwater		●			1
Manly	●			●	2
Nth Sydney		2			2
Northbridge	●	●	●		3
Pyrmont	●	●		●	3
R'wick/Coogee	●			●	2
Roseville		●			2
Sydney			2		2
The Spit	●	2			3
University	●	●	●		3
	7	7	11	10	35

Results of the Water Polo Competitions.

Grade	Premier		Runner-Up
1st	Bondi~6	d.	4~Balmain
2nd	Balmain~4	d.	2~Northbridge
3rd	Nth Sydney A~7	d.	5~Bankstown
Club Champions			BALMAIN / BONDI
Juniors	Northbridge~2	d.	1~Nth Sydney

▲ *The war had instilled discipline and fitness into the population and many young men were attracted by those qualities in the game of water polo.*

and University. The Association hoped that more teams would join in the future to enable this competition to reach the heights of pre-war days. In the play-offs, Randwick/Coogee defeated University (3~1) and Ben Buckler forfeited to Northbridge. The final was then won by Northbridge over Randwick/Coogee (6~4).

A Sunday Night Knock-out Handicap Competition was also contested this season with entries from Balmain, Ben Buckler, Bondi, Maroubra, Northbridge, Pyrmont, Sydney, The Boot and the University. The final was won by the old 'hard heads' from the Sydney club over Northbridge (4~2).[5]

1948-49

1948/49 NSWAWPA OFFICIALS: Dr. K. Kirkland (Patron); Dr. H.K. Porter (President); M. Campbell (Past President); A.P. Hart (Chairman); H. Duker (Registrar); H. Doerner (Secretary); J. Ferguson Jnr. (Asst. Secretary); R. Traynor (Treasurer).

The NSWAWPA extended their sincere sympathy to the relatives of Mr. J. Conlon, a vice-president and long supporter of the of the Association.

The Baths & Clubs

During this season, metropolitan matches were played at Bondi, Bankstown, Drummoyne, Elkington Park, Northbridge and The Spit.

In regard to new clubs, a team from North Narrabeen affiliated for the first time, while Ben Buckler, Birchgrove, East Sydney, Manly, Maroubra, Rozelle and The Boot all lapsed, primarily due to the abandonment of the Sunday Night Handicap Competition.

The Tuesday night competitions commenced in November and were comprised of 33 teams competing across four premiership grades. The 1st Grade competition consisted of only five teams and was played over three rounds. The Association introduced a 4th Grade for the first time which was strongly supported with eight different clubs.

After repeated and continual, but unsuccessful negotiations with the manager of the Coogee Aquarium, the week-end competition normally conducted on a Sunday night was abandoned.[6]

Representatives in NSW Teams

For the second time in the history of the NSW State team, the membership was dominated exclusively by just two clubs in Bondi and Balmain. Hermie Doerner (Bondi) racked up his 12th State team cap and created a record ten caps as captain/coach. Gordon Amadee (Balmain) was recalled and five encumbents held onto their places, while the new caps were Les Deveridge (Balmain), and Bondi teammates Ken Erickson and Asher Hart, the latter being a talented NSW swimmer in his youth.

This year again brought success for NSW as it claimed a second National Championship in Brisbane, by finishing ahead of Victoria and Queensland.

The Premierships

It was a two horse race again this season in the 1st Grade competition between the strong 'B' and 'B' clubs. Bondi eliminated Northbridge (2~1) and Balmain did the same to University (4~1) in the semi-finals. With no preliminary final both winners progressed directly to the grand-final, where Bondi ran out victors over Balmain (6~4) in a very closely contested match. Drummoyne won the 2nd Grade, and Balmain won both the 3rd's and were the inaugural winners of the 4th Grade competition. Balmain capped off a great season by also winning the Junior competition. It is worthy to record that the Balmain Club played in all five Association finals and were successful in three, a commendable record. The 'Club Champions' for overall performance across all grades, unquestionably went to Balmain.

Water polo stars "at sea" under new rules

First water polo matches under international rulings were played last night and many players, including Olympians, were "all at sea."

Players who hold, kick or "sink" a rival are now ordered out of the water. Previously only a free throw was given against them.

Under the new rule players are not allowed to "punch" the ball with clenched fists.

A goalkeeper can now carry the ball to half-way. Previously he was allowed to walk or swim only four yards.

Players may score a goal with any part of the body. In the past they had to score with their arms.

The new rulings were brought into force to comply with oversea regulations.

"The games last night were faster and better to watch," said secretary of the NSW Referees' Association (Mr. Harold Dukes).

"We will be sending a team to the Empire Games, and players must have the benefit of playing under the correct rulings.

"We lost matches overseas last year because the players were not conversant with the rules," he added.

Last night's results:—Bondi 10 (H. Doerner 4, A. Hart 2, J. Ferguson 2, R. Smee 2) beat University 4 (R. Taylor 2, R. Dutton 2); Balmain 6 (D. Pont 2 E. Johnson 2, L. Deveridge 2) beat Northbridge 4 (J. Dreelin 4); Pyrmont the bye.

(The Sun, 9th Nov 1949, p35).

NEW SOUTH WALES TEAM
National Champions
Brisbane, 1949
Hermie Doerner (c/Coach, Bondi)
Gordon Amadee (Balmain)
Les Deveridge (Balmain)
Owen Doerner (g, Bondi)
Ken Erickson (Bondi)
Jack Ferguson (Bondi)
Leon Ferguson (Bondi)
Asher Hart (Bondi)
Eric Johnson (vc, Balmain)
Mark Phillip (Manager)
Harold Duker (Referee).

BONDI
1948/49 - NSWAWPA 1st Grade Premiers
Hermie Doerner (c/Coach), Leon Ferguson, Jack Ferguson, Ray Smee, Clem Walsh, Owen Doerner (g), Asher Hart, A. Kirkman, Ken Erickson.

1948/49 Season Statistics
N.S.W.A.W.P.A.

Clubs in the Water Polo Competitions.

Clubs	Grades 1 2 3 4	Total
Balmain	● ● ● ●	4
Balmoral	●	1
Bankstown	●	1
Bondi	● ● ● ●	4
Drummoyne	● ●	2
Freshwater	●	1
Nth Narrabeen	● ●	2
Nth Sydney	● ● ●	3
Northbridge	● ● ●	3
Pyrmont	● ● ●	3
R'wick/Coogee	●	1
Roseville	●	1
Sydney	●	1
The Spit	● ● ●	3
University	● ● ●	3
	5 9 12 8	33

Results of the Water Polo Competitions.

Grade	Premier		Runner-Up
1st	Bondi~2	d.	1~Balmain
2nd	Drummoyne~6	d.	4~Balmain
3rd	Balmain~1	d.	0~Freshwater
4th	Balmain~4	d.	1~The Spit
	Club Champions		BALMAIN
Juniors	Balmain~7	d.	1~Nth Sydney

A Junior competition was played over two rounds and featured teams from Balmain, Balmoral, Drummoyne, Manly, Northbridge, North Sydney and The Spit. Balmain easily defeated North Sydney (7~1) in the grand-final.[6]

1949-50

1949/50 NSWAWPA OFFICIALS: Dr. K. Kirkland (Patron); Dr. H.K. Porter (President); M. Campbell (Past President); A.P. Hart (Chairman); M. Phillips (Registrar); H. Doerner (Secretary); J. Castle Jnr. (Asst. Secretary); R. Traynor (Treasurer).

The Association congratulated the following water polo players for their success in other fields of sport. R. Mattison (club unknown) for being a member of the Australian Surf Team that visited New Zealand, Roger Cornforth (Universities) who played Rugby Union for Australia against the British Isles team and Ron Lord (Drummoyne) who played for the NSW Soccer team against Queensland. Sincere sympathies were extended to the relatives of Mr. R. Hart, a vice-president of the Association on his passing.

The Baths & Clubs

The sport was really making headway and in some unexpected areas, as in this season half of the Associations clubs were from north of the harbour. During the year, metropolitan matches were played at Bondi, Bankstown, Drummoyne, Elkington Park, Northbridge and The Spit. In regard to new clubs, Cronulla, Narrabeen and the Shell Club affiliated for the first time, while Randwick & Coogee lapsed.

The Tuesday night competitions commenced in November and encompassed some 33 teams competing across four premiership grades. The 1st Grade competition consisted of only five teams and was played over three rounds. The University Penguins were particularly strong this season with an in-flux of ex-Hungarians in their ranks.[7]

Representatives in NSW Teams

In State team selection games, the Eastern District team won the Association's Interdistrict Competition and for the second year running, Bondi and Balmain clubs completely monopolised the membership of the NSW team. Leon Ferguson and Ken Erickson (Bondi) were omitted, but Hermie Doerner (Bondi) was still running the show as captain/coach. The selectors retained seven of its 1949 championship winning team and admitted only one new cap in a talented Bondi junior by the name of Ray Smee.

However, playing in Melbourne was always difficult and in the absence of entries from any other States, Victoria bounced back to narrowly reclaim the national title and their sixth Regal Cup (2~1; 2~2; 4~2).

The Premierships

The University Penguins were particularly strong this season with an influx of ex-Hungarians in their ranks. Bondi was once again the dominant 1st Grade team throughout the season, and took out it's 3rd straight minor premiership following completion of the preliminary rounds. In the play-offs, it was surprising to see Balmain eliminated with such ease by the University Penguins (11~4) and Bondi swept Northbridge aside (10~1) to progress to the competition decider. In the final, University did what they could but, there was no stopping a rampaging Bondi side who triumphed (9~2). The win gave Bondi their third successive 1st Grade premiership and established a record for the largest winning margin in a 1st Grade grand-final, that still stands. It is interesting to note that in this season, a different club was successful in each of the Associations' competitions, with Bondi taking out the Club Championship.

A Junior competition was played over two rounds and featured

NEW SOUTH WALES TEAM
Runners-Up at Nationals
Melbourne, 1950

Hermie Doerner (c/Co, Bondi)
Gordon Amadee (Balmain)
Les Deveridge (Balmain)
Owen Doerner (g, Bondi)
Jack Ferguson (Bondi)
Asher Hart (Bondi)
Eric Johnson (Balmain)
Ray Smee (Bondi)
Harold Duker (Mgr/Ref).

1949/50 Season Statistics
N.S.W.A.W.P.A.

Clubs in the Water Polo Competitions.

Clubs	Grades 1 2 3 4				Total
Balmain	●	●	●	●	4
Balmoral			●		1
Bankstown			●		1
Bondi	●	●	●		3
Cronulla			●		1
Drummoyne			●		1
Freshwater			●		1
Narrabeen			2		2
Nth Narrabeen			●		1
North Sydney	●		●	●	3
Northbridge	●	●		●	3
Pyrmont	●	●		●	3
Ramsgate		●			1
Roseville			●		1
Shell			●		1
Sydney		●			1
The Spit			●	●	2
University	●	●	●		3
	5	7	10	11	33

Results of the Water Polo Competitions.

Grade	Premier		Runner-Up
1st	Bondi~9	d.	2~University
2nd	University~3	d.	1~Bondi B
3rd	Bankstown~4	d.	2~Nth Narrabeen
4th	Northbridge~3	d.	2~Balmain
	Club Champions		BONDI
Juniors	Balmain~5	d.	3~The Spit

teams from Balmain, Bankstown, Drummoyne, Freshwater, Northbridge, Pyrmont and The Spit. Balmain eventually defeated The Spit (5~3) and crowned their undefeated season with the premiership.[7]

1950-51

1950/51 NSWAWPA OFFICIALS: Dr. K. Kirkland (Patron); Dr. H.K. Porter (President); M. Campbell (Past President); A.P. Hart (Chairman); M. Phillips (Registrar); H. Doerner (Secretary); E.B. Phillips (Asst. Secretary); R.Y. Traynor (Treasurer).

The 1950/51 season began with the 21st NSWAWPA Annual General Meeting, which was held at 7.45pm on Monday, 8th October 1951 in the Surf Life Saving Association Rooms, 16 Hunter St. Sydney. The NSW Association congratulated water polo players for their success in other fields of sport and this year the recipient was Ron Lord (Drummoyne) who was selected as goalkeeper for the Australian Soccer team against a visiting English side.

The Baths & Clubs

During this season, water polo was handicapped by a lack of pools. The acute shortage of pool space necessitated that some matches had to be played on weekends. Metropolitan matches were played at Bondi, Bankstown, Domain, Drummoyne, Elkington Park, Northbridge and The Spit.

UNIVERSITY PENGUINS WATER POLO TEAM
1949/50 - 1st Grade Runners-Up - NSWAWPA
Back row: F.J. Barnes, Roger Cornforth (g), Les Vessey, Zoli Szendro. Front row: Tibor Arvai, C.B. Phillips (Capt.), T. Murany Esq. (Coach), W.B. Phillips, F. Santos.
Photo - Bill Phillips Jr.

BONDI AMATEUR WATER POLO CLUB
1949/50 - 1st Grade Premiers - NSWAWPA
Back row (from left): Owen Doerner, Leon Ferguson, Ray Smee, Jack Ferguson. Front row: A. Kirkman, Hermie Doerner (c), Asher Hart. [Inset - Ken Erickson].
Photo - Ray Smee.

In regard to new clubs, Cabarita affiliated for the first time, East Sydney and North Ramsgate re-affiliated after a break of some years, while Balmoral, Cronulla, Freshwater, Narrabeen, Ramsgate and Roseville clubs all lapsed. Total NSWAWPA player registrations stood at approximately 240.

The Tuesday night competitions commenced in November as usual, but it wasn't long before power restrictions interfered with the schedule. As the season progressed, it became necessary to conduct games on weekends as both pools and referees became difficult to acquire.

Unfortunately, due to the severe shortage of pools, the Junior competition was not conducted, which in turn affected the overall number of teams entering the competitions.

As the season got underway, a new club from the north of Sydney was making waves and throwing plenty of goals. Only one round was played that year, but after the last game, it was The Spit Club that had gained the minor premiership. They had gone through their nine games undefeated with a superb goal average (36 goals for and only 7 against). The cause of this 'structural shift' in the Sydney water polo competition was the arrival of a number of post-war immigrants from Hungary.[8]

Representatives in NSW Teams

This years NSW team included an exciting new element in two ex-Hungarian players from The Spit Club. Under International rules, both Oscar Csuvik and Alez Kosegi (The Spit) could play within their adopted nation, but not for their adopted nation, which had the immediate effect of bolstering the NSW team tremendously.

> ### 'New' Spit side in polo win
>
> The Spit water polo team, in which six of the seven players are Hungarians, last night defeated Balmain, 9-1.
>
> For The Spit, Bela Vadas scored four goals, Oscar Csuvik and Alex Cosegi two each, and Tom Sendro one.
>
> Australian Empire Games representative G. Amedee scored Balmain's goal.
>
> *Daily Telegraph, 22nd Nov 1950*

▼ *Ex-Hungarian Olympian, Oscar Csuvik playing for the NSW Water Polo Team, brought a completely new approach to the game. Photo - Oscar (Csuvik) Charles.*

Roger Cornforth, also of The Spit Club was recalled along with Leon Ferguson (Bondi), while Victorian Peter Bennett (Melbourne), who was spending 12 months in Sydney, was also selected.

The 1951 Australian Championship and Regal Cup Series was contested from the 23rd to 28th February 1951, against Victoria over three matches played at Bankstown Baths, The Spit Baths and Elkington Park. The test match series was won by NSW (8~3; 4~5; 9~3).

The Premierships

In the metropolitan play-offs, The Spit eliminated Balmain (3~1) and Bondi A (the old heads) disposed of their second string side Bondi B (the young heads) by 5~1. Surprisingly, in the final Bondi A acquitted themselves remarkably well to defeat the talented Spit team (5~3). However, because The Spit club were minor premiers, they exercised their right to challenge Bondi A, but were again defeated (8~5) in the grand-final, which allowed Bondi to take their 4th successive 1st Grade premiership. The 'Club Champions' for overall performance across all grades, again went to Balmain.

During the grand-final, Alex Kosegi argued with and was ejected by the referee, Bob Traynor, and although eligible to return to the game, he took exception to the decision and remained on the bench, leaving The Spit team to play a man down for the remainder of the match. Some say this event led to discontent within the club and the eventual break-up of the Hungarian faction. But others, and particularly the Hungarians themselves, thought it prudent not to continue as water polo 'conquerors' in their newly adopted country. Oscar Csuvik commented... "we emigrated to Australia wanting to assimilate

BONDI AMATEUR WATER POLO CLUB
1950/51 - 1st Grade Premiers - NSWAWPA
Back row (from left): - Bill Jones, Keith Whitehead, Ray Smee, J. Gillies. Front row: Doug Laing (g), Jack Ferguson (c), G. Taylor, Col Smee. Inset: Peter Bennett. Photo - Ray Smee.

and develop friendships, not accumulate enemies!"

For this reason, the team decided to split and go their separate ways after their one and only successful season. Alex Kosegi, Zoli (Tom) Szendro and Elmar Szatmary transferred to Bondi. Bert (Momi) Vadas initially went to Bondi, but in 1954 transferred to a young but rapidly improving Bronte club. Oscar remained with The Spit club for a few more seasons, while Tibor Arvai and Roger Cornforth stopped playing altogether.[8]

The Europeans

Oscar Csuvic

Being a 1948 Olympic Games water polo silver medallist, 25 year old Oscar Csuvik was quickly snapped up by The Spit club when he arrived in Sydney in October 1950, primarily under the wing of Bill Berge Phillips. It was at The Spit club that Oscar also met Carl Phillips along with Alan Montgomery and his two year old son Peter, who went on to play in four Olympic Games for Australia.

At The Spit Club, the new recruit had the effect of catapulting, not only the club, but the game of water polo in Sydney and NSW, into a new era. Oscar was soon joined by a number of other water polo playing Hungarians, themselves emigrants, although none of whom were as well credentialled as Oscar. Banding together as people and cultures in unfamiliar environments often do, The Spit 1st Grade team effectively became an all Hungarian affair with the exception of ex-Australian water polo representative in Roger Cornforth. It was a very formidable team.

The Sydney Clubs Receive A Boost

The splitting up of The Spit team inadvertently delivered a tremendous boost for water polo in

---

1950/51 Season Statistics N.S.W.A.W.P.A.

Clubs in the Water Polo Competitions.

Clubs	Grades 1	2	3	4	Total
Balmain	●	●	●	●	4
Bankstown	●				1
Bondi	2	●	●		4
Cabarita				●	1
Drummoyne			●	●	2
East Sydney			●		1
Nth Narrabeen			●	2	3
Nth Ramsgate		●			1
Nth Sydney	●		●		2
Northbridge	●	●	●		3
Pyrmont	●	●	●		3
Shell			●		1
Sydney			●		1
The Spit	●	●	●	●	4
University	●	●		●	3
	9	8	8	9	34

Results of the Water Polo Competitions.

Grade	Premier		Runner-Up
1st	Bondi A~8	d.	5~The Spit
2nd	Balmain~4	d.	2~Northbridge
3rd	Nth Narrabeen	d.	Nth Sydney
4th	Balmain	d.	The Spit
Club Champions	BALMAIN		

THE SPIT WATER POLO TEAM
1950/51 - 1st Grade Runners-Up
NSWAWPA
Oscar Csuvik (c/Coach), Tibor Arvai, Elmer Szatmary, Les Vessey, Alex Koszegi, Bert Vadas, Zoli Szendro & Roger Cornforth (g).

Two Hungarian Olympic representatives and Frenchman Alex Jany will play in a water-polo match tonight.

They will play for a European team against New South Wales.

The match will be held during the swimming championships.

The Hungarian Olympic representatives are O. Csuvik and A. Kosegi.

A team of ten will represent New South Wales in the Australian swimming championships.

The championships will be held in Melbourne from February 17 to 24.

The team will be announced on Tuesday night.

(Daily Telegraph, 17th Jan 1951, p23).

Jany Was Water Polo Star

French swimmer Alex Jany yesterday scored three goals in a water-polo match which drew a big crowd to the Spit baths.

Jany played with a number of Australians against a team composed mostly of leading Hungarian players, now New Australians.

The match was not advertised, and was arranged when Jany said he would like a game if one were being played.

The Hungarian team won by eight goals to five.

Jany, who has ten times represented France in international matches, gave some idea of the high standard of his play.

He has played against Hungary twice, Holland twice, Spain, Belgium, Italy, Yugoslavia, Switzerland and Sweden.

Not Extended

Yesterday it was obvious that Jany was in the game for the fun of it, and he did not appear to extend himself at any stage.

NSW as the 'Hungarian style' was quickly adopted by a number of Sydney clubs. Essentially, the old method of passing the ball from player to player 'on the water' was brushed aside by the Hungarians, who showed how much quicker and spectacular water polo could be. Their players handled the ball in the air, passing from hand to hand rather than onto the water, as the Aussies had been accustomed. The other noticeable change was that the new 'Hungarian water polo techniques' were the exclusive domain of physically fit and self-disciplined players, and the victories of the Spit Club sounded a warning to those who weren't prepared to work hard at the sport.

Oscar was selected in the NSW team along with Alex Koszegi for a few seasons, but a FINA ruling in those years prohibited water polo internationals from playing for another country, even if they'd emigrated! Oscar was however, co-opted to coach the 1952 Australian team to the Helsinki Olympic Games although, apparently some players and officials were less than co-operative. Indeed, on the ship over, passengers had labelled some of the

◀Article on French water polo player Alex Jany (SMH, 8 Jan 1951, p6). ▼Training at The Spit club in 1951 were (from left): Szittya, Les Vessey, Oscar Csuvik, Tibor Arvai, Alex Kosegi, Bert Vadas, Bill Berge Phillips, Doug Laing, Keith Whitehead, Ray Smee. Photo - Robbie Vadas.

Australian Water Polo team as the 'Carlsberg Kids'.

Oscar wasn't used to this kind of behaviour, his attitude being far more professional, coming from a very disciplined and well drilled water polo background. He at one point, cabled his resignation to Bill Berge Phillips, who requested that Oscar hang on until he arrived, at which time the 'riot act' was summarily read to the Aussie team members.

After Helsinki, Oscar was nearing 30, and began studying accountancy, but without transport, found it increasingly difficult to maintain his commitment to water polo. His last season with The Spit club was in 1953/54, which sadly coincided with their demise.

Around ten years later, during the 1963/64 season, Oscar approached some young players led by Peter Primo and Dave Habler of Randwick Rugby Club, who were training one day, and enquired if they needed a coach. The Randwick boys didn't know who Oscar was, or his water polo credentials, but took him on his word, and were shocked by his prowess and skills. Oscar agreed and coached the Randwick Club to runners-up in their

Continuation of ... article on French water polo player Alex Jany (SMH, 8 Jan 1951, p6).
▼ *Players showing off their skills during a photo session at The Spit club in 1951.*
Photo - Robbie Vadas.

He scored the first goal of the match with a righthand backhand throw that left the opposing goalie no chance of making a save.

His second goal came from a smashing throw from nearly half way, then he added another from close in.

He was then content to pass the ball to his Australian teammates to give them opportunities to score.

The crowd was amused when Jany was penalised for wrapping his big legs around Hungarian player, Leslie Vessey.

The Hungarian team, which includes former internationals Oscar Scuvik, Alex Koszegy and Leslie Vessey, had a better understanding in the water than the Australian team.

To Play Again

But most spectators thought the result might have been closer if Jany had put all he knew into the game.

Jany has agreed to play in two water-polo matches during the State swimming championships.

He will play with the New Australians against the best team that can be selected from the Australians available.

The scores yesterday were: **Spit Hungarians**, 8 (O. Scuvik, 3; A. Koszegy, 2; L. Vessey, 3), beat **Spit Australians**, 5 (A. Jany, 3; A. Barnes, 1; J. Duncan, 1).

◀TOP: The 1948 Hungarian Olympic Games Team with Oscar Csuvic (bottom right). Photo - Oscar Charles. ABOVE: The Hungarian Olympian 'Kalman Markovits', became the poster boy for NSWAWPA and Bronte Water Polo Club with this impressive image (from 'Water Polo' by Bela Rajki, Museum Press, 1958).

first ever year in the 2nd Grade competition, and with only one season under their belt they entered the 1st Grade in season 1964/65... a profound achievement.

By 1967 Oscar was again in retirement from the sport, but Doug Laing, who was coaching a young and talented Universities team, approached Oscar to take over there. Oscar again agreed and thoroughly enjoyed the more professional attitude at Universities, where he continued on in that position for a number of years.

In 1968, Syd Grange (President of the ASU) approached Oscar to be manager of the Australian Water Polo team at the 1968 Mexico Olympic Games. Oscar thought this team to be much different to his previous stewardship, with most players exhibiting a very disciplined and focused approach, and so he agreed.[9]

In an odd twist, it was Peter Primo, then at Coogee Surf Club, who was asked to be water polo coach for a team of youngsters at Newtown

▶ABOVE: Caricature poster of the top Hungarian club team MTK (dated 1945), with Bert Vadas at bottom left. Their opposition on this occasion was the ILSA Club from Temesvar/ Timisoara (a Romanian town, near the Hungarian border). ILSA, a textile manufacturer and one of the city's largest employers, was also the builder of a 33.33m pool in 1933, and in no time at all, ILSA became one of Romania's strongest swimming and water polo clubs. The Romanian Water Polo Federation records show the original 1933 ILSA team as including amongst others Flesch Bonzo, being the father of our Rolly Flesch. The poster shows Jozseph Vértesi (1932 Gold Medal Olympian), who was the coach of MTK. A few years later some of the MTK players emigrated to Sydney including Vadas. But it just so happens that many years later, and following in his dad's footsteps, Rolly Flesch also joined the ILSA club where he received his first water polo training in that very same pool (see page 133). After arriving in Sydney and by sheer chance, Rolly's water polo coach at Randwick Boys High, Bob Cope who was himself a member of the strong Bronte Club, suggested that Rolly continue to build skills by joining him at Bronte, where it just so happened that Bert 'Momie' Vadas was by then the head coach… an uncanny chain of coincidence! BELOW: After World War II, water polo had become a major sport in Budapest.

ASC for the 1970/71 season. The following season, many of the Newtown team were introduced to Bronte Water Polo club by Peter Primo, myself included.

The contribution of men like Oscar Csuvik, Alex Kosegi, Anton Bolvary, Bert 'Momie' Vadas and many other European water polo players who emigrated to Australia in the 1950's and 60's, was enormous, and their influence had an immeasurable impact on both the style and the effectiveness of the Australian game.

A detailed account of Oscar Csuvik's contribution to Australian water polo is presented in 'Water Warriors: Chronicle of Australian Water Polo'. [10]

Bert Vadas

Bert Vadas was born about 1919, and received the nickname 'Momie' at a young age. In 1927, at age eight, he was inspired by some great players and tried to join the local water polo club, but despite rejection, Momie and his friends persisted.

In those days Hungary was the most professional water polo nation in the world, and their organisation was very advanced compared to other countries. All clubs had a system whereby young athletes weren't allowed to play until they'd trained and learnt the various skills and drills for three years, and this was before they were allowed to play even a practice game.

However, through persistence, Momie was eventually accepted into the MTK Club of Budapest, and went with the club on several trips around Europe.

Momie was married before the war, but being Jewish he was interred and taken to a labour camp in North-West Hungary, where he did what was needed to survive. There, the German staff once asked... "Who here can bake?" and despite no experience whatsover, Momie immediately raised his hand and was given the job... which ensured him work, as well as access to food. He did not play water polo during his detention.

Straight after the war Momie re-joined his teammates at MTK water polo club and played with them until he departed Hungary. His son Robbie came along in 1946. Momie himself was gifted, and played at the peak level of Hungarian water polo. He later told his son that he wasn't selected for the 1948 Hungarian Olympic team, because the authorities

TOP: Post-war photograph of Bert Vadas with the 1946 MTK champion water polo team from Hungary (from left): Les Vecsei, Tibor Arvai, Oscar Csuvik, Istvan Szatmary, Alex Kosegi, Santos, Bert Vadas and young Robbie Vadas. ABOVE: MTK Water Polo team with other Budapest players c.1935: Lagyi, Vadas, Laci, Lanyi, Schlenker, Hoffer, Nagy, and seated: Bert Vadas, Pacni & Saslaci. Photos - Robbie Vadas.

FUNDAMENTALS OF WATER POLO.

B. "(Momie)" VADAS.

ESSENTIALS TO REMEMBER.

1Swimming condition is vital
to good play.

2. Keep head up at all times
   and watch for the ball.

3. A quick pass always beats
   a swimmer,.. don't swim too
   far with the ball.

4. Always be ready to make a
   break in any direction.

5. Keep thinking ahead...
   anticipate any change in play
   and in possession of the ball.

6. Play to the rules at all
   times and never question the
   referee's decision.
   . . . .

1.

FOREWORD
These notes and illustrations are
designed to be a guide to both
coaches and players of water polo.
Considerable emphasis has been
placed on training methods, since
properly conducted training is both
interesting and instructive, and is
essential if the team is to improve
and enjoy the game.
The main features of positional
play are described, with methods
of attack and defence. It is
hoped that these notes will be
of assistance in improving the
standard of the game, and helping
to popularise this sport which is
ideally suited to Australian
conditions.
ORGANISATION OF TRAINING.
The various methods of training
are detailed below, If a large
number of players are practicing
at once, they should be divided
into groups, and while one is swimm
ing, for instance, another can be
passing the ball while a third is
shooting at goal etc.
These groups are then rotated, thus
bringing not only variety but also
planning so often missing in training.

Bert Vadas brought his water polo experience and skills learnt in Hungary to Australia and produced the 'Fundamentals of Water Polo.'

knew he wouldn't return to Hungary. This is interesting as many of the players who were actually selected for the London Games, didn't return to Hungary either, with many of them seeking refuge in Australia and America.

With Hungary now firmly under Communist rule, Momie's mother-in-law had already emigrated to Australia, so he tried a couple of times to escape with his family, and succeeded on his second attempt, entering Vienna in 1949. From there the Vadas's moved to Paris for almost a year before travelling to Italy, where they boarded a ship for Australia.

▲ *The Bronte team mates both played and socialised together (from left): Arthur Obey, Bert Vadas, Dick See and partners. Photo - Robbie Vadas.*

The Vadas's arrived in Sydney in late 1950, and moved temporarily in with their relatives at Glebe. They then bought a house in Matraville where they reamined until problems arose and they divorced, when Momie moved again about 1953/54 as a lodger into a place in Yanco Ave, Bronte. The Thornetts lived

▲*An 18 year old John Thornett was taken under Bert Vadas' wing, which was the genesis of Bronte Water Polo Club, circa 1953. ◄At just 5'9", but an absolute power pack, Bert Vadas demonstrated that being tall was not necessarily an advantage in water polo. Photo's - Robbie Vadas.*

just one block away in Thomas Street.

At that time, The Spit club, which was full of Hungarians... decided to disband and asked between themselves... "who'd like to help a bunch of young kids at Bronte?" Apparently... everyone stepped back except for Momie, who was then gifted the job. But he settled in very easily at Bronte... and grew to love the team, the players and their determined attitude. The real strength of the Bronte Club was that the players ate and socialised together, and became very close, which made them a loyal and powerful unit.

Momie's main strength was that he knew how to mould these young players. His soft speaking approach was never authoritarian, and always encouraging. He was definitely in command, but ruled in a friendly way. Momie himself was a water polo role model, and played in the NSW State team in 1954, 1955 and

1956... and he also coached the NSW team in 1960.

His greatest achievement however, was in shaping his athletically gifted Bronte boys into a skilled water polo team that rose from virtual unknowns, to become premiers of New South Wales, and arguably the most powerful water polo team in Australia from 1959 to 1962.

After Bronte's four consecutive 1st grade premierships, Momie remained on the scene as 1st Grade and head coach of Bronte for some time, frequently ferrying players to training and games in his 'coffee van.' But his involvement ended when Graeme Samuel took over the coaching reigns at the start of the 1969/70 season. Bert 'Momie' Vadas died about 2010, but he remains a revered water polo icon within the Bronte diaspora.[11]

Chapter 3
TALENTED LOCALS
(1952 - 1958)

Bronte Water Polo Club, 1st Grade (c.1955). Back row (from left): Dick Thornett, John Thornett, Vic McGrath, Ken Mills. Front row: Dick See, Bert 'Momie' Vadas, Ken Thornett, Jack Campbell.

"I was born in 1935, the eldest of three boys, and we had no particular predisposition to be athletes. But we were lucky that we were brought up at Bronte in Sydney near the beach and our early days were spent mostly in swimming. My father used to go down to the baths every morning and swam most days of the year in both summer and winter, and I went with him, so with some help from our Uncle, we all became swimmers at the Bronte Amateur Swimming Club, as it was called then."

John Thornett, 3 July 2008
Interviewed by Ian Warden [1]

By 1951 the lads that had played previously in the first Bronte water polo team, had grown into young men. The likes of Jack Campbell, Ken Mills and others were still on the scene, but joining them now was a 16 year old John Thornett, who was primarily responsible for reinvigorating water polo at Bronte. This group of talented young Bronte swimmers had role models to emulate in their State water polo representatives, and were most certainly inspired by the local Bondi boys, who were not only Sydney premiers, but later had three of their members selected in the 1952 Olympic Games team. This was what stirred them into entering a team of their own for the 1951/52 season.

1951-52

1951/52 NSWAWPA OFFICIALS: Dr. K. Kirkland (Patron); Dr. H.K. Porter (President); M. Campbell (Past President); A.P. Hart (Chairman); R. Gibson (Registrar); R.Y. Traynor (Secretary); H. Doerner (Asst. Secretary); R. Smee (Treasurer).

OLYMPIANS IN TEAMS

Candidates for the New South Wales water polo team for the Olympic Games trials and Australian Championships include former Olympic reps of Austria, Hungary and Holland. The former Olympians... will play a series of matches during the State Swimming Championships at North Sydney Olympic Pool, after which the NSW team will be named. Australian Olympians are J. Ferguson, E. Johnston and H. Doerner. Overseas Olympians are new Australians, A. Kosegi, O. Csuvik, B. Vardas (Hungary) and J. Hessing (Holland). The inter-district teams are:

NORTH: Goal, J. Dreelin; forwards, J. Ferguson, O. Csuvik, T. Sendro; backs, B. Vardas, L. Vessey, A. Ellean. Res: J. Barnes.

WEST: P. Fenech, J. Clothier, G. Amadee, E. Pierce, F. Jordan, E. Johnston, N. Cason. Res: A. Stringer, C. Phillips.

EAST: D. Laing, H. Doerner, R. Smee, K. Whitehead, A. Kosegi, J. Hessing, W. Jones. Res: A. Hart, E. Szatmary.

Unreferenced Newspaper,
Eric Johnston's Scrapbook
Jan/Feb 1952.

The 1951/52 season began following the NSWAWPA 22nd Annual General Meeting, which was held at 7.45pm on Monday, 29th September 1951, in the Surf Life Saving Association Rooms, 16 Hunter St. Sydney.

The Baths & Clubs

The premiership competitions commenced on the 20th November and games were played on Tuesday and Sunday evenings. The competitions were conducted across four grades with some 32 teams entering. This was the smallest number of teams entered with the NSW Association in a considerable number of years. The general standard of play however, was particularly good and the majority of teams that competed were very keen.

During the season, metropolitan matches were played at Bankstown, Drummoyne, Elkington Park, Northbridge and The Spit.

In regard to clubs, Balmoral, Bronte, Enfield and Roseville all re-affiliated after a break of some years, while Cabarita, North Ramsgate, Shell and The Sydney clubs lapsed. Player registrations dropped slightly to approximately 225.[2]

Representatives in NSW Teams

Bronte had only just re-entered the NSWAWPA competition this season with a team of youngsters, so none of the new brigade had any chance of selection in the NSW team, especially as they were playing in the 3rd Grade. At the age of 33, Bert Vadas did compete in an inter-district play-off match as a representative of The Spit Club, but he wasn't selected for the NSW team.

Being an Olympic year, jostling for places in the NSW team was intense, and the selectors had a field day. Only the two ex-Hungarians were retained from the previous side. Eric Johnson (Balmain) and Ray Smee (Bondi) were recalled, but six 1951 team members were let go and replaced by six young new caps in J. Clothier, Tony Fenech, Frank Jordan, Ted Pierce (Balmain), Keith Whitehead and goalkeeper Doug Laing (Bondi). It was the most radical overhaul of the NSW water polo team in history.

Unbeknown to the NSW selectors was that Victoria did almost exactly the same thing in admitting five new caps to their team. But the youth in the revamped NSW side made all the difference at the 5th Australian Championships in Melbourne, where they lost only one of their matches to take the title over Victoria and South Australia.

The 1952 Olympic Team

The Australian Olympic team was selected after these championships, with five players each from Victoria and NSW. The Aussies played through a European tour, and two matches at the Helsinki Olympics, where they placed 19th, but they lost only 16 of their 36 matches on tour, a very respectable tally for a novice team.

The Premierships

After four straight premierships in a row, many at the time might have asked "when will it

---

1951/52 Season Statistics
N.S.W.A.W.P.A.

Clubs in the Water Polo Competitions.

Clubs	Grades 1	2	3	4	Total
Balmoral			●		1
Bankstown		●	●		2
Bondi	2		●		3
Bronte			●		1
Drummoyne			●		1
East Sydney				●	1
Enfield				●	1
Nth Narrabeen		●	●	●	3
Nth Sydney			●	●	2
Northbridge		●	●		3
Pyrmont		●		●	3
Roseville				●	1
The Spit		●	●	●	3
University			●		1
	6	6	10	9	31

Results of the Water Polo Competitions.

Grade	Premier		Runner-Up
1st	Bondi A~5	d.	1~Balmain
2nd	Nth Narrabeen~2	d.	1~Balmain
3rd	Pyrmont~5	d.	1~Nth Sydney
4th	Pyrmont~10	d.	3~The Spit
Club Champions			BALMAIN

"I was winning championships at the Combined High Schools carnivals in sprints... never any good at long distance, but I won a few medals at CHS and swam in the inter-club series with Bronte. I did break the minute for the 100 metres during my early days, and so I had speed, but not the stamina for distance swimming. But... I found swimming a bit boring and water polo was the saving grace as I could actually do something with the ball..."

Dick Thornett, 9 August 2008
Interviewed by Ian Warden [3]

NEW SOUTH WALES TEAM
National Champions,
Melbourne, 1952

Ray Smee (c, Bondi)
J. Clothier (Balmain)
Oscar Csuvik (The Spit)
Tony Fenech (g, Balmain)
Eric Johnson (vc, Balmain)
Frank Jordan (Balmain)
Alex Kosegi (Bondi)
Doug Laing (g, Bondi)
Ted Pierce (Balmain)
Keith Whitehead (Bondi)
Bob Traynor (Manager).

▲ *M. Petrak of South Australia, tackling Ray Smee, NSW captain during the Australian Water Polo Championships at Richmond, Victoria. Petrak's tackle came too late because Smee's shot scored. (The Daily Telegraph, 15th Feb 1952).*

end?", but Bondi's domination of the 1st Grade competition was just shifting into high gear, and in this season they were all powerful. By the end of the preliminaries, Bondi A had won all of its 18 games, scoring 117 goals, with only 37 against.

In the play-offs Bondi A eliminated The Spit (8~3), and Balmain did the same to Bondi B (6~1). With no preliminary final both winners progressed straight to the grand-final where Bondi A ran out easy victors over Balmain (5~1) in an impressive display, to make it five straight premierships in a row for Bondi. North Narrabeen won the 2nd Grade, and Pyrmont won both the 3rd and 4th grade competitions, while Balmain again took out the Club Championship.

BONDI AWPC
1951/52 - NSWAWPA 1st Grade Premiers
Ray Smee (c), Bill Jones, Keith Whitehead, J. Gillies, Doug Laing (g), Jack Ferguson, Ken Erickson, G. Taylor, Col Smee, Fred Mayer.

A limited junior competition was re-introduced which only had two entries. This championship was won very convincingly by The Spit Club by a massive score over Balmain (15~0).[2]

Bronte AWPC

The Bronte Water Polo Club re-affiliated with the NSWAWPA this season, although the

"Our father was a very sincere and honest bloke, who did a lot of voluntary work. He was very supportive and genuine, and I suppose in his way he was quite determined. We had very supportive parents, so whatever we were doing, they gave us all the help they could. We weren't a wealthy family, a relatively poor family I suppose. In those days Bronte was a lower middle-class area, not like it is now. They rented their home down there until he was well over 50 and then finally bought it. He had musical interests, conducted choirs and things like that."

John Thornett, 3 July 2008
Interviewed by Ian Warden [1]

personnel was different and headed up mostly by John Thornett.

"The basis of Bronte water polo was of course, the swimming club. I started there in about 1950. The Sunday morning races were all handicaps, mostly 33 yards, but some 100 yards. You entered your name on arrival and the races began at about 9:00."
Bob Cope, Nov 2020

These young Bronte men entered a single team in the 3rd Grade, and although they didn't qualify for the semi-finals, they enjoyed themselves so much that they pledged to re-enter for the 1952/53 season.

1952-53

1952/53 NSWAWPA OFFICIALS: Dr. K. Kirkland (Patron); Dr. H.K. Porter (President); M. Campbell (Past President); A.P. Hart (Chairman); R. Gibson (Registrar); R.Y. Traynor (Secretary); H. Doerner (Asst. Secretary); R. Smee (Treasurer).

The 1952/53 season began following the NSWAWPA 23rd Annual General Meeting, which was held at 7.45pm on Monday, 29th September 1952, in the Surf Life Saving Association Rooms, 16 Hunter St. Sydney.

The question of country water polo was again raised this season, but remained a difficult task as the means of bringing country clubs together was a financial burden to the Association. It was decided that the various District teams should play off at the Country Swimming Championships, with the champion Country team then playing the champion Metropolitan team for the NSW premiership.

The Baths & Clubs

During the season, metropolitan matches were played at Rushcutters Bay, Bankstown, Roseville, Drummoyne, Elkington Park, Northbridge and The Spit. Before this season commenced, attempts were made to improve facilities at various baths so that the game could be more enjoyable for the players, referees and spectators. Improvements included the clear marking of goal, 2m, 4m and half way lines, as well as the repair and proper fastening of goals at each venue.

In regard to new clubs, Manly Old Boys and Parramatta affiliated for the first time and

"I started my swimming by joining the coach Evilyn de Lacey. Her married name was Whillier and there is a plaque to her memory on the beach pathway. She ran a squad that trained each week day at Bronte pool from about 6 am. I recall the three Thornetts, Ken and Barry Owens, Jack Brownjohn, Brian Hallinan, Terry Clarke, Vic McGrath, Dick and Bobbie See, Brian Ellison. So all these people influenced me to begin playing water polo, although my stepdad would not let me start until I was thirteen. There was another group in the polo club who had come from the surf club and included Ray Timewell, Pat McGrath (who was the surf club captain for years), Jack Campbell (a surf champion). There was a polo net at the Bronte pool for a while and some training occurred there, but it was really unsuitable so about 1960 training was moved completely to Rushcutters Bay Baths."
Bob Cope, 5th Nov 2020

"Us three brothers all played water polo. I actually started the Bronte Water Polo Club with another chap, and that club went on to be the Sydney premiers for quite a few years. Dick and Ken also joined as they were both good players and good swimmers. I was a good swimmer when I was young and at school, but deteriorated as I got older... I still played water polo, but couldn't swim very fast later on. The other two were very quick though, and Dick went on to play for Australia, but he had a lot of natural ball handling skills. We all were good at ball handling. I think we got that from a lot of practice as kids. We used to play ball games in the park down at Bronte, we threw tennis balls at each other in the back yard and did a lot of sport, just for fun."
John Thornett, 3 July 2008
Interviewed by Ian Warden [1]

"I was with the Bronte Swimming Club when Arthur Obey arrived, he was the most elite athlete I ever met. With the Thornetts, Vic McGrath, Dick See etc, who came later, the standard was pretty high, but Arthur was one level up again. We played table tennis upstairs in the club room and Arthur made everyone look like an amateur. At swimming races it was the same. He was offered a position as a golden junior with one of the major tennis companies, which meant he was destined for the world stage. But it meant nothing to Arthur. He gave it all up and turned to swimming by himself at Bronte at 4:30 in the morning and became a very talented decathlete. He died about 1990 and is buried at Waverley."
Brian Ellison, Oct 2018

1952/53 Season Statistics
N.S.W.A.W.P.A.

Clubs in the Water Polo Competitions.

Clubs	Grades 1	2	3	4	Total
Balmain	2	●			3
Bankstown	●	●			2
Bondi	2		●		3
Bronte		●		●	2
Cronulla		●			1
Drummoyne		●		●	2
East Sydney			●	●	2
Manly Old Boys			●		1
Nth Narrabeen	●		●		2
Nth Sydney		●			1
Northbridge	●		2		3
Parramatta				2	2
Pyrmont	●	●	●	●	4
Roseville				●	1
The Spit	●	●	●		3
University	●	●			2
	9	9	8	8	34

Results of the Water Polo Competitions.

Grade	Premier		Runner-Up
1st	Bondi~7	d.	3~The Spit
2nd	Balmain~4	d.	0~Bronte
3rd	East Sydney~8	d.	6~Pyrmont
4th	Parramatta B~8	d.	6~Parramatta A
	Club Champions		BONDI

Cronulla, re-affiliated after a lapse of several years, but Balmoral and Enfield clubs both lapsed. Player registrations increased to approximately 260.

While the Northbridge Juniors were the only undefeated team this season, a variety of teams were represented in the finals with eight different clubs filling out ten finals berths.

The Association again conducted its premiership matches over four grades which were played on Tuesday and Sunday nights. The old problem of forfeits soon became evident however, and a great deal of dissatisfaction was felt by teams travelling long distances only to find the opposition unable to field a side. This circumstance not only inconvenienced the visiting club, but affected the Association's income as many baths were contracted to provide a share of the gate. Some objections were also raised by various bodies to playing games on Sunday nights.[4]

Representatives in NSW Teams

This season Bronte managed to field two teams and was rapidly improving in both fitness and skill. But despite the fact that there were openings for the State team, any chance of selection was still way too ambitious for players from an emerging club, and consequently no one from Bronte was either invited or gained selection in the NSW team.

Some of the '52 Olympians opted for a rest this year, which opened up a number of slots in the NSW side. Eight of the successful 1952 NSW side were either let go or took the year off. While Alex Kosegi (Bondi) and Ted Pierce (Balmain) were retained, Gordon Amadee (Balmain) was recalled to fill the gap along with six more new caps in M. Best and Alan Stringer (Balmain), Bill Jones (Bondi), J. Quinn (Pyrmont), Tom Sendro (Universities) and goal keeper Peter Ashby (Northbridge).

SELECTION 0
STATE TEAM

New South Wales se tors will choose the St water-polo team tomo night.

They will choose team after having watc the Possibles v. Proba match at Elkington Baths, Balmain.

The State team compete in the Austra championships in Adela next month.

Daily Telegraph, 17th Jan 1953, p16

Hungarian State coach

Hungarian international, Alex Kosegi, will coach the New South Wales waterpolo team which will compete for the Australian title in Adelaide next month.

The selectors appointed Kosegi playing-coach when they chose the State team yesterday.

The team is: Goal, J. Barnes (Spit); backs, G. Amadee (Balmain), A. Stringer (Balmain); halves, A. Kosegi (Bondi), F. Jordan (Bankstown); forwards, W. Jones (Bondi), E. Pierce (Balmain), T. Sandros (Spit).

V.A.W.P.A.

REGAL CUP SERIES
to be held at the

RICHMOND BATHS
on

MONDAY, 2nd FEBRUARY, 1953
WEDNESDAY, 4th FEBRUARY, 1953
THURSDAY, 5th FEBRUARY, 1953

Season Ticket for
Reserve Enclosure, 15/-

Hon. Secretary:
B. LOVELOCK.
Phone: MX 3971.

Admit One, 5th February, 7.45 p.m.
Admit One, 4th February, 7.45 p.m.
Admit One, 2nd February, 7.45 p.m.

◄Announcement of the NSW State team for the 1953 Adelaide Australian Championships (Daily Telegraph, 20th Jan 1953, p18). ▲Official ticket to the Regal Cup Interstate Water Polo Series in Richmond, Victoria, 1953.

NEW SOUTH WALES TEAM
1953 - Runners-Up - National Championships, Adelaide
From left: Peter Ashby (g, Northbridge), Gordon Amedee (c, Balmain), Alan Stringer (Balmain), Bill Jones (Bondi), M. Best (Balmain), Ted Pierce (Balmain), J. Quinn (Pyrmont), Alex Kosegi (pl/Coach, Bondi), Bob Traynor (Manager/Referee). Missing: T. Sendro (Universities). Photo - Bill Jones.

Such profound changes on top of a similar mass turnover of personel in 1952 failed, when the Victorians scored an undefeated series win at the national titles in Adelaide, and NSW came in second ahead of West Australia and South Australia.

"At Bronte, everyone did everything together. We swam together, played table tennis together, played rugby with Randwick together and surfed together. Because I was a breaststroke swimmer Vic McGrath asked me to join the group that played water polo together, but as a goalkeeper."

Brian Ellison, Apr 2015

Eighteen-years-old former Sydney High School forward, John Thornett, will make his debut for University.

Thornett, a 14½-stoner, will play in the second row.

(Daily Telegraph, 22nd May 1953)

The Premierships

In 1st Grade, Bondi A only lost two games by the end of the preliminaries with their defence allowing only 25 goals against them all season, so they showed no signs of being de-throned. In the play-offs Bondi A eliminated Balmain A (8~1) without difficulty and The Spit did the same to Bondi B (7~3). With no preliminary final both winners progressed straight to the grand-final where Bondi A ran out victors over The Spit (7~3) to take an all time record sixth successive premiership. Balmain won the 2nd Grade over an emerging Bronte (4~0), East Sydney took out the 3rd Grade over Pyrmont (8~6), and Parramatta B surprisingly beat their big brother team Parramatta A (8~6) in the 4th Grade competition. The 'Club Champions' for overall performance across all grades went to Bondi.

BONDI AWPC
1952/53 - NSWAWPA 1st Grade Premiers
Ray Smee (c), Bill Jones, Keith Whitehead, J. Gillies, Doug Laing (g), Jack Ferguson,
Ken Erickson, Alex Kosegi, Col Smee, Fred Mayer.

A Junior competition was played over two rounds on a points basis only and featured teams from Balmain, Drummoyne, Northbridge and The Spit. Northbridge scored 24 goals with only four against, to conclude the season undefeated from Balmain.[4]

Bronte AWPC

Although they had recorded a number of wins, but missed the 1952 play-offs, Bronte had an enjoyable enough first season to re-enter the NSWAWPA, but in different grades. Due to an influx of new players, the club decided to enter a team in the 4th Grade, but at the same time they had a sufficient number of talented players to enter a team in the 2nd Grade.

Training out of Bronte Baths, these players certainly didn't have it easy and the 4th Grade failed to make to the play-offs, but the 2nd Grade qualified for the semi-finals and played themselves into the grand-final, where they were well beaten by Balmain (4~0), but the young Bronte side had showed its mettle, and they made plans to enter a team in the top grade for the 1953/54 season.

On the representative front, John Thornett was playing first class water polo, but few players could gain state team selection from the 2nd Grade, and so he had to content himself to the new season.

1953-54

1953/54 NSWAWPA OFFICIALS: Dr. K. Kirkland (Patron); Dr. H.K. Porter (President); M. Campbell (Past President); A.P. Hart (Chairman); R. Gibson (Registrar); I.J. Cantor (Secretary); H. Doerner (Asst. Secretary); R. Smee (Treasurer).

The 1953/54 season began following the NSWAWPA 24th Annual General Meeting, which was held at 7.45pm on Tuesday, 28th September 1953, in the Surf Life Saving Association Rooms, 16 Hunter St. Sydney.

The Baths & Clubs

During the season, metropolitan matches were played at Rushcutters Bay, Bankstown, Roseville, Drummoyne, Elkington Park, Northbridge and The Spit. In regard to new clubs, Navy and Garden Island affiliated for the first time, while Bankstown, Cronulla, Drummoyne and Manly Old Boys all lapsed. Due primarily to increases in affiliation fees, player registrations dropped markedly to approximately 200 this season.

The metropolitan premiership was conducted across three grades only in an effort to raise the standard of all teams, and considerable improvement was evident. Five teams competed in 1st Grade, eight in 2nd Grade and 15 in 3rd Grade. However, forfeits were again a major problem along with the playing of unregistered players and worst of all was the complete withdrawal of some teams mid-season.

Due to these problems, the financial needs of the Association had to be seriously considered and baths that provided the greatest financial return received a greater allocation of games. The Competition Committee also amalgamated the 3rd and 4th Grades and renamed them 3rd Grade North and 3rd Grade South, with a playoff between the winners of both districts to decide the premiership.[5]

> "I started playing water polo about October 1954, when as a swimmer at Roseville Swimming Club I was asked by some of the older guys (in their 20's) to help make up team numbers, which seemed to be a lot of the time. My memory of the early years was morning training in cold dirty water at low tide. Then, on Tuesday nights, being picked up and driven, dangerously, in their dad's car to a match at Manly, the Spit, Northbridge, Roseville, Greenwich or Balmain, to struggle with leather balls that swelled up with water and got very heavy. I was only 13."
> **Jon Kirkwood, June 2018**

> "I would've been around 14 when I began playing 1st Grade water polo, because I recall still being at Paddington School and was in about second year. There probably wouldn't have been anybody else playing 1st Grade at 14, but of course I was a bigger child and could handle myself better than most of the smaller kids."
> **Dick Thornett, 9 August 2008**
> **Interviewed by Ian Warden [3]**

1953/54 Season Statistics N.S.W.A.W.P.A.

Clubs in the Water Polo Competitions.

Clubs	1	2	3N	3S	Total
Balmain	●	●	●		3
Bondi	●	●			2
Bronte	●		●		2
Dee Why			2		2
East Sydney		●	●		2
Garden Island				●	1
Navy				2	2
Nth Narrabeen	●				1
Nth Sydney			●		1
Northbridge		●		●	2
Parramatta				●	1
Pyrmont	●	●	●		3
Roseville				●	1
The Spit	●	●		●	3
University		●	●		2
	5	8	7	8	28

Results of the Water Polo Competitions.

Grade	Premier		Runner-Up
1st	Bondi~5	d.	3~Bronte
2nd	Pyrmont~8	d.	5~East Sydney
3rd	Balmain~11	d.	2~Roseville
Club Champions			BALMAIN
3Nth	Roseville~7	d.	4~Northbridge
3Sth	Balmain~3	d.	2~Pyrmont

Representatives in NSW Teams

It is important to recognise how prestigious it was to be chosen to represent your club for the NSW State water polo team. Unlike today, which has no such competition, the significance of State team selection meant you were judged to be amongst the State's top 11 players. For New South Welshman, this also indicated that you were likely in the zenith of players across the country.

Wholesale changes were again made for the 1954 NSW State team with six players being dropped. Oscar Csuvik of The Spit club was recalled, along with Keith Whitehead and goalkeeper Doug Laing (Bondi), and Ken Lord (Balmain) was added as the second goalkeeper. However, Bronte's performance in just their third season was turning heads, and the form of both Bert Vadas and John Thornett also warranted their selection in this year's State team.

Momie and Thorn wouldn't have known it at the time, but their inclusion in the 1954 team began a tradition for Bronte, of having at least one player (and sometimes three or four) selected in the NSW team every year, over the next 22 seasons. They were the first Bronte players to be honoured with this significant achievement.

The strong NSW team concluded the 7th Australian Championships in Sydney, for the second only time in history as national co-champions with Victoria, while Western Australia and South Australia finished in equal third place.

The Premiership

Bronte had re-entered the Association competitions in 1951/52 and were growing rapidly in strength. They finished second on the points table after the preliminary rounds in the 1st Grade competition, and looked like the best chance to knock Bondi off their perch. In this season however, Bondi remained all powerful. In the play-offs Bondi eliminated their old rival Balmain (6~3) and Bronte disposed of Pyrmont B (6~4). With no preliminary final both winners progressed straight to the grand-final where Bondi showed their experience and skill by defeating the new boys from Bronte (5~3) to take their 7th successive premiership. Pyrmont won the 2nd Grade, and Balmain claimed the 3rd Grade competition. Balmain were again consistent enough across all grades to take out the Club Championship.

NSW State Premiership

For the very first time a true NSW Championship was held when Canberra ASC who had won the Country Water Polo Championships travelled to Sydney to play Bondi, the Metropolitan Champions. Even though Canberra were well beaten (14~4), they displayed true sportsmanship and their standard improved considerably for the experience.[5]

BONDI AWPC
1953/54 · NSWAWPA 1st Grade Premiers
Ray Smee (c), Jack Ferguson, Bill Jones, Alex Kosegi (player/Coach), Doug Laing (g),
Keith Whitehead, Col Smee, Fred Mayer.

Bronte AWPC

The early days of any new sporting team or club are fraught with danger as members often juggle the worth of their involvement, against their commitments across other aspects of their lives. But it was during this season that the relatively new Bronte Water Polo Club really consolidated themselves as a future force, both in the Sydney competition and within the sport itself.

Having gained a place in their first ever grand-final the previous year, Bronte threw their young players into the top grade this season and incredibly won their way through to the premiership game in their inaugural year in the 1st Grade. The young team had managed to achieve considerable success in a very short period, across three quite separate components of the sport.

Firstly, they had found a master player and coach in ex-Hungarian Bert Vadas, who gradually moulded the raw talent of the individual players and the teams into very skilled outfits. Secondly, after having played just two seasons, Bronte had managed to defeat both Balmain and The Spit and win most of their games in the 1953/54 season, which propelled them into their inaugural 1st Grade grand-final against the legendary Bondi Club. And finally, the talent of individual Bronte players like John Thornett and Bert Vadas was recognised by the selectors, and warranted their selection in the prestigious New South Wales team.

It was this combination of success that drew more and more players into the ranks of the Bronte club, and the previously loosely organised 'Bronte social club' began to expand with a common purpose. Bronte Water Polo Club became a remarkable example of how success brings success.

NEW SOUTH WALES TEAM
National Co-Champions
Sydney, 1954

Ray Smee (c/Coach, Bondi)
Oscar Csuvik (The Spit)
Jack Ferguson (Bondi)
Bill Jones (Bondi)
Alex Kosegi (Bondi)
Doug Laing (g, Bondi)
Ken Lord (g, Balmain)
Ted Pierce (Balmain)
John Thornett (Bronte)
Bert Vadas (Bronte)
Keith Whitehead (Bondi).

No Funds For Water Polo

N.S.W. will not be represented at the Australian water-polo championship in Perth in February because of lack of funds.

The registrar of the N.S.W. Water-Polo Association, Mr. J. E. Thornett, said last night it would cost more than £900 to send a team to Perth.

A N.S.W. team will visit Victoria in January.

The draw for to-night's round of A-grade matches at Drummoyne Baths is: 7.45 p.m., Association B v Bronte; 8.15, Association A v Pyrmont; 8.45, Bondi v Balmain.

SMH, 23 Dec 1954

Water Polo Team Loses Game

SYDNEY, Fri.—Western Australia suffered another defeat in the Australian water polo championship at the Balmain Baths last night.

The N.S.W. side, dominated by J. Thornett and V. Vardas, began well with several quick goals.

Western Australia, after good play by A. Calder and P. Atherden, looked likely to provide a close struggle.

However, the more experienced N.S.W. side tightened its grip on the match and won decisively.

N.S.W. 9 goals (Thornett 3, W Jones 2, Vardas 2, R. Smee 2) bv W.A 2 (Calder, A. Charlston).

The West Australian, 13 Feb 1954)

▲ Results from the 1954 Australian Championships in Sydney, showing the valued contributions of Bert Vadas and John Thornett.

"Before 1960, we trained at Bronte. We had a set of goals that we would bring down and put in at the turning board end of the baths. The pool was then deep enough so that you could not stand on the bottom... so we all had to swim. We would swim, then train for swimming and after played all the other sports and enjoyed polo through the week nights."

Brian Ellison, Apr 2015

1954-55

1954/55 NSWAWPA OFFICIALS: Dr. K. Kirkland (Patron); Dr. H.K. Porter (President); M. Campbell (Past President); A.P. Hart (Chairman); **J. Thornett (Registrar)**; I. Rolle (Secretary); H. Doerner (Asst. Secretary); R. Smee (Treasurer).

**NEW SOUTH WALES TEAM
Runners-Up, Exhibition Series
Melbourne, 1955**

Ray Smee (c, Bondi)
Bill Jones (Bondi)
Alex Kosegi (pl/Coach, Bondi)
Doug Laing (g, Bondi)
Ted Pierce (Balmain)
John Thornett (Bronte)
Bert Vadas (Bronte)
Keith Whitehead (Bondi).

The 1954/55 season began following the NSWAWPA 25th Annual General Meeting, which was held at 7.45pm on Monday, 15th November 1954, in the Surf Life Saving Association Rooms, 16 Hunter St. Sydney.

The NSW Association congratulated John Thornett (Bronte AWPC) for being selected to represent Australia at Rugby Union in the 1955 series against the New Zealand All Blacks.

The Baths & Clubs

During the season, metropolitan matches were mostly played on Thuirsday nights at Rushcutters Bay, Bankstown, Roseville, Drummoyne, Elkington Park, Northbridge and The Spit. In regard to new clubs, Sydney Teachers College under the stewardship of ex-Olympian Frank Jordan who was a Physical Education lecturer there, affiliated for the first time. Balmoral and Drummoyne re-affiliated after a one year lapse, but both Dee Why and The Spit, which entered three grades in the previous season, lapsed. Player registrations rose slightly to approximately 210.

Once again the Metropolitan competition was conducted across three grades in an effort to raise the standard of play and it was found that many teams benefited by this system. Six teams entered the 1st Grade competition, although two of these were comprised of teams selected by the Association, which played as Association 'A' and 'B'. The players who were fortunate enough to gain selection in the Association teams from 2nd and 3rd Grade derived great experience

1954/55 Season Statistics
N.S.W.A.W.P.A.

Clubs in the Water Polo Competitions.

Clubs	Grades 1	2	3N	3S	Total
Association	2				2
Balmain	●	●			2
Balmoral			●		1
Bondi	●	●			2
Bronte	●	●	2		4
Drummoyne				●	1
East Sydney	●			●	2
Garden Island				●	1
Navy				●	1
Nth Narrabeen		2			2
Nth Sydney	●	●			2
Northbridge		2	●		3
Parramatta		●			1
Pyrmont	●	●			2
Roseville	●	●			2
Teachers College				●	1
University		●			1
	6	11	6	7	30

Results of the Water Polo Competitions.

Grade	Premier		Runner-Up
1st	Bondi~4	d.	2~Bronte
2nd	East Sydney~7	d.	6~Balmain
3rd	Garden Island	d.	Balmoral
Club Champions			EAST SYDNEY
3Nth	Balmoral~10	d.	1~Roseville
3Sth	Garden Island~9	d.	4~Drummoyne

by being matched against the 1st Grade teams. Unfortunately, both forfeits and team withdrawals sorely affected some competitions.[6]

Representatives in NSW Teams

Bronte was invited this season to put forward a number of its members in the training squad for possible selection in the NSW team, with Dick See, Ray Burton, Vic McGrath, John Thornett and Bert Vadas, as a last minute inclusion, all being in contention. While three State players from 1954 were dropped without any new caps to replace them, the latter two Bronte players retained their places in the NSW team, which controversially did not travel to Perth for the 8th Australian Championships due to a lack of funds. Despite this setback, the NSW team journeyed instead to Melbourne to contest an Exhibition Series against Victoria, where they lost narrowly in all three matches.

The Premierships

In 1st Grade Bondi continued virtually unchecked with only one loss by the end of the rounds. In the play-offs, it was to be the exact replay of the previous season with Bondi squeezing past Balmain (5~4) and then Bronte disposing of Pyrmont (4~2). With no preliminary final both winners progressed straight to the grand-final where Bondi narrowly defeated Bronte (4~2) in a solid display of water polo. East Sydney won the 2nd Grade and Garden Island won the 3rd Grade. East Sydney also took home the Club Championship for the very first time.

NSW State Premiership

For the second successive year, a true NSW Championship was held when Canberra ASC, who had won the Country Water Polo Championship, were brought to Sydney at the expense of the Association to play off against the recent Metropolitan premiers, Bondi. Although Canberra were well beaten (12~2), the experience they gained helped bring their play to an even higher standard.[6]

BONDI AWPC
1954/55 - NSWAWPA 1st Grade Premiers
Ray Smee (c), Jack Ferguson, Bill Jones, Alex Kosegi (player/Coach), Doug Laing (g),
Keith Whitehead, Col Smee, Bill Roney, Fred Mayer, Brian Hutchings.

1954/55 RESULTS

WATER POLO ON SUNDAY

Water polo matches will be held at the Watson's Bay baths next Sunday afternoon in aid of the International Social Service.

State captain Ray Smee will lead Bondi against Bronte and East Sydney will play Pyrmont.

Daily Telegraph, 24th Dec 1954

WATER POLO

At Drummoyne Baths
Bondi, 8 (J. Ferguson 4, C. Smee 3, R. Smee 1), beat **Balmain**, 3 (M. Best 2, V. Peirce 1); **Pyrmont**, 10 (K. Lord 3, L. Hampson 4, J. Quinn 2, D. Lawler 1), beat **Association A**, 0; **Bronte**, 10 (B. Vadas 6, J. Thornett 2, R. Burton 1, R. See 1), beat **Association B**, 0

SMH, 24th Dec 1954

WATER POLO

DRUMMOYNE BATHS.—Bondi, 5 (W. Jones 3, A. Kosegi, J. Ferguson), beat Bronte, 3 (R. Burton, B. Badas, J. Thornett); Balmain, 5 (M. Best 4, E. Fitzgerald), beat Association A, 2 (K. Thornett, W. Rooney); Pyrmont, 5, beat Association B, 4.

N.S.W. team for annual Regal-Cup match, Victoria v N.S.W., at Bendigo (January 22) and Richmond (January 23); R. Smee (captain), K. Whitehead, backs; E. Pierce, K. Lord, halves; W. Jones, J. Thornett, forwards; D. Laing, goal. Coach, Alex Kosegi.

SMH, 15th Jan 1955

WATER POLO

DRUMMOYNE BATHS.—Bronte, 2 (R. Burton 1, B. Vadas 1), drew with Pyrmont, 2 (L. Hampson 1, K. Lord 1); Balmain, 5 (A. Stringer 2, E., Peirce, E. Fitzgerald, E. Best), beat Association B, 3 (R. Lake 1, D. Kennemoere 2); Bondi, 8, beat Association A, 3.

SMH, 21st Jan 1955

Water Polo

Bondi will meet Balmain in the second semi-final of the Sydney first-grade water polo competition at Drummoyne Baths at 8.30 p.m. to-day.

The winner will meet Bronte, who beat Pyrmont 4-2 in the first semi-final last week, in the final at Drummoyne to-night week.

SMH, 24th March 1955

WATER POLO

SEMI-FINALS.—**1st grade:** Bondi, 5 (J. Ferguson 2, K. Whitehead, A. Kosegi, W. Rooney), beat Balmain, 4 (A. Peirce 2, J. Clothier 2). **2nd grade:** Balmain, 7 (A. Beattie 4, V. Grant, W. Moss, R. Lake), beat East Sydney, 5 (K. Ross 4, J. Maher).

SMH, 25th March 1955

BRONTE AWPC
1954/55 - 1st Grade Team - NSWAWPA
Back row (from left): Vic McGrath, Dick See, John Thornett. Centre row: John Hartley, Ken Thornett, Jack Brownjohn.
Front row: Ray Burton, Arthur Obey, Bert Vadas. Photo - Jack Brownjohn.

Bronte AWPC

Entering its fourth year Bronte was going from strength to strength with players coming from all across Sydney's eastern suburbs, all wanting to be a part of this successful new water polo club. They had enough players to enter two teams in the 3rd Grade (South) competition, and another two teams in 2nd as well as 1st Grade for the 1954/55 season, more than any other club.

"I recall the three Thornetts, Ken Mills, Barry Owens, Jack Brownjohn, Brian Hallinan, Terry Clarke, Vic McGrath, Dick and Bobbie See, and Brian Ellison. All these people influenced me to begin playing water polo. There was another group in the polo club who had come from the surf club and included Ray Timewell, Pat McGrath (who was the surf club captain for years) and Jack Campbell (a surf champion), who were mostly 2nd and 3rd Grade players. There was a polo net at Bronte Baths and training occurred there, but it was really unsuitable."
Bob Cope, Nov 2020

"Over the years at Roseville, and especially from the mid 1950's, we created a good team by inducing a number of surf swimmers to play from Collaroy and Manly as well as some of the Dee Why players, when Fred Lamb became our coach."
Jon Kirkwood, June 2018

"I began playing with Bronte at age 13 in 1955. We had some informal sessions at Bronte pool where there was one goal, but training later moved to Rushcutters Bay. We of course played with leather balls that got more slippery and heavy as a game went on. The nylon balls appeared after the 1964 Olympic Games, and came out of America."
Bob Cope, March 2019

All grades had a great season, but only the 1st Grade managed to play themselves through to the grand-final, where they were led by their two State representatives, John Thornett and Bert Vadas, but thye were defeated by Bondi (2~4).

1955-56

1955/56 NSWAPA OFFICIALS: Dr. H.K. Porter (Patron); A.P. Hart (President); Dr H.K. Porter (Past President); H. Doerner (Chairman); R.See (Registrar); I.Rolle (Secretary); J. Flynn (Asst. Secretary); R. Smee (Treasurer).

The 1955/56 season began following the NSWAWPA 26th Annual General Meeting, which was held at 7.45pm on Tuesday, 26th September 1955, in the Surf Life Saving Association Rooms, 16 Hunter St. Sydney.

The Association congratulated John Thornett (Bronte AWPC) for being selected to represent Australia at Rugby Union in the series against South Africa and also in the Australian Rugby Union team, which toured Japan.

The Association held its first Annual Ball since 1946 at 'Cahill's' Ballroom, Elizabeth Street, where despite appalling weather over 150 supporters spent a very enjoyable evening.

At this time, the primary source of income for the NSWAWPA was the Olympic Games Fund with almost £190, followed by gate receipts at £145, then proceeds from Socials at £78, and entry & capitation fees at £66. Principal expenses were the 1955/56 Australian Championships run at a cost of £250, followed by Olympic Fund levies £100, and water polo equipment and goals at £60, with office expenses being £52. However, the Association finished the year in a healthy financial position with £415 in the bank.

The Baths & Clubs

During this season, metropolitan matches were played at Rushcutters Bay, Bankstown, Roseville, Drummoyne, Elkington Park, Northbridge and The Spit. Bankstown and Dee Why re-affiliated after a lapse of several years whilst Drummoyne, North Narrabeen and the Teachers College all lapsed. Player registrations climbed to approximately 225.

> "When I started playing, the 1st Grade goalkeepers were Arthur Obey and Ken Thornett. Arthur was a natural, but was too busy with his decathlon commitments to train. He represented Australia in the Olympics, was a policeman and of mixed race, possibly Fijian? Then Ken took over for a while until he left to play rugby league in England. Ken was a great goalkeeper, with magnificent reflexes and strength. No doubt he would have represented Australia if he had stayed with water polo. After Ken Thornett, Don Sarkies took over in goal."
>
> **Bob Cope, March 2019**

1955/56 Season Statistics N.S.W.A.W.P.A.

Clubs in the Water Polo Competitions.

Clubs	1	2	3N	3S	Total
Association	2				2
Balmain	●	●		●	3
Balmoral		●		●	2
Bankstown				●	1
Bondi	2			●	3
Bronte	2	●	2		5
Dee Why			●		1
East Sydney		●		●	2
Garden Island		●			1
Navy				●	1
Nth Sydney			2		2
Northbridge		●		●	2
Parramatta		●			1
Pyrmont	●	●		●	3
Roseville		●	●		2
University		●	●		2
	8	10	7	8	33

Results of the Water Polo Competitions.

Grade	Premier	Runner-Up
1st	Bondi A~5 d.	2~Balmain
2nd	Pyrmont~3 d.	2~University
3rd	Balmain~7 d.	3~Dee Why
Club Champions		BALMAIN
3Nth	Dee Why~3 d.	2~University
3Sth	Balmain d.	Navy

NEW SOUTH WALES TE TEAM
1956 - Co-Runners-up - National Championship - Melbourne
From left: Hermie Doerner (Referee), Ray Smee (c, Bondi), **Bert Vadas (Bronte)**, Doug Laing (g, Bondi), Alex Kosegi (Coach, Bondi), Rally Sarkies (Bondi), Ted Pierce (Balmain), Bill Jones (Bondi), Eric Fitzgerald (Balmain), Keith Whitehead (Bondi), **Dick See (Bronte)**. Photo - Ray Smee.

Once again the competition was conducted over three grades with seven teams in 1st Grade, ten teams in 2nd Grade and two 3rd Grade divisions: North with seven teams, and South with eight teams. An Association team, made up of selected 2nd and 3rd Grade players from various clubs, was again entered in the 1st Grade competition.[7]

Representatives in NSW Teams

With seven State players backing up from the previous year, the 1956 NSW team wasn't an easy one to crack. But Dick See was in awesome form and warranted his selection along with his Bronte mentor, Bert Vadas. Other new caps were Eric FitzGerald (Balmain) and Rally Sarkies (Bondi). Although he had an excellent chance of selection for the Australian Olympic team, Bronte's John Thornett made himself unavailable for State team selection in 1956, in favour of a Rugby Tour to Japan.

The rampaging Victorians took out the 9th Australian Championships from NSW and West Australia in equal second place, with South Australia in fourth.

AUSTRALIAN WATER POLO COUNCIL
(Affiliated with the A.S.U. of Australia)

Invites You to the

Farewell Barbecue

SUNDAY, 19th FEBRUARY, 1956

Donation: 10/

▲TOP: Official programs for the 9th Australian Water Polo Championships & 1956 Olympic Games Trials in Melbourne & Publication by the Victorian AWPA. MID: 1956 Olympic Games representatives from NSW (from left): Ted Pierce (Balmain), Keith Whitehead (Bondi), Ray Smee (c, Bondi), Eric FitzGerald (r, Balmain), Doug Laing (g, Bondi). ABOVE: Ticket to the Farewell barbeque for the 1956 national championships in Melbourne.

BRONTE AMATEUR WATER POLO CLUB
1955/56 - 1st Grade Team
Back row (from left): John Thornett, Dick Thornett, Dick See, Vic McGrath, Ken Mills.
Front row: Jack Campbell, Bert Vadas (c/Coach), Ken Thornett (g).

The 1956 Olympic Team

The Australian Olympic team consisted of six players from Victoria, four from NSW and one from West Australia. The Aussies played five trial matches, and a further five matches at the Melbourne Olympics, where they placed 9th, but they only won three of their ten matches in total. The sensation of these Games being the 'blood bath in the pool' between the Hungarian and Russian water polo teams.

The Premierships

In 1st Grade, Bondi played through the rounds without dropping a single game. The play-offs saw Bondi defeat Bronte, and Balmain disposed of Pyrmont. With no preliminary final, the winners progressed to the grand-final where Bondi gave a consummate performance to defeat Balmain (5~3), taking their record string of consecutive premierships to eight. Pyrmont won the 2nd Grade while Balmain won the 3rd Grade as well as the Club Championship.

No record of a State Premiership match between the premier Metropolitan and Country teams was recorded this year.[7]

"I was said to have had a chance of playing water polo for Australia, but I had to decide on whether I went on the Australian Universities Rugby Tour to Japan in 1956 or to play water polo at the Australian Championships in Melbourne, where they were selecting the team for the Melbourne Olympic Games. So, I elected to go on the rugby tour and made rugby my first choice after that. I had at that stage already been in the Australian Rugby team in 1955, so I already had a grounding in rugby."

John Thornett, 3 July 2008
Interviewed by Ian Warden [1]

"Bert taught us how to play and Bronte Water Polo club came into being. Vic McGrath started swimming 400m swims with his head up, groups began training in ball work, and the purely social games vanished. Polo became serious in it's own right not just as a minor part of the Bronte Swimming Club. Bondi was the major club in those days, but Bronte quickly developed into a formidable club."

Brian Ellison, Apr 2015

BONDI AWPC
1955/56 - NSWAWPA 1st Grade Premiers
Alex Kosegi c/Coach), Ray Smee, Bill Jones, Doug Laing (g), Keith Whitehead, Col Smee, Rally Sarkies, Bill Roney, Brian Hutchings, Nino Sydney.

▲ *The popularity of Bronte Beach and the baths in the foreground, can be seen in this photograph, taken sometime in the mid 1950s.*

Bronte AWPC

The club had doubled in size over the past two seasons and they now had a sufficient number of players to enter two teams in 3rd Grade (South), a 2nd Grade and also two teams in the 1st Grade. For the second year running, Bronte entered more teams in the NSWAWPA competitions than any other club.

Although John Thornett made himself unavailable for the State Water Polo Team this year, due to his growing commitment to rugby union, both Bert Vadas and Dick See were selected in the NSW side as Bronte's two representatives.

"We had sporting champions in our club like John Thornett, Ken Thornett, Dick See and the amazing Arthur Obey, but things changed dramatically with the arrival of Bert Vadas, who would enter the pool with a ball and make us all look and feel like idiots. We could all see that he was playing water polo a few levels above us. From then on, Bert taught us how to play and Bronte Water Polo Club really came into being."

Brian Ellison, April 2015

But despite their grandiose plans, 1955/56 proved to be an unsuccessful year with none of Bronte's five teams qualifying for grand-finals.

1955/56 RESULTS

WATER POLO

At Drummoyne Baths
First grade: Bronte A, 6 goals (B. Vadas 3, J. Thornett 2, R. Burton 1), beat Bondi B, 1 (R. Sarkies); Balmain, 9 (B. Peirce 3, D. Fitzgerald 2, M. Best 1, A. Stringer 1), beat Association, 1 (R. Thornett); Bronte B, 4 (K. Thornett 2, F. Mayer 1, G. Taylor 1), beat Pyrmont, 1 (K. Lord).

SMH, 25th Nov 1955

WATER POLO

Bondi B, 5 (R. Sharkey), Bronte B, 5 (F. Myers 3, R. Thornett 2); Pyrmont, 4 (Quinn 2, Hancock, Bowden), Association, 1 (T. Conolly); Bondi A, 4 (Koseki 1, Ferguson 1, Smee 1, C. Smee 1) beat Bronte A, 2 (B. Vadas, J. Thornett).

SMH, 16th Dec 1955

1956-57

1956/57 NSWAWPA OFFICIALS: Dr. H.K. Porter (Patron); A.P. Hart (President); Dr H.K. Porter (Past President); H. Doerner (Chairman); **R.J. Thornett (Registrar)**; Capt. F. Lamb (Secretary); R.Y. Traynor (Asst. Secretary); R. Smee (Treasurer).

"My brother John... who is five years older than me, started the Bronte Water Polo Club off after getting to know a few of the guys that played at Bondi, and they went to school together, but I wasn't playing initially because I was too young. With John playing there... Ken and I both also started playing water polo, but if you know Bronte at all, the facilities were pretty ordinary. It was a pretty small pool and shallow, and we kept losing balls out into the ocean, so you spent half the time swimming around in the surf, chasing balls. But about 1960 we moved to Rushcutters Bay. I did start water polo young and I think the ball skills I learnt there contributed to my football... of course the competitive swimming we were doing also helped with our speed around the water polo field. So, my ability was a combination of a few things."

Dick Thornett, 9 August 2008
Interviewed by Ian Warden [3]

The 1956/57 season began following the NSWAWPA 27th Annual General Meeting, which was held at 7.45pm on Tuesday, 23rd September 1956, in the Council Room at the National Fitness Building, Cnr. Bent & Macquarie Sts. Sydney.

The Association congratulated the following water polo players for their success in other fields of sport: John Thornett (Bronte AWPC) for being selected as a member of the Wallabies team to tour Britain and other distant parts. Col Smee (Bondi AWPC) for his selection to accompany the Colts during their series of football games in Ceylon.

Throughout the year the Association held a fund-raiser for the Olympic Training Squad, a Welcome Home party aboard the "Westralia" given in honour of the NSW State Team winning the Australian Championships in Adelaide, and the Annual Water Polo Ball, which was held at 'Cahill's Restaurant'. The Association ended the season in a very healthy financial position with over £500 in the bank.

The Baths & Clubs

During the season, metropolitan matches were played at Rushcutters Bay, Bankstown, Roseville, Drummoyne, Elkington Park, Northbridge and The Spit.

In regard to new clubs, Judean and the Rolls Royce Club (ex Domain Club) affiliated for the first time, while Manly, Narrabeen and The Spit re-affiliated after a lapse of several years. However, the Association team in 1st Grade was withdrawn and both Bankstown and Parramatta clubs lapsed. Player registrations leaped ahead this

1956/57 Season Statistics N.S.W.A.W.P.A.

Clubs in the Water Polo Competitions.

Clubs	1	2	3N	3S	Total
Balmain	●	●		●	3
Balmoral		2			2
Bondi	2			2	4
Bronte	●	●		●	3
Dee Why	●	2			3
East Sydney	●			2	3
Garden Island	●				1
Judean		2			2
Manly	●				1
Narrabeen		2			2
Navy			●		1
Nth Sydney		2			2
Northbridge	●	●			2
Pyrmont	●			●	2
Rolls Royce (Dom)			●		1
Roseville			●		1
The Spit			●		1
University	●	●			2
	5	8	12	11	36

Results of the Water Polo Competitions.

Grade	Premier		Runner-Up
1st	Bondi A~5	d.	1~Balmain
2nd	East Sydney~5	d.	3~Balmain
3rd	Nth Sydney A~3	d.	2~Pyrmont
Club Champions			BALMAIN
3Nth	Nth Sydney A~9	d.	2~Narrabeen A
3Sth	Pyrmont~2	d.	1~Balmain

NEW SOUTH WALES TEAM
1957 - National Champions - Adelaide
From left: Ted Pierce (vc, Balmain), Alan Stringer (Balmain), Nino Sydney 'Von Somogy' (Bondi), Eric Fitzgerald (Balmain), Alf Beattie (Balmain), Ron Preston (Pyrmont), Hermie Bakels (g, Balmain), Norm Cason (Balmain), Fred Lamb (Manager). Absent: Hermie Doerner (Coach, Bondi) and Keith Whitehead (c, Bondi). **Vic McGrath** **(Bronte)** was selected but withdrew. Photo - NSWAWPA Archives.

season to approximately 478 players across 36 clubs.

Once again the competition was conducted over three grades with five teams in 1st Grade, eight teams in 2nd Grade and two 3rd Grade divisions: North with 12 teams, and South with 11 teams. Only eight matches were played in 1st Grade this season

"Where did you say you learnt to play water polo?"

and the preliminary competition concluded with Balmain ahead of Bondi.[8]

Representatives in NSW Teams

John Thornett again concentrated on his rugby and made himself unavailable for the NSW State team, but Bronte's Vic McGrath played himself into the side, before having to withdraw due to illness. The selectors made wholesale changes to the NSW team this year as Alan Stringer (Balmain) was recalled, with five new faces in Hermie Bakels (g), Alf Beattie, Norm Cason (Balmain), Ron Preston (g, Pyrmont) and Nino Sydney (Bondi).

Nonetheless, the strategy worked as New South Wales wrenched the national title back from Victoria following a torrid series, with Western Australia and South Australia filling out third and fourth placings.

"Water polo wasn't really professional, but it was a game played for the love of it, and it was... a really hard game. People probably believe that by playing water polo you're in the water so you're not getting hot, but I used to perspire after a game of water polo... I'd get out and it'd take me half an hour to cool down. Your perspiration would be running from you so it was a very strenuous game, particularly when playing in deeper water. At Bronte it was shallow and you could stand up, but when we got to other pools it was something else again... it was a hard game."

"I played attacking forward most of the time because I was a strong goal shooter and my brother John played in centre forward. In those days, we were given positions when playing water polo, but this later changed. There was always a centre forward and I used to swim around my brother in the middle or in the half. Because I had speed and could connect the backs to the forwards who were shooting, so I was mostly in the position as a half forward, and goal shooter."

Dick Thornett, 9 August 2008
Interviewed by Ian Warden [3]

"When I first turned up to water polo training there were many others vying for inclusion in any team, but I was made 3rd Grade goalkeeper (a position no one wanted... even me), but I did it for the team. However, despite this sacrifice Karma was kind to me, so after two seasons I was promoted into the field by Burt Vadas, and never looked back."

Terry 'Lunk' Clark, April 2018

▼ *BELOW: Sharing in common great strength and sporting prowess, John Thornett and Ken Mills were also great mates. BOTTOM: Peter "The Flea" and Tommy Folden catch an octopus at their Rushcutters Bay Baths playground, c. 1957).*

The Premierships

In the play-offs, Balmain ended Bronte's hopes (5~3) and then Bondi A easily accounted for Bondi B (9~2). With no preliminary final both winners progressed straight to the grand-final where Bondi A were too strong for Balmain (4~2). As Balmain had finished the competition as minor premiers, they exercised their right to challenge Bondi A, but were defeated again by an even greater margin (5~1), in the grand-final. The win capped off a decade of water polo supremacy for Bondi and established a record for the NSW Mens competition that to this day has not been repeated. East Sydney backed up to win the 2nd Grade again, and North Sydney won the 3rd Grade. Balmain took home the Club Championship.

NSW State Premiership

The title of NSW State Champions 1956-57 went to the Bondi A team, which had won the 1st Grade Metropolitan premiership and were to meet the winners of the Country Championships Wagga Wagga, however Wagga forfeited on the match.[8]

BONDI AWPC
1956/57 - NSWAWPA 1st Grade Premiers
Alex Kosegi c/Coach), Ray Smee, Bill Jones, Doug Laing (g), Keith Whitehead, Rally Sarkies, Bill Roney, Col Smee, Brian Hutchings, Nino Sydney.

Bronte AWPC

This season saw Bronte radically drop back in numbers, the result being that only three teams were entered in the NSWAWPA competitions. But they managed to enter teams in 3rd Grade (South), 2nd and 1st Grade.

Unfortunately none of the Bronte sides qualified for the grand-finals this year, while Vic McGrath was their only player to gain selection in the NSW team, although he was later forced to withdraw due to illness.

1957-58

1957/58 NSWAWPA OFFICIALS: Dr. H.K. Porter (Patron); A.P. Hart (President); Dr H.K. Porter (Past President); H. Doerner (Chairman); R.Y. Traynor (Registrar); Capt. F. Lamb (Secretary); K. Langbien (Asst. Secretary); R. Smee (Treasurer).

"Long ago in the dark ages of water polo circa 1957, I got hooked into playing for Bronte and it changed my whole view on friendships, how they were built on and survived. My oldest water polo mate is Brian Hallinan… son of Tom Hallinan of Bronte Swimming Club officialdom fame. Brian and I met when we were about 5 years old, when our respective mothers hauled us off to The Nuns at St Clare's Convent for some discipline and holiness… needless to say in my case it didn't do much good. But Brian and I are still top mates 72 years on!"
Terry 'Lunk' Clark, April 2018

The 1957/58 season began following the NSWAWPA 28th Annual General Meeting, which was held at 7.30pm on Monday, 22nd September 1957, in the Council Room at the National Fitness Building, Cnr. Bent & Macquarie Sts. Sydney.

Throughout the year the Association held a reception for the visiting State teams at the Freshwater SLSC, a Farewell Party aboard the "Westralia" at the close of the Australian Championships, and the Annual Water Polo Ball, which was held at 'Cahill's Restaurant' in May. The Association ended the season in a very healthy position with over £600 in the bank.

The Baths & Clubs

During the season, metropolitan matches were played at Rushcutters Bay, Bankstown, Roseville, Drummoyne, Elkington Park, Northbridge and The Spit. Two new clubs in Coogee SLSC and Maroubra SLSC accepted invitations to enter the water polo competition and acquitted themselves extraordinarily well. The surf club players possessed all the necessary qualities of speed, strength, determination and good sportsmanship so essential to water polo. Drummoyne and North Narrabeen re-affiliated after a lapse, while the Rolls Royce Club transformed into the Wanderers (Domain Baths).

The media gave the sport of water polo more coverage this year with newspaper, radio and television all promoting the game. Once again the competition was conducted over three grades with nine teams in 1st Grade, eight teams in 2nd Grade and two 3rd Grade divisions: North with

1957/58 Season Statistics N.S.W.A.W.P.A.

Clubs in the Water Polo Competitions.

Clubs	Grades 1	2	3N	3S	Total
Balmain	2	●			3
Balmoral		●	●		2
Bondi	2	●		2	5
Bronte	●			●	2
Coogee SLSC				2	2
Dee Why		●	●		2
Drummoyne			●		1
East Sydney	●			●	2
Garden Island			●		1
Judean				●	1
Manly	●			2	3
Maroubra SLSC				●	1
Navy			●		1
Nth Narrabeen		●	●		2
Nth Sydney		●	●		2
Northbridge	●		●		2
Pyrmont	●	●			2
Roseville			●		1
The Spit			2		2
University		●		●	2
Wanderers (Dom)				●	1
	9	8	11	12	40

Results of the Water Polo Competitions.

Grade	Premier		Runner-Up
1st	Balmain A~4	d.	3~Bondi A
2nd	Dee Why~4	d.	3~Balmain
3rd	Manly A~7	d.	4~Dee Why
Club Champions			Balmain
3Nth	Dee Why~2	d.	0~Drummoyne
3Sth	Manly A~6	d.	4~Wanderers

TOP: Bronte 1st Grade Team began building in season 1957/58. Back row (from left): Dick Thornett, John Thornett, Vic McGrath, Ken Mills. Front row: Dick See, Bert Vadas (c/Coach), Ken Thornett (g), Jack Campbell. ABOVE: Bronte 1st Grade Team 1957/58.

11 teams, and South with 12 teams. Teams entering the competition reached 40 for the first time and player registrations across all clubs climbed again to 499.[9]

Representatives in NSW Teams

While remaining an avid clubman, John Thornett again made himself unavailable for representative honours this season, due to the 1957-58 Wallaby tour of Britain, Ireland and France. NSW retained the bulk of their 1957 national championship team, although Ray Smee, Bill Jones and goalkeeper Doug Laing (Bondi) were recalled. But forcing themselves into this NSW side with brilliant form were Vic McGrath and Dick Thornett (Bronte), who were the only new caps in the team. Despite the formidable Bondi combination returning for NSW, it was a well drilled Victoria that took a 5th national title home, with the Western and South Australians filling out third and fourth respectively.

The Premierships

The Association received nine entries in 1st Grade although Northbridge withdrew after some games. Balmain finished the preliminary rounds in front with Bondi a close second. In the NSWAWPA 1st Grade play-offs, Bondi A narrowly defeated Bondi B (3~1), while Balmain A easily disposed of Manly (8~0) in the semi-final. With no preliminary final both winners progressed straight to the final where Bondi A once again showed

NEW SOUTH WALES TEAM Runners-Up at Nationals Sydney, 1958
Keith Whitehead (c, Bondi)
Hermie Bakels (g, Balmain)
Eric Fitzgerald (Balmain)
Bill Jones (Bondi)
Doug Laing (g, Bondi)
Vic McGrath (Bronte)
Ted Pierce (vc, Balmain)
Ray Smee (Bondi)
Alan Stringer (Balmain)
Nino Sydney (Bondi)
Dick Thornett (Bronte)
Alex Kosegi (Coach, Bondi)
Fred Lamb (Manager).

"John and I used to spend a lot of time together away from club training. We'd go down to the Bronte pool and pick a deep area, then tread water, passing with two balls, left and right handed for an hour or so on end. I was only sort of 18, but that created timing, so it started early in my life, or probably even earlier. That's where I think you're timing, coordination and ball skills all go back to... that anticipation. And... you know... I was reasonably fast for a big fellow too, so I suppose that goes to down to all the early touch football. But I always relate back to the early Bronte days as I think there was a reason for it all."
Dick Thornett, 9 August 2008
Interviewed by Ian Warden [3]

▼ *Bronte 1st Grade Team of 1957/58, although these photos were taken after their premiership win in 1959. Back row (from left): Vic McGrath, Ken Mills, John Thornett, Dick Thornett. Front row: Ken Thornett (g), Bert Vadas (c/Coach), Jack Campbell, Dick See.*

"Dick Thornett was strange in terms of his growth pattern... because when he was younger he was very slightly built. But he didn't develop gradually, he grew from a 'dweeb' into the absolute biggest 'tank' you could imagine in a single year. This took him a couple of years to recover from...He grew into a huge man and very strong. Dick had a technique of pushing his opponent away gradually... and not being at all obvious, he was rarely caught by the referee."

Robbie Vadas, March 2019

"My first recollections of the game were around 1957-58 when my dad, Erick Folden went to play with his Hungarian friends like Bert Vadas, Oscar Csuvic, Alex Kosegi and the others..."

Peter Folden, Nov 2018

their experience to overwhelm Balmain (4~3). However, because Balmain were minor premiers, they exercised their right to challenge Bondi A in the grand-final. Bondi was expected to repeat their earlier performance and make it 11 straight premierships, but they faltered and lost to Balmain (4~3) in the closest of contests. The Balmain win brought an end to Bondi's 10 year stranglehold on the NSWAWPA 1st Grade water polo premiership. Dee Why won the 2nd Grade, and Manly A won the 3rd Grade, while Balmain took home the Club Championship.

NSW State Championship

The winners of the Country Championship once again qualified to meet the winners of the Metropolitan Championship for the title of 'State Champions' however, Canberra could not make the trip to Sydney and Balmain were declared '1957/58 State Champions' by forfeit. [9]

Bronte AWPC

By the 1957/58 season, Bronte was entering its seventh year in the NSW water polo scene, but hadn't yet tasted success. The club dropped in numbers again and only managed to enter two teams this season with a 3rd Grade (South) and 1st Grade.

This year Dick Thornett played himself into selection on the NSW State team along with Vic McGrath, while brother

---

1957/58 RESULTS

WATER POLO

METROPOLITAN PREMIERSHIP.
—First grade: Bronte beat Bondi A. 5-4; Manly beat Pyrmont, 4-3; Balmain A beat Bondi B, 14-2. 2nd grade: Deewhy beat Bondi, 4-2; Nth. Narrabeen drew with Balmoral, 2-all; Pyrmont forfeited to North Sydney.

SMH, 19th Feb 1958

WATER POLO

METROPOLITAN PREMIERSHIP.
—1st grade: Bondi A beat Balmain B, 12-4; Bondi B forfeited to Pyrmont. 2nd grade: North Narrabeen forfeited to University; Deewhy beat Balmoral, 7-3; Pyrmont forfeited to Bondi.

SMH, 26th Feb 1958

WATER POLO

METROPOLITAN CHAMPIONSHIP, 3rd grade, quarter-finals: South: Wanderers bt Coogee A, 5-1; Drummoyne bt East Sydney, 3-2; North: Deewhy bt Northbridge, 7-5; Manly A bt North Narrabeen, 14-5.
Competition points, grade 1: Balmain A, 100; Bondi A, 92; Manly, 82. (4th place still to be decided.) Grade II: Balmain, 70; Deewhy, 70; Balmoral, 60; Bondi, 56. Grade III (Sth. side): Wanderers, 62; East Sydney, 52; Coogee A, 50; Drummoyne, 46. (Nth. side): Northbridge, 66; Manly A, 62; Deewhy, 58 Nth. Narrabeen, 52.

SMH, 5th Mar 1958

WATER POLO

METROPOLITAN PREMIERSHIP
1st semi-finals.—1st grade: Balmain A beat Manly, 8-0. 2nd grade: Balmoral forfeited to Balmain. 3rd grade: Deewhy beat Drummoyne, 2-0.
Last competition round, 1st grade: Bondi B beat Pyrmont, 7-0.
Bondi B now fourth in the competition.

SMH, 11th Mar 1958

BALMAIN
1957/58 - NSWAWPA 1st Grade Premiers
Standing (from left): Alf Beattie, Alan Stringer, Balmain President, Eric FitzGerald, M. Best.
Seated: Hermie Bakels (g), Ted Pierce (c), Norm Cason.

John Thornett was still unavailable due to rugby union duties.

Both Bronte teams played some great water polo this year and the 1st Grade even defeated the great Bondi throughout the rounds, but neither team was able to win through to their respective grand-finals. However, persistence is a virtue and all the club had to do was to keep applying the pressure and be patient, as they could all feel that success lay just around the corner.

▲ *NSW goalkeeper Doug Laing (Bondi) makes a save against Western Australia at Elkington Park Baths during the 1958 Australian Water Polo Championships in Sydney.*

"Not so many years ago it was quite common to hear water polo referred to as 'The Cinderella of Sports', but members of the Association whose loyalty to the game has remained unshaken, derived great satisfaction from its steadily increasing popularity and acceptance as an essential part of swimming club activity.

A few die-hards, some of whom are in high places, are still reluctant to concede that the game is an integral part of organised swimming, but popular demand must prevail and eventually result in complete acceptance into the family circle of the hitherto 'unwanted child'."[7]

"I played through the grades, and remember playing 3rd Grade against a team from the Navy that was based in Nowra. They just played as an excuse to travel to Sydney each week. I distinctly remember them keeping their drinks cold in a string bag attached to the wooden walkway at Rushcutters Bay, just so refreshments were at hand at half time. There were no quarters in those days. But they used to stink of rum!"

Bob Cope, March 2019

Chapter 4

CHAMPIONS
(1959 - 1962)

▲ *From left: Bandi Kosegi, Frank Hoffer (goalkeeper), George Gulyas, Eric Folden and Alex Kosegi at Rushcutters Bay Baths about 1960. Photo - Tom Folden.*

"I was around 11 when I started to muck around with the leather balls down at Rushcutters Bay Baths. I was given the job of waxing the stitching on the balls to keep the water out. I thought I was the 'ants pants'. I began to play when I was 13, and had so much help from all the older team members."

Peter Folden, Nov 2018

"In the late 1950's, Vic McGrath took an interest in our team and often attended our weekday late afternoon training sessions, and gave us many hints and strategies that got us thru to grand finals, but we lost to Coogee."

Jon Kirkwood, June 2018

"At Rushy Baths was a starting stand for the swimming races. This consisted of a single board, 6x2" in the old system, held up by four supports coming up from the bottom of the pool. There was another board going along the supports at water level for the turning swimmers. As a youngster, I spent ages around this area holding my breath as I swam in and out between the supports."

Robbie Vadas, Aug 2019

By the late 1950's, Bronte Water Polo Club had managed to record a number of notable achievements. First and foremost, the Bronte teams were now part of a stable club within the NSW water polo scene and had grown from fielding just one 3rd Grade team in 1951/52 to maintaining permanent and talented sides in all grades of the NSWAWPA 1st Division competitions. Led by John Thornett and Bert Vadas, the Bronte 1st Grade had even reached the grand-finals of 1954 and 1955, but lost on both occasions to the rampaging Bondi teams that were in the midst of their record breaking 10 consecutive 1st Grade premierships.

The other notable achievement for Bronte was that the talents of both John Thornett and Momie Vadas had been recognised by their selection in the NSW teams of 1954 and 1955. So, many onlookers could sense a change coming over the Bronte club that was to propel them into dominance. By now they had attracted the talent, they had a master coach to direct them in Bert Vadas, and young Dick Thornett was now growing into a man, which proved to be the game changer.

1958-59

1958/59 NSWAWPA OFFICIALS: Dr. H.K. Porter (Patron); Mr. A.P Hart (President); H. Doerner (Chairman); J.E. Thornett (**Registrar**); Capt. F. Lamb (Secretary); T. Koolberg (Asst. Secretary); R.L. Smee (Treasurer).

The 1958/59 season began following the NSWAWPA 29th Annual General Meeting, but it was not necessary to look for justification of success in the Sydney area alone. During the 1958-59 season, when no less than 47 teams representing 23 clubs contested the three grades of the Metropolitan premiership, some 13 of the clubs nominated from two to five teams each.

The increasing popularity of the game was not without its problems however, as there were more swimmers wishing to play water polo than there were pools to accommodate them. This necessitated either the 'seeding' of players or teams, or restricting the number of games in the premiership competitions.

Then there was the shortage of referees, timekeepers and goal-judges, a problem which was resolved only by the players themselves.

"The kind of man required to control this most difficult of games, usually an ex-player, would not give of his time and pay his own

> "I remember one game when Bronte was playing Balmain and the Balmain goalkeeper was Herman Baykell... a very big man. And I got a penalty, which was on the four yard line, where you shoot for goal and the goalkeeper remains on the line. A lot of times you shoot around their head, or just above the shoulders, where it's the last position their hands will get to. So, as he came up with his arms, my shot was a bit misdirected and hit him square in the face, and the poor guy actually went down. He didn't go under but it knocked, and stunned him for a while. I had to push the ball through the net to make sure it was a goal first, and the went and helped him so. But yes, I guess you might say I had a pretty powerful shot.."
>
> ***Dick Thornett, 9 August 2008***
> ***Interviewed by Ian Warden [2]***

1958/59 RESULTS

WATER POLO

METROPOLITAN PREMIERSHIP. First Grade: East Sydney 3, Manly 2; Balmain "A" 12, University nil; Bondi "B" 7, Deewhy 3; Bronte 4, Bondi "A" 3. Second Grade: Wanderers 4, Deewhy 3; Balmain 3, Pyrmont nil. Third Grade: University 7, Coogee 4; Maroubra "B" 8, Judean nil; Bondi "A" 6, Wanderers 3.

SMH, 24 Nov, 1958

WATER POLO

Metropolitan Premiership Series.— 1st grade: Manly 6 beat University 0; Balmain forfeited to Balmain A. 2nd grade: Pyrmont 3, beat Bondi 1; 3rd grade: Manly A 5, beat North Narrabeen 4; Manly B 5, beat Collaroy 0; Navy 9, beat Maroubra A 2; Maroubra B 6, beat Bronte A, 1.

SMH, 1 Dec, 1958

WATER POLO

Metropolitan premiership.— 1st grade: Balmain B forfeited to University; Balmain A, 5, East Syd., 1; Bronte, 4, Bondi B, 3. 2nd grade: Spit, 5, Manly, 2; Garden Island forfeited to University; Coogee, 4, Wanderers, 3. 3rd grade: Manly A, 5, Deewhy, 2; Collaroy, 6, Spit A, 3; Manly B, 10, Spit B, 3; Balmain, 5, Maroubra A, 1; Bronte B, 4, North Sydney 1; Maroubra B, 13, University, 3; Bronte A, 4, Wanderers, 2; Judean forfeited to Coogee; Bondi B, 3, Drummoyne B, 1; Navy, 10, Cabarita, 2; Drummoyne A, 10, Bondi A, 9; Roseville forfeited to Narrabeen.

SMH, 3 Dec, 1958

WATER POLO

METROPOLITAN PREMIERSHIP. First Grade: Balmain A 10 beat University 2. Second grade: Spit 4 beat "Pyrmont 2; Deewhy 6 beat Garden Island 5. Third grade: Deewhy 6 beat Spit B 5; North Narrabeen 8 beat Spit A 1; Drummoyne B 2 beat Maroubra A 0; Cabarita 3 beat North Sydney 0; Maroubra B 9 beat Bondi A 1; Bronte B 8 beat Navy 2; Drummoyne A 4 beat Bronte A 0; East Sydney forfeited to University; Balmain 4 beat Clovelly 3. Judean 4 beat. Wanderers 2.

SMH, 10 Dec, 1958

WATER POLO

METROPOLITAN PREMIERSHIP SERIES, at Manly and Elkington Park Baths.—First grade: Bronte 8, Deewhy 2; East Sydney 3, University 1. Second grade: Spit 9, University 4; Manly 3, Deewhy 2; Garden Island 5, Pyrmont 3. Third grade: Manly B 3, drew with Manly A 3; Bronte B 10, Drummoyne B 2; Drummoyne A 10, Coogee 2.

SMH, 15 Dec, 1958

WATER POLO

Metropolitan premiership series.— First grade: Bondi A, 11, Manly, 2; Bondi B, 5, East Sydney, 3. Second grade: Manly 7, Bondi 0. Third grade: Manly A, 11, Spit B, 1; Bronte A, 4, University, 1; Bronte B, 8, Maroubra A, 0; Spit A, 5, Roseville, 4; Nth. Narrabeen, 7, Deewhy, 2; Balmain, 7, Drummoyne, B, 0; Maroubra B, 5, Drummoyne A, 2; Cabarita, 1, Bondi B, 0; Bondi A, 7, Judean, 1.

SMH, 17 Dec, 1958

"Remembering the first major game of my career at Elkington Park Baths back in early 1958, when I was only 15 years old. The NSWAWPA decided to stage a handicap tournament over two nights where each team consisted of one 1st Grader, two 2nd Graders and the rest from 3rd Grade. The teams played against each other, but there was a secret handicap number allocated to each team so that when you finished the game, an envelope was opened and that often determined the winner. For example, we played Balmain in the final and I think we drew 2~2, but when the envelope was opened, Bronte received one handicap goal, which meant we won and received the trophy. I don't recall another of these events ever being played since, but according to Dick See, I excelled that night... saving just about anything that was thrown at me. Balmain were also awarded two penalties (no doubt via Dick's rough marking), and I even saved one of those... a highlight of my career! I vividly recall this as it was my first water polo game for Bronte, during the pre-season and I was selected as 3rd Grade goalie (because no one else put their hand up) and so began my illustrious career as goalkeeper, then field player, then goalie again in Brisbane and finally field player once more. I can remember that Dick See was our 1st Grader and Bronte captain, Peter 'Rocky' Johnson was our 2nd Grader and I have a suspicion Warren Hurt was in the team (check with Ello and Billy McCarthy) etc. I know that one of the Balmain boys was State player Maxie Best, and I can remember faces but not the names of others."

Terry 'Lunk' Clark, Oct 2020

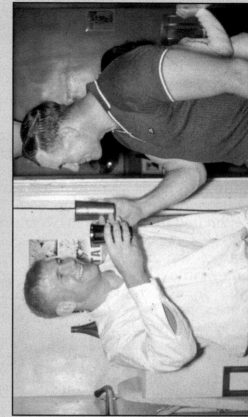

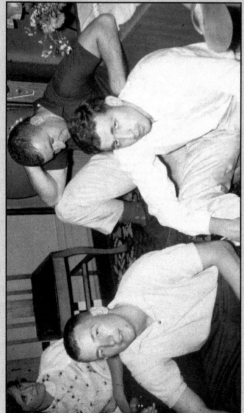

1959/60 - BRONTE AMATEUR WATER POLO CLUB

Four colour photographs of the Bronte boys socialising with their teammates and other club members. Photos - Viv Thornett.

expenses to make possible his services, for those who repay him with insults and by humiliating him in public."[1]

On a positive note, the boys from the surf clubs were adapting well to the game. The best example of this was Maroubra SLSC, who defeated all 27 teams in the competition to take out the 3rd Grade premiership this season.

An inter-services water polo championship was held at Nowra, which was won by the Royal Australian navy team.

The Baths & Clubs

In regard to new clubs, Clovelly SLSC followed the lead of the Coogee and Maroubra Surf Clubs from the previous year, and Collaroy affiliated for the first time, while Cabarita re-affiliated after a lapse of several years. Balmoral and Garden Island affiliated, but did not enter any teams and the Northbridge Club lapsed.

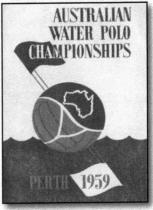

▶ABOVE: John Thornett standing up Hermie Bakels during the 1959 Australian Championships. BELOW: Program for Perth 1959 Australian Championships. ▼LEFT: Program excerpt showing notable players. RIGHT (Above): The 1959 NSW State team lines up at Crawley Baths for a photograph. (Below): The large crowd at Crawley Baths to watch the 1959 Perth Australian Water Polo Championships. Photos - NSWAWPA Archives.

NOTABLE PLAYERS IN THIS SERIES

WESTERN AUSTRALIA

ANTON BOLVARI—Played in 46 International games for Hungary before returning to Australia after Melbourne Olympic Games. Was a member of Hungarian 1952 and 1956 Gold Medal Teams and was Vice-Captain in 1956. Was a member of Victoria's Championship winning team last year. Now Captain-Coach of Melville Club and of W.A. Team.

ALLAN CHARLESTON—Has played 35 games for W.A. and represented Australia at Melbourne Olympic Games. Was State Captain-Coach in 1957 and 1958 and stood down for Anton Bolvari this season. Captain-Coach of Olympic Club, W.A. Premiers last season.

IMRE TAKACS—Played 9 International games for Hungary before immigrating to Australia in 1957. Was a member of Victoria's winning team last year. Now Captain-Coach of Fremantle Club.

VICTORIA

JOHN O'BRIEN—Has represented Victoria since 1951. Was a member of 1956 Australian Olympic Team.

JIM FARRELL—Was also a member of 1956 Olympic Team and has represented Victoria since 1954.

PAUL BANHIDY—Is a brilliant goalkeeper who has represented Hungary in International games.

KEITH WEIGARD—Has represented Victoria for three seasons. He is a noted League football ruckman with Fitzroy.

BILL McCABE—Was goalkeeper for Australia at the 1956 Olympic Games. He has played more than 30 games for Victoria. He plays League football with North Melbourne.

NEW SOUTH WALES

KEITH WHITEHEAD—Has represented N.S.W. since 1951 and played for Australia at 1952 and 1956 Olympic Games and New Zealand Centenary Games. (Known as Stein to all water polo people.)

DOUGIE LANG—Although only 5ft. 5½in. tall, Doug is one of the greatest Goalkeepers ever seen in this country. Represented Australia 1952 and 1956 Olympic Games and at New Zealand Centenary Games.

JOHN THORNETT—Is a Rugby International having toured Europe with the Wallabies last season.

NEW SOUTH WALES TEAM
1959 - 3rd Place - National Championships - Perth

Back row: (from left): Alan Stringer (Balmain), **John Thornett (Bronte)**, Alf Beatty (Balmain), Hermie Bakels (g. Balmain), **Dick Thornett (Bronte)**, Eric Fitzgerald (Balmain), Front row: Brian Hutchings (Bondi), Keith Whitehead (Bondi), Bob Traynor (Manager), Dr. H.K. Porter (NSW Patron), Doug Laing (g. Bondi). Missing: Alex Kosegi (Coach, Bondi). Photo - Nino Sydney. Photo - NSWAWPA Archives.

BRONTE AMATEUR WATER POLO CLUB
1958/59 - NSWAWPA 1st Grade Premiers
Back row (from left): Ken Mills, John Thornett, Dick Thornett, Ken Thornett. Front row: Vic McGrath, Ray Burton, Bert Vadas (c/Coach), Jack Campbell, Dick See. Photo - NSWAWPA 1958/59 Annual Report. Photo - NSWAWPA Archives.

Once again the competition was conducted over three grades with nine teams in 1st Grade, nine teams in 2nd Grade and three 3rd Grade divisions: North with eight teams, South with eight teams and West with nine teams. Teams entering the competition reached 43 and player registrations across all clubs jumped by 20% to 591. Games were scheduled at the following baths: Drummoyne, Elkington Park (Balmain), Granville, Manly, Northbridge, Rushcutters Bay, and The Spit. [1]

> "I started playing in 1959 when Ken Thornett went to England with the Kangaroos RL Team, he was the goalkeeper for Bronte 1st Grade, so I took his place."
> *Don Sarkies, 27 Jan 2015*

Representatives in NSW Teams

Only one new cap forced themselves into the NSW team this year in Brian Hutchings (Bondi). However, Alf Beattie (Balmain), Alex Kosegi (Bondi) and John Thornett (Bronte) were all recalled, giving Bronte two caps with Dick Thornett having been retained from the previous season.

The team travelled right across the country by train for the 12th Australian Championships at Crawley Baths in Perth. However, on their home turf and with ex-Hungarian Olympian, Anton Bolvari at the helm, it was

1958/59 NSWAWPA RESULTS

RESULTS

KEY: Pl.—Played; W—won; L—Lost; D—Drawn; F or D—Forfeited or Disqualified; For — Goals for; Agst — Goals against; Pts. — Points; Posn. — Position.

1ST. GRADE

	Pl.	W.	L.	D.	F.orDd	For	Agst	Pts.	Posn.
Bronte	14	12	1	1	—	100	33	78	1
Bondi "A"	14	10	2	2	—	93	29	72	2
Balmain "A"	14	9	4	1	—	81	41	66	3
Bondi "B"	14	8	5	1	—	56	39	62	4
Manly	14	7	7	—	—	58	63	56	5
East Sydney	14	5	9	—	—	41	62	48	6
Dee Why	14	2	12	—	—	29	107	36	7
Sydney University	14	—	14	—	—	16	101	28	8

Balmain 'B' withdrawn from competition.

1st Semi-Final:	Balmain "A"	5	v.	Bronte	4
2nd Semi-Final:	Bondi "A"		v.	Bondi "B" forfeit
Final:	Balmain "A"	5	v.	Bondi "A"	0
Grand Final:	Bronte	4	v.	Balmain	3

Premiers:— BRONTE

3RD. GRADE (South)

	Pl.	W.	L.	D.	F.orD.	For	Agst	Pts.	Posn.
Maroubra Surf "B"	14	12	1	1		74	18	78	1
Drummoyne "A"	14	12	1	1		78	21	78	2
Bronte "A"	14	10	4	—		49	30	68	3
Sydney University	14	7	5	—	2	27	46	52	4
Bondi "A"	14	6	5	—	3	39	44	46	5
Coogee Surf	14	4	7	—	3	17	59	38	6
Judean	14	3	9	—	2	22	52	30	7
Wanderers	14	—	11	—	3	14	51	22	8

Play-Off:	Maroubra "B"	13	v.	Drummoyne "A"	3
1st Semi-Final:	Maroubra "B"	5	v.	Bronte "A"	1
2nd Semi-Final	Drummoyne "A"		v.	University	2
Final:	Drummoyne "A"	4	v.	Maroubra "B"	0
Grand Final:	Maroubra "B"	3	v.	Drummoyne "A"	2

District Premiers:— MAROUBRA SURF "B"

3RD. GRADE (West)

	Pl.	W.	L.	D.	F.orD.	For	Agst	Pts.	Posn.
Bronte "B"	16	15	1	—	—	91	19	92	1
Balmain	16	12	2	1	1	49	25	80	2
Clovelly Surf	16	11	3	1	1	54	28	76	3
North Sydney	16	6	7	1	2	36	52	54	4
Bondi "B"	16	4	10	2	—	27	55	52	5
Maroubra Surf "A"	16	4	7	3	2	27	63	50	6
Cabarita	16	4	6	3	3	22	40	48	7
R.A.N.	16	6	4	—	6	49	42	44	8
Drummoyne "B"	16	3	10	1	2	19	54	42	9

1st Semi-Final	Balmain	6	v.	North Sydney	2
2nd Semi-Final	Bronte "B"	5	v.	Clovelly	2
Final:	Bronte "B"	4	v.	Balmain	3

District Premiers:— BRONTE "B"

3RD. GRADE INTERZONE FINALS

1.	Maroubra "B"	5	v.	Manly "A"	3
2.	Maroubra "B"	5	v.	Bronte "B"	4

Premiers:— MAROUBRA SURF "B"

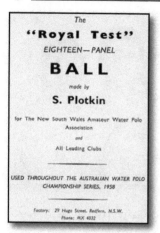

Western Australia that completed this tournament undefeated, with Victoria, NSW and South Australia filling out the placings. The win for WA stamped their state, from that point on, as a major force in Australian water polo.

The Premierships

The Association again received nine entries in 1st Grade although Balmain B withdrew after some games. Bronte had only lost one game and finished the preliminary rounds in front with Bondi A, a close second. In the play-offs, Bondi B forfeited to Bondi A and Balmain A to everyone's surprise defeated Bronte (5~4) in an upset. With no preliminary final both winners progressed straight to the final where Balmain A disposed of Bondi A (5~0) with ease. However, and even though they were knocked-out earlier, because they had finished the competition as the minor premiers, Bronte exercised their right to challenge Balmain A in the grand-final. Balmain weren't so lucky this time around, and lost to the very talented and well coached Bronte team (3~4), which included current and ex-State representatives in Bert Vadas, Vic McGrath, Dick See as well as, John and Dick Thornett.

The brilliant win was Bronte's inaugural 1st Grade water polo premiership and admitted them to an exclusive group of clubs that had attained that great honour since the NSW competition had begun back in 1892. Manly won the 2nd Grade, and Maroubra B won the 3rd Grade. The depth at Bronte this season also saw them take home the Club Championship.

NSW State Championship

By virtue of their having become the Metropolitan 1st Grade premiers, Bronte met the Country Champions, Dubbo, at Elkington Park Baths, Balmain.

1958/59 Season Statistics
N.S.W.A.W.P.A.

Clubs in the Water Polo Competitions.

Clubs	1	2	3N	3S	3W	Total
Balmain	2	●			●	4
Bondi	2	●		●	●	5
Bronte	●			●	●	3
Cabarita					●	1
Clovelly SLSC					●	1
Collaroy			●			1
Coogee SLSC		●			●	2
Dee Why	●	●	●			3
Drummoyne				●	●	2
East Sydney	●					1
Judean				●		1
Manly	●	●	2			4
Maroubra SLSC				●	●	2
Navy				●		1
Nth Narrabeen			●			1
Nth Sydney					●	1
Pyrmont		●				1
Roseville				●		1
The Spit		●	2			3
University	●	●		●		3
Wanderers (Dom)		●	●			2
	9	9	8	8	9	43

Results of the Water Polo Competitions.

Grade	Premier		Runner-Up
1st	Bronte~4	d.	3~Balmain
2nd	Manly~6	d.	5~Balmain
3rd	Maroubra B	d.	Bronte B
Club Champions	BRONTE		
3Nth	Manly A~6	d.	5~N. Narrabeen
3Sth	Maroubra B~3	d.	2~Drummoyne A
3Wst	Bronte B~4	d.	3~Balmain

The Dubbo players were no doubt overawed by the occasion, which undoubtedly contributed to their comprehensive defeat.[1]

Bronte AWPC

Bronte fielded an extra team this year, by entering two 3rd Grade teams, which had a marked effect on results from the previous season with all three teams qualifying for the play-offs.

Competing in the 3rd Grade 'South' Competition, Bronte A finished in third place, but lost to Maroubra B (1~5) in the semi-final. However Bronte B only lost one game on the season, to finish on top of the 3rd Grade 'West' Competition. They then defeated both Clovelly and Balmain to win the Division premiership, and only narrowly lost to Maroubra B in the 3rd Grade Inter-zone play off (4~5).

It was in 1st Grade however, that Bronte really demonstrated their mettle by finishing on top of the ladder. In the play-offs, they lost by a whisker to Balmain A (4~5), who then won through to the grand-final. But the competition rules back then gave a second chance to the minor-premiers, and after challenging Balmain A, Bronte turned the tables and snatched victory in the grand-final over Balmain A (4~3), capturing in the process their inaugural 1st Grade premiership. To cap off the stellar results, Bronte also won the the points based NSWAWPA Club Championship. The successful season placed Bronte on top of the Sydney water polo competition.

1959-60

1959/60 NSWAWPA OFFICIALS:
Dr. H.K. Porter (Patron); Mr. A.P Hart (President); H. Doerner (Chairman); **J.E. Thornett (Registrar)**; Capt. F. Lamb (Secretary); P.R. Lamb (Asst. Secretary); R.L. Smee (Treasurer).

The 1959/60 season began following the NSWAWPA 30th Annual General Meeting, which was held at 7.30pm on Tuesday, 6th October 1959, in the Surf Life Saving Association Rooms, 16 Hunter St. Sydney.

Not so many years previously, a high percentage of players were fully grown men, but recent years showed that just as each succeeding swimming champion appeared to be younger than their

"When I started playing, I'd catch the tram from the city to Bronte, often with John Thornett, and we would go down to Bronte Baths. We'd train there, but the ball often went into the ocean."
Don Sarkies, 27 Jan 2015

"I can clearly remember as a youngster in Romania… just trying to lift one of those water soaked heavy leather footballs that they called water-polo balls."
Roly Flesch, Feb 2019

"Touch football was another thing. The swimming club in my early years was a broad social and recreational club in the old tradition. You swam together, surfed together, played a monumentally high standard of touch football in Bronte Park together, played squash and badminton together in the surf club, table tennis in the swimming club and during the winter those who played football mostly went to Randwick."
Brian Ellison, Oct 2018

"I can remember we carried the goals down the stairs to Bronte Baths every time we trained, but the pool was far too shallow... and we could stand up."

Don Sarkies, 27 Jan 2015

predecessor, the Association also found an ever increasing number of 13 and 14 year olds taking part in the premiership competitions.

"At the present rate of progress, the time cannot be far distant when action will have to be taken to provide facilities for water polo. Two hundred and thirteen teams, including many from our High Schools, played water polo during the season in Sydney alone, a City which cannot boast a single full size Olympic Water Polo Pool and next season there will be more still."[2]

As an illustration of the urgency of the problem, in 1956-57 there were 18 metropolitan clubs and one country affiliation. But by 1958/59, that figure had risen to 28 metropolitan clubs and 22 country affiliations, an incredible 60% increase, or 31 new clubs had formed in just three years.

This season there was an influx of three more surf clubs in Cronulla, North Bondi and South Curl Curl. Cronulla won the 3rd Grade premiership at its very first attempt while Maroubra, having been advanced to 2nd Grade, went on to win it's second premiership in three years.

The Baths & Clubs

Fortunately, a brand new Olympic Pool was opened this season at Parramatta, which had the immediate effect of bringing the Parramatta Water Polo Club back into the competition. In regard to new clubs, Cronulla SLSC, Darlinghurst CYO, North Bondi SLSC, and South Curl Curl SLSC affiliated for the first time, while Northbridge re-affiliated after a lapse of one year. Both Garden Island and North Narrabeen clubs lapsed.

1959/60 Season Statistics
N.S.W.A.W.P.A.

Clubs in the Water Polo Competitions.

Clubs	1	2^N	2^S	3^N	3^S	3^W	Total
Balmain	●	●				●	3
Balmoral		●	●				2
Bankstown						●	1
Bondi	●		●	●			3
Bronte	●	2					3
Cabarita						●	1
Clovelly SLSC			●	●			2
Collaroy				●			1
Coogee SLSC				●			1
Cronulla SLSC				●			1
Darlinghurst CYO				●			1
Dee Why	●	●		●			3
Drummoyne			●		●		2
East Sydney	●						1
Judean				●			1
Manly	●	2		●			4
Maroubra SLSC			●		●	●	3
Navy			●				1
Nth Bondi SLSC	●			●			2
Nth Sydney				●			1
Northbridge			●				1
Parramatta City					2		2
Pyrmont	●						1
Roseville			●				1
Sth Curl Curl SLSC			●				1
The Spit		●	2				3
University	●	●		●		●	4
Wanderers (Dom)	●			●			2
	8	8	8	10	10	8	52

Results of the Water Polo Competitions.

Grade	Premier		Runner-Up
1st	Bronte~4	d.	1~Bondi
2nd	Maroubra~6	d.	4~Dee Why
3rd	Cronulla~4	d.	1~Balmain
Club Champions			BRONTE
2^{Nth}	Dee Why~7	d.	4~University
2^{Sth}	Maroubra~5	d.	4~Drummoyne
3^{Nth}	Balmoral~6	d.	4~Dee Why
3^{Sth}	Cronulla~4	d.	2~Bondi
3^{Wst}	Balmain~6	d.	5~Maroubra A

"Bronte polo also had the best touch football game ever! After Saturday polo at Rushcutters Bay, we would repair to the grassed park behind the beach for touch footy for an hour or so at about fourish. With so many footy first graders and internationals, it was a great game. Many non polo footballers joined in like Catchpole, Jimmy Lisle etc. Eventually the game moved to Burrows Park, next to the Clovelly Bowls Club."

Bob Cope, March 2019

◀ABOVE: The Rushcutters Bay Baths were completed in 1905 and served the residents of Woollahra Council. BELOW: The history of the Pyrmont Baths from their opening in 1877 to their demolition in 1946 was a remarkable journey (Pyrmont History Group).

THE HARBOUR BATHS

In the first years of the 1900s, the Sydney Harbour Trust approved the construction of a number of public bathing enclosures along the harbour foreshores, reflecting the increased popularity of bathing as a pastime, and the rising fear of shark attack. The earliest harbour enclosure established in Woollahra was the Rushcutters Bay baths, anchored off the eastern side of the Bay, north of the naval complex. Vaucluse Council built baths at Watsons Bay at the foot of Gap Street (now Robertson Place) in 1905, the same year that baths were built off the northern edge of Lyne Park in Rose Bay. Of these three, only the Watsons Bay facility survives today. The Rose Bay baths, a floating bathing enclosure clad in corrugated iron and extending 50 metres out into the Bay, operated variously as 'Pike's Crystal Baths' and 'O'Keefe's Crystal Waters', and included a high diving tower. The structure was demolished c.1942 when the area it occupied was required for an extension of the wartime Flying Boat base. The Rushcutter's Bay enclosure, for many years known as 'Farmer's baths', fell into disrepair and was eventually dismantled in 1974. While the original Watsons Bay baths were demolished in 1923, a new structure on the same site was completed by 1927 and enlarged in the early 1960s with the addition of a new section designed to meet the standards and dimensions required for NSW inter-club swimming competition. The Watsons Bay baths underwent a major refurbishment in 2010, providing an Olympic-sized swimming enclosure with many additional leisure features. [3]

Once again the competition was conducted over three grades with eight teams in 1st Grade. Second grade consisted of two divisions: North with eight teams; and South with eight teams. Third grade was divided into three divisions: North with ten teams, South with ten teams and West with eight teams. The number of metropolitan teams entering the competition reached 52 and player registrations across all clubs jumped another 20% to 692.[2]

Representatives in NSW Teams

Having won the NSW premiership in the previous year, Bronte succeeded in having both John and Dick Thornett retained, and Vic McGrath recalled for the NSW team. Both Ted Pierce (Balmain) and Ray Smee (Bondi) were also recalled, with Bill Roney (Bondi) being the only new cap in the side. However, NSW could only manage a second

NEW SOUTH WALES TEAM
1960 - Runners Up -National Championships - Melbourne
From left: **Vic McGrath (Bronte)**, **John Thornett (Bronte)**, Ted Pierce (Balmain), Hermie Bakels (g, Balmain), Keith Whitehead (Capt, Bondi), **Dick Thornett (Bronte)**, Ray Smee (Bondi). Missing: Eric Fitzgerald (Balmain), Brian Hutchings (Bondi), Bill Roney (Bondi), **Bert Vadas (Coach, Bronte)**. Photo - Nino Sydney.

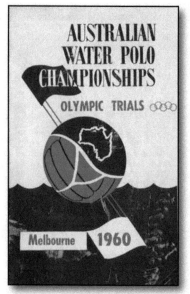

▲ Program and Official Pass for the 1960 Australian Water Polo Championships and Olympic Games Trials, Melbourne.

place to Victoria in the 13th Australian Championships held in Melbourne.

The Australian Olympic team was selected after these championships, with four players from Victoria, three each from NSW and West Australia, and one new boy from South Australia being chosen.

The 1960 Olympic Team

Being an Olympic year, there was great anticipation as to

whether Bronte could gain its first Olympic cap, and the players weren't disappointed when the great combination of Dick Thornett and Vic McGrath were both selected in the training squad. Although Vic McGrath didn't travel to Rome, he spent a couple of months training with the team as first reserve in Rockhampton.

The Aussies played against New Zealand, a number of pre games trials and three matches at the Rome Olympics, where they placed 15th, winning only five of their 12 matches in total.

Dick Thornett at the Rome Olympics [4]

"Being selected to play for Australia at water polo was a bit of a surprise... as I didn't really think I'd make it. It was about mid-February of 1960, and both John and I were at a barbeque after the final of the Australian Championships in Melbourne, where they announced the Australian side. That's when the team was announced, and yeah, it was a big thrill. I would have been 19 at the time."

"Before we flew off to the Olympics we had a training camp up at Rockhampton, which lasted quite a long time. It was supposed to be for the

"The fact that we didn't make it through to the finals had one saving grace, and that was we were able to watch Olympic sport all over the place, and I think most of the water polo team went to watch Tony Madigan (AUS) fight Cassius Clay. I knew Tony Madigan prior to the Olympics and he was a bit older than Clay, who got the decision in the semi-final bout. The win gave Clay the fight for the gold, and Madigan came back and fought for the bronze, but certainly all the Australian supporters, and a lot of the crowd thought it was the wrong decision against Clay... he later became Mohammed Ali of course."

Dick Thornett, 9 August 2008
Interviewed by Ian Warden [4]

"The Folden family arrived from Hungary in late 1956. Alex Koszegi was a friend of ours who was already in Sydney and he helped my mom & dad get settled while Peter and I started at Double Bay Public School. Every afternoon after school Pete and I made our way over the hill from Double Bay to Rushie to swim."

Tom Folden, Oct, 2020

AUSTRLIAN WATER POLO TEAM
1960 - OLYMPIC GAMES - ROME
Back row (from left): Keith Whitehead (vc, Bondi, NSW), Graham Sherman (Footscray, VIC), R. Jeffrey (r, g, Olympic, WA), Les Nunn (Maylands, WA), John O'Brien (c, Richmond, VIC), Ted Pierce (Balmain, NSW), **Vic McGrath (r, Bronte, NSW)**. Front row: Mick Withers (g, Kew, VIC), Allan Charleston (Olympic, WA), **Dick Thornett (Bronte, NSW)**, Hermie Doerner (Coach, Bondi, NSW), Des Clark (Ethelton, SA), Keith Wiegard (Kew, VIC), Tom Hoad (Melville, WA). Photo - Des Clark.

NEW SOUTH WALES AMATEUR WATER POLO ASSOCIATION
AFFILIATED WITH N.S.W.A.S.A.

METROPOLITAN PREMIERSHIP FIXTURES

1959 — 1960

FOR THE "ASCOT TROPHIES"

SPEEDO

Patron: Dr. H. K. Porter, M.B., Ch.M., F.R.C.O.G. *President:* Mr. Ashur P. Hart. *Chairman of Council:* Mr. H. A. Doerner. *Hon. Registrar:* Mr. J. E. Thornett, B.Sc., B.E., FW5959, BL5108. *Hon. Treasurer:* Mr. R. L. Smee. *Hon. Secretary:* Capt. F. Lamb, 28 Cabramatta Road, Mosman, XM7025. *Hon. Asst. Secretary:* Mr. P. A. Lamb XM7025, XM4684. *Hon. Comp. Secretary:* Mr. J. W. Ritchie, 99 Headland Rd., Curl Curl, XW7797, BL4081.

RUSHCUTTER BAY BATHS (Beach Rd. — FB 2964)

1959-60	Grade	Teams			Round	Time
Tues 8th Dec	3W	Parramatta City 'B'	v	Maroubra Surf 'A'	R4	7 p.m.
	3S	Maroubra Surf 'B'	v	Cronulla Surf	R5	7.30 p.m.
	3S	Clovelly Surf	v	Coogee Surf	R5	8 p.m.
	2S	Maroubra Surf	v	Bronte 'B'	R4	8.30 p.m.
Tues 15th Dec	3S	Maroubra Surf 'B'	v	Bondi	R6	7 p.m.
	3S	Judean	v	Darlinghurst C.Y.O.	R6	7.30 p.m.
	3S	Clovelly Surf	v	Domain Wanderers	R6	8 p.m.
	1	Bronte	v	East Sydney	R5	8.30 p.m.
Tues 22nd Dec	3S	North Bondi Surf	v	Bondi	R8	7 p.m.
	3S	Clovelly Surf	v	Judean	R8	7.30 p.m.
	2S	Clovelly Surf	v	R. A. Navy	R6	8 p.m.
	1	Dee Why	v	East Sydney	R7	8.30 p.m.
Tues 5th Jan	3S	Judean	v	Domain Wanderers	R9	7 p.m.
	3S	Clovelly Surf	v	Bondi	R7	7.30 p.m.
	2N	Domain Wanderers	v	Manly 'B'	R7	8 p.m.
	1	East Sydney	v	Sydney University	R6	8.30 p.m.
Tues 12th Jan	3W	Maroubra Surf 'A'	v	Sydney University 'A'	R8	7 p.m.
	3S	Clovelly Surf	v	North Bondi Surf	R10	7.30 p.m.
	2S	Maroubra Surf	v	Clovelly Surf	R8	8 p.m.
	1	East Sydney	v	North Bondi Surf	R8	8.30 p.m.
Tues 19th Jan	2S	Bronte 'A'	v	R. A. Navy	R9	7 p.m.
	2S	Clovelly Surf	v	Bronte 'B'	R9	7.30 p.m.
	3S	Maroubra Surf 'B'	v	North Bondi Surf	R12	8 p.m.
	1	Bronte	v	North Bondi Surf	R10	8.30 p.m.
Tues 26th Jan	3S	North Bondi Surf	v	Darlinghurst C.Y.O.	R13	7 p.m.
	3S	Maroubra Surf 'B'	v	Judean	R13	7.30 p.m.
	2S	Bronte 'B'	v	R. A. Navy	R10	8 p.m.
	2S	Bronte 'A'	v	Clovelly Surf	R10	8.30 p.m.
Sun 31st Jan	3S	North Sydney	v	North Bondi Surf	R11	7 p.m.
	3S	Coogee Surf	v	Darlinghurst C.Y.O.	R11	7.30 p.m.
	3W	Parramatta City 'A'	v	Maroubra Surf 'A'	R10	8 p.m.
	3S	Judean	v	Bondi	R11	8.30 p.m.
Tues 2nd Feb	3S	North Bondi Surf	v	Domain Wanderers	R14	7 p.m.
	2S	Bondi	v	Bronte 'A'	R11	7.30 p.m.
	2S	Maroubra Surf	v	Bronte 'B'	R11	8 p.m.
	1	Bondi	v	North Bondi Surf	R11	8.30 p.m.
Tues 9th Feb	3S	North Sydney	v	Domain Wanderers	R16	7 p.m.
	3S	North Bondi Surf	v	Judean	R16	7.30 p.m.
	2S	Bondi	v	R. A. Navy	R12	8 p.m.
	3S	Bondi	v	Cronulla	R16	8.30 p.m.
Tues 16th Feb	3S	Clovelly Surf	v	Judean	R17	7 p.m.
	2S	Bondi	v	Bronte 'B'	R13	7.30 p.m.
	2S	Clovelly Surf	v	R. A. Navy	R13	8 p.m.
	1	Bronte	v	Manly	R13	8.30 p.m.
Tues 23rd Feb	3W	Balmain	v	Maroubra Surf 'A'	R18	7 p.m.
	3S	North Bondi Surf	v	Coogee Surf	R18	7.30 p.m.
	3S	Maroubra Surf 'B'	v	Darlinghurst C.Y.O.	R18	8 p.m.
	2S	Maroubra Surf	v	R. A. Navy	R14	8.30 p.m.

SPEEDO — THE OFFICIAL OLYMPIC CHOICE

▲ *The fixtures card for the 1959/60 NSWAWPA Water Polo season, showing games scheduled at Rushcutters Bay Baths.*
▼ *Blazer pocket for Bronte AWPC - 1st Grade Water Polo premiers 1959/60.*

"It was not long after I joined in 1959 that we switched to Rushcutters Bay Baths. I trained at Bronte Baths for only a relatively short period, and water polo ceased to exist there from about 1960. After that we used to train and play matches at Rushie where during the week, anyone who wanted to train or play would turn up there. Dick Thornett's shot was so powerful, it made goalies shudder."

Don Sarkies, 27 Jan 2015

warmer water, but it was still bitterly cold in the local pool there. The water temperature was about 58 degrees in Fahrenheit, which was pretty cold, and every day was a real nightmare to try and get in the water for training. We had three months there, but developed team spirit."

"We were the first Australian Olympic team to travel by air to an Olympic Games. My first flight was actually coming back from Rockhampton into Sydney, as we had initially driven up there, but flying to Rome was by Qantas Boeing 707 and of course it took three separate jets to transport the entire team. We left early as we had a few trial games organised prior to the start of the Olympics, as our biggest problem in those days, was that we didn't have any international competition."

"It was only in an Olympic year that we would play against other countries and, of course our style of water polo was always about three or four years behind the Europeans. But in those times, from '52 to '56 and also from '56 to '60, we weren't playing against these teams regularly enough to pick up on their new style of water polo, so we were always behind. But things have changed as it's become much more international for Australia. Now, they're playing in world championships almost every year."

"When we arrived in Rome, we noticed a completely different technique used by the Italians and most other continental players. Our opponents weren't playing water polo the way they had done in 1956, ie. sitting in front of the goal post at one end and defending the same way. It had now developed into more of an up and down game. The Europeans were playing the full length of the field, with everyone up and everyone back... much more like the current style these days."

"We played about eight teams in pre-Olympics trial matches and beat South Africa, Egypt, Japan and Brazil, and we even beat France. The top teams were Hungary, Russia, Yugoslavia and Italy, the eventual winners. Of course we had players from Western Australia, Victoria, South Australia and New South Wales, but we weren't all that successful in Rome and finished low on the table in my estimation. We did alright for a team from the antipodes, but were narrowly beaten in the Olympics by South Africa and Holland, and Yugoslavia also beat us by 6~2, so we didn't qualify for the final round of eight, but we weren't far off."

"Because our water polo team had a match on the first night of the Games, we understandably weren't allowed to march in the Opening Ceremony, which being my one and only Olympic opportunity, has always been one of the biggest disappointments of my sporting career."

Dick Thornett [5]

The Premierships

The Association received eight entries in 1st Grade, although Sydney University withdrew after some games. Bondi bounced back after having their ten year winning streak broken by Balmain and Bronte over the previous two years, and by the conclusion of the preliminary rounds had only lost one game.

In the play-offs, Bronte defeated East Sydney (9~2) and Bondi disposed of Balmain (4~2). With no preliminary final both winners progressed straight to the play-off where Bronte defeated Bondi (4~3). However, because Bondi were minor premiers, they exercised their right to challenge

"I watched Dawn Fraser win her 100 metres and also John Devitt, who got the decision against Lance Larson in the 100 metres. I don't think times weren't used then with the actual placings being given by judges. But the other person we saw was Herb Elliott, who ran his gold medal mile in Rome. I actually took photographs of each of the four laps and Percy Cerutti, and got his old coach throwing the towel in the air... there was something special about it."

Dick Thornett, 9 August 2008
Interviewed by Ian Warden [4]

WATER POLO CLUB RETIREMENTS

The 1959/60 season saw the last appearance of two great Sydney water polo clubs in Pyrmont, and The Spit AWPC.

PYRMONT AWPC

Pyrmont ASC was amongst Sydney's earliest swimming clubs, and entered the water competition in 1902/03, winning the first of their ten (from 18) 1st Grade premierships in 1907/08. Pyrmont gained a total of 50 caps in the NSW team:

Name	# Caps	Span
J. Conlon	4 caps	1909-12
W. Carroll (g)	3 caps	1909-11
T. Woods	1 cap	1909
J. Watkinson Sr.	3 caps	1910-25
F. Anderson (g)	1 cap	1925
John Black (c)	7 caps	1925-32
Tas King	9 caps	1927-38
F. Pryke	2 caps	1927-29
J. Barrett	1 cap	1927
T. Gallecher	2 caps	1929-30
W. Kirke	1 cap	1929
Jack King*	12 caps	1932-48
J. Watkinson Jr.	2 caps	1934-46
J. Quinn	1 cap	1953
A. Preston	1 cap	1957

THE SPIT AWPC

The Spit Club operated out of The Spit Baths in Sydney, and entered the NSW competition shortly after the First World War recess. Although they never won a 1st Grade premiership, they were grand-finalists in 1942, 51 and 53, and were the first Sydney club to attract the Hungarians, through the efforts of their mentor Bill Berge Phillips. The Spit Club gained seven caps in the NSW team:

Name	# Caps	Span
K. Kirkland	1 cap	1925
O. Csuvic	3 caps	1951-54
R. Cornforth*	1 cap	1951
A. Kosegi	1 cap	1951
T. Sendro	1 cap	1953

Olympian or Australian Rep.

1959/60 NSWAWPA RESULTS

1st GRADE—

L., F., D.—Denotes Lost, Forfeit, Disqualified.

	Played	Won	Drawn	L.F.D.	Points	Posn.
Bondi	13	12	1	—	76	1
Bronte	13	9	2	2	66	2
Balmain	13	7	3	3	60	3
East Sydney	13	7	1	5	56	4
Dee Why	13	3	1	9	40	5
Manly	13	3	1	9	36	6
North Bondi Surf	13	3	1	9	36	6

Sydney University (withdrawn from competition).

Semi-finals: Bronte, 9, v. East Sydney, 2; Bondi, 4, v. Balmain, 2.
Final: Bronte, 4, v. Bondi, 3.
Grand Final: Bronte, 4, v. Bondi, 1.

Premiers: BRONTE.

2nd GRADE (NORTH)—

	Played	Won	Drawn	L.F.D.	Points	Posn.
Dee Why	14	11	—	3	72	1
The Spit	14	11	—	3	70	2
Sydney University	14	8	3	3	66	3
Pyrmont	14	7	3	4	60	4
Manly "B"	14	7	1	6	54	5
Domain Wanderers	14	3	—	11	40	6
Balmoral	14	2	—	12	26	7

Manly "A" (wthdrawn from competiticn).

Semi-finals: Sydney University, 3, v. Dee Why, 2; The Spit, 3, v. Pyrmont, 2.
Final: Sydney University, 9, v. The Spit, 3.
Grand Final: Dee Why, 7, v. Sydney University, 4.

Zone Premiers: DEE WHY.

2nd GRADE (SOUTH)—

	Played	Won	Drawn	L.F.D.	Points	Posn.
Maroubra Surf	14	13	1	—	82	1
Bronte "A"	14	10	2	2	72	2
Clovelly Surf	14	9	1	4	66	3
Drummoyne	14	8	2	4	64	4
Bronte "B"	14	4	1	9	46	5
Ba!main	14	5	—	9	44	6
R.A.N.	14	—	2	12	26	7
Bondi	14	2	1	11	26	7

Semi-fina!s: Maroubra Surf, 4, v. Clovelly Surf, 2; Drummoyne, 4, v. Bronte "A", 3.
Final: Maroubra, 5, v. Drummoyne, 4.
2nd Grade Fina! (Inter-Zone): Maroubra Surf, 6, v. Dee Why, 4.

Premiers: MAROUBRA SURF.

▼ *This season saw both Dick See and Bill Roney (Bondi), who was also a member of the NSW Water Polo team, play in the rugby league grand-final for Eastern Suburbs. Easts were runners-up to St. George that year, but both Dick and Bill avoided water polo banns by 'playing as amateurs'.*

"We used to play at both Bronte and Rushie, but Rushie was more suitable for water polo as you could play games there. We switched between the two pools, but Rushie became the centre of water polo in the Eastern Suburbs. Duncan MacLennan who was the Baths lessee used to allow us to train and do whatever we liked there. It was great as we used to play games every Saturday, often all afternoon with Bondi."

Don Sarkies, 27 Jan 2015

Bronte in the grand-final. As the match progressed, Bondi watched the game drift away and Bronte pulled away to give them their second successive premiership (4~1). After inter-grade playoffs, Maroubra won the 2nd Grade, and Cronulla won the 3rd Grade. Despite Bronte's domination of the 1st Grade, Bondi were consistent enough across all grades to take out the Club Championship.[2]

Bronte AWPC

Once again Bronte fielded two 3rd Grade teams, which after the elimination of the various zones, were forced to play in the same competition. Bronte B finished in fifth place and didn't proceed, but Bronte A qualified for the play-offs by placing second on the ladder, although they bowed out to Drummoyne (3~4) in the semi-final.

The reigning premiers in 1st Grade had a mixed season, winning only nine of their 13 matches, but lifted their performance to win through the play-offs and soundly defeat Bondi (4~1) in the grand-final, securing for Bronte their second consecutive NSWAWPA premiership.

Bronte Moves To Rushcutter's Bay

Over the years, summer crowds on the beaches and at Bronte in particular had restricted the possible training hours to late evenings, and the shallow draft of Bronte Baths had recently had its bottom raised twice by Waverley Council as a safety measure. The alterations obviously held back further development of the Bronte water polo teams. Therefore as Bronte Baths had become unsuitable, club members looked around for an alternate training venue. Bondi Baths was deeper, but was already taken up by the Bondi Amateur Water Polo Club, Watsons Bay and the Domain Baths were difficult to get to, and both Nielsen Park and Redleaf Baths had no protection from waves and boatwash. The club therefore settled on Rushcutters Bay Baths, which seemed like the best alternative, and what's more, the players were warmly welcomed by the Baths proprietor, Mr. Duncan MacLennan.

Dunc McLennan

During and after the War, the baths at Rushcutters Bay were owned by the Buckingham family, who also owned an extensive chain of retail stores in Sydney and around the country. But unable to make a go of it, they put the Baths up for sale in the early 1950's, which were quickly snapped up by Duncan McLennan.

The son of Scottish immigrants, Duncan MacLennan was born in Sydney in June 1921, and brought up in Bellevue Hill amid a well to do family in the butchery business. During World War II Dunc served in the AIF in the Middle East, but he was always an ideas man and entrepreneur.

RUSHCUTTERS BAY BATHS

Early 20th century maps and photographs of Yarranabee Park at Rushcutters Bay often include images of the Rushcutters Bay Baths, which were provided in the late nineteenth century under lease to private operators. Although greatly appreciated by swimmers, particularly the children who learnt to swim there, other local residents objected to the 'indecent exposure' of swimmers in the strictly gendered baths. In 1911 one prominent local resident requested that Woollahra Municipal Council plant some trees to hide the unsightly structure. The Baths were demolished in 1976. [6]

"About 1960, a 'game changer' occurred when Waverley Council filled in the bottom of Bronte Baths with concrete. You could now stand anywhere and water polo training became a farce, so the Club moved to Rushcutters Bay Baths."
Brian Ellison, Apr 2015

▼ *Early photograph of Rushcutters Bay, showing the Reg Bartley Oval in the background, with the early buildings of the Cruising Yacht Club of Australia in the foreground, c.1900.*

Photograph by Milton Kent.

An Aerial View of Rushcutter's Bay

▲ TOP: The Baths were situated on the eastern foreshore and at the head of Rushcutters Bay, as seen in this airial photograph circa 1928. ABOVE: The two storey Managers residence (left) and the Baths entrance and shop (right).

He set about expanding the operation of the Baths and built a boatshed and shop. Using Dunc's lease boats, his four daughters often visited Clarke Island, which they virtually adopted as their own.

Bronte Water Polo Club transferred their operations to Rushcutters Bay in 1960, when all the players quickly got to know Dunc and his family. But Dunc was a determined and assertive man, who had most of the players terrified as with a facility full of men, he had four young daughters to protect in Jean, Leslie (aka L), Belinda and Dawn (aka Lou).

For their part, the daughters couldn't resist taking the odd peek at the water polo boys and Leslie apparently once commented that 'if there was ever a man called Adonis... it was Brian Ellison", who according to her had the body to end all bodies with a perfectly formed physique!

As Darling Point residents and prior baths owners, the Buckinghams would often attend the Baths. And Belinda recalled that she would prepare their banana chairs and everything else

▼ *Keith Whitehead, coach of the 1960/61 NSW State Water Polo Squad, also represented Australia at Helsinki, Melbourne and Rome, talks to three of the squad at training at Rushcutters Bay Baths. They are from left, Warwick Lamb (Bondi), Alan Langford (Bondi) and Ken Owens (Bronte) (Sun-Herald, 8th Jan 1961).*

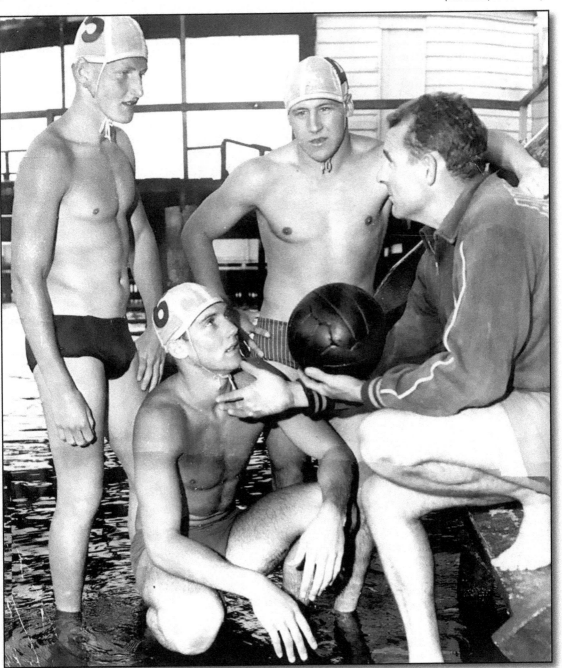

"I have very fond memories of 'Rushie' as we used to call it. Pete and I used to dive to retrieve Coca-Cola bottles around the baths to earn some pocket money. I had trained in Hungary with an Olympic coach John Gregory & I was soonafter picked up to train in a swimming squad at Rushie, run by Dr. Billy Roney. I also trained under John Conrad at Woollahra indoor pool for a short stint, who in 1965 pushed me to break 60 secs over the 100m sprint. The swimming led me to join North Bondi Surf Club and then Bronte Water Polo Club."

Tom Folden, Oct, 2020

▼TOP: *The Rushcutters Bay Baths on a busy day, showing the water polo goals that were raised to permit free swimming, and the big slippery slide. ABOVE: The individual change booths were a unique feature of 'Rushie.'*

they required, before rushing out to greet their chauffeur driven car... they among many others apparently loved the baths.

Dunc was very supportive of Bronte Water Polo Club and helped out wherever he could. He always immediately called the Maritime Services Board (MSB) to report oil spills, and they were apparently pretty good about coming out to rectify the problem by spraying or dispersion. It was Dunc who made the unique pulley system at Rushcutters Bay, which allowed the water polo goals to be raised and lowered when required, so it was no wonder when you heard him often shout...

"Get off the bloody goals!"

About 1975, socialite Dita Cobb among other Darling Point residents formed the opinion that the Rushie Baths were an eyesore and they complained to Woollahra Council and the MSB. The Council and MSB joined forces and an inspection was carried out, which condemned the facility, never mind the money Dunc had put into it

Dunc's Boomerang School

Boomerangs must be the most widely known Indigenous hunting tool, most likely because children love the idea of throwing something that spins around and returns, while tourists to Australia often buy boomerangs as a souvenir of their travels.

And that's probably why Duncan MacLennan's 'Boomerang School' sprang up some 50 years ago. Yep, 50 years. I only know this because as I stopped to look at the signs, the owner was locking up the front door and so we had a quick chat. The original owner Duncan MacLennan, who opened 'The Boomerang School' in the 1960s, ran the school with his daughter Belinda and son-in-law Frank, until his death in 2018.

Because most of the big hotels in the area have closed in the past decade or so (the Rex, Top of the Town, Sebel Town House and Hyatt Kingsgate come to mind) there aren't so many tourists seeking boomerang lessons or souvenirs these days. And sadly, the backpackers prefer to spend their money on other things.

I wish now that I'd visited 'The Boomerang School' earlier and perhaps encouraged people to visit or take part in one of their free boomerang throwing lessons, which were held at Rushcutters Bay Park every Tuesday. [7]

LEFT: The long time proprietor of the Rushcutters Bay Baths, Duncan McLennan in his later years... he passed away in 2018 at the grand old age of 97! RIGHT: Dunc's Boomerang School at the top of William St, Kings Cross.

over many years, or the livelihood and residence that he and his family had invested. On top of that, he was levied a $54,000 demolition bill. But Dunc fought them through the courts and won, although he had to walk away without any compensation.

While running the Baths, Dunc started a Boomerang School in the adjacent park, which became quite successful. After the Baths closed Dunc expanded his Boomerang School from a shop at the top of William St, in Kings Cross, where he sold aboriginal artefacts as well. Dunc's wife, Gloria (nee Farquhar) died in 2012 and her ashes were scattered in the sea on the site of the old Baths. Then in July 2018, at the grand old age of 97, Dunc also died, and his daughters intend to soon do the same as a permanent memorial for their father.

1960-61

1960/61 NSWAWPA OFFICIALS: Dr. H.K. Porter (Patron); Capt. F. Lamb (President); A.P. Hart (Past President); R. Traynor (Chairman); H. W. Langford (Registrar); A.E. Richards (Secretary); W.D. Allen (Asst. Secretary); **J.E. Thornett (Treasurer)**.

The 1960/61 season began following the NSWAWPA 31st Annual General Meeting. It is perhaps worthwhile at this point to take a snapshot of how the NSWAWPA functioned as an entity at the beginning of the 1960's, as with a spike in player registrations from 479 to 709 over the previous five years, water polo at this time was witnessing a meteoric rise in popularity.

In addition to the above office holders, there were ten Association vice-presidents who could be called upon to help out, with Bronte's Bert Vadas amongst them. There were further honorary positions for 'Medical Officer, Solicitor, Competition Secretary, Public Relations and Auditors, as well as a Minute Secretary.' The Association elected delegates to the NSW Amateur Swimming Association (3 members); the Australian Water Polo Committee (1); and the Australian Water Polo Referees Board (1).

The Association also ran no less than seven standing committees for the following specific functions: The Executive Committee (14); The Judiciary Committee (10); The Selection Committee (5); The Country Committee (3); The Schools Committee (6); The Competition Committee (5); and The Referee Appointments Board (4), had some 29 referees to call from on the Referees Panel (John Thornett, Vic McGrath & Dick See of Bronte amongst them).

1960/61 Season Statistics
N.S.W.A.W.P.A.

Clubs in the Water Polo Competitions.

Clubs	1^1	1^2	1^3	2^2	2^3	3^3	Total
Army (RAE)					●		1
Balmain	●	●	●				3
Balmoral/Dee Why	●	●	●			●	4
Bankstown						2	2
Bondi	●	●	●				3
Bronte	●	●	●				3
Cabarita						●	1
Clovelly SLSC				●	●		2
Collaroy SLSC				●			1
Coogee SLSC				●	●		2
Cronulla SLSC				●	●		2
Drumm/East Sydney	●	●	●				3
Judean						●	1
Manly		●	●				2
Maroubra SLSC	●	●	●				3
Navy				●			1
Nth Sydney				●			1
Northbridge					●		1
Parramatta City				●	●	●	3
Roseville					●		1
Sth Curl Curl SLSC	●						1
University				●	●		2
Wanderers (Dom)						2	2
	7	7	7	8	8	8	45

Results of the Water Polo Competitions.

Grade	Premier		Runner-Up
1st	Bronte~7	dr	7~Bondi
2nd	Balmoral/Dee Why~6	d.	4~Clovelly
3rd	Clovelly~9	d.	2~Bronte
	Club Champions		BRONTE
D1 2nd	Balmoral/Dee Why~3	d.	1~Drummoyne/East Syd
D2 2nd	Clovelly~5	d.	4~Parramatta City
D1 3rd	Bronte~4	d.	3~Balmain
D2 3rd	Clovelly~10	d.	2~Roseville
D3 3rd	Cabarita~6	d.	2~Wanderers A

The hard work of the Country Committee over a number of years was responsible for introducing no less than 25 clubs and Associations being affiliated with the NSWAWPA from the regional areas.

The success of the six Surf Life Saving Clubs in the competition to this point had been astounding. Maroubra Surf Club were finalists in 1st Division-3rd Grade; Clovelly Surf, Coogee Surf and Cronulla Surf were all finalists in 2nd Division-2nd Grade; and Coogee Surf and Clovelly Surf were finalists in 2nd Division-3rd Grade. From those finals, Clovelly Surf Club took out the 3rd Grade title and were runners-up in the 2nd Grade, an amazing achievement![8]

The Baths & Clubs

Although the NSWAWPA water polo competitions got off to a late start this season, they came to a satisfactory conclusion with a general improvement in the lower grades. Metropolitan player registrations climbed to 709, which came from 45 teams representing 23 clubs.

There would appear to be little doubt that with the influx of several young players and the upgrading of leading 2nd Grade teams, the 1st Grade competitions in the years ahead should be of immense interest.

The absence of suitable pools was again a bugbear, but it was hoped that with the opening of several freshwater pools in the suburbs, some measure of relief might occur. The Association expressed their desire that Councils contemplating the building of new pools and the extension of present swimming facilities would follow the lead taken by Parramatta City Council who installed a pool suitable for diving and water polo, measuring up to international standards as adopted by the ASU.

In regard to new clubs, The Royal Aust. Engineers (Army) and Collaroy SLSC affiliated for the first time. Two club amalgamations occurred between Balmoral/Dee Why, and also between Drummoyne/East Sydney. Both Darlinghurst CYO and North Bondi SLSC lapsed after their one and only appearance.

Worst of all however, was to see the end of two of Sydney;'s greatest water polo clubs with

1960/61 NSW COUNTRY AFFILIATIONS	
Bathurst City	Moree
Blue Mtns	Muswellbrook
Canberra	Narrandera
Casino	Nowra
Cessnock	Parkes
Condobolin	Singleton
Dubbo	Temora
Goulburn	Wauchope
Grafton	Wagga Wagga
Gunnedah	Wellington
Inverell	West Wyalong
Kurri Kurri	Young
Maitland	

"We had lots of barbeques at different homes down at Bronte. At the end of the season in those days, the younger players were given ping pong balls, painted like water polo balls with ribbons attached for 'best & fairest', and 'most improved' etc. written on them. It was like 'wow' to receive one and it made you feel special, so we tried even harder in the next season. My nick name was the 'flea'... Bronte club was like one big family."
Peter Folden, Nov 2018

"The outer wall at Rushie was mostly at the level of the water, but there was a section which stepped up to house a diving board. Throwing the ball at this section resulted in the ball coming back to you. It was here that Vic McGrath would practice shooting including many bat shots. He did this after training sessions were over and the rest of the team had left."
Robbie Vadas, Aug 2019

NEW SOUTH WALES TEAM
1961 - 3rd Place - National Championships - Adelaide
Back row (from left): Bob Traynor (Manager), **Dick Thornett (Bronte)**, David Woods (Balmain), Nino Sydney [Von Somogy] (c, Bondi), **Vic McGrath (Bronte)**, Peter Ritchie (Universities), Keith Whitehead (Coach, Bondi). Front row: **Ken Owens (Bronte)**, Alan Langford (Bondi), Brian Hamill (Drummoyne), **Don Sarkies (g, Bronte)**, Nick Barnes (Universities), Tom Laws (Balmain). Absent: Tex Rickards (A/Manager). Photo - NSWAWPA Annual Report 1960/61 at Rushcutters Bay Baths..

"In 1961 we played at North Sydney Olympic Pool and Dick See and Billy Roney were told they had better not play because they were professional rugby league players. They were not allowed to play in the game."

"Bronte always had about three grades and we were strong in all three. We won the 1st Grade grand final in 1961 - it was a drawn game. We played three extra time periods against Bondi at North Sydney Pool, but at 11.30pm, the Baths Manager said stop... and it was all over."

Don Sarkies, 27 Jan 2015

"Ken Mills was a very hard player and 'Momie' Vadas was such a great coach, role model and leader for the club."

Phil Bower, 29 Jan 2019

The Spit and Pyrmont both dropping out of the competition. Existing members from both these clubs were mostly subsumed into the amalgamated clubs mentioned above.

This season the premierships were conducted across three divisions. Division I consisted of a 1st Grade with seven teams, a 2nd Grade with seven teams and a 3rd Grade with seven teams. Division II consisted of a 2nd Grade with eight teams and a 3rd Grade with eight teams. The III Division consisted of one 3rd Grade only of eight teams.[8]

Representatives in NSW Teams

This season a total of 23 players were invited to join the NSW training squad under coach, Keith Whitehead (Bondi). Being the reigning 1st Grade premiers, Bronte was fortunate in supplying more than a quarter of the roster, which included Dick Thornett, Vic McGrath, Don Sarkies (g), Ken Owens, Bob Cope and Ray Timewell. While Vic McGrath and Dick Thornett were retained from the previous year, seven new caps were awarded to Alan

Langford (Bondi), Brian Hamill (Drummoyne), David Woods (Balmain), Nick Barnes and Peter Ritchie (Universities), and both Ken Owens and goalkeeper Don Sarkies (Bronte). But despite the drastic shake-up, NSW unfortunately still placed third in the 14th Australian Championships in Adelaide, behind Victoria and Western Australia.

The Premierships

By the end of the preliminary rounds, Bronte led the six other entries in 1st Grade, with Bondi a close second. In the play-offs, Bronte defeated Bondi (6~5), while Balmain disposed of Drummoyne/East Sydney (5~3). Bondi then eliminated Balmain in the final (5~4) to gain a grand-final berth. For the first time, the NSWAWPA conducted the finals series in conjunction with the 1st Speedo Water Polo Carnival at North Sydney Olympic Pool, and the innovation proved to be very successful, although the pool was too shallow.

In what became rather controversial for the NSW Association, after a torrid encounter in the 1st Grade final, and having played a number of periods of extra time, Bronte and Bondi were surprisingly declared joint premiers (7~7).

In actual fact, there had been two other instances of drawn 1st Grade water polo premierships in NSW in the past. One had taken place way back in the 1892/93 season when Balmain and the Wentworth club played a five all draw to be declared joint premiers. The other drawn premiership was a two all draw between Pyrmont and Sydney clubs for the 1925/26 grand-final although, Pyrmont gained the premiership on a countback, having been undefeated throughout the season.

The highly unusual joint premiership in March 1961 was not actually due to competition rules, or because of player

SPEEDO WATER POLO CARNIVAL

Wednesday, 29th March, 1961

North Sydney Olympic Pool

SOUVENIR PROGRAMME

"The game had changed dramatically from the influence of the Hungarians who kept the ball in the air with a "ball beats the man" style of play, but sometimes "the man... 'Dick or John Thornett'... beat the ball" and especially if you got in their way!"
Jon Kirkwood, June 2018

1960/61 NSWAWPA RESULTS

1st DIVISION

1st GRADE—
L., F., D.—Denotes Lost, Forfeit, Disqualified.

	Played	Won	Drawn	L.F.D.	Pts.	Posn.
Bronte	12	10	1	1	33	1
Bondi	12	9	1	2	31	2
Balmain	12	7	2	3	28	3
Drummoyne-East Sydney	12	6	3	3	27	4
Maroubra Surf	11	2	2	7	17	5
Manly	12	1	2	9	16	6
Balmoral-Dee Why	11	—	1	10	12	7

Semi-finals: Balmain 5 v. Drummoyne-East Sydney 3.
Bronte 6 v. Bondi 5.
Final: Bondi 5 v. Balmain 4.
Grand Final: Bronte 7 v. Bondi 7.
Co-premiers: BRONTE and BONDI.

2nd GRADE—

	Played	Won	Drawn	L.F.D.	Pts.	Posn.
Bronte	12	9	2	1	32	1
Drummoyne-East Sydney	12	8	1	3	29	2
Balmain	12	6	2	4	26	3
Balmoral-Dee Why	12	6	—	6	24	4
Manly	12	3	3	6	21	5
Bondi	12	3	4	5	21	5
Maroubra Surf	12	1	—	11	14	7

Semi-finals: Balmoral-Dee Why 7 v. Balmain 3.
Drummoyne-East Sydney 2 v. Bronte 1.
Final: Balmoral-Dee Why 5 v. Bronte 4.
Grand Final: Balmoral-Dee Why 3 v. Drummoyne-E. Sydney 1.
Premiers: BALMORAL-DEE WHY.

3rd GRADE—

	Played	Won	Drawn	L.F.D.	Pts.	Posn.
Balmain	12	9	1	2	31	1
Bronte	12	9	—	3	30	2
Drummoyne-East Sydney	12	8	—	4	28	3
Maroubra Surf	12	7	1	3	26	4
Balmoral-Dee Why	12	5	—	7	22	5

Bondi (withdrawn from competition.
Sth. Curl Curl Surf (withdrawn from competition).
Semi-finals: Maroubra Surf 2 v. Drummoyne-East Sydney 1.
Balmain 6 v. Bronte 1.
Final: Bronte 6 v. Maroubra Surf 5.
Grand Final: Bronte 4 v. Balmain 3.
Premiers: BRONTE.

PROGRAMME OF EVENTS

| 7.30 p.m. | "GOD SAVE THE QUEEN" |
| | St. George-Sutherland Shire Band |

Event No. 1

WATER POLO

COMBINED HIGH SCHOOLS v. N.S.W. ASSOCIATION COLTS

1. J. HARRISON (North Sydney)	1. G. MILLER (Dee Why)
2. N. STEVENS-JONES (Balgowlah)	2. R. COPE (Bronte)
3. R. GREENAWAY (Sydney Tech.)	3. G. LEO (Balmain)
4. C. McGRAW (Drummoyne)	4. G. HARDY (Clovelly)
5. M. HUMPHREYS (North Sydney)	5. W. PHILLIPS (Balmoral)
6. P. GALLAGHER (Fort Street)	6. I. SAINT (Bankstown)
7. A. WARD (Manly)	7. R. BEACHLEY (Dee Why)
8. D. WOODS (Drummoyne)	8. R. TREVENAR (Cabarita)
9. W. MOORE (Balgowlah)	9. C. PHILLIPS (Cabarita)
10. S. SHEAVES (Rozelle)	10. N. WINTERTON (Balmoral)
11. W. LAMB (North Sydney)	11. T. LAWS (Balmain)

Referee: Mr. R. Smee.

Goal Judges: Mr. R. Stephens, Mr. J. Dolly.

Event No. 9

METROPOLITAN FIRST GRADE PREMIERSHIP GRAND FINAL

"Ascot" Trophy: presented by W. D. and H. O. Wills (Aust.) Ltd. and The "Speedo" Shield for N.S.W. Champions.

Referee: Mr. R. Y. Traynor

Goal Judges: Messrs. R. Stephens, J. Dolly.

BRONTE (Title Holders

Cap		Age	Weight	Height
†1.	D. SARKIES	26	10.12	5. 8
†2.	V. McGRATH	25	13. 7	5.11
3.				
4.	K. MILLS	31	15.10	6. 2
†5.	K. OWENS	19	11. 7	5. 8
*6.	R. THORNETT	20	16. 4	6. 1
7.	R. TIMEWELL	19	12. 0	5. 9
†8.	B. VADAS	42	12. 0	5. 7
†9.	J. THORNETT	25	15.10	6. 0
	Average	26	13. 6	5.10

versus

Cap		Age	Weight	Height
1.	P. WATERMAN	20	13. 7	6. 2
*2.	R. SMEE	30	15. 0	6. 0
*3.	K. WHITEHEAD	29	13. 7	6. 0
†4.	W. JONES	29	14. 0	5.10
†5.	E. FITZGERALD	26	12. 0	5.10
†6.	N. SOMOGY	26	12. 7	5.11
†7.	B. HUTCHINGS	24	12. 0	5.11
†8.	W. RONEY	23	11. 7	5.10
	Average	26	13. 0	5.11

* Denotes Olympic Representative.

† Denotes State Representative.

▲TOP: Teams for the CHS v Association Colts lead-up match at the 1961 grand-final. ABOVE: Teams and statistics for the 1961 NSWAWPA 1st Grade Water Polo grand-final. ▶The highly unusual joint water polo premiership of 1960/61, which was held at North Sydney Pool, was not actually due to NSWAWPA competition rules, or because of player fatigue. The drawn decider occurred at the pool manager's insistence that his facility had to close punctually at 11pm! Therefore, with the scores level and the lights being turned off, play was stopped at 7~7, with Bronte and Bondi teams being declared joint premiers.

fatigue. The drawn decider occurred at the pool manager's insistence that his facility had to close punctually at 11pm! Therefore, with the scores level and the lights being turned off, play had to be stopped with the two teams being declared joint premiers. The win made it three premierships in a row for Bronte who had finished undefeated throughout the season, despite drawing with Bondi on two previous occasions. For Bondi, the win became their 19th 1st Grade premiership.

BONDI AWPC
1960/61 · NSWAWPA Joint 1st Grade Premiers
Peter Waterman (g), Ray Smee, Keith Whitehead, Bill Jones, Eric FitzGerald, Nino von Somogy, Brian Hutchings, Bill Roney (Speedo Water Polo Carnival Program - 29th March 1961, Nth Sydney Pool).

After the intergrade playoffs, Balmoral/Dee Why won the 2nd Grade, and Clovelly Surf won the 3rd Grade.

BRONTE AWPC
1960/61 - NSWAWPA Joint 1st Grade Premiers
Back row (from left): Vic McGrath, Don Sarkies (g), Ken Mills, John Thornett (c), Dick Thornett. Front row: Ray Timewell, Dick See, Ken Owens, Bert 'Mommy' Vadas (Coach). Photo - National WP News, August 1986, Vol 2(2).

The Club Championship was also won by Bronte demonstrating the depth of talent in their lower grades.[8]

Bronte AWPC

By the 1960/61 season the sport of water polo and the NSWAWPA had risen like a mountain out of the sea, and Bronte AWPC was the eruption at the top of that volcano.

Unfortunately however, Bronte received a blow when their State representative, Dick See, was prevented from competing in the water polo grand-final after being declared professional by the NSWASA for having played a rugby league game with Eastern Suburbs Rugby League Football Club.

Once again entering all three Division I grades, the Bronte 3rd Grade finished second in the competition, but won through the play-offs to defeat Balmain (4~3) and take the premiership. The 2nd Grade finished on top and took the minor-premiership, but lost by one goal to Balmoral-Dee Why (4~5) in the final.

Finishing on top of the table this year, the

"The venue for the 1961 grand-final, was disastrous as you could stand up for almost half of North Sydney pool. I remember during the third quarter… that Nino Sydney held and sank Vic McGrath, which should have been a major foul. But next thing… Nino was launched into the air, as Vic had submerged and lifted him completely out of the water… which was incredible! The result was that Vic was ejected rather than Nino… and Bronte went to man down. But the game ended at 7-7… after 3 sets of extra-time, and the Pool Manager turned the lights out!"
Robbie Vadas, March 2019

▼ *Blazer pocket for Bronte AWPC - 1st Grade Water Polo joint premiers with Bondi 1960/61.*

"Things at Rushie were very different as all you were there for, was to train and play water polo. There was still a social aspect, but not to the same degree as at Bronte, and there were few other activities to be shared. Polo was never my major interest so after a couple of seasons I joined Drummoyne to experience the role of coach and then retired from polo and took a job in New Guinea. But all in all, the years at Bronte were some of the best of my life. I made many lifelong friends from those days and they remain some of the best friends I have."

Brian Ellison, Apr 2015

reigning 1st Grade premiers Bronte, had a better season and won through the play-offs and into the grand-final against Bondi. But with scores level at 7~7, the match was called off with Bronte and Bondi being declared joint premiers.

1961-62

1961/62 NSWAWPA OFFICIALS: Dr. H.K. Porter (Patron); Capt. F. Lamb (President); A.P. Hart (Past President); R. Traynor (Chairman); H. W. Langford (Registrar); A.W. Hamill (Secretary); A.E. Richards (Asst. Secretary); **J.E. Thornett** (Treasurer).

The 1961/62 season began following the NSWAWPA 32nd Annual General Meeting.

In this season, the NSWAWPA Executive decided to launch a 'match of the week' program to be played on Wednesday evenings. The program ran well from the outset, but the initiative had to be abandoned after considerable financial losses. Despite the failure, this season brought the greatest-ever coverage in terms of newspaper publicity. The Sunday Mirror's 'Water Polo' section written by 'The Skipper' was very helpful in promoting the game, informing the public of results and recruiting new players. This season the number of teams entering the metropolitan competitions totalled 46 from 22 clubs, although there was a serious fall off in registrations to 591 players due to the Associations new 10/- registration fee. However, the most serious problem faced by the NSW Association remained the allocation of suitable pools, despite Leichhardt Council making vast improvements to Balmain Baths. On a more positive side, advice was received from Ashfield Council that their new baths were well underway and being constructed deep enough to allow for virtually all water polo competitions.[9]

1961/62 Season Statistics N.S.W.A.W.P.A.

Clubs in the Water Polo Competitions.

Clubs	1¹	1²	2²	2³	2³	3³	Total
Balmain	●	●		●			3
Balmoral			●				1
Bankstown			●	●			2
Bondi	●	●		●			3
Bronte	●	●	●			●	4
Clovelly SLSC	●	●		●		●	4
Collaroy SLSC			●				1
Coogee SLSC			●		●	●	3
Dee Why			●				1
Drumm/East Sydney	●	●		●			3
Fairfield				●			1
Freshwater			●				1
Judean			●				1
Liverpool			●				1
Maroubra SLSC	●	●		●			3
Nth Sydney			●				1
Northbridge					●	●	2
Parramatta City	●	●	●				3
Ryde						●	1
Roseville					●	●	2
Sydney					●	●	2
University	●	●	●				3
	8	8	8	8	7	7	46

Results of the Water Polo Competitions.

Grade	Premier		Runner-Up
1st	Bronte~4	d.	3~Balmain
2nd	Balmain-?	d.	?~Universities
3rd	Bronte A~?	d.	?~Bronte B
	Club Champions		BRONTE
D1²ⁿᵈ	???		???
D2²ⁿᵈ	???		???
D2³ʳᵈ	???		???
D2³ʳᵈ	???		???
D3³ʳᵈ	???		???

The Baths & Clubs

This season the premierships were again conducted across three divisions. Division I consisted of a 1st Grade of eight teams, a 2nd Grade with eight teams. Division II consisted of a 2nd Grade of eight teams and two separate 3rd Grades, one with eight teams and the other with seven teams. The III Division consisted of one 3rd Grade only of seven teams.

In regard to new clubs, Fairfield, Liverpool and Ryde affiliated for the first time. The amalgamation between Balmoral and Dee Why the previous year had failed, but both clubs re-entered separately. Freshwater re-affiliated after a gap of some years, and it was heartening to see the old Sydney Club re-incarnated from the remains of the Domain Wanderers. Unfortunately six clubs including Army, Cabarita, Cronulla SLSC, Manly, Navy and South Curl Curl SLSC all lapsed.

Lamentably, the NSWAWPA Annual Report this season only listed the results tables for each competition with minor premierships. No semi-final or final results were recorded, so the results listed in the Annual Report were for minor premierships only, with the winners only being known from newspaper results.[9]

A Bondi player hits for goal in the Bondi-Bronte first grade water polo premiership clash.

NUARY 21, 1962   32

▲ A 1st grade premiership clash between Bondi & Bronte (SMH, 21 January, 1962).

Representatives in NSW Teams

In stark contrast to the previous season's 'blood-letting', the only new cap selected in the 1962 NSW team was Bill Phillips Jr. (Universities). Bronte's Dick Thornett and Vic McGrath made themselves unavailable, but both Kenny Owens and goalkeeper Don Sarkies retained their places in the side. This year however, brought success for NSW as it claimed their first national championship for five long years, when they finished in a unique three way tie for first place with Victoria and Western Australia. But New South Wales managed to take home the trophy by defeating Victoria in the tournament play-off (3~2), which was a first ever occurrence for the event.

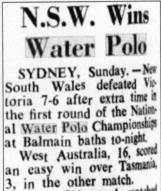

N.S.W. Wins Water Polo

SYDNEY, Sunday. — New South Wales defeated Victoria 7-6 after extra time in the first round of the National Water Polo Championships at Balmain baths to-night.

West Australia, 16, scored an easy win over Tasmania, 3, in the other match.

About 500 people watched the titles matches which will continue until Saturday.

(Canberra Times, 5th Feb 1962)

NEW SOUTH WALES TEAM
1962 - National Champions - Sydney
Back row (from left): Bill Phillips (Universities), Alan Langford (Bondi), **Don Sarkies (g, Bronte)**, Peter Ritchie (Universities). Middle row: David Woods (Balmain), Brian Hamill (Drummoyne), Nino Sydney (Bondi), Nick Barnes (Universities). Sitting: Eric Fitzgerald (Balmain), Ted Pierce (c, Balmain), **Ken Owens (Bronte)**. Missing: Keith Whitehead (Coach, Bondi). Photo - Nino Sydney.

D. Sarkies, the NSW goalkeeper, makes a great save in the water polo match against Victoria yesterday. NSW won 5-4.

The Premierships

The problem with the 1961/62 competition is that the NSWAWPA Annual Report only listed the results as they stood at the end of the rounds, and unfortunately no play-off data was ever published.

We know that the 1962 NSWAWPA grand-finals were played at Drummoyne Baths where Bronte defeated Balmain (4~3) to take out their fourth consecutive 1st Grade premiership. However, the 2nd Grade result is much less certain, and although there is a photograph of the Bronte 2nd Grade (indicating a possible premiership), newspaper results reveal that Bronte was defeated by Universities (3~5) in the preliminary final. This would probably have meant that Universities would have played

1961/62 RESULTS

WATER POLO

BALMAIN BATHS.—3rd div.,
2nd grade: Coogee A, 6 beat
Sydney A, 2; Northbridge A, 3
beat Roseville A, 2. 3rd grade:
Bronte B, 5 beat Clovelly Surf A,
2; Coogee Surf B, 4 beat Sydney
B, 0.

(SMH, 2 Feb 1962)

WATER POLO

DRUMMOYNE. — 1st grade:
Bondi, 4 (W. Jones 2, B. Hutchings, W. Lamb), beat Bronte, 3
(J. Thornett, V. McGrath, R.
Thornett). 2nd grade: Bronte, 5,
beat Drummoyne-East Sydney, 1;
3rd grade: Coogee Surf A, 6,
beat Roseville A, 4.

(SMH, 26 Feb 1962)

WATER POLO

At Drummoyne.
1st GRADE, semi-final. 6 no.
4 (Hutchings 2, Fitzgerald, Smeal)
beat Balmain 1 (Woods); 3rd
DIV. final. Bronte B, 6 beat
Clovelly B, 1. 3rd GRADE. Div.
1, Drummoyne-East Sydney, 5
beat Universities, 1. Div. 2: Sydney A, 5, beat Northbridge A, 3.

(SMH, 7 Mar 1962)

WATER POLO

FINALS.—First div., second
grade: Universities 5, Bronte 3.
Second div.: Bankstown 7, Deewhy
Penguins 1. First div., third grade:
Bronte 3, Drummoyne-East Sydney
nil. Second div.: Coogee 7, Sydney
A 3.

(SMH, 13 Mar 1962)

Balmain in the grand-final, but without any data, the result remains unknown.

However, the 3rd Grade results are known, as it was an all Bronte affair. In the 3rd Grade, Bronte A defeated Bronte B to claim the premiership, after both teams had progressed through their respective inter-divisional play-offs. Although the 2nd Grade result remains unknown, the Bronte Club played consistently well enough across all grades to also take home the Club Championship.

▲ABOVE & MID: The 1962 Australian Championships were held at Drummoyne Baths in Sydney (above & middle), and also at Elkington Park at Balmain.

BRONTE AMATEUR WATER POLO CLUB
1961/62 - 2nd Grade - NSWAWPA
From left: Brian Ellison, Warren Hurt, John Walker, Terry "Lunk" Clark, Ken Emerton, Peter "Rocky" Johnson, Robert Foster, Dave Steer, Warren "Wick" Riley. Photo - Brian Ellison.

BRONTE AMATEUR WATER POLO CLUB
1961/62 - 3rd Grade Premiers - NSWAWPA
Back row (from left): Dave Steer, Kevin Walker, Brian Fitzpatrick, Mick Downey, Pat McGrath. Sitting: Ken Davidson, Ron Mandelson (c), Tom Folden (c), Brian Hallinan, Robert See. Insets: Left - Terry 'Lunky' Clark, Right - Vic McGrath (Coach). Photo - Tom Folden.

BRONTE AWPC
1961/62 - NSWAWPA 1st Grade Premiers
Back row (from left): Dick Thornett (c), Ken Mills, John Thornett, Vic McGrath, Dick See.
Front row: Bob Cope, Don Sarkies (g), Roland Hill, Ken Owens. Inset: Bert Vadas, coach. Photo courtesy of Bronte AWPC Archives.

Bronte AWPC

Bronte entered four teams this season, a feat only equalled by the Clovelly Club, which was also experiencing an upswing at the time. The performances of the Bronte teams this year was truly outstanding with both 3rd Grades finishing on top of their respective competitions, and the Bronte A and B team bagged a premiership and runner-up in that grade respectively.

Despite finishing in second place on the ladder, the play-off performance of Bronte's 2nd Grade that season remains unknown. However the 1st Grade extended their winning streak to four consecutive premierships.

Both Dick Thornett and Vic McGrath were unavailable for NSW State team selection this season, but Ken Owens and Don Sarkies played great polo to gain selection in the side.

"Dick Thornett and Vic McGrath, understood each other so well, they could swim and pass between them without even looking at one another… they had such a great understanding and combination. Team rosters were usually small back then… and many teams only had seven players. Those were the days where the club had to provide a referee… with only one referee per game."
Robbie Vadas, March 2019

"When you walked up the path beside the pool at Bronte, you came to the male change rooms. Then continuing past them was a two story construction, called the club house. Going inside and up the stairs was always a major question of faith. I never knew whether the building would collapse while I was inside or if it would remain intact until I'd left."
Robbie Vadas, March 2019

"The thing I learned was communication with your mates, so I took up writing Weekly articles for the Bondi Weekly and the Wentworth Courier about the goings on at training and the match results for Bronte Water Polo Club."
Terry 'Lunk' Clark, April 2018

"When we trained at Rushcutters Bay, Peter Johnson was the instigator...we used to train after 6 o'clock when less bathers would come down to the pool. It was fun, we just did our own thing and there was plenty of space. Afterwards we would go back to Bronte Baths and play touch football. We had a lot of International rugby players like John Thornett, Dick Thornett, Peter Johnson, Kenny Owens, Ted Heinrich, Dick See and Terry Curley... all star internationals and a very formidable touch football side. It was great times!"

Don Sarkies, 27 Jan 2015

▶ *The Victorian Schoolboys & NSW Combined High Schools teams played a series of matches against one another in 1962, which concluded in match each. The NSWCHS team of 1962 was Tom Folden (Vaucluse), Tom Hardy (g, Randwick) Robert Langford (Randwick), Colin McGraw (Drummoyne), Stephen Sheaves (Ibrox Park), Alan Ward (Manly) Ron de Groot (Granville), Warwick Lamb (North Sydney), M. Little (Cleveland Street), Graham Olde (Manly), R. Talmacs (Sydney Tech).*

1961/62 NSWAWPA RESULTS

1st GRADE—

	P	W	D	L	F	Points
Bronte	13	9	2	2	—	33
Maroubra	13	—	2	11	—	15
Universities	13	4	1	7	1	21
Bondi	13	9	2	2	—	33
Parramatta	13	3	—	10	—	19
Drummoyne	13	9	—	5	—	32
Balmain	13	11	2	1	—	38
Clovelly	13	1	3	7	2	16

1st DIVISION

2nd GRADE—

	P	W	D	L	F	Points
Bronte	13	11	1	1	—	35
Maroubra	13	2	1	10	—	18
Universities	13	6	2	5	—	27
Bondi	13	7	—	5	1	26
Parramatta	13	—	1	12	—	14
Drummoyne	13	4	—	9	—	21
Clovelly	13	7	1	4	1	27
Balmain	13	12	—	1	—	37

2nd DIVISION

3rd GRADE—

	P	W	D	L	F	Points
Bronte	13	9	1	3	—	32
Maroubra	13	7	—	5	1	26
Universities	13	9	—	4	—	31
Bondi	13	2	—	9	2	15
Parramatta	13	—	—	13	—	13
Drummoyne	13	9	1	2	1	31
Balmain	13	9	—	4	—	31
Clovelly	13	5	—	8	—	23

3rd DIVISION

3rd GRADE—

	P	W	D	L	F	Points
Bronte B	12	11	—	1	—	34
Sydney B	13	5	2	6	—	25
Ryde	13	4	1	6	1	20
Roseville B	13	4	2	7	1	23
Northbridge B	13	4	2	5	2	21
Clovelly B	13	10	1	2	—	34
Coogee B	13	9	—	3	1	30

"Although I'd been attending games with my father since I was born, my first actual water polo competition season was 1961-1962 at the age of 16, when I played in the 3rd Grade 'B' team. Vic McGrath was the coach of both Bronte 3rd Grades that season, but we had to play separate from the other three grades and all over the place across Sydney. I recall that we lost our first game at Manly... but then won every game after that, including the divisional final. We then won the inter-divisional final, but after that we were defeated by Bronte 'A' 3rd Grade (2-4) in the grand-final. I can remember Vic's impartial advice to both teams being… "I can't say anything, you're going to have to coach yourselves tonight!"

Robbie Vadas, March 2019

The Thornetts

It's not a common thing to befriend or even know of a talented athlete, national representative or Olympian, and much less common to find siblings who have achieved the same sporting greatness. But it is stratospherically rare to come across three siblings that have all represented their country at international sport. One such unique trio of sporting brotherhood however, came to prominence out of the Sydney beachside suburb of Bronte during the 1950's in John, Ken and Dick Thornett.

Backed by their supportive parents the Thornett boys all attended local schools and developed a healthy, but very competitive mindset to sport, which accompanied their many achievements right throughout their lives. Their individual and combined sporting achievements were both impressive and formidable, but a common thread for the Thornett boys was that they all helped to develop and played for Bronte Amateur Water Polo Club.

John Thornett [10]

John Edward Thornett, MBE (1935-2019) was an Australian rugby union player, who played 37 tests for Australia between 1955 and 1967 and made an additional 77 representative match appearances. He captained Australia in 16 test matches and an additional 47 tour matches during the eight international rugby tours he made with Wallaby squads.

Thornett was born in Sydney, and educated at Sydney Boys High School, graduating in 1951, where he was school Captain. A champion swimmer, rowing in the 1st VIII, and captain of the rugby 1st XV. John also competed for Bronte Swimming Club before being coaxed into playing water polo for the newly formed Bronte Amateur Water Polo Club for the 1951-52 season.

Representing Bronte, John was selected at the age of 18 in the NSW State water polo team in 1954 where he competed at the Australian Water Polo Championships in Sydney. John also represented NSW on three other occasions at the Australian Water Polo Championships in Melbourne (1955), Perth (1959)

▶TOP: Portrait of John Thornett, known as the 'Captain of Captains' for the Wallabies Rugby Union team. From 1955 to 1967 John represented Australia on 114 occasions, and was captain for 16 of his 37 tests. MID: Playing for Northern Suburbs. BOTTOM: Working for NSWAWPA as Hon. Treasurer and Secretary.

▲ In addition to his rugby union career, John Thornett was selected in the NSW State water polo teams in 1954, 1955, 1959 and 1960, and spearheaded the Bronte AWPC to their four consecutive 1st Grade NSWAWPA premierships from 1959 to 1962. ▼ The immensely talented Thornett brothers (from left) Dick, John and Ken.

and Melbourne (1960). He was a member of Bronte's inaugural 1st Grade water polo winning team in the NSWAWPA premiership season of 1958-59, which they repeated again in 1959-60, 1960-61 and 1961-62. John was also actively involved with the NSWAWPA where he worked as the Hon. Registrar and Treasurer, but despite focusing on rugby union John loved water polo and he remained a loyal and active club member with Bronte AWPC until 1970.

However, despite his obvious water polo talent, rugby union was his passion and in 1954 John toured with the Australian Universities team to New Zealand, and in 1955 he first played for New South Wales Waratahs. That same year he made his representative debut for Australia touring to New Zealand and playing in all three tests. The following year he again toured with the Australian Universities side to Japan.

In 1956 he appeared for the Waratahs against the visiting Springboks and also played in both tests. He made the 1957-58 Australia rugby union tour of Britain, Ireland and France and played in four of the five tests. In 1958 he made his second tour of New Zealand for two test appearances including an unexpected victory in the 2nd Test in Christchurch. He made further test appearances in 1959 (twice against the British Lions) and in 1962 (twice against Fiji). On the 1961 tour of South Africa captained by Ken Catchpole, Thornett played in both tests and made his debut as Australian captain in a tour match against South-West Africa where a draw was achieved.

From 1963 to 1967 Thornett was entrenched as Australia's leader captaining the Wallabies more times than any player to that point in Australia's rugby history. By this point in his career and with his pace slowing, Thornett had moved from flanker to second-row and then settled into the front-row. He captained the Wallabies on the 1962 tour of New Zealand playing in all three tests and in 11 of the total 13 matches. In 1963 he captained Australia to an 18~9 victory in a one-off test match at the Sydney Cricket Ground against England. Then in 1963 he led the Wallabies on a 24 match tour of South Africa, playing in 16 of the matches including the drawn four test match series, a highlight of Australia's dour international record

over the 50s and 60s. He played in all eight matches of the 1964 tour to New Zealand, including three tests and then in 1965 he led New South Wales and Australia (twice) to victory over the visiting Springboks, followed the next year by matches at home against the British Lions.

Thornett's rugby career concluded at the end of the 1966-67 Australia rugby union tour of Britain, Ireland and France which he captained. John Thornett was only the second Australian player, after Nicholas Shehadie, to play 100 games for his country. He was made a Member of the Order of the British Empire in 1966 and inducted into the Sport Australia Hall of Fame in 1985. He received an Australian Sports Medal in 2000. In 2005 he was honoured as one of the inaugural five inductees into the Australian Rugby Union Hall of Fame. Upon his induction the Australian Rugby Union president, Paul McLean, referred to Thornett's name as: "synonymous with Australian pride and great leadership". Thornett was additionally honoured by the International Rugby Board in 2013 with induction into the IRB Hall of Fame. His portrait hangs in the offices of the Australian Rugby Union.

Ken Thornett [11]

Ken Thornett (1937-2016), also known by the nickname of "The Mayor of Parramatta", was an Australian rugby league fullback. He represented the Kangaroos in 12 tests during 1963 and 1964 and on the off-season Kangaroo Tour.

As his summer sport, Ken was initially devoted to water polo along with his two brothers John and Dick. Under the tutorship of ex-Hungarian international Bert Vadas, he became an excellent goalkeeper with lightning quick reflexes, and was a member of Bronte's inaugural 1st Grade water polo premiership team in season 1958-59, which feat the club repeated with Ken again as goalkeeper in 1959-60. Unfortunately he lost contact with water polo after departing for England to play rugby league professionally in mid 1960.

Ken Thornett began his football career playing 1st Grade rugby

▲John, Ken & Dick Thornett, in 'Tackling Rugby', by Ken Thornett & Tom Easton, Lansdowne Press (1966). ▼ Ken Thornett signed with the Parramatta Rugby League Club after returning from Leeds, England in 1962.

▲ His Royal Highness, Prince Phillip, Duke of Edinburgh shakes the hands of Peter Dimond (left), Ken Thornett and Ken Irvine (right) prior to the 1963 1st Rugby League Test at Wembley (in 'Tackling Rugby', by Ken Thornett & Tom Easton, Lansdowne Press [1966]).

union with Randwick DRUFC, and was the youngest player ever to be selected to play in a 1st Grade union side. After switching to rugby league, Ken travelled to the UK and played with Leeds for several seasons.

Ken Thornett played fullback in Leeds' 25~10 victory over Warrington in the Championship Final during the 1960-61 season at Odsal Stadium, Bradford on Saturday 20 May 1961, in front of a crowd of 52,177. He played fullback in Leeds' 9~19 defeat by Wakefield Trinity in the 1961 Yorkshire County Cup Final during the 1961-62 season at Odsal Stadium, Bradford on Saturday 11 November 1961.

Ken Thornett then returned to Australia and signed with the Parramatta club. Thornett played only seven games in his first season, but the resultant six wins and a draw from those games lifted Parramatta to their first-ever finals position, following eight "wooden spoons" and a paltry 20 percent win record in all their previous matches in seasons 1952 to 1961. Thornett played regularly with Parramatta from 1963, and totalled 136 games for the club. He was the prominent Australian rugby league fullback in the early 1960s after Keith Barnes, and before Les Johns and Graeme Langlands.

Ken played in all six tests of the 1963 Kangaroo tour and in 10 minor tour games. He made a further six test appearances and by the end of his representative career in 1964 had played three tests each against Great Britain and New Zealand, five against France and one against South Africa.

He went on to captain-coach Parramatta in 1965 and 1966, but a dispute with the club saw him seek a transfer to Eastern Suburbs, but the blue and golds would not release him from the two years remaining on his contract without a large transfer fee. Ken Thornett retired at the end of 1968, but returned for one more season under Ian Walsh in 1971 and helped Parramatta rise from last to fourth.

In 1965 he was named NSW Player of the Year. The western grandstand of Parramatta Stadium was named the Ken Thornett Stand in his honour. In February 2008, Ken Thornett was named in the list of Australia's 100 Greatest Players (1908-2007), which was commissioned by the NRL and ARL to celebrate the code's centenary year in Australia.

Dick Thornett [12]

Richard Norman Thornett (1940-2011) was one of just five Australians to have represented their country in three sports. He was an Olympic water polo player before becoming a rugby union and rugby league player, a triple code international representative.

Dick followed in the footsteps of his two older brothers and was drawn to playing water polo for Bronte Amateur Water Polo Club. Under the leadership of his brother John Thornett and the expert coaching of ex-Hungarian international Bert Vadas, Dick became an excellent water polo player with a legendary shot at goal, and was a member of Bronte's inaugural 1st Grade water polo winning team in the NSWAWPA Premiership season of 1958-59, which they repeated in the 1959-60, 1960-61 and 1961-62 seasons. Representing Bronte at the age of 17, Dick was chosen in the NSW State water polo team in 1958 where he competed at the Australian Water Polo Championships in Sydney, and was selected to represent NSW on three other occasions at the Australian Water Polo Championships in Perth (1959), Melbourne (1960) and Adelaide (1961). Dick was also selected to represent Australia at water polo at age 20 for the 1960 Rome Olympic Games. Unfortunately, he was later banned from playing water polo by the Australian Swimming Union after he turned 'professional' by joining Parramatta Rugby League Club in 1962.

However, like his older brothers, Dick was a natural at football and played as a forward for Randwick DRUFC. In his two senior seasons in rugby union in 1961 and 1962 Dick Thornett made 11 national representative test appearances for the Wallabies. On the 1961 Wallabies tour of South Africa, Dick Thornett was in the squad with his brother John Thornett and they played test matches together. But Dick left the amateur code after just two years to join his brother Ken Thornett at the Parramatta Eels Rugby League Club.

As mostly a second-rower, Dick Thornett played with the Eels until 1971, making 168 appearances for the club, being a master ball player informing the style-changing ball skills that Arthur Beetson would bring to forward play shortly after Dick Thornett. In a club game against Canterbury in 1968 Thornett matched the then standing club record of four tries in a match.

In 1969 he appeared as a guest player for Auckland in a match against the New Zealand national rugby league team to mark the New Zealand Rugby League's diamond jubilee. He made national representative appearances for the Kangaroos in Tests against South

◄ Dick Thornett's profile from 'Water Warriors: Chronicle of Australian Water Polo' (13, p. 180), confirming him as one of Australia's most talented water polo players. Dick was guest of honour at the launch of 'Water Warriors' at Sydney International Aquatic Centre, Homebush in January 2009. [12] ▼ Dick Thornett had an outstanding career in rugby league, but he was also selected in the NSW State water polo teams in 1958, 1959, 1960 and 1961, and was the only Bronte Olympian, being chosen in the Australian water polo team for the 1960 Rome Olympic Games. He also starred for Bronte AWPC in their four consecutive 1st Grade NSWAWPA premierships in 1959, 1960, 1961 and 1962.

DICK THORNETT
BRONTE AWPC (NSW)
~ ~ 🌢 ~ ~

Dick Thornett and his brother John Thornett were instrumental in helping the Bronte club to dominate the NSWAWPA 1st Grade water polo premiership from 1959 to 1962. Dick was a naturally gifted athlete and was selected for the Australian water polo team at the Rome Olympic Games (1960). Having already played 11 tests for the 'Wallabies' in rugby union, Dick signed to play with the Parramatta Rugby League Club in 1962, but was banned by the NSWASU for turning professional and therefore excluded from any further NSW or Australian teams. Made in the interests of preserving amateurism, the decision prematurely ended the water polo career of one of Australia's most talented and skilled athletes.

Dick Thornett went on to be chosen as a 'Kangaroo' in the Australian rugby league team, becoming an Australian representative in three different sporting codes; a truly remarkable achievement. Dick's older brother John Thornett, also represented NSW in water polo in 1954, 1955, 1959 and 1960, but proved his mettle in rugby union by gaining 37 international caps (16 as captain) with the 'Wallabies.' Photo - NSWAWPA Archives.

Surprise selection is heavy-weight second rower Dick Thornett, who will represent Australia before playing for his State, N.S.W.

Dick joins his brother Ken in the team.

Their older brother John is at present captain of the Australian Wallaby side touring South Africa.

Dick Thornett, who changed codes at the beginning of this season, has played only 17 rugby league competition matches, five of which were in the pre-season competition.

He replaces his clubmate Brian Hambly.

(Canberra Times, 24 June 1963)

Dick Thornett

A Northern Star

In the Rugger game social clubs abound but few are better known than the North of the Harbour Briars' Kentwell Cup team in the Union sub-district competition.

And who is their 1975 coach? None other than Dick Thornett!

Although Dick has not previously done any coaching he will bring to the Briars the benefit of a wealth of experience.

From 1958 to 1962 Dick played 60 first grade games with Randwick R.U.

In 1961 he played his first rep. game, and his first R.U. tests against Fiji, South Africa, and France, all in the one season.

In 1962 Dick played 5 tests against New Zealand both in Australia and N.Z.

In 1963 Dick changed from R.U. to R.L. and immediately played for Australia against Great Britain in 3 tests.

May all good Northsiders and particularly the Briars reflect on Dick's impressive record of 11 R.U. Internationals and 14 R.L. tests.

And, for good measure, Dick represented Australia at the Rome Olympics at Water Polo playing in three matches of the series.

As mine host of the North Star Hotel at North Sydney it would appear that the hostelry is most appropriately named.

Australian Test Side

ILKLEY, Yorkshire. Sunday (A.A.P.). — The Kangaroos have made only one change in their Test side for the third and final rugby league Test against Britain at Leeds next Saturday.

Brian Hambly comes into the second row in place of Ken Day who played in the Second Test.

Australia's team is: Ken Thornett, Ken Irvine, Graeme Langlands, Reg Gasnier, Peter Dimond, Earl Harrison, Barry Muir, Johnny Raper, Dick Thornett, Brian Hambly, Paul Quinn, Ian Walsh (captain), Noel Kelly.

With Peter Gallagher again injured, Paul Quinn retains the prop position for the Test. Day injured a thigh muscle in training last week.

(Canberra Times, 25 Nov 1963)

▶ABOVE: At the end of his career Dick Thornett took on the coaching role at Briars (City Tattersalls Magazine, May 1975).
BELOW: Dick Thornett shown here at his beloved Dolphin Hotel in Surry Hills. His outstanding sporting achievements followed him throughout his life. Dick Thornett was the only member of Bronte AWPC to be selected in an Australian Olympic Water Polo team, which he achieved for the 1960 Rome Olympic Games.

Africa in 1963, on the 1963-64 Kangaroo tour and in three matches of the 1968 World Cup.

His international rugby league debut in the 1st test against South Africa in Brisbane on 20 July 1963 saw Dick Thornett become Australia's 28th dual code rugby international, following Michael Cleary and preceding Jim Lisle. Ken Thornett also appeared in that test match, making the brothers the first to play together in an Australian test side since Bill and Viv Farnsworth in 1912. Thornett's final two club seasons at Parramatta were affected by a bout of hepatitis and he saw out the final year of his career with a season at Easts. While playing rugby, Thornett also served in the New South Wales Police Force and in 2008, rugby league's centennial year in Australia, he was named as a reserve in a NSW Police team of the century.

John and Dick Thornett both played together for the Wallabies in 1961-62, and Dick and Ken Thornett both played together in three tests during the 1963-64 Kangaroo Tour. Dick Thornett is one of five Australians to have represented their country in three sports. He played Olympic water polo before becoming a rugby league and rugby union international, a triple code international representative.

"In those days a lot of funny things happened in water polo. We used to play in tidal harbour pools at Rushcutters Bay, Balmain and Northbridge, which were a bit muddy on the bottom and became slimy and dirty at low tide. But you could do a few things under the water that you could get away with. So, yeah... it was a hard game, but also a fun game."
Dick Thornett [5]

The fame of the Thornett brothers mirrored the development of Bronte Water Polo, where the three brothers became the backbone of the club. As their sporting prowess and reputations developed, other talented sportsman like Ken Mills, Dick See and Vic McGrath gravitated to Bronte and the club became legendary in its own time. In many ways the development and success of Bronte Water Polo Club ran exactly parallel with the sporting success and achievements of the three Thornett brothers.

"About 1959, Dick See ran for Council and was elected, but he couldn't stop the filling in of the Bronte Baths. Later both he and Dick Thornett were banned by the NSWASA, when they became professional rugby league players... However Dick See, who also played for Newtown RLFC, quietly slipped back into playing water polo. Dick Thornett was too high profile and sadly was never re-admitted to play the great game."
Robbie Vadas, March 2019

Bronte Water Polo Club

(By "LUNKY")

At Cabarita last Saturday afternoon, Bronte first grade proved that they are hot favourites to take out competition honours when they defeated Bondi in the first semi-final, the margin being 6 goals to 5.

Bronte, attacking from the outset, held a slight lead until the last quarter, when Bondi hit the front 5-4. Then John Thornett scored a good goal to equalise, and with only a minute of play left Bondi' centre-back, Keith Whitehead was sent from the water as the result of a foul. With an extra man it was only a matter of time before Bronte scored again and clinched the match.

Scorers for the match were R. Thornett (3), J. Thornett (2), K. Owens (1).

Congratulations are extended to Warren Hurt, who celebrated his 21st birthday last Saturday.

Bondi Weekly, Undated, 1962?

Chapter 5
RETIREMENTS & REBUILDING
(1963 - 1966)

Preparing for water polo training at "Rushcutters Bay Baths", by Jeffrey Smart (1961).

"My nickname was originally "Lunkhead", which was shortened to 'Lunky' as I aged, and then became Lunk when I moved to Queensland to team up with Magyars under the captaincy of Brian "Barney the Bear" Lyndon. How I got the nickname "Lunkhead" was... one Saturday training arvo at Rushy, when I was 17 and still in goals, a shot was released by Dick Thornett, who was in his prime, which hit me squarely on the forehead and flew out over Dunc's kiosk and across the park outside. Kenny Owens was despatched for the search and found the ball in the gutter of Yarranabee Road, well over 200m away... and it was one of the old leather balls! When Kenny returned, he came up to me and simply said "Gee... you must have a Lunk head", and that's where my nickname came from... and I wear it with pride, as it came from a real mate."

Terry 'Lunk' Clark, April 2018

Commencing just their 12th season in the NSWAWPA competitions, the Bronte club had made tremendous strides in its few short years, and had already captured four 1st Grade and two 3rd Grade premierships. But more than that, Bronte had amazing depth as evidenced by their various teams achieving no less than 26 play-off appearances since their inception.

By the start of the 1962/63 season, Bronte were the number one water polo club in Sydney, in New South Wales, and very probably right across the country, which was an incredible achievement.

1962-63

1962/63 NSWAWPA OFFICIALS: Dr. H.K. Porter (Patron); Capt. F. Lamb (President); A.P. Hart (Past President); R. Traynor (Chairman); **J. B. Kirkwood (Registrar)**; A.W. Hamill (Secretary); R. Sherwood (Asst. Secretary); **J.E. Thornett (Treasurer).**

The greatest problem faced by the Association this season remained the allocation of suitable pools in the metropolitan area, which severely hindered further development of the sport. They did however, attain the co-operation of Ashfield Council and their new swimming pool complex, which had a full sized water polo pool. Also, the Association Executive abolished the 10/- player registration fee, which allowed clubs to register as many eligible players as they wanted.

An interesting fact this year was that many of the successful teams had secured the services of an 'out of the water' coach. This was a departure from previous seasons where most teams had been content to play each week off their own initiative, or with a player/coach. It appeared that in many cases, such coaches considerably improved the standard of play.

RANDWICK BOYS HIGH
1963 - 1st Grade Premiers - Phillip Zone
Back row from left: Robert Langford (c), Colin Campbell, Len Harris, Dennis Speed. Front row: Keiran Speed, N. Parker, Mr. Bob Cope (Coach), Adrian Hall, Rolly Flesch. Absent: Brian Powell
(Pegasus - RBHS Yearbook, Dec 1963)

Future Bronte great, 12 year old Rolly Flesch (right) was inspired by the athleticism and skill of water polo at an early age. These images were taken from Rolly's involvement with Timisoara Swimming & Water Polo Club (ILSA), Romania. Photos - Rolly Flesch.

John Thornett (Bronte AWPC), who was also the NSWAWPA Hon. Treasurer at that time, was again congratulated on his selection as captain of the touring Wallabies Rugby Union Team to South Africa.

The Baths & Clubs

During this season water polo games were conducted at Ashfield, Drummoyne, Elkington Park, Cabarita, Gunnamatta Bay, Liverpool, Manly, Roseville, Ryde and Rushcutters Bay Baths.

In regard to new clubs, Ashfield and Eastwood/ Epping affiliated for the first time. Both Cronulla and Manly re-affiliated after a gap of some years, but unfortunately Balmoral, Dee Why and the Sydney Club all lapsed.

The premiership nomenclature was altered for the 1962/63 season when the NSWAWPA competitions were separated by divisions, across three grades. Division I had three grades: 1st Grade consisted of seven teams; 2nd Grade consisted of seven teams; and 3rd Grade consisted of seven

1962/63 Season Statistics
N.S.W.A.W.P.A.

Clubs in the Water Polo Competitions.

Clubs	1¹	1²	1³	2ˢ	3ᴺ	3ˢ	3ᵂ	Total
Ashfield				●	●			2
Balmain	●	●	●					3
Bankstown				●		●		2
Bondi	●		●					2
Bronte	●	●	●	●				4
Clovelly				●	2			3
Collaroy	●			2				3
Coogee				●	2			3
Cronulla				●		●		2
Drumm/East Sydney	●	●	●					3
Eastwood/Epping							●	1
Fairfield							●	1
Freshwater				●				1
Judean						●		1
Liverpool							2	2
Manly	●	●	●					3
Maroubra				●	●			2
Nth Sydney				●				1
Northbridge				●				1
Parramatta	●	●	●					3
Roseville					2			2
Ryde						2		2
Universities	●	●	●	●				4
	7	7	7	7	8	8	7	51

Results of the Water Polo Competitions.

Grade	Premier		Runner-Up
1ˢᵗ	Bondi~6	d.	5~Balmain
2ⁿᵈ	Bronte B~4	d.	3~Balmain
3ʳᵈ	Coogee A~11	d.	7~Balmain
Club Champions			BRONTE
D1²ⁿᵈ	Balmain~3	d.	2~Universities
D2ˢᵗʰ	Bronte B~3	d.	2~Maroubra
D1³ʳᵈ	Balmain~2	d.	1~Manly
D3ᴺᵗʰ	Roseville A~4	d.	2~Universities
D3ˢᵗʰ	Coogee A~6	d.	3~Judean
D3ᵂˢᵗ	Liverpool A~7	d.	2~Eastwood/Epping

"In October 1962 I was invited to join Bronte. From memory, I began in 2nd Grade in the 62-63 competition. Then in October 63, Bronte entered two first grade teams as an "A" and a "B" team. I was put into the "B" team with John Thornett, Ken Mills, Dick See, Brian Ellison, Gary Cawood and others..."
Jon Kirkwood, June 2018

teams. Division II had only one 2nd Grade consisting of seven teams. Division III had three grades: 3rd Grade (North) consisted of eight teams; 3rd Grade (South) had eight teams; and 3rd Grade (West) also consisted of seven teams.

Leading teams in 2nd Grade from both Divisions were to play off for an inter-divisional premiership; and leading teams in 3rd Grade from both Divisions were also to play for an inter-divisional premiership. The number of teams entering the metropolitan competitions totalled 51 from 23 clubs with a total of 753 registered players. [2]

Representatives in NSW Teams

Kenny Owens (Bronte) lost his place in the State team this year along with Ted Pierce (Balmain) and Peter Ritchie (Universities), while Bill Phillips (Universities) was unavailable. However, Bronte's Vic McGrath was reinstated, while Don Sarkies remained secure as the number one goalie for the Blues. The two new caps in the team, Warwick Lamb and goalkeeper Peter Waterman were both from Bondi. Regrettably the new combination for the Blues didn't perform as well as predicted and NSW finished third in the limited three State competition, behind Victoria and Western Australia.

The Premierships

By the end of the preliminary rounds, Bronte was undefeated and led the six other entries in 1st Grade with Bondi and Balmain, well behind in equal second place. In the play-offs, Balmain

NEW SOUTH WALES TEAM
1963 - 3rd Place - National Championships - Perth

Back row (from left): Bob Traynor (A/Manager), Warwick Lamb (Bondi), Alan Langford (Bondi), David Woods (Balmain), **Vic McGrath (Bronte)**, Brian Hutchings (Bondi), Bert Trevennar (Manager).
Front row: Peter Waterman (g,Bondi), Nino Sydney (player/Coach, Bondi), Nick Barnes (vc,Universities), Brian Hamill (c,Drummoyne),
Don Sarkies (g,Bronte), Eric Fitzgerald (Bondi). Photo - NSWAPWA Annual Report 1962/63.

"I always said you could play water polo in summertime and football in the winter. The seasons might have overlapped by two or three weeks, but it didn't take long to adjust to the other sport and that made it very easy. It's probably one of the reasons why I was able to represent Australia in three sports, but you couldn't do it these days. The muscles you use are much the same so I think, it was quite easy to adapt from one sport to the other."

Dick Thornett, 9 August 2008
Interviewed by Ian Warden [1]

"About 1959, Dick See ran for a seat on Waverley Council and was elected, but he couldn't stop Bronte Baths being filled in. Later, both he and Dick Thornett were banned by the NSWASA when they became professional rugby league players. Despite playing league for Newtown RLFC, Dick See was able to quietly slip back into playing water polo. However, Dick Thornett was too high profile and was never re-admitted... which was a huge loss to the sport."

Robbie Vadas, March 2019

▼ Don Sarkies against WA during the 1964 national championships in Perth. Don was the main goalkeeper for NSW from 1961 to 1966, and for Bronte from 1960 to 1973. He possessed extremely fast reflexes and was a superb 'reader' of the play... he knew all the tricks of goalkeeping. (Sun-Herald, 27th Feb 1964).

disposed of Drummoyne (5~1), and Bondi played a brilliant game to defeat Bronte, the reigning premiers (5~2). Balmain repeated the insult in the final by eliminating Bronte (3~2) to gain a grand-final berth. The competition decider was a battle royale, but it was Bondi who emerged as the victors over Balmain (6~5). The win brought the sum total of Bondi's 1st Grade premierships to a record breaking 19. This Bondi team also established a unique record by fielding a team of 11 players who had all represented New South Wales at some stage. However, unbeknown to them at the time, this victory was to be their last.

It was to be a big year for Sydney's Eastern Suburbs clubs as after the intergrade playoffs, Bronte 'B' won the 2nd Grade, and Coogee 'A' won the 3rd Grade competition. Bronte played consistently across all grades to take home the Club Championship.[2]

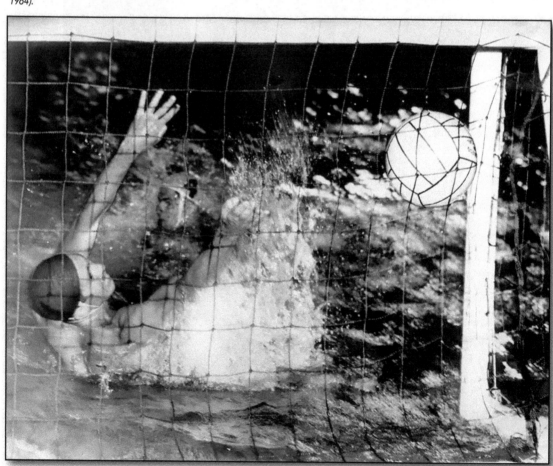

Bronte AWPC

It was hard to beat the performance of the Bronte teams following their enormously successful results of the previous season, but Bronte once again finished this season with solid results across all grades.

Finishing in fourth place, the 3rd Grade won through to the final, but lost to Manly (2~4). Bronte fielded two 2nd Grade teams with the Southern Division Bronte 'B' team finishing second on the ladder. However, led by Peter 'Rocky' Johnson, they won through the play-offs and defeated Balmain (4~2) in the grand-final to take the premiership. The Bronte 'A' 2nd Grade also finished second on the table, but lost to Universities in the final (2~6). Despite an undefeated season, the morale of 1st Grade was badly affected by the banning of Dick Thornett just prior to their semi-match against Bondi, which they lost (2~5). The team tried to pull themselves together, but narrowly bowed out a week later to Balmain in the final (2~3).

Dick Thornett Banned

It was at the end of the 1962/63 summer season, when Dick Thornett had a brush with water polo officialdom, which severed his connections with water polo forever. There had been a lot of publicity at that time about Dick, his possible changeover from rugby union to rugby league, and his signing with the Parramatta Rugby League Club.

BONDI AWPC
1962/63 - NSWAWPA 1st Grade Premiers
From left: Eric Fitzgerald, Brian Hutchings, Ray Smee, Alex Kosegi, Alan Langford, Nino Sydney, Warwick Lamb.
Insets: Keith Whitehead, Doug Laing, Bill Jones and Peter Waterman. Photo - Ray Smee.

DICK THORNETT (17)
SECOND-ROW FORWARD

Rugby League
SYDNEY, Wednesday. — A contract will be signed to-morrow between Rugby Union forward Dick Thornett and Parramatta Rugby League Club.

(Canberra Times, 31st Jan 1963)

"It was very disappointing... to be banned from playing water polo. The comradeship you get through team sport is magnificent, and its one thing that sticks with you all through your life, your friends that you through rough times is really something, and I found that to be one of the beauties of water polo."

Dick Thornett, 9 August 2008
Interviewed by Ian Warden [1]

▲ *Dick Thornett in Parramatta livery, was one of the most popular 'Scanlans trading cards' of the 1960's.*

BRONTE 'B' AWPC
1962/63 - NSWAWPA 2nd Grade Premiers
Back row (from left): John Walker, Terry "Lunky" Clark, Brian Ellison (g), Dave Steer. Seated: Ken Emerton, Warren Hurt, Peter "Rocky" Johnson (c), Warren "Wick" Riley, Robert Foster. Photo - Brian Ellison.

▲ Peter 'Rocky' Johnson enjoyed a long State and International rugby union career throughout the 1960s, making 92 national appearances and he captained the Australian side in five test matches, but was also a great water polo player and Bronte club stalwart.

"It happened just before a semi final water polo match at Drummoyne Pool when one of these petty amateur officials walked up and asked me to sign a statutory declaration, saying that I was still an amateur. I told him where, and what to do with it, and I walked out... and I never saw another game of water polo for years.

They could've let it run until the end of the season, but no... it was just the pettiness of it all, which existed in amateur sport very strongly then. If you compare that with professionalism in Olympic sports today... it was only 28 years ago. My experiences could've been of more benefit to remain playing the game, sharing my skills with younger kids rather than being treated like that. There were a lot of rugby league players that remained playing water polo then, so it was a terrible precedent that this fool made... I won't call him anything more. It was the most ridiculous thing, and John and I have talked about it many times. Anyway, that experience ended my involvement with water polo... a game I loved."

Dick Thornett [1]

Another member of Bronte Water Polo with a superb sporting pedigree was Peter 'Rocky' Johnson, who captained Bronte 2nd Grade to a premiership in the 1962/63 season. Rocky was a great clubman for Bronte, but like the Thornetts his forte was rugby union.

Peter 'Rocky' Johnson [3]

1st GRADE WATER POLO TEAM
ZONE PREMIERS CITY OF SYDNEY WINNERS
Back Row: R. Gadge, H. Engleman, R. Flesch, D. Jackson.
Front Row: R. Bratton, N. MacDonald, Mr. R. Cope, R. Maxwell,
G. Rodgers. Absent: R. Langford (Captain), D. Speed

▲ 1964 Water Polo report from Randwick BHS, which featured Rolly Flesch and Bob Cope (Coach) from Bronte (Pegasus - RBHS Yearbook, Dec 1962).

Peter George Johnson (1937-2016) was an Australian international rugby union player. Schooled at Waverley Public in Sydney's east, Johnson gained entry to Sydney Boys High School and learnt his rugby from the former rugby league international Frank O'Rourke. He was selected in the GPS 2nd XV in his last year of high school. He started his senior rugby at the Eastern Suburbs club, then moved to Randwick before playing at Sydney Uni for a spell. At Randwick he deputised at hooker behind the first-grade rake Jim Brown who was also the Wallaby incumbent. Johnson was selected out of 2nd Grade to trial for the 1957–58 Australia rugby union tour of Britain, Ireland and France but did not make the squad.

Johnson started featuring in representative sides from 1958 playing for South Harbour and for the Australian Barbarians against the visiting New Zealand Maori. That year he was selected in the squad for the 1958 Australia rugby union tour of New Zealand, and played in five matches. Howell asserts that Johnson made an affable tourist, was witty and humorous and was warmly welcomed in the rugby tour environment.

In 1959 Johnson appeared for New South Wales and then for Australia in two Test matches against the visiting British & Irish Lions. In 1960 the All Blacks visited and Rocky played against them for the NSW Waratahs. The following year he met France in a Test match, then Fiji for three Tests and was afterwards selected on the Wallabies 1961 Australia rugby union tour of South Africa, where he played in both Tests and two other tour matches.

In 1962 Johnson played in a New South Wales team that defeated the visiting All Blacks. Then in the first Test against those same visitors Johnson was honoured as Australian captain for the New South Wales captain Jim Lenehan, who withdrew due to injury. On Lenehan's return for the 2nd Test he took the captaincy. Johnson played in that game, his tenth Test appearance for the Wallabies. Later that year the Wallabies embarked on the 1962 Australia rugby union tour of New Zealand with John Thornett as squad captain. Johnson played in eight

"It was an easy link to Bronte water polo club for me, through Bob Cope, who was my school water polo coach at Randwick Boys High, and also an established 1st grade player with the top Sydney club at the time... Bronte."

Rolly Flesch, Feb 2019

1962/63 NSWAWPA RESULTS

FIRST GRADE

At the completion of the Competition Rounds, the points stood as follows with the finals' results recorded after each group.

FIRST DIVISION—

	P	W	D	L	F	Points
Bronte	12	12	—	—	—	36
Bondi	12	7	2	3	—	28
Balmain	12	8	—	4	—	28
Drummoyne	12	6	1	5	—	25
Universities	12	4	—	8	—	20
Manly	12	1	2	9	—	16
Parramatta	12	1	1	10	—	15

First Semi: Balmain 5 def Drummoyne 1.
Second Semi: Bondi 5 def Bronte 2.
Final: Balmain 3 def Bronte 2.
Metropolitan Premiership Grand Final: Bondi 6 def Balmain 5.
First Grade Premiers: BONDI.

SECOND GRADE

FIRST DIVISION—

	P	W	D	L	F	Points
Balmain	12	10	1	1	—	33
Bronte	12	10	—	2	—	32
Universities	12	5	2	5	—	24
Drummoyne	12	6	—	6	—	24
Manly	12	5	—	7	—	22
Collaroy	12	2	2	6	2	16
Parramatta	12	1	1	10	—	15

First Semi: Universities 4 def Drummoyne 2.
Second Semi: Balmain 6 def Bronte 4.
Final: Universities 6 def Bronte 2.
Grand Final: Balmain 3 def Universities 2.
Divisional Premiers: BALMAIN.

SOUTHERN DIVISION—

	P	W	D	L	F	Points
Cronulla	12	10	1	1	—	33
Bronte B	12	8	1	3	—	29
Maroubra	12	8	1	3	—	29
Bankstown	12	5	—	6	1	21
Coogee	12	3	—	7	2	16
Ashfield	12	2	—	10	—	16
Clovelly	12	4	1	1	6	15

First Semi: Maroubra 10 def Bankstown 3.
Second Semi: Bronte B 7 def Cronulla 3.
Final: Maroubra 10 def Cronulla 1.
Grand Final: Bronte B 3 def Maroubra 2.
Divisional Premiers: BRONTE B.
Second Grade Metropolitan Premiership—
Bronte B 4 def Balmain 3.
Second Grade Premiers: BRONTE B.

THIRD GRADE

FIRST DIVISION—

	P	W	D	L	F	Points
Balmain	12	10	2	—	—	34
Manly	12	9	1	2	—	31
Universities	12	6	2	4	—	26
Bronte	12	6	1	5	—	25
Drummoyne	12	3	2	7	—	20
Parramatta	12	3	1	8	—	19
Bondi	12	—	1	11	—	13

First Semi: Bronte def Universities on disqualification.
Second Semi: Balmain 3 def Manly 2.
Final: Manly 4 def Bronte 2.
Grand Final: Balmain 2 def Manly 1.
Divisional Premiers: BALMAIN.

of the thirteen games including all three Test matches.

Johnson was in a victorious Wallaby side in 1963 that defeated England before he then was selected for the 1963 Australia rugby union tour of South Africa. He played in sixteen matches and in all four Tests was the dominant Australian forward and matched it with the Springboks' best. Howell quotes the rugby writer Phil Tressider: "Peter Johnson showed once again that he is the outstanding hooker in international Union today.....his all round forward play was so sound that he could have held down a Test position simply as prop forward". The following year he made his third tour to New Zealand on the 1964 Australia rugby union tour of New Zealand where he played in six of eight total matches including the three Tests, the 3rd an Australian victory.

Johnson was capped in further Test appearances in 1965 against South Africa and the British & Irish Lions who both visited and then in 1966 he was picked for the 1966–67 Australia rugby union tour of Britain, Ireland and France on which he played in all five Tests and sixteen other matches. He appeared in a domestic Test against Ireland in 1967 and then made his fourth visit to New Zealand for the 1967 75th anniversary Test match.

Johnson returned to the national captaincy in 1968 being honoured with the leadership of the Wallabies in the 2nd Bledisloe Cup Test against the All Blacks in the June, in a victorious Test when the French visited in August and then in two Test matches on the 1968 Australia rugby union tour of British Isles. He made five further Test appearances (none as captain), one in 1970 when Scotland toured, two against the Springboks in 1970 and two Tests on the 1971 Australia rugby union tour of France. He played in six of the ten matches of that tour and was replaced in the 2nd Test against France which, at 34 years of age, marked the end of a remarkable representative career.

All told, Peter 'Rocky' Johnson played 92 matches for his country between 1958 and 1971, with 42 of those being Test matches. It was a record number of appearances at the time. Johnson made eight Wallaby tours and played 215 first grade games for his Randwick club and 24 in lower grade games. When the Randwick team of the century was chosen Johnson was selected as a hooker. He died of a heart attack on 12 July 2016. Later that year he was inducted into the Australian Rugby Hall of Fame.

1963-64

1963/64 NSWAWPA OFFICIALS: Dr. H.K. Porter (Patron); G. R. Woods (President); Capt. F. Lamb (Past President); R. Traynor (Chairman); **J. B. Kirkwood (Registrar)**; A.W. Hamill (Secretary); G. Dent (Asst. Secretary); **J.E. Thornett/B. Ellison (Treasurer)**.

"I often think of the times when playing water polo at Rushie, Dunc the owner used to turn the lights out, and we would all go crazy calling out to him from the water. When playing at low tide, we could stand in places and feel the mud oozing under our feet, and at certain times of the year we would train or play while surrounded by hoardes of invading jellyfish. I was notorious for using the mirky water of the baths to duck underwater, then suddenly pop up and call for the ball in front of the oppositions goal."

Tom Folden, Oct, 2020

The 1963/64 NSWAWPA season witnessed the greatest volume of water polo publicity ever seen in New South Wales. Press, radio and television coverage was widespread with most of the credit going to the new NSWAWPA Publicity Officer, Gary Dent of the Parramatta club.

The possibility of having some 1st Grade matches televised was first floated by Fred Lamb and carried out by the Publicity Officer, Gary Dent. This took place one afternoon with Bondi, Balmain, Bronte and Drummoyne playing two rounds of five minute games. Bondi won the tournament and the broadcast was very well received.

An exhibition water polo match between Parramatta and a pick-up Universities side was played at the official opening of the Springwood Olympic Pool on Sunday 27th October, 1963. Having been defeated by Universities in the rounds of the metropolitan competition just a week previous to this game, Parramatta vowed revenge and played for their lives. With the official party admiring the spectacle unfolding before them, the game soon got out of hand and descended into kicking and punching. The commentator tried in vain to make out that the blood and brutality being let loose in the water was all part of a normal water polo match. Unfortunately, the result wasn't recorded, but the team rosters were fortunately printed in the event program.

The deepest and sincerest sympathies of the Association were extended to the family and friends of

Exhibition Match

at
**Springwood Olympic Pool
27th October 1963**

PARRAMATTA: Garry Dent, Frank O'Brien, John Curran, Joe Konic, Alan Purdue, Ron De Groot, Ben Schmidt and Chiro Zorich & A.E. Tex Richards (Coach).

UNIVERSITIES: Bohden Bilinsky, Don Sarkies, Nick Barnes, John Harrison, Peter Ritchie, Fecko Bowman, Carl Phillips, David Cohen, Warren Staude, Ian Bund, Peter Fox, Brian Baker, Bill Ford (Coach).
[4]

▼ *Joe Konic and Frank Jordan (Parramatta) reach for the ball, while training with the NSW State team.*

Mr. A.E. 'Tex' Rickards, the late Country Water Polo Secretary. He was Assistant Manager of the NSW team for the 1961 National Championships and his popularity and assistance to the country clubs as well as his work with the younger players elevated much interest in the sport, particularly in the country regions.[5]

First NSW Women's Water Polo Competition

Throughout the 1962/63 season in New South Wales, requests had been received concerning the possibility of conducting a women's water polo competition. A vast amount of planning, organisation and publicity was required to launch the competition, which had to be achieved in a short space of time. Fred Lamb, the immediate past President of the NSWAWPA, put a great deal of effort into the early development of the women's competition in NSW, and was coach of the Balmoral women's team from its inception. Gordon Woods (NSWAWPA President) was also wholeheartedly behind the new initiative.

After much hard work, the inaugural Ladies Water Polo Premiership attracted six teams from three existing clubs in Bondi, Bronte and Balmoral, with three new clubs in Birchgrove, Randwick and Victoria Park joining. The teams were far from even in strength, but they never lost their spirit and the Association felt there was a tremendous future for the Ladies Competition and subsequently extended every encouragement to those concerned.

At many clubs the ladies had watched the men playing water polo and had even jumped in for a throw of the ball on some occassions. But they became serious in November of 1963 when the first NSW Ladies Water Polo competition finally commenced.

1963/64 Season Statistics
N.S.W.A.W.P.A.

Clubs in the Mens Water Polo Competitions.

Clubs	1¹	1²	1³	2ˢ	3ᴺ	3ˢ	3ᵂ	Total
Ashfield				2				2
Balmain	●	●	●					3
Balmoral			●		●			2
Bondi	●	●	●					3
Bronte	2	●	●					4
Canterbury				2				2
Collaroy				2				2
Cronulla			●		●			2
Drummoyne	●	●	●					3
Enfield						2		2
Eastwood/Epping				●		●		2
Freshwater				●				1
Gymea Bay					●			1
Judean			●					1
Leichhardt						●		1
Liverpool						2		2
Maroubra Seals			●					1
Maroubra Surf			●					1
Nth Palm Beach					●			1
Nth Sydney				●				1
Parramatta	●	●	●					3
Randwick Rugby		●	●	●	●			4
Roseville					●			1
Universities	●	●		●	●			4
	7	7	7	7	7	7	7	49

Results of the Mens Water Polo Competitions.

Grade	Premier		Runner-Up
1st	Balmain~6	d.	5~Bondi
2nd	Balmain~10	d.	4~Eastwood/Epp
3rd	Balmain~9	d.	8~Gymea Bay
	Club Champions		BALMAIN
D1²ⁿᵈ	Balmain~7	def	5~Randwick Rugby
D2²ⁿᵈ	Eastwood/Epp~8	def	6~Cronulla
D1³ʳᵈ	Balmain~4	def	0~Universities
D3ᴺᵗʰ	Collaroy A~5	def	1~Roseville
D3ˢᵗʰ	Gymea Bay~4	def	2~Canterbury A
D3ᵂˢᵗ	Enfield A~7	def	6~Liverpool A

▲ *New Zealander J. Harvey (left), stretches for a high pass as NSW goalkeeper Brian Ellison (Bronte), watches closely in the International fixture at Ashfield Pool, where the teams drew 3-all (Sun-Herald, 24 Feb 1964).*

Although initially the womens teams were looked upon with some element of ridicule by the men, in time they developed to influence the game in a profound way.

The Baths & Clubs

The previous season saw a large number of players transferring between clubs. Fortunately, many of these players started up new clubs or revived older ones with the end result being an increase in the number of clubs in the competition. Forfeits were also much less frequent than in previous seasons.

The Competition Committee administered seven men's and one ladie's competition this season, amounting to 340 games, which were played at Balmain Baths, Drummoyne, Canterbury, Liverpool, Rushcutters Bay, Roseville, Gunnamatta Bay, Manly and a brand new swimming complex with a separate water polo/diving pool at Ashfield.

In regard to new clubs, Canterbury, Gymea Bay, Leichhardt, Maroubra Seals, North Palm

"Kenny Owens bought a pub and many was a Saturday night that the pub was a springboard to a party somewhere or other, and always lots of fun. I have vivid memories of parties in the shed at the back of Ello's place where I provided music recorded on reel to reel tapes, especially the Beatles, who by then had changed the music scene significantly. There were also "dance nights" with my reel to reel tapes at Bronte Surf Club, but some of those nights degenerated into fights when the 'locals' gatecrashed our party."

Jon Kirkwood, June 2018

"Donny Sarkies and Brian Ellison went to try out as goalkeepers for the State team in 1964 at Balmain Baths. They played a trial game and every one waited after for the selectors to emerge… Don was selected, but Ello initially missed out, although he was later added to the team. It was the only ever time that the NSWAWPA selected two State team goalkeepers from the same club."

Robbie Vadas, March 2019

Bronte Water Polo Club

(By "LUNKY")

This season the Club is in the enviable position of having a dearth of topline coaches. Chief coach is Mr. Burt Vadas, a former Hungarian Representative Polo player and current President of the Club. Burt came to Bronte in its early stages and by his play and coaching piloted the Club to its first Premiership.

Deputy coaches are Mr. Richard Thornett who represented Australia in Water Polo at the Rome Olympiad in 1960; and Mr. John Thornett, Australia's current Rugby Union Captain and former State Water Polo player. Then last but not least, Mr. Vic McGrath, another State Representative. With the knowledge and experience of these men and the talent available, it appears the Club is set for its most successful season.

Don't forget the first training session, 2 p.m., Saturday, October 10, at Rushcutter Bay Pool.

And a happy week to all especially to the "B.R." who celebrated his 22nd birthday this week.

For any inquiries ring Mr. Brian Ellison on 665-6581.

Bronte Water Polo Club

(By "LUNKY")

Further reminder to all Members that the first official training session will be held at the Rushcutter Bay Pool on Saturday, October 10, 1964. A General Meeting will also be held on this date to discuss the number of teams to be entered by the Club in the Metropolitan Competition and the date of the Club's first Social outing.

Rumours have it that an injury prone, Bill "Sonny" McCarthy, is making a desperate effort to be fit for the opening competition matches by engaging in strenuous work.

This season will see the new type Water Polo Ball formally introduced into competition play. Last season this ball, which is much more lighter and durable than the older design, proved successful, so Bronte has purchased 5 of these balls. These balls will be used in all games and training sessions so that Club members will be able to become accustomed to their lightness.

Remember—If you have a friend interested in playing Water Polo, bring him along to the Official Training and if you have any further inquiries contact Brian Ellison on 665-6581.

Bronte Water Polo Club

(By LUNKY)

The First grade, fresh from its win in the pre-season knockout comp., was sadly outclassed by a strong Drummoyne side, in the first competition match last Tuesday. Under pressure from the outset, the First's never recovered from being down 0-3 at the end of the 2nd quarter and were finally defeated 4 goals to 1.

The 2nd's, lacking understanding between its players, ran out losers by the odd goal.

In the 3rd's, the A team showed that it is a very strong candidate for Premiership honours by "whitewashing" Drummoyne 4-0.

The "B's" with only 3 members who had played before staged an upset by defeating Ashfield 3-1 at Balmain. Down 0-1 in the first quarter they staged a great fightback to be 1-all going into the last quarter and proved too strong for their opposition to add two more goals. Great work fellas—keep it up!

Oscar of the Week — Newcomer—Chris Williams who in his first match displayed initiative and power to notch two goals in his team's win.

Results of games — 1st's—defeated 1-4; 2nd's—defeated 3-4; 3rd "A"—won 4-0; 3rd "B"—won 3-1.

Lunky (Terry Clark) wrote weekly articles about the performance of the Bronte Water Polo teams, which were published in the Bondi Weekly; 8th Oct 1964; 1st Oct 1964; 26th Nov 1964.

Old Myths, New Realities

The water polo public throughout Australia has been thunderstruck by some of the more glaring omissions with the biggest and strongest four players being left out of the team. Allan Charleston (WA), John O'Brien (VIC), **Vic McGrath** and David Woods (NSW) are players with such a wealth of experience that it is suicide to send a team away without them... The reality of it all is that the best water polo team Australia could produce is not going to Tokyo......and doubt that the team will win a game!

J.C. Hannan,
The Australian Swimmer, June 1964, p.2.

Beach and Randwick Rugby affiliated for the first time. Both Balmoral and Enfield re-affiliated after a gap of some years, and Drummoyne dropped East Sydney as a partner club. Unfortunately Bankstown, Clovelly, Coogee, Fairfield, Manly, Northbridge and Ryde all lapsed. The number of teams entering the metropolitan competitions totalled 49 with 707 registered male players, and a further six teams of ladies, representing 26 clubs in all.

The premierships were conducted across three divisions, and separated by grades. Division I consisted of a 1st Grade of seven teams, a 2nd Grade of seven teams and a 3rd Grade of seven teams. Division II consisted of one 2nd Grade of seven teams. Division III consisted of three competitions separated by region; 3rd Grade (North) with seven teams, 3rd Grade (South) with

NEW SOUTH WALES TEAM
1964 - 3rd Place - National Championships - Sydney

Back row (from left): Alex Kosegi (Coach, Bondi), Brian Hutchings (Bondi), **Vic McGrath (Bronte)**, David Woods (Balmain), **Brian Ellison (g, Bronte)**, Frank O'Brien (Parramatta), Gordon Woods (Manager, Balmain). Front row: Nino Sydney (Bondi), **Don Sarkies (g, Bronte)**, Brian Hamill (vc, Drummoyne), Ted Pierce (c, Balmain), Nick Barnes (Universities), Bill Phillips (Universities). Photo - NSWAPWA Annual Report 1963/64.

seven teams, and 3rd Grade (West) also with seven teams. The winners of 2nd Grade and 3rd Grade qualified for inter-divisional playoffs. An odd feature of this season was the greatest number of drawn games for many years.[5]

Representatives in NSW Teams

NSW were hoping for a turnaround this season and retained seven players from 1963, the only new caps being Frank O'Brien (Parramatta) and Brian Ellison (Bronte), who joined Vic McGrath and Don Sarkies as Bronte's two other respresentatives. It was the only time in the history of NSWAWPA that two goalkeepers had been selected in the State team from the same club!

▼ BELOW (Left): Official Program for the 1964 Australian Water Polo Championships and Olympic Games Trials. (Right): The NSW roster for the 1964 National Championships. BOTTOM: Joe Konic and his junior squad. Back row (from left): Allan Young?, Ted Baldock, Neil McDonald, Tom Folden, Paul ?, ??? Front row: Chris Butt, Joe Konic, Robert Langford, Graham Gairns, Ray from Germany, Doug Grevitt, ???, Ray Mendels.

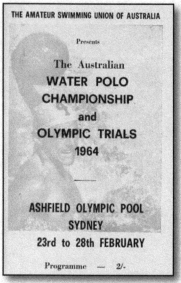

THE AMATEUR SWIMMING UNION OF AUSTRALIA

Presents

The Australian
**WATER POLO
CHAMPIONSHIP**
and
**OLYMPIC TRIALS
1964**

ASHFIELD OLYMPIC POOL
SYDNEY
23rd to 28th FEBRUARY

Programme — 2/-

AUSTRALIAN WATER POLO CHAMPIONSHIP
SYDNEY 1964

COMPETING TEAMS

TITLE HOLDERS VICTORIA

NEW SOUTH WALES

Cap Numbers

1.	D. SARKIES	(Goalkeeper)
2.	V. A. McGRATH	
3.	F. O'BRIEN	
4.	N. BARNES	
5.	B. HUTCHINGS	
6.	D. M. WOODS	
7.	E. J. PEIRCE	(Captain)
8.	N. SYDNEY	
9.	B. W. HAMILL	(Vice-Captain)
10.	W. J. BERGE PHILLIPS	
1.	B. ELLISON	(Reserve Goalkeeper)

A. Kosegi — Coach   G. R. Woods — Manager

But Western Australia were outstanding this year, to not only take the title, but they had five of their side selected in the Australian Olympic team.

The 1964 Olympic Team

The Australian Olympic team was selected after these championships, with five players from Western Australia, and three each from Victoria and NSW. The Aussies played four trial matches, but at the Tokyo Olympics they lost to both Russia (0~6) and East Germany (1~3), in what was a nightmare draw for them, to finish in tenth place, winning only one of their six matches on tour.

The Premierships

By the end of the preliminary rounds Bondi had won the minor premiership from Balmain and Bronte in the 1st Grade. In the play-offs, Bronte 'A' just scraped past the highly experienced Bronte 'B' (4~3) in the minor semi, and Balmain defeated Bondi (5~4) in the major semi. Bondi then regrouped to eliminate Bronte 'A' (5~4) to gain a grand-final ticket. The 1st Grade grand-final was as close as they come, with Balmain eventually defeating Bondi (6~5) to take their first premiership since 1958.

Balmain also won both the 2nd Grade and the 3rd Grade. The Club Championship was also annexed by Balmain who achieved the remarkable feat of

1963/64 NSWAWPA RESULTS

1st DIVISION 1st GRADE—

	Played	W.	D.	L.	Forfeit or Disq.	Goals For	Against	Pts.	Pos.
Bondi	12	8	2	1	1	65	36	29	1
Balmain	12	8	1	3	—	77	45	29	2
Bronte A	12	6	3	3	—	47	40	27	3
Bronte B	12	4	3	5	—	46	54	23	4
Drummoyne	12	4	1	7	—	37	52	21	5
Parramatta	12	3	1	8	—	40	63	19	6
Universities	12	3	1	8	—	31	53	19	7

First Semi-final: Bronte A 4 def Bronte B 3.
Second Semi-final: Balmain 5 def Bondi 4.
Final: Bondi 5 def Bronte A 4.
Grand Final: Balmain 6 def Bondi 5.

First Grade Metropolitan Premiers — BALMAIN.

1st DIVISION 2nd GRADE—

	Played	W.	D.	L.	Forfeit or Disq.	Goals For	Against	Pts.	Pos.
Randwick	12	8	2	2	—	56	29	30	1
Bronte	12	8	2	2	—	49	27	30	1
Balmain	12	8	2	2	—	40	27	30	3
Universities	12	5	4	3	—	35	22	26	4
Drummoyne	12	5	1	6	—	37	31	23	5
Parramatta	12	1	—	11	—	24	59	14	6
Bondi	12	1	1	6	4	16	62	11	7

First Semi-final: Balmain 2 def Universities 1.
Second Semi-final: Randwick 3 def Bronte 1.
Final: Balmain 3 def Bronte 2.
Grand Final: Balmain 7 def Randwick 5.
Inter-Divisional Play-off: Balmain 10 def Epping 4.

Second Grade Metropolitan Premiers — BALMAIN.

1st DIVISION 3rd GRADE—

	Played	W.	D.	L.	Forfeit or Disq.	Goals For	Against	Pts.	Pos.
Balmain	12	9	3	0	—	75	16	33	1
Drummoyne	12	9	3	0	—	65	15	33	2
Universities	12	8	2	2	—	59	23	30	3
Bronte	12	5	1	6	—	49	37	23	4
Parramatta	12	3	1	8	—	47	44	19	5
Randwick	12	3	—	9	—	21	77	18	6
Bondi	12	0	—	10	2	7	111	10	7

First Semi-final: Universities 9 def Bronte 1.
Second Semi-final: Balmain 5 def Drummoyne 4.
Final: Universities 3 def Drummoyne 0.
Grand Final: Balmain 4 def Universities.
First Inter-Divisional Play-off: Balmain 5 def Collaroy 4.
Second Inter-Divisional Play-off: Balmain 9 def Gymea Bay 8

Third Grade Metropolitan Premiers — BALMAIN.

BALMAIN AWPC
1963/64 - NSWAWPA 1st Grade Premiers
Back row (from left): Ken Laws, Paul Dunford, Alf Beattie, David Woods, Gordon Woods (President). Front row: Alan Stringer, Ted Pierce (c), ???, Max May. Photo - Balmain AWPC Archives.

▲ Members of the 1963-64 Australian Kangaroos Rugby League touring team and heroes to many young Australians, featuring Dick Thornett (1) and Ken Thornett (2).

winning the Metropolitan Premiership in all three Division I grades. The runners-up in the Club Championship were Bronte, who had gallantly fielded two 1st Grade teams. The inaugural Ladies competition was won by Birchgrove (*see chapter 7*).[5]

Bronte AWPC

Bronte was one of the six pioneer clubs to field a team in Sydney's first ever Ladies' competition this season (*see chapter 7*).

In the mens events, Bronte had so much depth that they offered to field two teams in 1st Grade to make up numbers for the competition.

The Bronte 3rd Grade finished in fourth place, but were easily eliminated by Universities in the semi-final (1~9). The 2nd Grade completed the season in second place, but lost both their play-offs, bowing out to Balmain in the final (2~3). The two 1st Grade teams finished third and fourth on the table, and both qualified for the play-offs. But they were matched against each other in the semi-final, with Bronte B being eliminated (3~4). Bronte A then advanced to the final, but lost narrowly to Bondi (4~5). It was the first time in five years that Bronte had failed to win a premiership.

WATER POLO TEAM FACES TOUGH TEST

The A.C.T. water polo team to play in the New South Wales Country championships will have a severe test this weekend when it plays six matches against a Sydney club team.

A squad of 15 Bronte players will come to Canberra for the matches, which will be played on Saturday and Sunday.

The Bronte team led by N.S.W. captain-coach Vic McGrath, is particularly strong and is at the head of the Sydney inter-club competition at present.

There will be five other N.S.W. representative players in the visiting squad besides McGrath — John Thornett, Roley Felch, Don Sarkies, Dick See and Brian Hamil.

With such a strong team to compete against the A.C.T. squad will have a fierce work-out in preparation for the Country championships.

The championship will be

Printed by the Federal Capital Press of Australia Pty. Limited at Pirie Street, Fyshwick, A.C.T. for the publishers, The Federal Capital Press of Australia Pty. Limited and John Fairfax & Sons Limited.

played in Moree on January 30 and 31, and will be contested by country teams from all over N.S.W.

Eleven players have been named in the A.C.T. side, which is regarded as the strongest chosen yet to represent the A.C.T.

The players named are Alf Tye (captain-coach), Bruce Gibson, Jim MacFarlane, Geoff Hosie, Tony Irvine, Bob Pearse, Mike Hickey, Graham Robinson, Kippa Simpson, Pat Armstrong and Ralph Dean.

They have been practising together for two hours each night and have been moulded into a formidable combination.

It is expected the games against Bronte will add a vital edge to the A.C.T. team.

Three matches will be played on Saturday — at Duntroon at 11 a.m., and two games at the Canberra pool, starting at 4 p.m.

The remaining matches will be played on Sunday — with two games at Quean-

beyan, beginning at 10.30 a.m., and the final match at Duntroon at 3 p.m.

The A.C.T. players have a tough schedule ahead of them in the next few weeks. They will drive the 505 miles to Moree on Friday week, play in the tournament then return to Canberra on February 1, in time to play in the local inter-club competition, which starts on February 2. — GRAEME KELLY.

Flat 5, No. 7 Brae Street, Bronte.

19th February, 1965.

Dear

As you know a Barbecue was held at John Thornett's home to raise funds to send club-members Don Sarkies, Vic McGrath and Rolly Flesch to the Australian Championships in Hobart.

Owing to the fact that the Club's finances are not very substantial, the Social Committee has decided to hold another Barbecue at the Bronte Baths on Saturday, March 6th, 1965; commencing at 6p.m. The Splashers Hall has also been obtained for dancing and adequate tarpaulin cover has been arranged in case of threatening weather.

The entry fee, which will include steaks, sausages liquid refreshments (both hard and soft) and entertainment music- wise is a moderate £1 single and 30/- double.

At these prices you can't afford not to be there and enjoy yourself.

Yours,

TERRY CLARK.

(Lunk.)

SOCIAL SECRETARY.

▲ Bronte WPC played the ACT in Canberra (The Canberra Times, 21 Jan 1965, p28). ▶ There was always something going on and just a month after the Canberra trip, a barbeque was held at John Thornett's home to raise funds to send Bronte's reps to the 1965 Australian Championships.

1964-65

1964/65 NSWAWPA OFFICIALS: Dr. H.K. Porter (Patron); G. R. Woods (President); Capt. F. Lamb (Past President); R. Traynor (Chairman); R. Webb (Registrar); G. Dent/P. Derwent (Secretary); L. Papps (Asst. Secretary); **J.B. Kirkwood (Treasurer).**

Due primarily to the recent Olympic Games in Tokyo, this season saw a marked increase in the number of entries for the various NSWAWPA competitions. Not only was there a substantial increase in participation, but the enthusiasm and keenness of the competition was highlighted in the very close results often produced during the play-offs.

"Getting to training at Rushie or to games at Balmain, Ashfield, Drummoyne etc, was a real ordeal undertaken by endless lifts from our coach, Momie Vadas, especially for someone who got carsick in the rear. A free lift depended on the amount of space available in the cargo area of his coffee van, where I'd squeeze in between other players and the hessian bags of coffee."

Rolly Flesch, Feb 2019

In an attempt to obtain television publicity, the Association again experimented with a round of 1st Grade competition games at Ashfield Pool on Saturday afternoons. This was quite successful as Channel 7 were able to broadcast these afternoon games and the show highlighted footage for their evening sport wrap-up. However, Saturday afternoons proved to be unpopular with the players and often clashed with other commitments.

In another coup, the National Fitness Council of NSW made an instructional film on water polo, which was shown in six parts on Channel Nine's 'Focus on Sport'. Commentary was provided by Ray Smee and John Thornett.

The possibility of televising some 1st Grade matches had been first put forward by Fred Lamb and carried out by the Publicity Officer, Gary Dent in the previous season. This year, Bondi, Balmain, Bronte and Drummoyne played two rounds with five minute quarters with Bondi taking out the tournament.

It was with the deepest regret that the Association recorded the passing of Fred Lamb, the Immediate Past President. He had been an active water polo player in the United Kingdom in his youth and later became interested in coaching junior water polo before moving into administration.

The late Fred Lamb first appeared on the water polo scene in Australia in January 1956. Fred was Honorary Secretary from 1956 to 1960, and President from 1961 to 1963, then under the rules of the Assn was retired and became Immediate Past President, accepting once again, an active office-bearing role in becoming Country Secretary.

He was very successful in publicising water polo and wrote a

1964/65 Season Statistics
N.S.W.A.W.P.A.

Clubs in the Mens Water Polo Competitions.

Clubs	1^1	1^2	1^3	2	3^N	3^S	3^W	Total
Army						●		1
Ashfield						●	●	2
Balmain	●	●	●	●				4
Balmoral				2				2
Bondi	●	●	●					3
Bronte	●	●	●			●		4
Canterbury						●	●	2
Collaroy				●	●			2
Drummoyne	●	●	●					3
Eastwood/Epping					●		●	2
Enfield						●	●	2
Judean					●			1
Lane Cove							●	1
Leichhardt							●	1
Liverpool					●	●		2
Maroubra Seals					●			1
Maroubra Surf							●	1
Nth Palm Beach							●	1
Nth Sydney				2				2
Northbridge					●			1
Parramatta	●	●	●					3
Randwick Rugby	●	●	●					3
Roseville					●			1
St. George	●	●	●					3
Sans Souci						●		1
Universities	●	●	●					3
	8	**8**	**8**	**6**	**7**	**7**	**8**	**52**

Results of the Mens Water Polo Competitions.

Grade	Premier		Runner-Up
1st	Balmain~4	d.	3~Universities
2nd	Collaroy~7	d.	6~Balmain
3rd	Balmoral A~4	def	3~Balmain
Club Champions			UNIVERSITIES
D1²	Balmain~3	def	1~Bronte
D2²	Collaroy~2	def	1~Maroubra Seals
D1³	Balmain~3	def	2~Universities
D3ᴺᵗʰ	Balmoral A~7	def	2~Northbridge
D3ˢᵗʰ	Enfield B~3	def	2~Army
D3ᵂˢᵗ	Enfield A~5	def	3~Ashfield A

TOP (Left): 1965 National Championship bronze medal. (Right): Pennant for the Hobart 1965 Australian Water Polo Championships. ABOVE (Left): Captain/coach, Vic McGrath (Bronte) at left, calms the NSW team at the 1965 Hobart National Championships. (Right): The yellow ribboned, 3rd place National Championship medal for Don Sarkies (NSW).

column in the Sunday Mirror under the heading of 'Skipper'. Fred Lamb greatly stimulated interest in water polo in his own clubs, Dee Why, then later Balmoral. It was nice to see the last team Fred coached in Balmoral Ladies, win their grand final. Fred Lamb's contribution to the sport ranked very high indeed, along with other stalwarts like Harry Grose, Cecil Chapman, Asher Hart and Hermie Doerner.[6]

The Baths & Clubs

Altogether, 462 games were arranged this season by the Competition Committee at the following pools: Ashfield, Balmain Baths, Canterbury, Drummoyne, Gunnamatta Bay, Liverpool, Manly, Roseville and Rushcutters Bay Baths.

Blow To A Proud Record

Bondi water polo club has failed to get a representative in the state team for the first time in 30 years. The team comprises representatives from five other Sydney clubs. Bondi's failure to gain representation comes after many years as one of Sydney's top teams. Brian Hutchings and Nino Sidney represented Bondi last year. State officials have cleared doubts about Bronte representatives Vic McGrath, Don Sarkies and Rowley Flesch, who due to a mix up between the Water Polo Association and the NSW ASA, were not affiliated. McGrath is captain/coach of the State team. Former Yugoslav international, Joe Konic (Parramatta) is in the side. The team will compete in the Australian Championships in Hobart from February 20th to March 1st.

Unreferenced Newscutting

NEW SOUTH WALES TEAM

1965 - 3rd Place - National Championships - Hobart

Back row (from left): Bill Phillips (Universities), Ken Laws (Balmain), **Don Sarkies (g, Bronte), Rolly Flesch (Bronte)**, John Harrison (g, Universities), Nick Barnes (vc, Universities). Front row: Bert Trevenar (Manager), Ron De Groot (Parramatta), David Woods (Balmain), Joe Konic (Parramatta), Brian Hamill (Drummoyne), **Vic McGrath (c/Coach, Bronte)**, Gary Dent (A/Manager).

Photo - NSWAPWA Annual Report 1964/65.

There was a marked improvement in the standard of play generally, but particularly in the 1st Grade competition. Many experienced players, together with a number of younger players were willing to train more seriously for the sport and this commitment was reflected in better standards of play in all competitions.

In regard to new clubs, St. George and Sans Souci affiliated for the first time. Army, Lane Cove (Greenwich) and Northbridge re-affiliated after a gap of some years. Unfortunately Freshwater, Cronulla and Gymea Bay lapsed although the latter two clubs amalgamated for the most part with the new St. George super club. The number of teams entering the metropolitan competitions totalled 62 from 28 clubs, a substantial increase with 988 registered players.[6]

"With Don Sarkies in goals, defending was a breeze… you could take off on counter-attack as an opponent was winding up to shoot, because you just knew that Donny would save it. I can remember a game against Balmain where they intercepted and David Woods charged down the field with no one between him and Donny. Woodsy picked up the ball at great height and threw with all his power into the bottom right hand corner… but Donny knew exactly where he'd shoot, and neatly plucked the ball out of the air with both hands, saying… "Thank You!" I could never score against Donny at training."

Robbie Vadas, March 2019

Representatives in NSW Teams

Brian Ellison unfortunately lost his place to John Harrison (Universities), but a new approach was taken this year with Vic McGrath being appointed captain/coach of the NSW State team. Joining him from Bronte and showing terrific form was Don Sarkies and a very talented youngster in Rolly Flesch. Other new caps for this year's side were Ron De Groot and Joe Konic (Parramatta), and Ken Laws (Balmain). But once again, NSW could only win four of their eight games, and placed third in the 18th Australian Championships in Hobert, behind an undefeated Victoria and Western Australia.

The Premierships

In the 1st Grade competition, every match was hard-fought and no game was a foregone conclusion as had been the case in previous years. By the end of the preliminary rounds, Universities and Balmain were

1964/65 NSWAWPA RESULTS

1st Grade

	Played	W.	D.	L.	Forf. or Disq.	Goals For	Against	Pts.	Pos.
Universities	21	17	1	3	—	136	66	56	1
Balmain	21	16	3	2	—	142	74	56	2
Bronte	21	12	5	4	—	100	64	50	3
Drummoyne	21	12	3	6	—	69	63	48	4
Parramatta	21	7	2	12	—	81	93	37	5
Randwick	21	6	1	14	—	51	96	34	6
Bondi	21	3	3	12	3	58	97	27	7
St. George	21	2	—	18	1	45	132	24	8

1st Semi-final: Bronte 8 def. Drummoyne 7.
2nd Semi-final: Universities 8 def. Balmain 7.
Final: Balmain 6 def. Bronte 5.
Grand Final: Balmain 4 def. Universities 3.

1st GRADE METROPOLITAN PREMIERS — BALMAIN

1st Division—2nd Grade

	Played	W.	D.	L.	Forf. or Disq.	Goals For	Against	Pts.	Pos.
Universities	14	12	—	2	—	70	11	38	1
Balmain	14	11	1	2	—	60	29	37	2
Bronte	14	10	—	4	—	70	27	34	3
Drummoyne	14	7	2	5	—	39	36	30	4
St. George	14	5	1	8	—	33	48	25	5
Parramatta	14	4	1	9	—	40	57	23	6
Randwick	14	2	2	10	1	27	72	20	7
Bondi	14	1	1	7	5	30	79	12	8

1st Semi-final: Bronte 4 def. Drummoyne 3.
2nd Semi-final: Balmain 3 def. Universities 2.
Final: Bronte 2 def. Universities 1.
Grand Final: Balmain 3 def. Bronte 1.

1st DIVISION PREMIERS — BALMAIN

3rd Grade—1st Division

	Played	W.	D.	L.	Forf. or Disq.	Goals For	Against	Pts.	Pos.
Universities	14	14	—	—	—	96	7	42	1
Bronte	14	11	—	2	1	52	16	35	2
Balmain	14	9	1	4	—	52	30	33	3
Drummoyne	14	8	1	3	2	38	32	29	4
Parramatta	14	4	1	8	1	24	51	22	5
St. George	14	4	—	9	1	34	58	21	6
Bondi	14	3	1	9	1	24	56	20	7
Randwick	14	1	—	10	3	18	82	13	8

1st Semi-final: Balmain 4 def. Drummoyne 2.
2nd Semi-final: Universities 5 def. Bronte 2.
Final: Balmain def. Bronte (forfeit).
Grand Final: Balmain 3 def. Universities 2.

3rd GRADE 1st DIVISION PREMIERS — BALMAIN

FIRST GRADE

	BALMAIN	BONDI	BRONTE	DRUMMOYNE	PARRAMATTA	RANDWICK	St. GEORGE	UNIVERSITIES
BALMAIN		7-1 2-2 9-3	10-5 4-4 3-6	7-3 3-2	5-2 15-6	9-3 12-3	11-3	6-4
BONDI	1-7 2-2 3-9		2-2 2-3	FORF 0-5	FORF 0-5 1-6 2-3	3-4 FORF 0-5 3-2	2-6 6-4	2-4 4-5
BRONTE	5-10 4-4 6-3	2-2 3-2		1-4 4-1 2-2	4-4 6-3 11-6	6-2 2-3 7-0	5-0 6-2 10-2	2-5 3-2 3-3
DRUMMOYNE	3-7 2-3	5-0 1-4 2-2	4-1 1-4 2-2		2-1	7-1 3-2	3-0 6-2	4-12
PARRAMATTA	2-5 6-1 6-15	5-0 3-2	4-4 3-6 6-11	1-2		4-4 3-0 5-3	6-3 7-2	2-8 2-5
RANDWICK	3-9 3-12	4-3 5-0 2-3	2-6 3-2 0-7	1-7 2-3	4-4 0-3 3-5		5-4	5-9 3-6
St. GEORGE	3-11	6-2 4-6	0-5 2-6 2-10	0-3 2-6	3-6 2-7	4-5		2-7 2-6 1-12
UNIVERSITIES	4-6	4-2 5-4	5-2 2-3 3-3	12-4	8-2 5-2	9-5 6-3	7-2 6-2 12-1	

FIRST DIVISION
SECOND GRADE

	BALMAIN	BONDI	BRONTE	DRUMMOYNE	PARRAMATTA	RANDWICK	St. GEORGE	UNIVERSITIES
BALMAIN		8-1 3-3	3-4 2-8	3-2	11-2 3-2	5-2 7-0	1-0	2-0
BONDI	1-8 3-3		1-4	FORF 0-5	2-10	5-4 3-5	3-4 FORF 0-5	0-1
BRONTE	4-3 8-2	4-1		3-4 1-2	6-0 5-1	9-3 7-1	6-0 4-2	2-4 0-3
DRUMMOYNE	2-3	5-0	4-3 2-1		1-1	2-2	2-3 6-2	1-5
PARRAMATTA	2-11 2-3	10-2	0-6 1-5	1-1		0-2 6-2	3-4	0-10 0-5
RANDWICK	2-5 0-7	4-5 5-3	3-9 1-7	2-2	2-0 2-6		2-3	0-11 1-8
St. GEORGE	0-1	4-3 5-0	0-6 2-4	3-2 2-6	4-3	3-2		1-5 1-6
UNIVERSITIES	0-2	1-0	4-2 3-0	5-1	10-0 5-0	11-0 8-1	5-1 6-1	

THIRD GRADE

THIRD GRADE	BALMAIN 'A'	BONDI	BRONTE 'A'	DRUMMOYNE	PARRAMATTA	RANDWICK	St. GEORGE	UNIVERSITIES
BALMAIN 'A'	/	3-2 6-1	0-3 1-2	3-2	4-2 6-1	8-1	4-3	2-6
BONDI	2-3 1-6	/	0-4	1-4	1-1 3-2	4-3 2-3	4-3 3-4	0-6
BRONTE 'A'	3-0 2-1	4-0	/	4-0 2-0	5-0 5-1	7-0 5-1	2-1 9-0	0-4 1-2
DRUMMOYNE	2-3	4-1	0-4 0-2	/	6-0	6-2	3-2 6-0	FORF 0-5
PARRAMATTA	2-4 1-6	1-1 2-3	0-5 1-5	0-6	/	3-1 4-1	4-1	2-9 0-6
RANDWICK	1-8 3-2	3-4 1-5	0-7	2-6	1-2 1-4	/	1-5	0-9 0-13
St. GEORGE	3-4	3-4 4-3	1-2 0-9	2-3	1-4	5-1	/	1-9 0-6
UNIVERSITIES	6-2	6-0	4-0 2-1	5-0	9-2 6-0	9-0 13-0	9-1 6-0	/

THIRD DIVISION SOUTH

THIRD DIVISION SOUTH	ARMY	ASHFIELD 'B'	BALMAIN 'B'	BRONTE 'B'	CANTERBURY 'B'	ENFIELD 'B'	MAROUBRA SURF 'B'	SANS SOUCI
ARMY	/	9-4	FORF 0-5	2-1 1-5	14-2 7-1	5-7	W	6-4 2-4
ASHFIELD 'B'	4-9	/	FORF 0-5 3-2	1-3 0-2	4-1	2-11 1-7	I	4-8
BALMAIN 'B'	5-0	5-0 2-3	/	4-2 2-2	7-2	1-6	T	4-6
BRONTE 'B'	1-2 5-1	3-1 2-0	2-4 2-2	/	7-2 10-0	0-2 2-5	H	1-9 2-2
CANTERBURY 'B'	2-14 1-7	1-4	2-7	2-7 0-10	/	0-11	D R A	4-7
ENFIELD 'B'	7-5 7-1	11-2	6-1	2-0 5-2	11-0	/	W	6-1 6-3
MAROUBRA SURF 'B'	W	I	T	H	D	R	A — W	N
SANS SOUCI	4-6 4-2	8-4	6-4	9-1 2-2	7-4 14-3	1-6 3-6	N	/

In the days before computers, progress score sheets were kept by the NSWAWPA Secretaries. The above results for Season 1964/65 being rigorously recorded by our very own Robbie Vadas, who worked quietly behind the scenes for Bronte, over many years.

"I was always intrigued by the nicknames of some Bronte teammates, and we made up new nicknames for many others, which were borne with pride and mostly stuck with those they were bestowed upon. Here are just a few:

Jon Kirkwood	"Oscar"
John Gahagan	"Superman"
John Keane	"Allah"
John Solomons	"Sollo"
Graeme Robinson	"Cheetah"
Robbie Vadas	"Robi X"
Bert Vadas	"Momie"
John Power	"Bighead"
John Walker	"Mother"
Warren Hurt	"Wazza"
John Thornett	"Thorn"
Peter Johnson	"Rocky"
Chris Simpson	"Kipper"
Ken Emerson	"Nose"
Peter Folden	"Foldini"
Brian Hallinan	"The Rat"
Warren Riley	"Wick"
Billy McCarthy	"Sonny"
Brian Ellison	"Ello"
Dennis Morgan	"Morgo"
Billy Parsons	"The Sheik"
John de Leon	"Schnozzel"
Brian Fitzpatrick	"Big Fitz"
Ken Mills	"Millsy"
Terry Clark	"Lunky"
Don Sarkies	"Sarkies"

Terry 'Lunk' Clark, April 2018

▼ *A cup for winning the NSW Country Championship with the Canberra club in 1966, owned by Chris 'Kipper' Simpson.*

joint leaders with the six other entries in 1st Grade, well behind on points. In the play-offs, Bronte disposed of Drummoyne (8~7), and Universities played a brilliant game to defeat Balmain by the same margin (8~7). Balmain then recovered to eliminate Bronte (6~5) in the final, and gain a grand-final berth. The decider was played on the 21st March 1965 and was a typically tight affair with Balmain eventually prevailing after a titanic struggle over a talented Universities (4~3) to take the title for the second year in a row.

Collaroy were undefeated to win the 2nd Grade, and Balmoral 'A' took out the 3rd Grade premiership as well as the Ladies' competition, with both these sides being undefeated on the season.

The Club Champion for consistency across grades was won for the first time by Universities, who were minor premiers in all three grades in Division I.[6]

BALMAIN AWPC
1964/65 - NSWAWPA Men's 1st Grade Premiers
Ken Laws, Paul Dunford, Alf Beattie, David Woods, Alan Stringer, Ted Pierce (c), Tom Laws, Max May, Hermie Bakels (g).

Bronte AWPC

On the 21st December 1964, Robbie Vadas reported to the NSWAWPA that Bronte Club had a highly successful trip to Wagga to promote the sport to the country club.

Bronte had another successful season with all teams qualifying for the play offs. The 3rd Grade finished in second place, and won through to the final, but forfeited to Balmain. The 2nd Grade completed the season in third place with the equal best goal scoring record. They managed to win through the play-offs, but lost to Balmain in the grand-final (1~3). The 1st Grade team also finished third on the table, but was only narrowly eliminated by Balmain in the final (5~6).

1965-66

1965/66 NSWAWPA OFFICIALS: Dr. H.K. Porter (Patron); G. R. Woods (President); Capt. F. Lamb (Past President); R. Traynor (Chairman); **R. Vadas (Registrar)**; P.A. Derwent (Secretary); L. Papps (Asst. Secretary); H.J. Bund (Comp. Secretary); O. Charles (Treasurer).

During the 1965/66 season, water polo continued to progress and the NSWAWPA conducted almost 500 metropolitan competition games across three grades together with a Junior, as well as a Ladies' competition. The increase in the number of players showed a steady and consistent growth over past seasons and metropolitan registrations climbed to over 1,000 for the first time.

It was pleasing to see that forfeits and disqualifications were minimal especially in the two top grades. The major sponsors for the Association were W.D. & H.O. Wills for the metropolitan trophies, Speedo Knitting Mills, Sterling Swimwear Pty. Ltd. and Jantzen (Aust.) Ltd.

The Baths & Clubs

For the very first time, the Association experimented with a pre-season competition which commenced in the 2nd week of October and concluded on the 21st of November. The competition was played between 24 teams for the A.E. 'Tex' Rickards Trophy and was won by the Bronte Club. The pre-season contest was such a success that the Association recommended making it an annual event.

In regard to new clubs, Eastern Suburbs Police Boys and Western Suburbs affiliated for the first time. Unfortunately Army, Ashfield and Enfield all lapsed although the latter two clubs amalgamated for the most part with the new Western Suburbs Club. The number of entries received for the Men's Metropolitan competitions came to 50 teams from 25 clubs.

1965/66 Season Statistics N.S.W.A.W.P.A.

Clubs in the Mens Water Polo Competitions.

Clubs	1^1	1^2	1^3	2	3^N	3^S	3^W	Total
Balmain	●	●	●				●	4
Balmoral				●				1
Bondi		●	●					2
Bronte	●	●	●					3
Canterbury							●	1
Collaroy	●	●	●					3
Drummoyne	●	●	●					3
Eastwood/Epping				●	●			2
East Subs Police BC					●			1
Judean						2		2
Lane Cove					●			1
Leichhardt							●	1
Liverpool				●				1
Maroubra Seals				●				1
Maroubra Surf					●			1
Nth Palm Beach					●			1
Nth Sydney				2				2
Northbridge					●			1
Parramatta	●	●	●				●	4
Randwick Rugby		●	●					2
Roseville					●			1
St. George	●	●	●					3
Sans Souci						2		2
Universities	●	2	●					4
Western Suburbs				●		2		3
	8	9	9	6	6	6	6	50

Results of the Mens Water Polo Competitions.

Grade	Premier		Runner-Up
1st	Balmain~4	d.	3~Universities
2nd	Universities A~10	d.	3~Maroubra Seals
3rd	Balmain A~8	d.	1~Eastwood/Epping
Club Champions			BRONTE
D1 2nd	Universities A~3	d.	2~Bronte
D2 2nd	Maroubra Seals~4	d.	2~Western Suburbs
D1 3rd	Balmain A~6	d.	5~Bronte
D3 Nth	Eastwood/Epping~2	d.	1~Lane Cove
D3 Sth	Judean A~5	d.	3~Sans Souci A
D3 Wst	Western Suburbs A~3	d.	2~Canterbury

NEW SOUTH WALES TEAM
1966 - Runners-Up - National Championships - Brisbane

Back row (from left): Bob Traynor (Manager), Ron De Groot (Parramatta), **Don Sarkies (g, Bronte)**, John Harrison (g, Universities), Peter Ritchie (Universities), Warwick Lamb (Universities), Alex Kosegi (Coach, Bondi). Front row: Ken Laws (Balmain), Brian Hamill (vc, Drummoyne), David Woods (c, Balmain), Nick Barnes (Universities). Absent: Bill Phillips (Universities).
Photo - NSWAPWA Annual Report 1965/66.

TOP: The 1966 NSW State team at the Australian Water Polo Championships in Brisbane, with Don Sarkies at the end of the line, Bronte's sole representative that year. MID: The 1966 Australian Water Polo Championships were held at the Valley Pool in Brisbane. BOTTOM (Left): 1966 National Championship silver medal. (Centre): Pennant from the 1966 Host State. (Right): 2nd place National Championship medal for Don Sarkies (NSW).

The competition this season was intense and any one of Universities, Bronte, Bondi, Balmain or even Drummoyne could have been premiers.

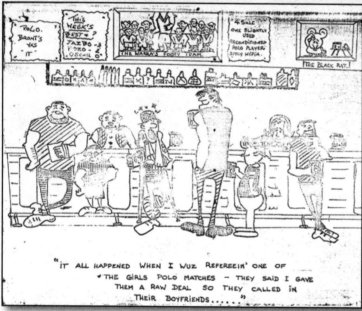

"IT ALL HAPPENED WHEN I WUZ REFEREEIN' ONE OF
• THE GIRLS POLO MATCHES — THEY SAID I GAVE
THEM A RAW DEAL SO THEY CALLED IN
THEIR BOYFRIENDS....."

▲TOP: Joe Konic (left) and a number of the boys from Bondi including... (back row) Chris Butt, Ted Baldock, Tom Folden; (front row) Ray Mendels, Ray from Germany, Robert Langford. ABOVE: Cartoon on the back page of the 1965/66 Bronte AWPC Annual Report.

Possibly the best game of the year was Bondi's 2~1 defeat of Universities in the first round. It was a personal triumph for former Australian captain, Ray Smee's tactics, leadership and personal drive and every member of the Bondi team for their part in executing the plan. The win was a copy-book lesson that few spectators present would ever forget.[7]

Representatives in NSW Teams

In an attempt to retain its more experienced members, NSW held onto seven players this year, including Bronte's Don Sarkies as goalkeeper, which gained for him a sixth consecutive State team cap. However, while there were no new caps, both Vic McGrath and Rolly Flesch lost their places, with both Warwick Lamb and Peter Ritchie (Universities) being recalled. Unfortunately, Victoria were just too good yet again, and claimed their 10th National title.

The Premierships

By the end of the preliminary rounds, Universities had gained the minor premiership dropping only their first round game against Bondi. In the play-offs, the reigning premiers, Balmain knocked out Bondi (8~3) in the minor semi, and Universities played a clinical game to defeat Bronte (6~4) in the major semi-final. Balmain then accounted for Bronte (6~3) in the final, to secure a grand-final berth. All premiership finals that year were played at the 'home' of NSWAWPA, the 'Dawn Fraser Swimming Pool' at Balmain and this definitely suited the 'Tigers'. Despite coming into the match as underdogs, Balmain outplayed Universities in a torrid encounter, to make it three 1st Grade premierships in a row.

Universities 'A' took out the 2nd Grade premiership and Balmain 'A' were undefeated to claim the 3rd Grade title. Although not successful in any one grade, the Club Championship for consistency across all grades was won by the beachsiders from Bronte Water Polo Club.

BALMAIN AWPC
1965/66 - NSWAWPA Men's 1st Grade Premiers
Ken Laws, Paul Dunford, Alf Beattie, David Woods, Alan Stringer, Ted Pierce (c), Tom Laws, Max May, Hermie Bakels (g).

An outstanding Association achievement for the year was the inauguration of a new Junior Competition, sponsored by the Shell Company of Australia, which commenced late in the season, but concluded on Sunday, 21st March, 1966. The last time the Association had run a Junior competition was back in 1953.

Fourteen teams competed in two divisions. The Eastern Division consisted of teams from Balmain A and B, Bronte, Bondi, Judean and Eastern Suburbs Police Boys Club. The Southern Division consisted of teams from Cronulla A and B, Sans Souci, Canterbury, Como, North Ramsgate, Hurlstone and the John Edmondson Club. In the playoffs, Cronulla A defeated Bronte (6~0) and Balmain A disposed of Sans Souci

1965/66 NSWAWPA RESULTS

Division I, 1st Grade

	Played	W.	D.	L.	Forf. or Disq.	Goals For	Against	Pts.	Pos.
Universities	14	13	—	1	—	89	32	40	1
Bronte	14	10	—	4	—	70	31	34	2
Balmain	14	9	2	3	—	91	44	34	3
Bondi	14	9	1	4	—	74	46	34	4
Drummoyne	14	6	2	6	—	63	40	28	5
Collaroy	14	4	—	10	—	37	69	22	6
Parramatta	14	2	1	11	—	36	76	19	7
St. George	14	—	—	14	—	19	141	14	8

1st Semi-final: Balmain 8 def. Bondi 3.
2nd Semi-final: Universities 6 def. Bronte 4.
Final: Balmain 6 def. Bronte 3.
Grand Final: Balmain 4 def. Universities 3.

1st GRADE METROPOLITAN PREMIERS — BALMAIN

2nd Grade, 1st Division

	Played	W.	D.	L.	Forf. or Disq.	Goals For	Against	Pts.	Pos.
Bronte	16	11	5	—	—	79	31	43	1
Universities A	16	12	2	2	—	86	31	42	2
Balmain	16	10	3	3	—	89	47	39	3
St. George	16	8	3	5	—	53	43	34	4
Drummoyne	16	8	2	6	—	60	30	34	5
Universities B	16	7	1	6	2	52	58	29	6
Parramatta	16	5	1	10	—	47	57	27	7
Collaroy	16	1	—	15	—	23	85	18	8
Randwick	16	1	1	11	3	14	121	16	9

1st Semi-final: Balmain def. St. George (disq.).
2nd Semi-final: Bronte 5 def. Universities A 4.
Final: Universities A 7 def. Balmain 3.
Grand Final: Universities A 3 def. Bronte 2.

1st Division Premiers—Universities A

3rd Grade, 1st Division

	Played	W.	D.	L.	Forf. or Disq.	Goals For	Against	Pts.	Pos.
Balmain A	16	12	12	—	2	51	23	40	1
Bronte	16	9	4	2	1	44	33	37	2
Bondi	16	9	1	6	—	51	28	35	3
Universities	16	8	1	6	1	46	33	32	4
St. George	16	5	3	8	—	45	46	31	5
Parramatta A	16	6	3	5	2	46	41	29	6
Drummoyne	16	6	2	5	3	28	40	27	7
Collaroy	16	5	3	4	4	37	56	25	8
Randwick	16	2	1	10	3	29	77	18	9

1st Semi-final: Bondi 8 def. Universities 2.
2nd Semi-final: Bronte 5 def. Balmain (disq.).
Final: Balmain A 2 def. Bondi 1.
Grand Final: Balmain A 6 def. Bronte 5.

3rd Grade 1st Division Premiers—Balmain A

JUNIOR COMPETITION:

Eastern Division: Balmain A (15 points), Bronte (11), Balmain B (11), Bondi (8), Judean (7), Eastern Suburbs Police Boys (6).
Southern Division: Cronulla A (18), Sans Souci (18), Cronulla B (17), Canterbury (10), Como (10), North Ramsgate (9), Hurlstone (6), John Edmondson (6).
Play-offs: Cronulla A 6 def. Bronte 0.
Balmain A 4 def. Sans Souci 3.
Cronulla A 8 def. Balmain A 4.

JUNIOR COMPETITION PREMIERS — CRONULLA A

Pre-Season Competition
A. E. Richards Memorial Trophy

Bronte A		26 points	First
Collaroy		25 points	Second
Bondi		24 points	Third
Parramatta A		20 points	Fourth
St. George		20 points	Fifth
Universities A		20 points	Sixth

Winners—Bronte A

NEW SOUTH WALES COMBINED HIGH SCHOOLS
1966 - 1st XI Water Polo Team

Back row (from left): ???, Ken Brandon (g), Peter Montgomery (vc), John McFarlane, Keith McIndoe, ???, Mr. Casey (Manager). Front row: Brett Gooley, ? Chapman, Bruce Falson, Roger Wilkinson, ???. Absent: Ray Mullins (Coach). Photo - Peter Montgomery.

A Polo Players Dream
by
Terry 'Lunk' Clark
Bronte AWPC, 1965

Tonight's the night of my big game; the chance to hit the top
I hit the water, swim two laps, my blood is running hot
The whistle blows, the game is on and I win the swim for ball
The centre back looks up the field, awaiting my loud call
And there I am in front of goal about to take the pass
My biggest chance in all the season to really show my class
I spin around and note contempt within the goalie's glance
And from the side our coach is calling, 'shoot low it's your only chance'
With ball at the ready and muscles taught, I gaze at the goalie's face
But in my mind is indecision, should I lob or try for pace?
My shoulder lunges, my arm whips hard and the ball speeds t'ward the net
I tell myself, 'it's going in', but alas it isn't yet
For I see the goalie lift himself, his arm glide through the air
And in a flash my joyful feeling, is changed quickly to despair
That dreaded 'whump' is heard by me, and all the crowd afar
As I see the ball fly from the goalie's arm, high above the bar
I swim my hardest to take the corner, but the referee signals time
The chance to be a top flight star, seems never to be mine
But all my worries are not as bad, as to you they all may seem
As all these happenings are just a part, of a polo players dream.

(4~3). The competition was won easily however, by Cronulla A over Balmain A (8~4).

The 1966 NSWCHS Water Polo team embarked upon a tour to Melbourne in Victoria, where they defeated a Victorian Schoolboys team in a two match series.[7]

Bronte AWPC

Once again, Bronte put in a polished performance with all three grades qualifying for the finals. The 3rd Grade finished second on the table and won through to the play-offs, but lost by one goal to Balmain A (5~6) in the grand-final. Our 2nd Grade finished undefeated at the top of the table, but lost narrowly in the grand-final to Universities A (2~3), while 1st Grade finished second on the table, but lost in the final to Balmain (3~6).

CRAVEN FILTER TROPHIES

Presented to the Association by W. D. & H. O. Wills (Australia) Ltd., for the winners of the Metropolitan Premiership Competitions.

The main achievement this year was that Bronte had once again taken out the NSWAWPA Club Championship.

Although Bronte had not won a 1st grade premiership since 1962, the past four seasons had brought two NSWAWPA Club Championships for overall consistency, with not one of its grades missing a finals series in that period. Most pleasing was that the Bronte Junior team of 1965/66 collected the A. E. 'Tex' Richards Memorial Pre-Season Trophy and also finished the competition in the final four. Even without winning premierships, Bronte remained a formidable water polo club.

THE BRONTE AMATEUR WATER POLO CLUB
YEAR BOOK — 1965/66
FOREWARD

Since the Bronte Club began it has had to rely on the generosity of the Bronte Amateur Swimming Club for the publication of its Annual Report. This year, it was decided to produce a more comprehensive and informative report of our own, which we hope will be improved upon in seasons to come.

Included in this report is a short history of the Club and details of some of the players who have helped to lift it from a virtual unknown to the coveted Premiership by their knowledge and leadership. Well, enough said.... Read on!

* * * * * * * * * *

THE FORMATION AND HISTORY OF THE CLUB

Contrary to what you may have heard the first Bronte Water Polo team was founded in 1948 and not in 1952. The 1948 team was a mixture of both Surf and Swimming Club junior members, who banded together and entered the 1st Grade Competition in that year. Although the team boasted four Australian Surf Champions - Ken Baret_ Ken Mills, Dara Drewett and Rod Chapman and two State swimming champions - Jack Campbell and Jack Gilmore, plus outstanding surfer Roy Falson; they suffered defeat after defeat which proved the old saying - "Champion swimmers don't always make good water polo players". The team_ finished the season with only one win to its credit which put a damper on the enthusiasm of some members and caused the team to disband. Ken Mills and Jack Campbell then transferred to Pyrmont Club for several seasons before returning to their home club----Bronte.

Then in 1952 a group of keen youngsters who, although members of the Bronte Swimming Club, decided water polo was the game for them and so they formed the current Bronte Amateur Water Polo Club. In that year the team entered the 3rd Grade Competition, but, owing to the fact that they were only learners, did not succeed in capturing the Premiership. In 1953/54 the same team advanced to 2nd. Grade, but success in this competition also eluded them. So, in 1954/55 after only two seasons in water polo,the team entered the 1st Grade Competition and at the same time was joined by Bert (Momi) Vadas, a seasoned player who had represented Hungary in European Competition and had migrated to Australia with other members of the famous "M.T.K." Budapest" team.

The impact of Bert upon the Club was fantastic and so, under his leadership the team of "green kids" were moulded into a viable combination. The team improved with every game and only just failed to realize a "fairy tale" climb up the ladder when they were beaten in the Grand Final.

It has been said by many experienced players that Bert was one of the freak players of the game, possessing uncanny ball sense and positional skill; and a shot so fast and so well directed that goalkeepers were left astonished as the ball flew past their ears. Bert was also the first player to successfully introduce the famed bat-shot into Australian Water Polo. This particular shot is accomplished by flicking the ball up in front of the player during the glide motion of a swiming stroke and then hitting, it with the stiffened fingers of the other hand as it comes through to commence its normal swimming stroke.

The original team of 1952 comprised of Roy Burton, Dick See, Arthur Obey, Jack Brownjohn, Ken and John Thornett and Vic McGrath. Then Bert joined the Club in 1954/55 and set about moulding a Premiership team. From that day onward the team spent its time learning tactics, gaining experience and mastering the finer points of the game. Then in the 58/59 Season with the acquisition of "wonder boy", Dick Thornett and last of the "originals", Ken Mills - the team hit top gear, reached the Grand Final, defeated Bondi and so clinched its first Premiership. In the 1959/60 Season the 1st Grade team again emerged as the holder of the Premiership. The 1960/61 Season saw the Club grow and as a result three teams were entered in the Competition. They were a 1st Grade, 2nd Grade and a 3rd Grade - the only successful one being the 1st Grade, who drew the Grand Final with Bondi and so became Co-Premiers for that year.

It was the 1961/62 season which was to prove Bronte's best ever. That year four teams were entered, being 1st Grade, 2nd Grade and two 3rd Grades. When the Premierships had been decided the results were follows:

1st Grade - Premiers.
2nd Grade - Runners Up.
3rd Grade "A" - Premiers.
3rd Grade "B" - Runners Up.

In 1962/63 the 1st Grade after being undefeated in both rounds were surprisingly eliminated in the Final by the ultimate winners .... Balmain, but the Club received some consolation when the 2nd Grade finally took off the Premiership after being runners up for the previous three seasons. The 1963/64 season proved unsuccessful for the Club owing to the fact that the 1st and 2nd Grades were undergoing a rebuilding process after losing some of the "old brigade". At the end of the 1964/65 season the 1st's were narrowly defeated by Balmain..6-5 in the Final. The 2nd Grade suffered the same fate losing to Balmain 1-3 in the Grand Final. The 3rd Grade "A" team reached the Finals and the 3rd Grade "B" team narrowly failed to reach the Semi-Final on averages.

* * * * * * * * * *

THANKS

Thanks must go to Rushcutter Bay Baths Proprieter, Mr. Duncan McLennan, known to members of all Clubs simply as "Dunc"; his wife Gloria and his daughters Leslie, "Duch" and Belinda for the way in which they have helped our Club over the years. After being pestered by many small children throughout a long day, they always seem to have a big smile for all the Bronte 'kids' whose antics may well try anyone's patience!

THE THORNETT FAMILY

As this is our first Annual Report it is an opportune time to realise the achievements and efforts of the Thornett family. If you peruse the newspapers any day of the week you will most certainly come across the name of either John, Dick or Ken Thornett, but never any mention of their parents.

Believe me, the Bronte Water Polo Club is highly indebted to both Mr. and Mrs. Thornett, not only for the fact that they have given the Club three highly talented players, but for the way in which they have stuck with the Bronte Club through lean times. It is common knowledge amongst the older members that whenever the Club was in need of finance Mr. and Mrs. Thornett would always unselfishly volunteer their home and help for a fund raising function and when the Semi's and finals rolled around two keener barrackers you would never find!

To Mr. and Mrs. Thornett the Club can only express its gratitude in one word...   Thanks!

JOHN THORNETT

The eldest of the three sons and Captain of the Bronte Club, John is a man held in high esteem for his gentleman approach to both sport and civilian life. He was one of the original 1952 team and devoted all his spare time over the years to water polo both as an official and as a player. Through hard training and perseverence John received his just reward when he was selected to represent N.S.W. in the Australian Championships and made such an impression that it was regarded as a formality that he would be included in an Olympic team in the near future, but then fate stepped in! Later that season John was selected to represent his country in another field of sport Rugby Union.

After several matches on the International tour he became an instant success and it was unfortunate that his chances of representative polo were jeopardised owing to the fact that he was on tour with the Wallabies at the time of the 1956 Olympic Selection Trials. In the field of Rugby Union, John went from strength to strength and finally realised his boyhood ambition when he captained the Australian Wallaby Tourists in the 1963 series against the all conquering South African Springboks, and with his fine leadership and play bought his team within an ace of inflicting a series defeat upon the 'Boks.

John is also the captain of the current Sydney Rugby Union Premiers, Northern Suburbs and early in his career was a member of the University Team which also gained Premiership honours. Apart from his football and water polo achievements John is also an accomplished boxer and tennis player and like the rest of us, just a golfer!

KEN THORNETT

Also a member of the 1952 team, Ken was a very competent field player, but it was in the position of goalkeeper that Ken really made his mark, possessing uncanny reflexes which enabled him to pull balls out of the net, that against other goalkeepers would be certain goals. After stringing together a long line of outstanding displays he was finally chosen to play in the selection Trials for the State Team and was considered unlucky to not make the team. Ken, apparently bitten by the Rugby Union bug, started to make his name as a fullback for the Randwick Club and after spending several years knocking on the door for International Selection he decided to venture to Great Britian to further his football career. In England he decided to change to Rugby League and after a couple of matches was rated as a player of outstanding potential and later rated by experts as one of the best fullbacks in the world.

Ken then returned to Australia and joined the Parramatta Club where he lived up to the experts expectations and was finally selected to represent Australia against the touring New Zealand Kiwis. After starring for his country in this series he was then selected as a Kangaroo Tourist to England later that year and was one of the players instrumental in the team's Ashes victory.

RICHARD THORNETT

The "baby" of the family, Dick has won fame as a triple international,. having represented his country in Water Polo at the 1960 Rome Olympic Games; in Rugby Union on tours of South Africa and New Zealand; in Rugby League against New Zealand, France, England and South Africa. As soon as Dick handled a water polo ball he was an instant success and possessed a shot so powerful that it made most goalkeepers shudder just at the thought of it. At the Olympic Games he gained the respect of seasoned internationals by his vigorous play and scoring potential. Dick, like Ken and John received the call of Rugby Union and commenced his career as a second-rower for the Randwick Club and after many top class, perfomances eventually gained his Test Cap. After a highly sucessful tour of New Zealand, Dick turned to the Rugby League code, and joined brother Ken in the Parramatta team, where he took to the game like a duck takes to water and he achieved the unique distinction of representing Australia in only his first Season, against the Kiwi's. Later that year, he toured England with brother Ken and helped Arthur Summons Boys wrest the Ashes from England.

KEN OWENS

Young brother of Barry Owens who came up through the ranks of the Club during the '50's and finally secured himself not only a permanent first grade spot, but also a berth in the 1960 State Team. Ken, like the Thornett Brothers and Peter Johnson was also a prominent Rugby Union player with the Randwick Club. Ken started this season in fine style with Bronte and was producing the form which won him the State trip but England. He has the unique distinction of having not one, but approximately five sendoffs before leaving.

KEN MILLS

On our front cover you will probably recognize the facial features as those of the one and only Ken Mills. We feel it is only fitting that Ken's happy grin should adorn our initial issue as he is the only member of the 1948 "originals" still playing.

Now... we are not going to state his age, although we believe that it's around the 21 mark, but one fact we feel should be mentioned is that Ken has played over 15 years of water polo which is an achievement that not too many can boast of, and what's more he's still going strong. Ken's other sporting accomplishments are that he was an Australian Surf Teams Champion (in the days when the surf's were big) and also a top flight golfer (although he'll never admit it).

RON MANDELSON

Although Ron left our Club at the beginning of the 1964/65 Season because of residential and travelling difficulties we are of the opinion that his service to the Club should not go unsung. In his career with the Club Ron was both Secretary and Treasurer and the way in which he carried out these duties was one to be admired by all. Ron had the uncanny talent of being there every time asking for your fees so you could never give him the same excuse twice.

Now that Ron is gone we only just realise the amount of work he accomplished and the time and effort he devoted to his job and it is the opinion of all the Committee members that St.George's gain has been our unfortunate loss.

MR AND MRS ELLISON

Mr. and Mrs. Ellison are two more people who are to receive recog:nition for their servicesto the Club over the years. Some of our ncw members may not have met the Ellison's, hut they may have had the frustrating cxperieace of trying to score a goal against the goalkecper son, Brian, during the Competition.

In the same way as Mr. & Mrs. Thornett, the Ellisons would always volunteer their home for social functions, which were always an outstanding success   due mainly to the wonderful organisation of Mr. and Mrs. Ellison. They had the happy knack of adding little touches and effects which turned the particular evening from a moderate success to a social knockout!

Over the years their interest in the Club has never waned which is shown in their attendance at all our Social functions. Mr. and Mrs. Ellison...... from all the boys......Thanks again for your help and support!

* * * * * * * * * *

ASK YOUR FAMILY CHEMIST - HE KNOWS!

Six little words which together spell out Commonsense.
So, if you are experiencing a minor bout of sickness,
or
You have a few of those little aches and pains.
Remember, we've got our own Dick See at 83 Erskinville Road (51-2137)
* * * * * * * * * *

PLAYERS PARADE

AMER, John Prominent squash player; first season with the Club; John is a good social man and proved a leading light on the Wagga Trip.

ANDERSON, Alan Visited Sydney with the N.Z. Waitamata Club in '63/64; returned to join Bronte this season and played solidly.

ASHLEY, Kevin A vigourous centre forward; "Ash" won social best and fairest at the Wagga and Canberra Trips.

BULLOCK, Dave Outstanding young goalkeeper; unfittest man in the Club as he trains only twice daily.

CAWOOD, Gary One of the "Wood" brothers; rugged centre forward; another prominent squash player; spends spare time in various social endeavours.

CLARK, Lunk In career with Club has played all positions including "left right out"; Lunk's weekly articles provide Competition info and a few laughs for members; his only claim to fame - his head!

COULSON, Greg During early part of season captained 3rd's; also a Club selector; a calm, experienced player; now our unfortunate loss to Newcastle.

FLESCH, Rolly Schoolboy player represented N.S.W. in his first season in senior water polo competition.

FOLDEN, Eric Senior active player; head of his own "water polo family'. An outstanding example of coolheadness under pressure ant a player to be watched by all young members.

FOLDEN, Peter Rapidly improving young player who represented the N.S.W. Schoolboys in Australian Championships during '64/65 season.

FOLDEN, Tommy Regular first grader; strong swimmer; selected to represent at the 1965 World Judean Games.

GAHAGAN, John Played all grades in his initial season; an "iron man" who looks to have an outstanding future with the Club.

HICKMAN, Chris Welcome capture from Bronte Swimming Club; overcame lack of size with courageous displays.

HILLIER, Bob Club stalwart; always gives of his best, both in sport and social activities.

KEANE, John Centre forward - find of the season (non-swimming variety). Socially a regular "keg king"!

KIRKWOOD, Jon The other half of the "Wood" brothers; swimming forward acquired from Roseville; 'Oscar' will go to any extreme for the Club - even the shirt off his back!

De LEON, John Reaped the benefits of two years grade experience now a Combined High School representative.

MILLS, Ken Veteran campaigner; rugged hack; dependent upon cigarettes between quarters (sometimes not even bothering to leave the water). Always on the social scene.

McCARTHY, Bill Public relations player of water polo; still finds time during games to dictate letters to his secretary from the water. "Sonny" is another strong social man and ardent trip supporter.

McGRATH, Vic State Captain-Coach last season; known for his antipathy to drink; also fishes with a Jaguar.

NORTHCOTT, Wal Showed promise in his first season with the Club.

OWENS, Barry Randwick Rugby player; a Club stalwart and strong player; part of the team of "Baz & Maz".

PARSONS, Bill In his first season with the Club was selected as a C.H.S. representative; spends his spare time beachcombing.

POWER, John Schoolboy gain who shows outstanding potential as a utility player; acquitted himself well in his initial season in grade water polo.

SARKIES, Don Seasoned state goalkeeper; active Club official and a keen golfer. Now, would the real Don Sarkies please stand up!

SEE, Dick	One of our original first graders who has held his position right through. Our popular family chemist — "Bones" is widely known for drawing up the "Dick See Rules of Sport".
SEE, Bob	Carrying on the See tradition — Well known on the surfie scene.
SOLOMONS, John	"The Mayor of Tokyo" ; showed marked improvement in his second season with the Club; always prominent on country trips and is always in attendance at all social events.
THORNETT, John	Club Captain; our strongest centre forward; an inspiration to the first grade; also the Club champion firewood gatherer.
THOMAS, Dave	Another player to show improvement this season; Dave is reported not to have missed a social event during the season — ours — or anybody else's.
VADAS, Bert	Club President and Coach; originator of Bronte's style of play and also Of the "American Coffee Safe Driving Award".
VADAS, Robbie	Club Registrar and representative on the NSWAWPA Executive. Usually a center back or half; always a reliable player at any time.
WARDROP, John	Strong swimmer and rapidly improving player. When on a country trip "minuteman" never fails to obtain a receipt for his "purchase".

* * * * * * * * * *

FEELING TIRED AND LISTLESS AFTER THAT HARD GAME?
Well, believe me it's high time for a cup of COFFEE….and man, - - -
when I say coffee I mean the real McCoy… you know - - the bean type.
It's a real drink - puts blood into your bloodstream …. And all that jazz
Seeing you sold on coffee.
Now I'll tell you where to get it!
THE AMERICAN COFFEE BAR
SITUATED AT...... 36 DARLINGHURST ROAD, KINGS X
REMEMBER.…FOR YOUR FRESHLY GROUND COFFEE
DON"T FORGET - RING THE KING - - - BERT VADAS on 35-5780
ALL FAMOUS BLENDS AND QUALITIES AVAILABLE.

* * * * * * * * * *

A POINT TO REMEMBER
ANYONE CAN BE A GOOD VICTOR
BUT ONLY A SPORTSMAN CAN BE A GOOD LOSER

DON'T WORRY
   If by chance your name doesn't appear in this year book — just remember that next year's will be bigger and better and already with this season only half-way through — there is enough interesting information on each member to fill a volume of the Encyclopedia Brittanica!

* * * * * * * * * *

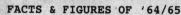

FACTS & FIGURES OF '64/65

Listed below in alphabetical order you will find each player's figures. Goalkeepers are itimised also.

NAME	GAMES PLAYED	GOALS	QUARTERS	SENT OUT
AMER, John	9	nil	21	nil
ANDERSON, Alan	14	3	40	3
ASHLEY, Kevin	10	6	27	nil
BULLOCK, Dave	28	2-32 against	103	nil
CAWOOD, Gary	19	13	50	nil
CLARK, Lunk	19	7	62	4
COULSON, Greg(g)	7	8-3 against	22	nil
FLESCH, Rolly	16	11	64	2
FOLDEN, Eric	21	6	65	2
FOLDEN, Peter	28	23	83	nil
FOLDEN, Tommy	20	14	82	2
GAHAGAN, John	30	43	90	1
HICKMAN, Chris	10	6	37	nil
HILLIER, Bob(g)	14	20 against	45	nil
KEANE, Jack	10	9	37	1
KIRKWOOD, Jon "0"	18	4	54	nil
DeLEON, John	13	1	42	nil
McCARTHY, Bill(g)	15	7-12 against	53	nil
McGRATH, Vic	17	19	68	4
MILLS, Ken	21	7	76	1
NORTHCOTT, Wally	5	2	17	nil
OWENS, Barry	9	1	25	nil
PARSONS, Bill	12	4	31	1
POWER, John(g)	12	2-2 against	45	1
SARKIES, Don(g)	23	71 against	92	nil
SEE, Dick	20	6	80	1
SEE, Bob	10	5	32	nil
SOLOMONS, John	15	nil	39	nil
THOMAS, Dave(g)	15	2-2	53	nil
THORNETT, John	21	44	80	4
VADAS, Robbie	27	5	81	1
WARDROP, John(g)	14	7-2 against	44	1

SOCIAL ACTIVITIES

Well it is my pleasure to tell you that the Social Committee is really in full swing with its Social turns. The first function was a Barbecue held at Bronte Baths in March which proved a big success both socially and financially.

Then our next evening was a film night at the Bronte Splasher Clubrooms in April which for all who attended proved quite enjoyable. The next promotion was in the form of a Cabaret-Dance at the Bronte Surf Club in early May which proved another unqulified success. Between these two functions we squeezed in our Annual Golf Day on Good Friday which for many reasons received a poor rollup - but still all who attended had a great day... mostly in the rough!

On the 27th May the Social Committee ventured into a new field arranging a Squash exhibition and Social Evening at the Bondi Waverley Squash Club who kindly allowed the use of their amenities to aid our fund raising campaign. In all there were 80 people in attendance and if the other 79 had as good as night as I did Boy, What a night!

Don't worry there's more to come - much more and as usual your will be notified in advance by letter of the date and location of the function. If you would like lee to bring your friends along remember - Your friends are our friends, so the more the merrier.. See you at the next turn!

Lunk...

* * * * * * * * * *

HEARD THAT TUNE ?
SAVE FOR TOMORROW TODAY at BANK E.S.& A.
Well, if you're single and have a grand to spare; Or
If you're like the rest of us with only 10 bob to spare;
You'll be amazed the way it GROWS in the E.S. & A. BANK... Remember
For the personal touch - Ring Bill McCarthy (Public Relations)
The Phone No. 28 2573.

* * * * * * * * * *

ACKNOWLEDGEMENTS

The Social Committee would like to thank the following people, Clubs and organizations for the way they have helped the Bronte Water Polo Club in their various capacities.

The Bronte Splashers Swimming Club; the Lessee of Bronte Baths - Mr. Andy Cleland and his wife Nora; the Bronte Surf Lifesaving Club; Mr. and Mrs. J. Ellison; Brian Ellison; Miss Ann Driver; Miss Sandra Driver; Mrs. Cawood; Mrs. Hillier; the Randwick Rugby Club; Miss Jan Ryan; Mr. and Mrs Ron King; Mr. Gary Quinlan; Mrs. Joan McCarthy; the Bondi-Waverley Squash Club; Miss Valda Page; Lorna and all the boys at the E.S .&.A! and last but not least... our accomplished barman... Sid Lockwood!

* * * * * * * * * *

HEADLINES OF LUNK'S NOTICES - '64/65

WATCH OUT FOR MINUTEMAN: Heralding John Wardrop's 6 goal scoring spree.
MOST VERSATILE PLAYER: Who in one night could not put a foot right whilst refereeing and then could not put a foot wrong as a player in the next game, "Oscar Wood".
MOST RELIEVED MEMBER: Tommy Folden, after hearing of his Leaving Certificate Pass.
QUESTION OF THE WEEK: Headline from Sydney newspaper "Solomons now available". We all know John is available so why put it on the sport's page of the paper?
OSCAR OF THE YEAR: John (Three Cheers Boys!) Amer, for leading the 3 "B" Team to a win over "Australia's Best", The Army.

The baths on the Darling Point side of Rushcutters Bay were erected in 1902, and were under the private ownership of Duncan MacLennan from the early 1950's until they were closed down in 1976. From left to right can be seen the Boatshed, from where Dunc leased small boats, the two storey residence (where Dunc & Gloria slept on the main level while their four daughters shared the two upstairs bedrooms); the main entrance and shop, which sold hot food. In the early days, the sectioned pool to the right was known as the Ladies Baths, which featured individual change cubicles. Photo - Belinda MacLennan.

Chapter 6
THE RESURGENCE
(1967 - 1971)

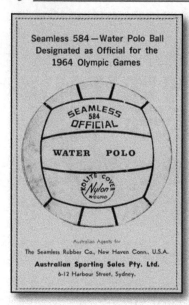

Seamless 584 — Water Polo Ball
Designated as Official for the
1964 Olympic Games

SEAMLESS
584
OFFICIAL

WATER POLO

KOLITE COVER
Nylon
WOUND

Australian Agents for
The Seamless Rubber Co., New Haven Conn., U.S.A.
Australian Sporting Sales Pty. Ltd.
6-12 Harbour Street, Sydney.

By the beginning of the 1966/67 season Bronte had maintained their respected standing as one of Sydney's top water polo clubs, having gained no less than 30 State representative caps since their inception in 1952. Despite changes in personnel, every single grade had qualified for the play-off series over each of the previous four seasons, and by this time they had regained the NSWAWPA Club Championship. However, the club had only captured one 2nd Grade premiership since 1962, and were looking for a resurgence.

1966-67

1966/67 NSWAWPA OFFICIALS: Dr. H.K. Porter (Patron); H.J. Bund (President); G. R. Woods (Past President); R. Traynor (Chairman); J. McFarlane (Registrar); R.N. Steer (Secretary); L. Papps (Asst. Secretary); **R. Vadas (Comp. Secretary)**; O. Charles (Treasurer).

The new season got underway after the 38th NSWAWPA Annual General Meeting. The major sponsors for the Association were again W.D. & H.O. Wills for the metropolitan trophies, Speedo Knitting Mills for the Pre-Season competition and the Shell Company of Australia for the Junior Championships.

By this time the Americans had developed a new lightweight rubber water-proof ball, which revolutionised the sport and was adopted internationally in the mid-1960's. The new ball was adapted as the official NSWAWPA game ball and replaced the old leather balls.

The Baths & Clubs

The Competition Committee capably organised the competitions which were conducted in three divisions with the first grade playing three rounds, and two each for the lower grades.

Almost 550 games were played throughout the season at Ashfield, Balmain, Drummoyne, Gunnamatta Bay, Manly, Roseville and the recent new pool at Parramatta.

In regard to new clubs, Illawarra affiliated for the first time and Gymea Bay re-affiliated after a break. Unfortunately Maroubra SLSC, Sans Souci and Roseville lapsed. The number of entries received for the men's metropolitan competitions climbed to a record 54 teams from 24 clubs, with player registrations reaching 1030.

"I have spent many years in QLD after leaving Bronte, but you can never take Bronte out of the boy. I have told many tales, but one that sticks to mind is of a brash young teenager who I saw score a fantastic goal with an overhead scissor kick at Rushy, and that was Rolly Flesch...never saw anyone do it again."

Terry 'Lunk' Clark, Jan, 2019

"I joined Bronte in 1967, when I was 16, after playing a couple of years for Randwick. My stepfather, Jack Campbell, had played for Bronte for a number of years and had won 1st Grade premierships with them."

Phil Bower, 29 Jan 2019

The pre-season competition, inaugurated the previous year was again conducted and won by Bondi 'A' from Drummoyne. Once the 1st Grade competition got rolling, it quickly became apparent that there wasn't too much difference between the top five clubs in Balmain, Bondi, Bronte, Drummoyne and Universities.[1]

Representatives in NSW Teams

Despite Balmain taking out the last three premierships, the lion share of players for the State team was furnished by the Universities club. While Don Sarkies lost his place to Peter Waterman (Bondi), Rolly Flesch and Peter Folden from Bronte played themselves into the team, with Max May also gaining a new cap for Balmain. But it seemed there was nothing NSW could do to stem the Victorian onslaught, and they powered on to take their 11th National title in Adelaide.

The Premierships

In the play-offs, Drummoyne qualified for the 1st Grade finals series for the first time in many years, but was unluckily defeated by Bondi (7~5) in the minor semi, while Universities disposed of Balmain (5~4) in the major semi-final. Balmain then defeated Bondi (8~4) to set up a re-match against the Universities Club in the competition decider. All premiership finals were once again played at the home of NSWAWPA, the renamed 'Dawn Fraser Swimming Pool' at Balmain.

Balmain had lost six games on the season against Universities' three, and were once again underdogs, but with great determination and passion, they swept Universities aside (6~3) to claim their fourth 1st Grade premiership in a row.

Bronte were successful in the 2nd Grade

1966/67 Season Statistics
N.S.W.A.W.P.A.

Clubs in the Mens Water Polo Competitions.

Clubs	1¹	1²	1³	2²	3N	3S	3W	Total
Balmain	•	•	•		•	•		5
Balmoral				•				1
Bondi	•	•	•					3
Bronte	•	•	•					3
Canterbury							•	1
Collaroy	•	•	•					3
Como						•		1
Drummoyne	•	•	•					3
Eastwood/Epping				•	•			2
Illawarra				•		•		2
Judean				•	•			2
Lane Cove			2					2
Leichhardt						•		1
Liverpool				•		•		2
Maroubra Seals				•				1
Nth Palm Beach						•		1
Nth Sydney			2					2
Northbridge				•				1
Parramatta	•	•	•			2		5
Penrith						•		1
Randwick Rugby						•		1
St. George	•	•	•					3
Universities	•	•	•	•				4
Western Suburbs			2		•	•		4
	8	8	8	8	7	7	8	54

Results of the Mens Water Polo Competitions.

Grade	Premier		Runner-Up
1st	Bondi A		Pre-Season Comp.
1st	Balmain~6	d.	3~Universities
2nd	Bronte~5	d.	0~Western Suburbs B
3rd	Balmain A~3	d.	1~Balmoral
Club Champions			BALMAIN
D1²ⁿᵈ	Bronte~5	d.	2~Universities
D2²ⁿᵈ	Western Suburbs B~6	d.	5~Maroubra Seals
D1³ʳᵈ	Balmain A~8	d.	3~Bronte
D3ᴺᵗʰ	Balmoral~6	d.	4~Lane Cove A
D3ˢᵗʰ	Balmain B~5	d.	2~Randwick
D3ᵂˢᵗ	Canterbury~6	d.	5~Penrith

"Dick and Ken Thornett had retired by the time I started playing, but legends like Dick See, Vic McGrath and Don Sarkies we're all still playing. Peter Folden, Rolly Flesch and Bill Parsons were the younger, up and coming players... while Tom Folden was then playing for Bondi."

Phil Bower, 29 Jan 2019

"Bronte had many good players in the 60's and the 70's, but their golden period was in the late 1950's and early 60's, when the Thornett brothers made their contribution to the club and its four consecutive premierships."

Peter Montgomery, July 2020

NEW SOUTH WALES TEAM
1967 - Co-runners-up - National Championships - Adelaide

Back row (from left): **Peter Folden (Bronte)**, **Roley Flesch (Bronte)**, Ron De Groot (Parramatta), Nick Barnes (c, Universities), Warwick Lamb (Universities), John Harrison (g, Universities). Front row: Max May (Balmain), David Woods (vc, Balmain), Alex Kosegi (Coach, Bondi), Bert Trevenar (Manager), Brian Hamill (Drummoyne), Bill Phillips (Universities), Peter Waterman (g, Bondi). Photo - Roley Flesch.

AMATEUR SWIMMING UNION OF AUSTRALIA

AUSTRALIAN WATER POLO CHAMPIONSHIP

HENLEY OLYMPIC POOL

FEBRUARY 15th to 25th, 1967

SESSIONS NIGHT 15, 18, 19, 20, 21
DAY 16, 17, 23, 24, 25

TICKETS AVAILABLE — JOHN MARTIN'S — ALLAN'S

THE NATIONAL WATER POLO CHAMPIONSHIP

HENLEY POOL ADELAIDE

PROGRAMME 20c 15th FEBRUARY TO 25th FEBRUARY

TOP: Signed poster advertising the 1967 Australian Water Polo Championships in Adelaide, signed by many representatives from the different States. ABOVE (Left): The NSW Team relaxes prior to a match at the 1967 Adelaide National Water Polo Championships. (Right): Official Program for the 1967 National Championships.

competition, being undefeated on the season. Balmain A also took out the 3rd Grade premiership in an undefeated display, as well as the Club Championship.

BRONTE WATER POLO - TASMANIAN REPORT.

by Sonny.

OVERSEAS PLAYERS RETURN HOME.

Last Sunday afternoon our team of sixteen seasoned "internationals" jetted into 105 degree Mascot Airport from cool, cool Hobart. Most were very weary but all were delighted to see the group of relatives and friends there to meet them.

The tour was a most enjoyable one, during which the team had good success in its matches and developed a wonderful "tour spirit" which will never be forgotten by the players. This spirit which developed through training and games, carried on at all social occasions and sight seeing trips.

Not enough good things can be said about the local water polo people in Hobart. The officials, players and supporters treated our boys as their own which made the tour a success. The locals keenly contested each match and organised barbecues and parties so we could meet with them socially afterwards.

Hotel life was made very pleasant by licensee, Milton Searle, who turned out to be a former Bondi water polo - surf club man of the Mills era. Dick See kept all on their toes by organis -ing darts, chinese checkers, draughts tournaments for the team in their leisure hours at the hotel, played of course, under "Dick See Rules".

TASSIE SAYINGS.

Apart from all noticing the pleasant Tassie accent, several sayings became prominent on the tour for various reasons. Some of these are:-

Cobber	More toast Ruth
Ring a Cab	Roundabouts?
Let's walk across the Bridge	The Greasy Spoon
Training is at Clarence not	Easy .... Easy
How many for lunch?	Dawn / Dawn /
"In 1830" (Port Arthur Guide)	Play it cool
Rickety Split	Morgo
No curfews	Let's play the girls
24 knock on the door	Intellectual dishonesty
Irving Hargraves (hero of the tour)	

TOUR RECORD

The most important feature of the tour was the team's excellent match record. Success in this regard was due mainly to Vic McGrath's leadership and coaching with an end result of eight games played - seven wins and a draw. Major contributing factor to the team's wins was a two hour training session each morning at Clarence Pool under Vic's coaching. He made these sessions both strenuous and interesting and all players showed good improvement in the week.

SUNDAY, JAN. 15   Vs   TASMANIAN STATE SQUAD

In what was virtually a trial match we used all sixteen players in a six quarter game. The freshwater troubled most of our boys and several were found at the bottom after the match. Jack Gahagan was the first scorer of the tour and we managed to finish a couple of goals in front. After this match the Tasmanian State Team was selected.
WON 5 - 3 (Messider 2, McGrath 2, and Gahagan)

MONDAY, JAN. 16   Vs   CLARENCE

We saw our main centre forwards, Messider and Cawood, begin to adjust their style to suit local interpretations which were found to be very severe on centre-forwards throughout the tour. Clarence were a young side, excepting their coach, Dave Salter, who received no quarter from our forwards, and they lacked the experience to cope with our team.
WON 5 - 0 (Messider 3, Cawood 2)

TUESDAY, JAN. 17   Vs   UNIVERSITY

McCarthy at centre-forward led our younger players in the first half, scoring a fine left-hander. Here we saw distinct improvement from Vadas, Morgo, Kritzler, Hofbauer, and both Hickmans. Most were replaced in the second half and McGrath and Cawood brought our score up to six goals. Good effort in this match from Uni. skipper and State player, Peter Briscoe.
WON 6 - 3 (McCarthy 2, Cawood 2, McGrath 2)

In only its second year, the Junior Competition, was proving to be a phenomenal success. Some 17 teams competed across two divisions. The Central Division consisted of teams from Balmain, Bondi, Canterbury, Eastern Suburbs Police Boys, South Sydney Police Boys, Sydney High School A and B and Western Suburbs. The St. George Division consisted of teams from Cronulla A and B, Illawarra, Carss Park, Como, Gymea, North Cronulla, Sylvania Heights and North Ramsgate. The reigning premiers Cronulla, eventually defeated Balmain in a keenly contested final (7~5). The enthusiasm and commitment of these talented junior players was inspiring.[1]

Bronte AWPC

Although Bronte had only won a 2nd Grade premiership since their triple crown in 1962, the club remained a potent force in the Sydney competition and this was apparent in their winning of the NSWAWPA Club Championship during the 1965/66 season.

This season 3rd Grade finished in second place, but were beaten by Balmain A (3~8) in the grand-final. However, 2nd Grade finished on top of the ladder, and beat Universities in the grand-fnal (5~2) to cap off an undefeated season. Despite having the best defensive record in the competition, the 1st Grade slumped to fifth place, which was the first time in ten years that they had missed the play-offs. This was a concerning development, especially when combined with the lack of juniors coming into the club.

Tasmanian Tour

By this time Bronte Water Polo Club had racked up a few visits to the country areas, partly to build club morale, but also to help develop the growth of water polo in the NSW districts. But a plan was hatched at the beginning of the 1966/67 season to send a club squad to Tasmania for a full week, which was quite an large expansion on the usual weekend car trips to country towns.

The project was taken on by Bill 'Sonny' McCarthy, who diligently arranged all the relevant details from travel, accommodation, meals and touring,

WEDNESDAY, JAN. 18   Vs   TASMANIA

The State Team became a little over-confident early and we were able to score from breaks from the halfway more than in previous matches. With McGrath, See and Gahagan active halves and swimming too strongly for the locals, the match was always in our grasp. McGrath more than matched his opposite, Tassie captain -coach, Ross Leighton, scoring four goals. Power had his best match.

       WON 5 - 3   (McGrath 4 & Messider)

THURSDAY, JAN. 19   Vs   SANDY BAY

Sandy Bay, the top club side, fielded five State players in their team and were expected to provide tough opposition. Weakened early by playing some younger players with their State reps. they allowed us to shoot to a big lead by half time, and we didn't let up. Dick See, one of the best players of the tour, had a great match, being rewarded with a good goal. All our boys played well, in particular backs Wills and McCarthy, and our fantastic goalies, Ellison and Bullock. Messider and McGrath kept up their averages.

       WON 9 - 2 (McGrath 4, Messider 4 & See)

               Vs   GLENORCHY

Half an hour after the conclusion of the above match and about eight miles away we met Hobart's No. 2 club side, Glenorchy, led by Ross Leighton. They proved a stronger combination than Sandy Bay and with most of our senior players playing only a quarter or so, it was left to the younger brigade to win what was one of the best matches of the tour. Wills was man-of-the-match, scoring three goals from centre-forward, and despite comments from Messider and See, his efforts were sheer skill. Hofbauer was an excellent swimming forward and Morgo was great. Bullock was almost invincible and Ross Leighton was subdued by the Octopus (Curly Kritzler). Best game of the tour from the Hickmans with Chris scoring a clever lob.

       WON 5 - 2   (Wills 3, C. Hickman & McGrath)

FRIDAY, JAN. 20   Vs   HOBART   (TAS. STATE TEAM)

An outstanding water polo match of high Sydney First Grade level provided the large crowd with plenty of excitement. All players in both teams showed big improvement on their earlier clashes and the goalkeepers were in magnificent form. Bullock and then Ellison played "shut the gate" games making seven l brilliant saves. They only slightly overshadowed the State goalie, Ian Martin, who is probably Tasmania's most valuable player.

The difference between the teams was our ability to score goals under pressure and the larger size of our team. Turning point in the game was an Ellison save followed by quick pass to centre-forward Messider who with a huge break scored his third goal.

       WON 3 - 0   (Messider 3)

Comment should be made here re the excellent presentation of this match and the facilities at Clarence Pool. Our match was played midway through the Hobart competition roster games which were conducted in a highly efficient manner. As for Clarence Pool, our State reps. and club players agreed that it is the best pool available for water polo in Australia. We did all our training and played all matches, except the Glenorchy game, at Clarence where the pool manager, Ray Vare, was tremendously helpful at all times.

SATURDAY, JAN. 21 ' Vs   TASMANIA

In the final match of the tour the Tasmanian team led in clever fashion by Ross Leighton were all over us in the first half to lead three nil. Their backs and goalie gave nothing away and it was only when our team threw off their lethargy that we were able to catch up and salvage a lucky draw. Full marks to the Tassie boys, Phil Bird, Bruce Wilkinson, Peter Briscoe, Gunther Schmafles, Ian Martin, John Wilkinson and the rest for their fine displays in this match and proceeding matches. Comment of the match - "Mills you idiot .... lovely goal Ken".

       DRAW 3 - 3 (Messider 2 & Mills)

TASMANIAN LADIES TEAM

As far as some of our younger players were concerned, their most enjoyable games were the two matches against the Tasmanian State girl representatives. Both games were recorded as draws and provided plenty of entertainment for both teams. With Danny, Chris and Morgo as attacking forwards and Rob, Mick and Curly as grappling backs they and the girls had the time of their lives. Special thanks to all the girls for their good sportsmanship and interest, in particular to our favourites, the famous team of Jan & Jan.

FAREWELL

We were farewelled by members of the various men's and ladies' clubs at a cabaret at the Ingomar Hotel on Saturday night. The evening was great fun and our appreciation cannot be expressed in words. Several organised and private parties followed to put a suitable end to the tour.

1966/67 NSWAWPA RESULTS

1966-67 Pre-Season Competition
For
Speedo Perpetual Trophy
F. Lamb Memorial Trophy

1st Division

Bondi 'A'	25 points	First
Drummoyne	25 points	Second
Bronte 'A'	20 points	Third
Balmain 'A'	19 points	Fourth

Winners—Bondi 'A'

Division I, 1st Grade

	Played	W.	D.	L.	Forf. or Dis.	Goals For	Against	Pts.	Pos.
Universities	21	17	1	3	—	116	62	56	1
Balmain	21	14	2	5	—	98	54	51	2
Bondi	21	13	3	5	—	103	48	50	3
Drummoyne	21	12	4	5	—	83	62	49	4
Bronte	21	11	3	7	—	69	44	46	5
St. George	21	2	4	15	—	42	103	29	6
Collaroy	21	2	4	14	1	53	108	28	7
Parramatta	21	2	1	17	1	33	117	25	8

1st Semi-final: Bondi 7 def. Drummoyne 5.
2nd Semi-final: Universities 5 def. Balmain 4.
Final: Balmain 8 def. Bondi 4.
Grand Final: Balmain 6 def. Universities 3.

1st GRADE METROPOLITAN PREMIERS 1966-67—BALMAIN

Division 1, 2nd Grade

	Played	W.	D.	L.	Forf. or Dis.	Goals For	Against	Pts.	Pos.
Bronte	14	12	2	—	—	62	20	40	1
Drummoyne	14	8	2	4	—	48	17	32	2
Balmain	14	8	2	4	—	53	28	32	3
Universities	14	7	3	3	1	57	36	30	4
St. George	14	6	4	4	—	48	33	30	5
Bondi	14	3	2	9	—	42	51	22	6
Parramatta	14	1	1	8	2	27	72	18	7
Collaroy	14	1	—	12	1	12	76	15	8

1st Semi-final: Universities 2 def. Balmain 1.
2nd Semi-final: Bronte 5 def. Drummoyne 3.
Final: Universities 6 def. Drummoyne 4.
Grand Final: Bronte 5 def. Universities 2.

1st Division Premiers—Bronte

2nd Division Premiers—Western Suburbs "B"
Interdivisional Play-off: Bronte 5 def. Western Suburbs 'B' 0.

2nd GRADE METROPOLITAN PREMIERS 1966-67—BRONTE

Division 1, 3rd Grade

	Played	W.	D.	L.	Forf. or Dis.	Goals For	Against	Pts.	Pos.
Balmain 'A'	14	14	—	—	—	71	15	42	1
Bronte	14	7	3	4	—	38	25	31	2
St. George	14	6	5	3	—	39	32	31	3
Bondi	14	8	1	4	—	54	28	30	4
Parramatta 'A'	14	6	2	6	—	34	36	28	5
Drummoyne	14	5	2	7	—	27	33	26	6
Universities	14	3	—	9	2	20	55	18	7
Collaroy	14	—	1	11	2	10	67	13	8

1st Semi-final: St. George 5 def. Bondi 3.
2nd Semi-final: Balmain 'A' 5 def. Bronte 2.
Final: Bronte 8 def. St. George 4.
Grand Final: Balmain 'A' 8 def. Bronte 3.

1st Division Premiers—Balmain "A"

"One of the highlights of my time at Bronte was winning the 3rd Grade premiership in 1968, the other was our trip to Tasmania in January 1967. This tour was organised in my first season with the club and having never been interstate before, it was a real adventure for me. It was also an opportunity to play and mix socially with the more experienced players, including some Bronte legends like Vic McGrath, Dick See and Ken Mills. We played some difficult Tassie club sides and also the Tasmanian State team, but we remained undefeated in all matches. Vic McGrath gave us younger players some water time in most matches and I learnt so much from playing and watching the game. The younger brigade also had fun playing twice against a Tassie girls' team. I also remember the wonderful hospitality of the Tasmanian water polo fraternity."

Dennis Morgan, Nov 2020

as well as the competition schedule.

The trip was arranged for mid-January 1967 when many were still on their summer holidays. Sonny and coach Vic McGrath were able to put together a formidable squad, which included... Ken Mills, Dick See, Peter Messider, Vic McGrath, John Gahagan, Gary Cawood, Dave Bullock (g), Robbie Vadas, Dennis Morgan, Brian Ellison (g), Steve Kritzler, Danny Hofbauer and both Michael and Chris Hickman... as well as Billy himself.

Basing themselves in Hobart, the Bronte boys trained every morning at the Clarence Pool under the guidance of Vic McGrath, who made the sessions both strenuous and interesting.

But the most impressive feature of the tour was their match record. Bronte managed to play undefeated throughout their eight matches, the only blemish being a 3~3 draw against the Tasmanian State team on the final day of the tour. Their success was again mainly due to Vic McGrath's leadership and coaching abilities, and all in all the tour was an outstanding success.

1967-68

1967/68 NSWAWPA OFFICIALS: Dr. H.K. Porter (Patron); H.J. Bund (President); G.R. Woods (Past President); R. Traynor (Chairman); J.W. McFarlane (Registrar); D.J. Cohen (Secretary); L. Papps (Asst. Secretary); **R. Vadas (Comp. Secretary)**; O.N. Begg (Treasurer).

The new season got underway after the 39th NSWAWPA Annual General Meeting, which was held at the usual venue in the Aquatic Club, Cnr. Riley and Cathedral Sts., East Sydney.

The NSWAWPA promoted a 'new look' for the game during the 1967/68 season and succeeded across a number of spheres. The competitions for the Ladies and Country divisions were expanding and new developments were taking place at the representative level. The number of entries received for the men's metropolitan competitions climbed to 59 teams from 26 clubs.

The Pre-Season competition was again well contested by most of the conventional clubs and won this season by Balmain. As the traditional summer premierships got underway, the first division matches were switched to Wednesday nights to assist the increased workload on the referees.

After only four years of metropolitan competition, the Ladies inaugurated a representative Interstate series with the Victorians and for the first time, a NSW Colts team was formed and also competed against Victoria. Furthermore, visits by Czechoslovakian club team 'Kosice' in January and the Canterbury Provincial team from New Zealand were additional highlights of this very successful season.

In terms of publicity, water polo received more than its usual allocation with monthly full-page articles in Speedo's "International Swimmer" and newsprint coverage for the Olympic Games fiasco *(see page 184)* as well as the Kosice tour. On the social scene, a Sydney Harbour Cruise and a Christmas Party was held.

During the season, the Referees Board conducted a number of examinations. Mr. Frank Jordan, ex-Olympian and PE Lecturer of the Sydney Teacher's College, requested that the Referee's Board examine student teachers and teachers in the rules of Water

▼ BELOW: Rare cartoon showing how to block with hands up water polo. BOTTOM: Bronte players Fred Mayer (Bondi) and Tom Folden jumping for the ball in training (Tharunka, 1st Oct 1968, p15).

1967/68 Season Statistics
N.S.W.A.W.P.A.

Clubs in the Mens Water Polo Competitions.

Clubs	1^1	1^2	1^3	2^1	2^2	3^N	3^S	3^W	Total
Balmain	●	●	●	●	●				5
Balmoral				●					1
Bondi	●	●	●				●		4
Bronte	●	●	●				●		4
Canterbury				●	●				2
Collaroy	●	●	●						3
Drummoyne	●	●	●						3
Eastwood/Epping				●	●				2
East Sub Police BC							●		1
East Sub Surfers							●		1
Glebe Police BC							●		1
Illawarra				●	●				2
Judean				●	●				2
Lane Cove				●	●				2
Liverpool							2		2
Maroubra								●	1
Nth Palm Beach					●				1
Nth Sydney						2			2
Northbridge						2			2
Parramatta	●	●	●						3
P'matta Memorial							2		2
Penrith							2		2
St. George	●	●	●				●		4
Sydney University							●		1
Universities	●	●	●						3
Western Suburbs			2	●					3
	8	8	8	8	7	6	8	6	59

Results of the Mens Water Polo Competitions.

Grade	Premier		Runner-Up
1st	Balmain		Pre-Season Comp.
1st	Universities~3	d.	2~Bronte
2nd	Bronte~2	d.	1~Balmain
3rd	Bronte~3	d.	2~Balmain
	Club Champions		BALMAIN
D2 1st	Balmain~1	d.	0~Western Suburbs A
D2 2nd	Balmain~1	d.	0~Illawarra
D3 Playoff	Maroubra Seals~5	d.	1~Penrith
D3 Nth	Balmoral~5	d.	4~Northbridge A
D3 Sth	Maroubra Seals~2	d.	0~St. George
D3 Wst	Penrith~6	d.	4~P'matta Memorial

Polo. It was most appropriate that teachers be able to referee as, after all, the NSW High Schools were a primary nursery for the sport. With the assistance of Gordon Woods, a number of other examinations for referees were held to alleviate the problem. The Referee's Board also proposed the idea that each club be obliged to nominate a non-playing referee for each team that was entered in the Association's competitions.[2]

The Baths & Clubs

Matches this season were played at Ashfield, Balmain, Drummoyne, Gunnamatta Bay, Manly, Parramatta and Roseville Baths. New clubs to the metropolitan competition were Eastern Suburbs Surfers, Glebe Police Boys, Parramatta Memorial and a student based Sydney University Club, which all affiliated for the first time. Leichhardt and Randwick Rugby Clubs lapsed, and due to the abandonment of the previously successful Junior Competition, the following Junior Clubs also failed to affiliate: Carss Park, Cronulla, Gymea Bay, North Cronulla, North Ramsgate, South Sydney Police Boys, Sydney BHS and Sylvania Heights. The number of entries received for the men's metropolitan competitions climbed to 59 teams from 26 clubs.

The Competition Committee proficiently organised the competitions, which as in past seasons were conducted across three divisions, although the large number of teams and organisation thereof, was becoming burdensome, particularly when compared to the Victorian and Western Australian competitions, which had approximately 30 teams. The number one problem for the NSW Association however, remained the lack of suitable referees.

Graham 'Cheetah' Robinson began his water polo in Canberra, but joined Bronte in 1968 after moving to Sydney. 'Robbo' began as a solid 2nd Grade player with a powerful shot, but was called up to Bronte's 1st Grade on numerous occasions, and finished his water polo with Northbridge.

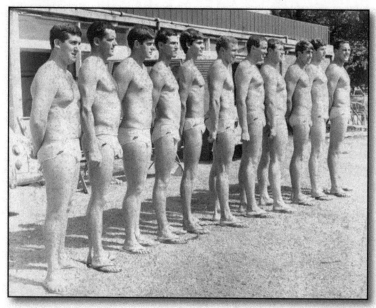

▲ *Photograph of the 1968 NSW Water Polo team in Melbourne, Victoria.*

WATER POLO

AUSTRALIAN CHAMPIONSHIPS
In Melbourne

NSW. 15 (W. Parsons 3, R. de Groot 2, P. Folden 2, R. Langford 2, D. Woods 2, N. Barnes, M. May, W. Phillips, A. McLaughlin) beat Tasmania 1 (Leighton). Western Australia 15 beat South Australia 0; Victoria 6 beat Queensland 1. Points: Victoria 14, W.A. 12, N.S.W. 10, Tasmania 4, Queensland 2, South Australia 0.

'One cannot let 1968/69 pass without reflecting upon the effort by water polo people in all States, towards the 1968 Olympic Team, which did not receive the opportunity to demonstrate the result of their preparation. Estimates of outlays by Water Polo bodies, the players and supporters towards the 1964 and 1968 Olympic Teams as well as the 1965 and 1967 European Tours amounted to over $60,000. To compete at the 1968 Mexico Games, players sacrificed income from work and some who were students even had to repeat University courses."

1968/69 NSWAWPA Annual Report

The Pre-Season competition was again contested and won this year by Balmain. As the summer competitions got underway, to assist the workload being placed on referees, the Division I matches matches were played on Tuesday nights and Division III matches on Thursday nights. The main organisational change was that the Inter-Divisional play offs were no longer held.

Representatives in NSW Teams

The 21st Australian Championships in Melbourne set the scene for a tight competition, with the added incentive of 11 Olympic berths up for grabs.

NSW turned their back on nine time State and national coach Alex Kosegi, and reverted to using a player/coach in David Woods (Balmain). Unfortunately Rolly Flesch was dropped again, but his place was filled by teammate Billy Parsons, who was shooting as good as anyone in Sydney. Peter Folden was also improving and worked himself into the top seven. Three other new caps were gained by Robert Langford (Bondi), Ian McLauchlain (Balmain) and Mick Withers (Balmain), the latter transferring from the Kew club with seven Victorian caps already under his belt.

But there was no stopping Victoria, who annexed yet another Australian Championship by defeating Western Australia in a play-off (6~5), to bring their total number of titles to 12, with NSW in third place.

The 1968 Olympic Team

The Australian Olympic team was selected after the National Championships, with only two Victorians included, while four were from Western Australia and incredibly five, from NSW, although one of those was the ex-Victorian goalkeeper, Micky Withers. The Aussies played one match in

NEW SOUTH WALES TEAM
1968 - 3rd Place - National Championships - Melbourne
Back row (from left): Nino Sydney (Asst/Manager, Bondi), Robert Langford (Bondi), **Bill Parsons (Bronte)**, Ron De Groot (Parramatta), Michael Withers (c & g, Balmain), Bill Phillips Jr. (Universities), David Woods (vc, Balmain). Front row: J. McFarlane (Manager), **Peter Folden (Bronte)**, Max May (Balmain), John Harrison (g, Universities), Ian McLauchlain (Drummoyne), Nick Barnes (Universities), Alex Kosegi (Coach, Bondi), Photo - Jack Hickson.

AUSTRALIAN WATER POLO TEAM
1968 - Mexico City Olympic Games
From left: Coach/Manager - Oscar Charles (Csuvic), Michael Withers (Balmain, NSW), Tom Hoad (Melville, WA), Graeme Samuel (Dolphins, WA), David Neesham (Melville, WA), John Harrison (g, Universities, NSW), Bill McAtee (Applecross, WA), Tony Harrison (Melbourne, VIC), Nick Barnes (Universities, NSW), Ian Mills (Richmond, VIC), Bill Phillips Jr. (Universities, NSW), David Woods (Balmain, NSW). Photo - Oscar Charles. NOTE: After qualifying, this team was blocked from competing at Mexico City by the Australian Olympic Committee. Photo - Oscar Charles.

"Playing for Bondi, I remember the Bronte players were as tough as teak. In that era... I recall Dick See threw the first bounce shot I ever saw in a grand-final at Drummoyne pool and as a young player, I was inspired... With one referee it was a violent sport in those days, especially against Balmain, but Bronte teams always played fair and to the rules."

Lindsay Cotterill, July 2020

[At age 15, Lindsay was the youngest player to ever score a 1st Grade goal for Bondi v Parramatta, in 1967.]

▼ *Chris 'Kipper' Simpson passing the ball for Canberra against Bronte, who visited the ACT in early 1968 (The Canberra Times, 10th Feb 1968). Kipper and Graham Robinson later joined Bronte when they relocated to Sydney.*

New Zealand and engaged in a European tour, losing only four of their 16 matches on tour.

Tragically, the Australian Olympic Committee denied their participation in the Mexico Olympic Games. However, the controversial circumstances of the Australian Water Polo team leading up to, but then not being permitted to play at the 1968 Mexico Olympic Games, is beyond the scope of this publication (see 'Water Warriors', p.206 by Tracy Rockwell).[3]

New South Wales Colts Team

An invitation was extended this season from the Victorian AWPA for the 1st Interstate Colts Series, which was played during the National Championships in Melbourne, with NSW winning both matches.

1968 NSWAWPA COLTS
Bruce Falson (c, St. George), Peter Montgomery (v/c, Universities), Peter Kerr (St. George), Graham Facey (St. George), W. Frost (St. George), K. McKinder (St. George), Ian McLauchlain (Drummoyne), Peter Smith (Drummoyne), Andrew Chapman (Drummoyne), Ted Baldock (Bondi), Harry Merkur (Judean), Bill Phillips Jr. (Coach/Manager, Universities).

The Premierships

Balmain finished top of the table in 1st, 2nd and 3rd Grades in Division I, and were favourites in all three. In the 1st Grade play-offs, Bronte defeated Bondi (6~4) in the minor semi-final, while Universities upset Balmain (7~5) in the major semi-final. With exciting players like Peter Folden, Rolly Flesch and Billy Parsons, Bronte used their distinctive style of play to soundly defeat Balmain (5~1) in the final, who took the game much too casually.

The premiership grand-finals were played at Drummoyne Olympic Pool on Saturday 16th March,

Water polo matches against top teams

The ACT water polo team, recently successful in the defence of the NSW Country water polo title, will have a busy weekend playing against State and Metropolitan teams.

Most matches will be played at the Canberra Olympic Pool.

On Saturday and Sunday, ACT will play a series of matches against Bronte.

Bronte will bring two men's teams and one ladies' team.

Well - known Bronte players include John Thornett and Vic McGrath.

These matches will be a prelude to a more important fixture on Monday evening when ACT will play the Queensland State team en route to contest the Australian State championships in Melbourne.

This match is probably

While the Queensland team is at full strength in preparation for the Australian championships, ACT is probably not the best representative team on paper.

The team is made up of available players from the Country championship team and the third place getter in the Country title, Canberra.

Nevertheless, ACT should not be outclassed by the Queensland team, because the available players are of good calibre.

One of the ACT's top players, J. Martin, is unfortunately unavailable. Also not apparently available is Chris Lord, the ACT goalie.

But I. Conding is at his best, a most difficult goalie to beat, and he may turn out to be the trump card against Queensland.

J. Hanrahan is another doubtful starter.

Other ACT and Canberra players in the weekend matches are G. Robinson, (captain), Hugh Crawley, Chris Simpson, P. Lores, M. McIntosh, N. de Mestre, A. Hawke and P. Charlton.

1968 - BRONTE AMATEUR WATER POLO CLUB

From left: Bert 'Momi' Vadas, Dick See, Brian Ellison, Eric Folden, ??? (obscured), John Thornett, Billy MacCarthy, Don Sarkies, Jon Kirkwood (back), Ross Sellick, Ernie Kritzler, Robbie Vadas (front), Peter O'Hara, Steve Kritzler, John Keane, Billy Parsons, ???, Denis Morgan, George Gulyas, Danny Hoffbauer. In front: Paul Sarkies, John Power, Oliver Barta, Phil Bower.

CZECH goal-keeper Kladek rises out of the water to parry a shot from a Sydney player in his team's water polo match at Drummoyne pool last week. See story left.

THE SPIRIT OF BRONTE.   67-68
By "Morgo".

Well, here we are again -- at the beginning of a brand new season and this one looks like being the Club's biggest and most successful ever.

The enthusiasm already shown by committee members and coaches has been tremendous and if all club members are willing to get behind them and support them, then "Bronte will win three Flags". (First grade coach Vic McGrath's quote.)

TEAMS.

This year the club has entered 5 teams in the Metropolitan Competition, with a Ladies' Team and a second 3rd grade team, (consisting of Bronte Surf Club Members) having been added.

LADIES TEAM.

A special welcome is extended to all members of the Ladies' Team. These girls have mostly been recruited from the Bondi Club and they are confident of winning the competition for their new club. I'm sure everyone is looking forward to their participation in all club activities.   Once again -- welcome girls!

TRAINING.

This year a new approach has been adopted with regards to training and selection of teams. Attendance at training will be essential for team selection and this policy will be maintained throughout the whole season.

A 1ST SQUAD has been selected comprising:-
D. Sarkies, J. Wardrop, V. McGrath, R. Sec, K. Mills, R. Flesch, P. Holden, W. Parsons, J. Power, P. O'Hara, G. Cawood, J. Gahagan.
This squad, under coach Vic McGrath, will train:-
Monday and Friday mornings, 6.00 a.m. at Rushcutter's Bay (Nov. start.)
Tuesday and Thursday evenings, 6.00 p.m.   "   ".
Unofficial training, Monday and Friday evenings, 6.00 p.m. -- Rushy.
The first grade team will be selected from this squad on the basis of both form and attendance at training.

▲ TOP: A combined Drummoyne/Bronte team played against the touring team from Kosice in Czechoslovakia in mid-January 1968. The team was Brian Hamill, Ian McLauchlain, Terry Chapman, Darren Bogg (Drummoyne), and Brian Ellison, Don Sarkies (g), Bill Parsons, Peter Folden, Rolly Flesch and Gary Cawood (Bronte).

before a record crowd of over one thousand people. Victory in the 1968 1st Grade premiership fell to Universities by the leanest of margins over a very talented Bronte club (3~2). It was the inaugural 1st Grade premiership for Universities in their fourth attempt at the title.

The Association was delighted to see that the crowd at the grand-final was greater than at any session of the NSW Swimming Championships and concluded that the sport of water polo was at long last 'starting to lift its head.' Balmain couldn't claim a trick in the other two Division I competitions, with Bronte victorious in taking out both the 2nd and 3rd Grade premierships. Balmain's overall consistency won them the Club Championship.[2]

▼ BELOW: Tom Folden prepares himself for a shot. BOTTOM: "The Spirit of Bronte" was a weekly Club Bulletin written by Dennis 'Morgo' Morgan (from 1967 to 1969), which communicated information and results to members.

UNIVERSITIES AWPC
1967/68 - NSWAWPA 1st Grade Premiers
Bill Phillips Jr, John Harrison (g), Nick Barnes, Peter Fox, Warwick Lamb, Peter Montgomery, Peter Ritchie, Dave Cohen, Jim Skekdah, Oscar Charles (Coach).

Bronte AWPC

Wrting under the pen name of 'Morgo', Dennis Morgan was elected Bronte Publicity Officer for the period spanning 1967 to 1969, and his weekly bulletins headed, "THE SPIRIT OF BRONTE" were keenly read by all club members.

Tamworth Trip (Nov 1967)
By "Morgo"

The trip to Tamworth proved highly successful both competitively and socially. I think we have at last found the ideal way to travel, and this is of course by coach. I'm sure everyone will agree that the trip up and back in the coach really made the weekend, and furthermore the coach was at our disposal the whole time up there, to take us wherever we wanted to go. Our coach-captain, I mean 'Coach-Captain Barry Atkinson' was very co-operative, and seemed to enjoy himself as much as we did ourselves.

The journey going started off rather quietly and it was only after "refreshments" had been served that things livened up. 'Screamin Al Davis and Mick 'Tokyo' Hickman provided most of the entertainment with their wide range of choruses, while card sharks Lorraine Grills and Ross Selleck cleaned

2ND SQUAD— club members not above and new members.

    Coach : George Glenn.

    Training:-

        Monday and Friday evenings, 6.00 p.m. at Nushcutter's Bay.

        Unofficial training, Tuesday and Thursday evenings, 6.00 p.m. - Rushy.

In addition everyone will train as usual on Saturday afternoons at 2.00p.m.

FEES.

    As everyone knows, the club, at the moment, has some outstanding commitments. It is thus imperative that club fees are paid promptly. So how about it fellas— pay either Don Sarkies or John Gahagan today or as soon as possible.

        Fees $3. $ 2 Students.

SOCIAL HAPPENINGS.

    The social committee this year comprises:-

    W. Parsons (Sec.), R. Dawson, C. Hickman, J. Keane, D. Morgan, J. Power, W. Riley, J. Solomons, and 2 members of the Girl's team.

    It can be seen that the committee contains much new blood and the enthusiasm already shown augurs well for a highly enjoyable social season. Many functions are at present in the making and details will be announced later.

HARBOUR CRUISE.

    The Water Polo Association is holding a Harbour Cruise on 21st. October. Ferry leaves Circular Quay Wharf 2 at 7.30. p.m.

        Band.   Food and refreshments available on board. $ 5 double. ALL WELCOME.

MATCHES.

    Sat. 14th Oct. vs St. George (Practice match) 2.00 p.m. at Rushy.

    Wed. 18th Oct. First pre-season match.

    Sat. 21st Oct. vs Drummoyne (Practice match) 2.00 p.m. at Rushy.

The first competition match is on Wednesday 15th Nov.

BRONTE WATER POLO.

C/- J. Gahagan,
144 Beach St.
COOGEE. 2034.
665-5812.

Dear Denis,

Below is a draw for '67/68.

DRAW 1967/1968....   3rd grade ... 7.00 p.m.
                            2nd   "   ... 7.35 p.m.
                            1st   "   ... 8.20 p.m.

Round		Day	Date		v			1st	2nd	3rd
Round 1	....Wednesday	15th November	....v....	Drummoyne	....Drummoyne		W.5-2	D.1-1.	W.5-0.
2	....	22nd November	....	Bondi	Balmain		L.8-9	W.	W.3-2
3	....	29th November		Collaroy	Manly		W.2-0	W.11-4	W.9-1
4	....	6th December		Parramatta	Parramatta		W.6-0	W.6-0	W.11-1.
5	....	13th December		St George	Gunnamatta Bay		L.3-4	W.6-1	W.7-3
6	....	20th December	.	Balmain	Balmain		L.3-4	W.1-0	L.2-5.
7	....	3rd January		Universities	Balmain		L.5-6	W.4-2	W.9-0
8	....	10th January		Drummoyne	Ashfield		W.11-4	W.10-2	W.8-0
9	....	17th January		Bondi	Ashfield		D.2-2	W.4-0	W.4-2
10	....	24th January		Collaroy	Balmain		W.8-2	D.3-3	W.4-1
11	....	31st January		Parramatta	Ashfield		W.4-2	W.4-5	W.5-3
12	....	7th February		St George	Ashfield		W.5-1.	D.5-5	W.4-2
13	....	14th February		Balmain	Balmain		W.6-5	L.6-1	D.3-3
14th		21st February		Universities	Ashfield		W.9-6	W.5-3	W.6-0
								Balm. W.1-0	
1st Semi-Final.....		28th February			Balmain				
							Bondi W.		Balm. L.2-4
2nd Semi-Final.....		6th March			Balmain		Balm. W.5-1		St.G. W.5-1
FINAL....SUNDAY 10th MARCH					Balmain		Uni. L.2-3	Balm. W.2-1	Balm. W.3-2
GRAND FINAL		16th MARCH .... SATURDAY.....			BRUMMOYNE				

1) All players should be in attendance no less than 15 minutes before the game, is
    due to start.
2) All players should report to their respective coaches.
              3rds to Bill McCarthy
              2nds to George Glenn
              1st to Vic McGrath or Bert Vadas.
3) First and Second Graders should try to be there to watch the 3rds in action.
    They appreciate the support and all the advice we can give them.
4) A Reminder about Training :- Although Saturday's training is well attended,
    the training of a Monday, 2 days before the game, is vital. An effort should
    be made to be in attendance at both.
5) All games will continue to be played on Wednesday Nights so these nights will
    of course be kept free.
6) The First Grade will on occasions be called on to play the State Team. Usually,
    these occasions will be on a Sunday Night and your secretary will endeavour
    to supply a timely warning.
7) A reminder about FEES - Pay John Kirkwood.

Best wishes for a successful season.

                                    Yours faithfully

                                    JACK GAHAGAN.

up at 'Slippery Sam'.

There was some confusion over accommodation when we arrived with not enough billets having been arranged for the girls, but one of the Tamworth boys came to the rescue and offered to put up five girls in his caravan (kind of him, wasn't

"On our first ever trip to Tamworth we had a great bus driver who did the right thing and didn't drink, but the whole weekend he looked after us. No stubbies in those days, but he let us have a 44 gallon drum in the back of the bus for our 8 hour trip up to Tamworth. We arrived half stonkered, and although we won, our first game on arrival was obviously far from ideal."

Bill Parsons, Oct, 2020

BRONTE AMATEUR WATER POLO CLUB.

C/- J. Gahagan,
144 Beach St.,
COOGEE. 2034.
665 5812.

The Election of Officers was held early in September and the results were as follows:

Patron :	A. Cleland.			
President :	B. Vadas.	Club Coach :	B. Vadas.	
Secretary :	J. Gahagan.	1st Grade :	V. McGrath.	
Treasurer :	D. Sarkies.	2nd " :	G. Glenn.	
Social Secretary:	. Parsons.	3rd " :	W. McCarthy.	

Congratulations to all those elected.

B. Vadas - Life Member - and Bronte's First. After about 14 years dedication to the game the highest honour the Club could bestow on one of its members was awarded to Bert at the Annual General Meeting. Much more could be said about Bert's work for the Club by others with longer membership than the writer. "Congratulations - Bert".

Finance - The Club begins this season with a considerable deficit which is mainly a carry-over from the Tasmanian tour in 1967. The Social Committee will be meeting on the 7th Oct. to discuss methods of reducing this.

One way in which we can all help is to pay our Fees promptly to EITHER Don Sarkies (Treasurer) or myself. Fees incidentally remain unchanged at $3.00 Seniors and Juniors $1.00

TRAINING : Official Training will commence on Sat. 7th Oct. 1967.

Some members have taken advantage of the excellent conditions at Canterbury Pool on Sunday afternoons where for 20c you can choose between 3 pools, all warm. Hot showers also are available.

GAMES : vs St. George on the 14th Oct. in all 3 Grades.

vs Drummoyne on the 21st Oct. in all 3 Grades.

Both dates are Saturdays and Games begin at 2.00 p.m.

Training has been reorganised this season with the aim being to bring all grades through to the Grand-Final instead of only the 3rds and 2nds. A brief outline appears below.

Saturday afternoons as usual.

1ST SQUAD TRAINS   Monday and Friday morning 6.00 a.m. (November start)
Coach V. McGrath.   Tuesday and Thursday afternoon 6 p.m.
              Unofficial training Mon. and Fri.

2ND SQUAD
Coach G. Glenn.   Monday and Friday 6 p.m.

TEAMS.   There are 5 Teams.   1 First Grade
              1 2nd Grade
              2 3rd Grade
              1 Ladies.

it?). The Bronte boys were put up in a rugby union club hall, but not many slept there on the Saturday night as the 'dawn brigade' seized it for one of their infamous games of 'rickety split'.

Our main game against Tamworth was played on the Saturday night. The local boys put up good

1st	2nd	3rd	4th
G. Robinson P. O'Hara	J. Thornett	G. Robinson P. O'Hara	G. Robinson · J Kirkwood
J. Folden J. Kirkwood	G. Rob P O'Hara J. Power	T. Folden R. Vadas	J. Power · T Folden
R. Vadas J Power P. Bower	R. Vadas J. Kirkwood P. Bower	J. Power J. Thornett P. Bower	R Vadas J. Thornett P. Bower

▲TOP: A reunion photo of members of the 1968 Bronte 1st Grade team: Tom Folden, Rolly Flesch, Irwin Vegg, Peter Folden (behind), Bert 'Momie' Vadas and Don Sarkies. ABOVE: John Thornett's team organisation for a 1968 Bronte 2nd Grade match.

"My first memories of the Bronte Club were very positive and I know I fell in love with the game because of that first year at Bronte. I played goals in 3rd Grade and we won the premiership that year (1967/68). It was not just because we won, but that as a 16 year old I got to play and train with some great people and players. Bill McCarthy was our coach and I'm sure without his mentoring and inspiration I wouldn't have achieved what I have done in the sport."

Phil Bower, 29 Jan 2019

opposition in the first two quarters, but Bronte gradually wore them down and eventually ran out winners 13~1. John Gahagan top scored with five goals, good games also from Ross Selleck (3), Bill Parsons (3) and Gary Cawood (2). We attended a barbecue after the match and finished off the night at the local Services Club.

Next morning everyone somehow made it to the pool by 8am and our junior boys team played the Tamworth side. This proved to be a very close game with our boys acquitting themselves very well. Chris Hickman and Dave Stapleton, in particular had good games. That morning also, our girl's team played the Tamworth junior boy's side. Our girls turned on a really first class performance, and were unlucky to go down by the odd goal. They seem to be improving with every match.

Later on the Sunday morning we visited the Farrar Agricultural College, with John Gahagan and Brian Ellison giving the local boys a few pointers in the pool there. The rest of the team invented a new game called water rugby (or 'all-in-brawl'), and we're sure it will catch on.

On the return journey we stopped at Scone for a dip in the pool there. I'm afraid I must report that here someone misbehaved. That person (he/she shall remain anonymous) actually swam in their sacred pool, and was promptly told to cease - shame!! We left the pool in disgrace.

We arrived back in Sydney at about midnight on Sunday. I'm sure everyone thoroughly enjoyed the trip and we hope others can be arranged in the not too distant future.

The Bronte club took two men's and one ladie's team on a development visit to play against ACT teams in Canberra over the weekend of 10th to 12th February 1968. The ACT side was a formidable outfit captained by Graham Robinson and included Chris Simpson. Both being sons of Army

---

THE SPIRIT OF BRONTE.

by "Morgo."

VERSUS COLLAROY.

Well, Bronte really turned it on against Collaroy last week, winning all 3 grades and scoring in all 22 goals while conceding only 5. The standard of play seems to be improving with every match.

1st Grade.

After a comparatively slow start, this match proved to be a fast and furious one, with much close marking from both sides. Neither side was able to gain an advantage for any length of time and it was only the accurate shooting of Bill Parsons that pulled Bronte through. Good games from Dick See and Rolly Flesch who continually got the attack moving and from Gary Cawood who defended sternly.

Bronte 2 (W. Parsons 2) bt Collaroy 0.

2nd Grade.

Second's on Wednesday showed a glimpse of the form that won them the premiership last season. They were quite impressive in attack, but their defence at times tended to lapse, allowing Collaroy to score 4 goals. John Thornett showed what a sitting centre-forward should do, and good games also from Bob See, Peter O'Hara and Wayne Reilly.

Bronte 11 (J. Thornett 5, Bob See 3, P. O'Hara 2, J. Kirkwood 1) bt. Collaroy 4.

3rd Grade

Third's proved too strong for a young Collaroy team. Jack Campbell and John Havas were able to dominate the halves and this gave the forwards John De Leon and Ross Selleck numerous scoring chances. Jack Keane proved a tower of strength in the backs and was ably assisted by Dave Stapleton.

Bronte 9 (J. De Leon 5, R. Selleck 3, J. Havas 1) bt Collaroy 1

FEES.

QUITE A FEW CLUB MEMBERS HAVE YET TO PAY THEIR FEES. PLEASE DO SO AS SOON AS POSSIBLE FELLAS, AS THE CLUB STILL HAS SOME OUTSTANDING COMMITMENTS. SEE JOHN GAHAGAN TODAY!!

FEES---£3.

SOCIAL HAPPENINGS.

Water Polo Association Xmas Party next Monday night (4th Dec.) at Aquatic Club. All welcome. £3 Double. Food, refreshments available.

Next Sat. night the club is holding a Xmas-Get-together at Gary Cawood's place. Come along with all your friends and make this a really great night. Refreshments are available.

The address is:- 16 Tilba St.,
Berala.
(see Gary for directions.)

OSCAR OF THE WEEK.

To the two Johns - Thornett and De Leon- for their 5 goals each in Wednesday's matches against Collaroy. John Thornett overcame the handicap of 3 or 4 opponents clinging to his back, arms, and legs for most of the night. John De Leon used his famous "bat" shot to score most of his goals (we all know what he used for a bat!!)

COMING MATCHES.

Next Wednesday vs Parramatta at Parramatta.
Sun Dec.10--- 1st Grade vs State Squad at Balmain, 8.00 p.m.

"THE SPIRIT OF BRONTE"
By "Morgo"

VERSUS BALMAIN

Our clash with Balmain as usual produced some very good and hard water polo. This time I'm afraid that the owners went to Balmain with them winning two matches to our one.

1st Grade

This was truly an excellent game with both sides playing fine water polo. Bronte matched Balmain in every department and we are really unlucky to go down 3-4 (a draw would have been a good result). The whole Bronte team played well, in particular Peter Folden who scored two excellent goals, and Gary Caywood who stuck to Dave Woods like glue.

Balmain 4 bt. Bronte 3 (P. Folden 2, W. Parsons 1)

2nd Grade

Seconds played well to defeat a strong Balmain side 1-0. The game was highlighted by close marking from both sides, and it was not until the final quarter that Bob See won the game for Bronte with a fine goal. John Power had another good game, as did Eric Folden and goalie John Wardrop.

Bronte 1 (Bob See 1) bt. Balmain 0

3rd Grade

Bronte got off to a bad start when to early errors allowed Balmain to go to a 2-0 lead. Balmain were able to keep up the pressure in Bronte never really recovered. Bill McCarthy continually rallied the players and scored to fine goals himself. Thirds can play better than they did last Wednesday and next time they meet Balmain it will be a different story.

Balmain 5 bt. Bronte 2 (W. McCarthy 2)

OSCAR OF THE WEEK

To the whole 1st Grade side for their great performance against Balmain last week. Although they went down, 1sts turned in the best display of the season and here's hoping for many more like it.

COMING MATCHES

Friday 29th December   Combined Bronte/Drummoyne vs The Czechoslovakian Team
at Drummoyne Baths 7:30pm
Wednesday 3rd January vs Universities at Balmain Baths

▲Match reports for Bronte v Collaroy played at Manly Baths on Wed, 29th Nov 1967 & v Balmain played at Balmain Baths on Wed, 20th Dec 1967.

THE SPIRIT OF BRONTE.
by "Morgo".

VERSUS UNIVERSITIES.

Despite the absence of a number of players, Bronte was able to record 2 good wins and a close defeat against Universities last Wednesday and thus remain in second place in the Club Championship behind Balmain.

(Club Championship points: Balmain 118, Bronte 98, Bondi 93, Uni. 91, St.George 83, Drummoyne 76, Collaroy 61, P'matta 52).

1st Grade.

Firsts last Wednesday went down for the fourth time this season by the single goal. Luck does not seem to be with them. They looked set for a win when John Gahagan scored a great goal early in the 1st quarter, but then their game deteriorated and Uni shot ahead. Bronte however rallied in the last 2 quarters with some fine penalty shooting by Bill Parsons and nearly bridged the gap. Gary Cawood played his usual hard game, while John Gahagan tried for a break all night.

Universities 6 bt. Bronte 5 (W. Parsons 4, J. Gahagan 1).

2nd. Grade.

This proved to be a very hard and close game with both sides fairly evenly matched. The scores were tied at 2 all right into the last quarter, and then 2 quick goals by Bob See gave Bronte the match. Bob had a great game scoring all 4 goals, and he was well backed up by Peter O'Hara, Robbie Vadas and Eric Folden.

Bronte 4 (Bob See 4) bt. Universities 2.

3rd. Grade.

Thirds returned to their old form with a 9-0 win over Uni. The team combined very well, with the backs and halves moving the ball up quickly so as to give the forwards numerous scoring chances. Ross Selleck had another fine game scoring 6 goals. Good games also from Chris Hickman, Lindsey Watson, and John Havas.

Bronte 9 (R.Selleck 6, W. McCarthy 2, L. Watson 1). bt. Universities 0.

OSCARS OF THE WEEK.

To Gary Cawood, who after much arm-twisting (ha-ha) has finally agreed to take over as coach for the girl's team while Bill McCarthy is away. One wonders if a certain blonde named Sandra will also be at every training session.

COMING MATCHES.

Next Thursday (11th Jan.) a combined Bronte and Drummoyne team will be playing the Czechoslovakian team at Drummoyne Baths. There are other matches on as well and the programme starts at 7.00. We want everyone to be there to cheer for the club in this international match.

Wed 10th Jan. vs Drummoyne at Ashfield.

FEES.

There are still a few club members who have not paid their fees. Please do so immediately fellas. See John Kirkwood or John Gahagan with your $3 today.

THE SPIRIT OF BRONTE.
By "Morgo".

VERSUS DRUMMOYNE.

Well, this club really turned it on in our first visit to Ashfield Pool this season, with Drummoyne being the unlucky opponents. Bronte convincingly won all three grades and in doing so scored 31 goals to Drummoyne's 6. Let's hope this can continue.

1st Grade.

First's played some really excellent water polo to defeat Drummoyne. The scores were fairly close up to half-time, but in the last two quarters Bronte took control of the match and virtually walked away from their opponents. The whole team played well, with particular mention to newcomer Irwin Veg, who gave a fine display of off-the-water shooting, and to Alex Kasco who had his best game for the club so far.

Bronte 11 (I. Veg 3, A. Kasco 3, W. Parsons 3, P. Folden 1, J. Gahagan 1) bt. Drummoyne 4.

2nd Grade.

Second's made amends for their first round draw with Drummoyne, by defeating them 10-2. Bronte were far too strong for their opponents in all departments and controlled the match throughout. John Thornett scored 4 good goals, and John Kirkwood had his best game this season -- he seems to be finding some of last year's form.

Bronte 10 (J. Thornett 4, Bob See 3, J. Kirkwood 2, W. Reilly 1) bt. Drummoyne 2.

3rd Grade.

Third's coasted to an easy 8-0 win over Drummoyne, but never really got into top gear. They just played well enough to win. Chris Hickman and John De Leon turned in good games in the forwards, while Jack Keane controlled operations in the backs.

Bronte 8 (C. Rickman 3, J. De Leon 3, R. Selleck 2) bt. Drummoyne 0.

BRONTE GIRL'S VERSUS BALMAIN.

Last Sunday night the Bronte girl's team scored a well-earned 2-1 win over Balmain. Bronte should have won by an even greater margin but lack of experience let them down on a couple of occasions. The whole team played well, in particular captain Lorraine Grills who directed play from the halves and Carol Scandrett in the forwards. This team seems to be improving with every match and the girls are now confident of taking out the premiership in their first season with the club.

Bronte 2 (L. Grills, C. Scandrett) bt. Balmain 1.

OSCARS OF THE WEEK.

The oscars this week of course go to Peter Folden and Bill Parsons who were selected in the State team last Sunday night. Both have been playing excellent water polo this season and thoroughly deserve the honour of representing their state at the Australian Championships in Melbourne next month. I'm sure all club members join me in congratulating them and wishing them the best of luck.

COMING MATCHES.

Sun 14th Jan. Bronte girls VS University at Balmain.

Wed 17th Jan. Bronte VS Bondi at Ashfield.

▲ *Match reports for Bronte v Universities played at Balmain Baths on Wed, 3rd Jan 1968 & v Drummoyne played at Ashfield Pool on Wed, 10th Jan 1968.*

---

fathers, these lads had learnt the game while residing at Duntroon Military College, and were assisted by the likes of Neville de Mestre.

Bronte took many trips over the years to help develop water polo in the country areas, but what came out of this visit was that both Graeme 'Robbo' Robinson and Chris 'Kipper' Simpson soon after left Canberra and headed to Sydney, where they joined up and played from then on with Bronte.

Death of Vic McGrath

It was with great sorrow that both the Bronte Club and the Water Polo Association mourned the passing of the great Mr. Vic McGrath, and all members were shocked to hear of his tragic motor vehicle accident in New Zealand. Vic was a devotee of water polo, a reserve for the 1960 Olympic Team, a NSW State player for many years and a captain and coach of the NSW State Team. He was a greatly respected player and valued member of the water polo community.

Bronte bounced back in the 1967/68 season, confirming themselves as one of the strongest Sydney water polo

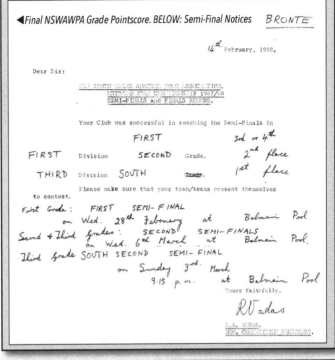

Final NSWAWPA Grade Pointscore. BELOW: Semi-Final Notices — BRONTE

14th February, 1968.

Dear Sir:

NEW SOUTH WALES AMATEUR POLO ASSOCIATION.
METROPOLITAN CHAMPIONSHIP 1967/68
SEMI-FINALS and FINALS ROUNDS.

Your Club was successful in reaching the Semi-Finals in

FIRST — 3rd or 4th

FIRST Division — SECOND Grade. — 2nd place

THIRD Division — SOUTH — 1st place

Please make sure that your team/teams present themselves to contest.

First Grade: FIRST SEMI-FINAL on Wed. 28th February at Balmain Pool

Second & Third Grades: SECOND SEMI-FINALS on Wed. 6th March at Balmain Pool.

Third Grade SOUTH SECOND SEMI-FINAL on Sunday 3rd March 9.15 p.m. at Balmain Pool

Yours faithfully,

R Vadas

R.A. VADAS.
HON. COMPETITION SECRETARY.

1967/68 NSWAWPA RESULTS

METROPOLITAN COMPETITION FIRST DIVISION

1st Grade

	Played	Won	Drawn	Lost	For	Against	Points
Balmain	14	11	1	2	73	49	37
Universities	14	9	2	3	75	49	34
Bondi	14	9	2	3	77	49	34
Bronte	14	9	1	4	70	50	33
St. George	14	7	1	6	46	63	29
Drummoyne	14	4	2	8	27	65	24
Parramatta	14	1	1	12	44	55	17
Collaroy	14	0	2	12	44	77	16

1st SEMI	Bronte, 6, defeated Bondi, 4
2nd SEMI	Universities, 7, defeated Balmain, 5
FINAL	Bronte, 5, defeated Balmain, 1
GRAND FINAL	Universities, 3, defeated Bronte, 2

2nd Grade

	Played	Won	Drawn	Lost	For	Against	Points
Balmain	14	11	2	1	65	19	38
Bronte	14	10	3	1	68	27	37
Universities	14	7	3	4	47	44	31
St. George	14	4	4	6	56	49	26
Collaroy	14	4	4	5	47	54	25
Drummoyne	14	2	4	8	33	53	22
Parramatta	14	3	1	11	40	73	22
Bondi	14	3	1	8	14	57	19

1st SEMI: Universities, 3, defeated St. George, 2
2nd SEMI: Bronte, 2, defeated Balmain, 1
FINAL: Balmain, 4, defeated Universities, 2
GRAND FINAL: Bronte, 2, defeated Balmain, 1

3rd Grade

	Played	Won	Drawn	Lost	For	Against	Points
Balmain	14	13	1	—	71	14	41
Bronte	14	12	1	1	80	23	39
St. George	14	8	2	4	45	31	32
Bondi	14	5	3	6	30	30	27
Collaroy	14	5	1	8	34	49	25
Drummoyne	14	4	—	10	23	50	22
Parramatta	14	3	1	10	27	58	21
Universities	14	—	2	12	10	65	16

1st SEMI: St. George, 5, defeated Bondi, 4
2nd SEMI: Balmain, 4, defeated Bronte, 2
FINAL: Bronte, 5, defeated St. George, 1
GRAND FINAL: Bronte, 3, defeated Balmain, 2

DIVISION 3 — "SOUTH"

	Played	Won	Drawn	Lost	Forfeit	Points
Bronte	14	12	1	1	—	39
Maroubra	14	10	1	3	—	35
Eastern Suburbs Surfers	14	9	1	4	—	33
St. George	14	8	1	5	—	31
Bondi	14	8	—	5	1	29
Sydney University	14	5	—	8	1	23
Eastern Suburbs Police Boys' Club	14	1	—	12	1	15
Glebe Police Boys' Club	14	1	—	11	2	14

1st SEMI	St. George, 4, defeated Eastern Suburbs Surfers, 2
2nd SEMI	Maroubra, 3, defeated Bronte, 2
FINAL	St. George, 5, defeated Bronte, 4
GRAND FINAL	Maroubra, 2, defeated St. George, 0

3rd DIVISION GRAND FINAL: MAROUBRA, 5, defeated PENRITH, 1

clubs with all three Division I teams qualifying for the grand-finals, although they went into the play offs as underdogs in all three grades.

With only one loss on the season, 3rd Grade finished in second place, but managed to defeat Balmain (3~2) in the grand-final to take the premiership. The Bronte 2nd Grade then repeated the feat and also defeated Balmain (2~1) in the grand-final.

Bronte 1st Grade had obtained the services of two talented imports this year in Irwin Vegg, a top American water polo player from the New York Athletic Club, and a tall lanky Englishman by the name of Peter Messider. Despite finishing fourth on the ladder, they also advanced through to the grand-final, recording wins over Bondi (6~4) and Balmain (5~1) in the preliminaries, but still went into the grand-final as underdogs. But although they played brilliantly, Bronte could not thwart the polish of Uni's Australian representatives in Nick Barnes, Bill Phillips and goalkeeper John Harrison, and they lost narrowly in the decider (2~3).

NEW SOUTH WALES AMATEUR WATER POLO ASSOCIATION

METROPOLITAN COMPETITION DRAW 1968 — 1969

BOX A81
P.O. SYDNEY SOUTH
N.S.W. 2000

▲ *1968/69 NSWAWPA Metropolitan water polo draw.* ▼ *The 1968 Water Polo Report for Randwick BHS, which featured the legendary John 'Fiji' McLure, seated 3rd from left. (Pegasus - RBHS Yearbook, 1968).*

1968-69

1968/69 NSWAWPA OFFICIALS: H.K. Porter (Patron); H.J. Bund (President); G.R. Woods (Past President); F. Falson (Chairman); J. W. (Registrar); D. J. Cohen (Secretary); L. Papps (A/Secretary); **R. Vadas (Comp. Secretary)**; A. Sparkes (Country Secretary); O. Bogg (Treasurer).

The new season got underway after the 40th NSWAWPA Annual General Meeting, which was held at the Aquatic Club, Cnr. Riley and Cathedral Sts., East Sydney.

This season saw much progress for the game with the growth of the Interstate series for both NSW Ladies and NSW Colts teams. Travelling also became popular this season with the St. George District WPA spending a memorable few days in New Zealand, while the Collaroy Devils also ventured across the Tasman to compete against the Kiwis.

The Country Clubs were again invited to select a representative team at the Country Championships and to trial for places in the 1969 NSW State team as the improvement by many country players had been remarkable. Structural changes during this season reformed the competition so that Division I now consisted of four grades, with two grades each in Divisions II and III. Due credit was passed on to the referees as well as the Competition Committee, for making these changes which

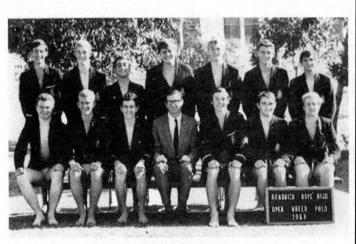

WATER POLO

FIRST GRADE WATER POLO

The 1st Grade side had another most enjoyable and successful season in the Zone competition. The team was defeated only by one side—Sydney High—but only went down after torrid and close competition. Despite this, Randwick went on to win all other games, defeating some teams as much as 10 to nil. Team members would like to gratefully acknowledge the aid given by our coach and "chauffeur"—Mr. Young. Best players can't be distinguished—but John Anderson, John McLure, Gary Jones and Ron Rogers were prominent players who will be missed next year. However, with young players showing potential in lower grades, next year's side should be top class and sure to be capably led by Bob Barrie, a Zone team representative last year.

RON ROGERS and JOHN McLURE.

OPEN WATER POLO

Back Row (left to right): B. Grimshaw, P. Bath, R. Raftos, V. Hazir, G. Simms, J. Stone, R. Raftos.
Front Row (left to right): J. Anderson, R. Barrie, C. McLure, Mr. R. K. Young, P. Craig, G. Jones, G. Vaughan.

gave more emphasis to the first division. The major sponsors for the Association were again W.D. & H.O. Wills for the metropolitan trophies, and Speedo Knitting Mills for the Pre-Season competition.

The Baths & Clubs

In regard to clubs joining or re-joining the competitions... Bilgola, Blacktown, Clovelly, Hawkesbury, HMAS Nirimba, South Sydney Police Boys and University of NSW all affiliated. However, Balmoral, Eastwood/Epping, Eastern Suburbs Police Boys, Eastern Suburbs Surfers, Glebe Police

Water polo match off

By JOHN HOLLAND

The important water polo match between Queanbeyan and Cardinals to be played at the Queanbeyan pool tomorrow morning has been postponed until Tuesday night.

The decision to postpone was prompted by the absence of several key players in Sydney.

The ACT representative squad will play a series of games against the top Sydney first grade team Bronte today and tomorrow.

The ACT team is: Hugh Crawley, Ben Smith (Cardinals), Paul Jones, Roger Martin (Dolphins) Chris Lord, Fraser Graham, (Norths) and Jim Hanrahan (Workmens).

The match between Queanbeyan and Cardinals is expected to be a key one as Cardinals are at present leading the competition with Queanbeyan in equal second place with Dolphins.

This is the final match of the pre-Christmas competition and the greatly improved Queanbeyan combination is expected to be a strong test for the unbeaten Cardinals.

(Canberra Times, 7th Dec 1968)

1968/69 Season Statistics
N.S.W.A.W.P.A.

Clubs in the Mens Water Polo Competitions.

Clubs	1	2	3	4	2¹	2²	3E	3W	Total
Balmain	●	●	●	●	●	●	●		7
Bilgola						●			1
Blacktown								●	1
Bondi	●	●	●	●					4
Bronte	●	●	●	●	●				5
Canterbury					●	●			2
Clovelly						●			1
Collaroy	●	●	●	●	●	●			6
Drummoyne	●	●	●	●					4
Hawkesbury							●		1
HMAS Nirimba							●		1
Illawarra						●	●		2
Judean						●	●		2
Liverpool						●	●		2
Maroubra						●			1
Nth Palm Beach							●		1
Nth Sydney					●	●	●		3
Northbridge					●	●			2
Parramatta	●	●	●					●	4
P'matta Memorial							2		2
Penrith						●	●		2
St. George	●	●	●	●					4
Sth Sydney Police BC							●		1
Sydney University							2		2
University of NSW							●		1
Universities	●	●	●	●					4
Western Suburbs	●	●		●					3
	9	9	9	9	10	9	8	6	69

Results of the Mens Water Polo Competitions.

Grade	Premier		Runner-Up
1st	Bronte		Pre-Season Comp.
1st	Balmain~2	d.	1~Universities
2nd	Balmain~4	d.	3~Bronte
3rd	Bondi~3	d.	2~Balmain
4th	Balmain~6	d.	5~St. George
Club Champions	BALMAIN		
D2 1st	Balmain~10	d.	1~Maroubra Seals
D2 2nd	Clovelly Eskimos~2	d.	1~Collaroy
D3 Playoff	P'matta Memorial A~6	d.	4~Sth Sydney PBC
D3 Est	Sth Sydney PBC~5	d.	3~Nth Palm Beach
D3 Wst	Parramatta Mem A~6	d.	1~Parramatta Mem B

NEW SOUTH WALES MENS TEAM
1969 - 3rd Place - National Championships - Perth

Back row (from left): **Peter Folden** (Bronte), **Dave Bullock** (g, St George), Ian McLauchlain (Balmain), Graham Hannan (Parramatta), Bill Gooley (Manager, St George), David Woods (c/Coach, Balmain), Peter Montgomery (Universities), **John Gahagan** **(Bronte)**. Front row: John Harrison (vc/g, Universities), Max May (Balmain), Ken Laws (Balmain), Bruce Falson (St George).
Photo - NSWAPWA Annual Report 1968/69.

Boys and Lane Cove all lapsed. Despite the attrition, the number of entries received for the men's metropolitan competitions increased to 69 teams from 27 clubs.

Bronte were quick off the mark to take the Speedo Perpetual Trophy for the pre-season competition. After this warm-up competition, the premiership began in earnest and as the season wore on, the 1st Grade competition developed into a race between the 'big four' clubs in Balmain, Bondi, Bronte and Universities.[4]

AMATEUR SWIMMING UNION OF AUSTRALIA

— ★ —

AUSTRALIAN CHAMPIONSHIPS
BEATTY PARK AQUATIC CENTRE
NORTH PERTH

PASS

14th - 23rd FEBRUARY, 1969

THE AMATEUR SWIMMING UNION OF AUSTRALIAN PRESENTS

THE NATIONAL WATER POLO CHAMPIONSHIP

BEATTY PARK   AQUATIC CENTRE   NORTH PERTH

PROGRAMME 20c   16TH FEBRUARY TO 23RD FEBRUARY 1969

LEFT: Official Pass for the 1969 Perth Australian Championships . BELOW (Left): Representing St George, Dave Bullock played brilliantly throughout the 1968/69 season to earn selection in the NSW Men's team, but had learnt most of his skills during his former years with Bronte. (Right): Program for the 1969 Australian Championships in Perth.

BALMAIN AWPC
1968/69 - NSWAWPA 1st Grade Premiers
Back row (from left): Kevin Stapleton, John Waddington, Iain MacLaughlain, Graeme Samuel, John McFarlane, Mick Withers (g), Terry Jansen. Seated: Eric Fitzgerald, Max May, David Woods (c), Ken Laws. Photo - Balmain WPC Archives.

Jon 'Oscar' Kirkwood

▲ *Jon 'Oscar' Kirkwood began playing water polo with Roseville Club about 1954, but through Vic McGrath was invited to join Bronte Water Polo Club in 1962, where he remained until 1967, later transferring to Northbridge. Jon was not only a solid player and a great club man for Bronte, but he also worked as both Hon. Treasurer and Registrar for the NSWAWPA from 1963 to 1965.*

Representatives in NSW Teams

In an attempt to regain the Australian Championship after only having won it once, over the previous 12 years, wholesale changes were made to the NSW State team. Only Dave Woods, Max May, Iain McLauchlain (Balmain), John Harrison (Universities) and Peter Folden (Bronte) were retained from 1968. Ken Laws (Balmain) was resurrected, along with five new caps in Bruce Falson and goalkeeper Dave Bullock (St George), Graham Hannan (Parramatta), Peter Montgomery (Universities) and John Gahagan joined Peter Folden as Bronte's two representatives. Dave Bullock had learnt all his skills while at Bronte, but had transferred to St George a few months before.

This year the 22nd Australian Championships were held at Beatty Park in Perth, but the

ACT beats Bronte in water polo

By JOHN HOLLAND

An outstanding display of goalkeeping by Chris Lord enabled the ACT representative water polo team to beat one of the top Sydney club sides, Bronte, by five goals to four on Saturday.

Lord executed a series of fine saves and interceptions

Young side in water polo

A young Queanbeyan water polo side is expected to be a strong force in the 1968-69 competition which begins next month.

The team performed well last year and should be more formidable this year.

The ACT representative side have lost Graham Robinson and Chris Simpson who have been transferred to Sydney. They have been nominated for the NSW training squad and will play with Bronte.

during a torrid final quarter in which the Sydney team consistently attacked the ACT defence in an attempt to equalise.

The Canberra team was playing in an invitation three-way competition between Bronte, Bondi and ACT.

In its other two games it was narrowly beaten 2-1 and 8-6 by the strong Bondi club.

Against Bronte, the ACT skipper and coach, Jim Hanrahan, scored a well-deserved hat trick to give his team a winning chance.

Surprise lead

Additional goals by Hugh Crawley and Graham Robinson enabled it to take a surprise 5-3 lead into the final quarter.

Robinson, the former ACT skipper, was playing by invitation, having decided to move to Sydney a few weeks ago in an attempt to make the State squad.

Apart from Lord, the most impressive of the Canberra players were Hanrahan and Crawley, who each scored four goals.

The only senior game played in Canberra over the weekend was between Wests and Services at Queanbeyan yesterday.

After a dull, scoreless first half, Wests gained the upper hand to win 3-1.

Once again the Services team showed early promise, but it tired badly to allow Wests to break through.

Best for Wests was John Donohue, who scored two goals, and best for Services was goalkeeper Ray Ovenell.

The junior knockout competition at the Canberra Olympic pool on Saturday was considered a great success by officials.

In the first game, Canberra ran to an early lead against Manuka and despite a spirited finish was

able to hold out for a well-deserved 4-3 win.

Queanbeyan showed the benefit of regular coaching classes in its match against Duntroon to take a two-goal lead at half-time and ran out winners 4-0.

Drawn game

The final was a thrilling game as both teams matched each other goal-for-goal throughout.

Enthusiasm was the order of the day rather than finesse and the game ended in a 3-3 draw.

Sydney (Saturday): ACT 5 (Hanrahan 3, Crawley, Robinson) d Bronte 4. ACT 6 (Crawley 2, Tribe, de Mestre 2, Hanrahan) lost to Bondi 8. ACT 1 (Crawley) lost to Bondi 2.

Competition: Wests 3 (Donohue 2, Lindeman) d Services 1 (Rayner).

Junior knockout: Canberra 4 d Manuka 3; Queanbeyan 4 d Duntroon 0. Final: Queanbeyan 3 drew with Canberra 3.

Two articles about Bronte v Queanbeyan (The Canberra Times, 1st Oct 1968) and v Canberra water polo teams (The Canberra Times, 18th Nov 1968).

competition was attended by just four States. By the end of the week, Western Australia at home, proved their dominance to take their third national title, with NSW coming third once again behind Victoria.

The Premierships

In the 1st Grade play-offs, Universities who were the reigning premiers, defeated Bondi (8~5) in the minor semi-final, and Balmain comfortably disposed of Bronte (8~3) in the major semi-final. Universities then had to draw upon all its collective experience and talent to narrowly defeat a very talented Bronte team (9~8) to qualify for the competition decider. Balmain hadn't lost a game on the season and with great determination and a passionate crowd behind them, they narrowly overcame Universities (2~1) to claim the 1st Grade premiership, which crowned their undefeated season record. Balmain were also successful in the 2nd and 4th grades and annexed the Club Championship. Bondi took out the 3rd Grade Premiership.

Officials from the St. George District Association once again conducted a Junior water polo competition and by offering overnight

Duel ahead for Dolphins in water polo

By JOHN HOLLAND

Competition leader Dolphins will be hard-pressed to beat the greatly improved Workmens side in tonight's water polo competition round at Canberra Olympic Pool.

Led by the ACT representative skipper, Jim Hanrahan, Workmen have shown gradual improvement in recent games.

With Hanrahan in attack it has a good chance of upsetting the smooth Dolphin combination, which will be without its star goal scorer, Chris Simpson.

Simpson has probably played his last game for Dolphins as he is involved with university examinations tonight, and plans to move to Sydney in the next week or so.

He is hoping to join another former Dolphins and ACT star, Graham Robinson, with the top Sydney first grade club, Bronte.

One of Canberra's leading clubs in the past four years, Dolphins will no doubt find it hard to maintain their position on the table following the loss of its best two players.

Strenuous late game

However, their coach, Paul Jones, claims he has a ready-made replacement in reserve grader, Eddie Parks.

With Malcolm McIntosh and Roger Martin giving him plenty of the ball tonight, Parks could be a danger to the Workmen's defence.

Following a narrow loss to Cardinals in last week's match, Hanrahan has been concentrating on tightening the Workmen's defence.

It has an able goalkeeper in Dave Bullivant, and if Mike Craft, John Tydeman and Bill Beale can give him better support, the game could go Workmen's way.

The late game between Cardinals and Norths is expected to be a strenuous affair.

Cardinals is a formidable side and although it did not impress in attack last week, it has the ability to lift its game.

Cardinals defence

The Norths defence, which has been erratic in recent games, will be hard pushed to keep Crawley, Bedford, Martin and de Mestre out of scoring range.

Norths have a trump card in their goalkeeper, Chris Lord, who was the star of the ACT side which played in Sydney last weekend.

In attack it has a trier in Fraser Graham, but he will need more support from his team mates if he wants to breach the strong Cardinals defence.

Against Services in the last round Norths failed to get going in the first half, but redeemed themselves with a whirlwind final quarter which had Services defending desperately.

The second grade game between the unbeaten leaders Dolphins and Cardinals will commence at 5.30pm.

Both teams outclassed their opponents in earlier games and even at this stage, tonight's winner will become favourite to take out the competition.

Canberra Times, 20th Nov 1968

Tuition by water polo experts

Two members of the NSW Amateur Water Polo Association referees' appointments board will be in Canberra this weekend to conduct courses and examinations for local players and officials.

They are Mr Jim Mac-Farlane and Mr Alf Sparkes.

A general meeting of all players has been called for 6pm at the club rooms at Olympic Pool.

Bronte, a top Sydney club, will play Canberra today at 10.30am at the Olympic Pool and also in the afternoon at the temporary pool set up at Weston Park, Yarralumla.

Former ACT representatives Graham Robinson and K. Simpson will play with Bronte, and their clash with the local players will be a highlight of the weekend.

Bronte will be unable to bring its womens team.

Canberra Times, 22nd Feb 1969

THE SPIRIT OF BRONTE.
by "Morgo".

68-69

Let me begin the column this year with an apology for its lateness in getting under way. Due to other commitments I was unable to get along for the first few matches of the season. But from now on, if you care to glance at this column every Saturday, you will find out how Bronte fared in the previous week's matches and also the events that are coming up on the Bronte calendar.

VERSUS COLLAROY.

Two wins, a draw and a loss was Bronte's record against Collaroy last Wednesday---not bad, but the club's overall play was nowhere near the high standard that it set last year. Let's hope we can find this form quickly.

1ST. GRADE.

This match proved to be a very ordinary one with neither side gaining the upper hand for any length of time, and I guess a draw was the best result. Bronte played well in patches, but also made some foolish mistakes and it was from these that Collaroy's goals resulted. Peter Folden played well in the forwards, while Gary Cawood defended sternly in the backs.
Bronte 4 (I. Veg 2, P.Folden, R. Flesch) drew with Collaroy 4.

2ND GRADE.

Second's on Wednesday showed a glimpse of the form that won them the premiership last season. They were quite impressive in attack, but also missed many scoring opportunities. Graham Robinson had a fine game, scoring 3 goals, and he was well backed up by Peter O'Hara, Robbie Vadas and John Power. In addition Phil Bower had a great game in goals.
Bronte 6 (G.Robinson 3, P.O'Hara, J.Kirkwood, R.Vadas) bt. Collaroy 2.

3RD GRADE.

Third's played quite well in going down to a very experienced Collaroy side. This team can, however, play much better and I think it should concentrate on moving the ball about more quickly in the water. Bill McCarthy and Ross Selleck tried hard in the forwards, while Danny Hofbauer had a good game in defence.
Collaroy 4 bt. Bronte 3 (C.Hickman, W.McCarthy, R.Selleck)

4TH GRADE

Fourth's won on a forfeit, and in doing so are credited with 5 goals.
Bronte 5 bt. Collaroy 0.

OSCAR OF THE WEEK.

To a certain hotel at Manly which showed such "excellent" hospitality to our club members last Wednesday night. Why, they even took us on a guided tour of the establishment!!

SOCIAL HAPPENINGS.

Next Saturday (Dec.21st)__immediately after training.
Everyone is invited to stay on at Bushy after training for a few Xmas drinks, which will be provided by the club. Even if you plan to go out later in the evening, there will still be plenty of time for a bit of socialising poolside.

RAFFLE.

Please return your raffle butts and money to Gary Cawood today.

COMING MATCHES.

Wed 18th Dec.   Bronte vs.   Universities at Ashfield.

FEES.

QUITE A FEW CLUB MEMBERS HAVE YET TO PAY THEIR FEES. PLEASE DO SO IMMEDIATELY FELLAS. SEE JOHN KIRKWOOD TODAY!!
FEES -- £5   (£2 for school students).

THE SPIRIT OF BRONTE.
by "Morgo".

VERSUS WESTERN SUBURBS.

Bronte had quite a successful night against newcomers Western Suburbs last Wednesday, winning 3 grades and drawing one.

1st. Grade.

First's win over Wests was not really convincing. Wests fielded a very young and inexperienced side, but they put up a good display and were able to hold Bronte for most of the match. It was only in the last quarter that Bronte really got on top. Irwin Veg scored 3 good goals and narrowly missed quite a few others. Dick See and Alex Kasco also played well.
Bronte 6 (I.VEG 3, W.Parsons, R.See, A.Kasco) bt. Wests 0.

2nd. Grade.

Second's played well. they moved the ball about quickly and defended well, but they just couldn't seem to finish off movements. Perhaps this needs looking into. Peter O'Hara, Gary Cawood and Eric Folden all had good games.
Bronte 4 (P.O'Hara 2, A.Kasco, J.Kirkwood) bt. Wests 0.

3rd. Grade.

Thirds hit top form and recorded a good 9-1 win over Wests. The team combined particularly well, with the backs and halves moving the ball up quickly so as to give the forwards numerous scoring chances. Bill McCarthy and Ross Selleck both found shooting form while Jack Keane defended well.
Bronte 9 (W.McCarthy 4, R.Selleck 3, C.Simpson 2) bt. Wests 1.

4th. Grade.

After a good start Fourth's fell away and they had to be content with a 1-1 draw. The defence was quite sound, but many scoring opportunties were missed through inexperience. Lindsey Watson had a good game first up, while Paul Aisbett and Steve Kritzler also played well.
Bronte 1 (P.Aisbett) drew with Wests 1.

OSCAR OF THE WEEK.

To Peter Folden who was selected in the State team last Sunday night. I'm sure all club members join me in congratulating him and wishing him the best of luck in the Australian Championships in Perth next month.

SOCIAL HAPPENINGS.

Tonight (Sat. 11th Jan.) Bob Langford is holding a party for the Tamworth Water Polo team who is down here for the weekend. He has invited Bronte to come along. Food and refreshments are supplied. The address is :-
18 Tyrwhitt St.
Maroubra.

COMING MATCHES.

Wed 15th Jan.   Bronte vs Parramatta at Parramatta.
Wed 22nd Jan.   Bronte vs St.George at Gunnamatta Bay.

▲ Match reports for Bronte v Collaroy played at Balmain Baths on Wed, 11th Dec 1968 & v Western Suburbs played at Ashfield Pool on Wed, 8th Jan 1969.

---

accommodation at Cronulla, were even able to attract the Goulburn club to the contest. The competition was conducted at Gunnamatta Bay and after a series of elimination games, a most exciting final was won by Bondi, who defeated St. George (2~1). The Shell Company again provided the trophies apart from making an additional donation towards the promotion of the junior competition.[4]

Bronte AWPC

The club continued with its development work in the country districts with further successful trips to Canberra and Brisbane this season.

"Something jagged a lost memory recently of a Bronte Under 21 team, headed up by Billy Parsons, Peter Folden and Peter O'Hara, which was coached by myself in the late 60s, where over a weekend in Brisbane we played undefeated against all the local teams. An Ashes trophy was presented at the farewell barbecue of one my treasured white buckskin boots!"

Bill McCarthy, Oct 2020

"I remember it well. I think we beat every team and even drew against the Queensland State team. At one stage we had lunch at the famous Breakfast Creek Pub where we were told

to put our shirts on when in the beer garden, even though it was stinking hot!! We also couldn't get over that you had to be 21 to get into licenced premises back then. We stayed at Lunky's place and I think we (Billy McCarthy, Graham Robinson (Cheeta), myself and one other... maybe Chris Simpson (Kipper) hastened the birth of his son, who arrived the day after we left. After a night out and a day stopping a runaway horse we re-decorated Lunky's lounge room with newspapers and flags from a car dealership and a Real Estate sign. Of course this did precipitate a retaliation. I was also involved with the help of Lunky in almost selling Billy McCarthy's house without him knowing, which could have brought on a nervous breakdown for Mrs. McCarthy. Lunky could recount the finer details I'm sure, including the huge Real Estate sign we transported back to Sydney from Lunky's dining room for the occasion, which was hung across the front of Billy's house... Great memories."

Bill Parsons, Oct, 2020

Although a water polo premiership eluded them, in terms of performance, the club had another fruitful season. In the NSWAWPA competitions, Bronte fielded five teams, but the team competing in the Division II-1st Grade comp struggled throughout the season, and finished well down on the ladder.

THE SPIRIT OF BRONTE.
by "Morgo."

VERSUS BONDI.
Bronte and Bondi finished up all square last Wednesday, with 2 wins apiece. The scores in all games were close, and as a result the water polo was hard and exciting.

1st Grade.
This game was a really good one. It was close throughout, and each team scored some really good goals. Bronte, however, always seemed to have a slight edge. Don Sarkies brought off some great saves in goals, while Holly Flesch and Dick See played well in the field.
Bronte 4 (W.Parsons, R.Flesch, I.Veg, P.Folden) bt. Bondi 3.

2nd Grade.
Seconds were beaten by an unexpectedly strong Bondi side. They seemed to lose confidence after a couple of goals were scored against them, and it was only in the last half that they really fought back. Peter O'Hara and Robbie Vadas both had fine games.
Bondi 3 bt. Bronte 2 (P.O'Hara 2).

3rd Grade.
Thirds always looked the better side in this match and should have scored a few more goals. Again Bronte's forwards dominated the opposition while Dave Stapleton and Jack Keane defended well.
Bronte 5 (W.McCarthy 3, R.Selleck 2) bt. Bondi 3.

4th Grade.
Bondi proved too strong in this match and Bronte just couldn't seem to get moving. Steve Kritzler and Alan Webb played well, while John Boniface scored 2 good penalty goals.
Bondi 5 bt. Bronte 2 (J.Boniface 2).

OSCAR OF THE WEEK.
A somewhat belated oscar this week goes to Rhonda Flower who almost singlehandedly arranged last week's Harbour Cruise. Although the Harbour Cruise did not turn out to be a success financially (due to lack of support by club members), it was a great success socially. Those who went agree that it was one of the best turns the club has had. Thanks Rhonda!

SOCIAL HAPPENINGS.
A coach trip to Canberra has been arranged for the weekend of the 23rd of February. I'm sure that those who went on these trips last year will agree that they are well worth it. Those wishing to come along, please see John Power.

COMING MATCHES.
Wed. 5th Feb vs Drummoyne at Drummoyne.
Wed. 12th Feb vs Balmain at Balmain.

ooooooOOOOOOOOOOOooooooo

THE SPIRIT OF BRONTE.
by "Morgo'.

VERSUS DRUMMOYNE.
Last Wednesday was another successful night for Bronte with 3 wins and a loss against Drummoyne. Next week is the big one though, when we take on Balmain at Balmain (of course).

1st Grade.
First's defeated Drummoyne 6-0 in quite an uninspiring match. Both sides were allowed many liberties and this probably contributed to the scappiness of the game. John Gahagan played really well and scored 2 great goals while Holly Flesch and Don Sarkies also had good games.
Bronte 6 (J.Gahagan 2, A.Kasco, I.Veg, W.Parsons, R.Flesch) bt. Drummoyne 0.

2nd Grade.
Second's were never really extended in defeating Drummoyne 7-0. They scored some good goals, but overanxiousness prevented them from scoring quite a few others. John Kirkwood and Robbie Vadas both had good games.
Bronte 7 (J.Kirkwood 2, P.O'Hara 2, G.Robinson, R.Vadas, C.Simpson) bt. Drummoyne 0.

3rd Grade.
Third's, despite being depleted, had no trouble in defeating Drummoyne 7-3. Drummoyne's goals were scored as a result of silly mistakes on Bronte's part, which will have to be rectified. Ross Selleck, Jack Campbell and Wayne Reilly all played well.
Bronte 7 (R.Selleck 4, W.Reilly 2, W.McCarthy) bt. Drummoyne 3.

4th Grade.
Fourth's had a win snatched from their grasp when they tired in the last quarter. They had played well in the first half and looked all set for a win. Ernie Kritzler, Lindsey Watson, and Bruce Selleck had good games.
Drummoyne 3 bt. Bronte 2 (E.Kritzler, L.Watson).

OSCAR OF THE WEEK.
To John Gahagan on his selection in the State team. I'm sure everyone will agree that no one deserves this honour more than John. He now joins Peter Folden, Bronte's other representative in the team. Best of luck in Perth fellas!

SOCIAL HAPPENINGS.
The coach is still not full for the trip to Canberra yet, so anyone else wishing to go please see John Power immediately.

COMING MATCHES.
Wed 12th Feb. vs. Balmain at Balmain.
Wed 19th Feb. vs. Bye.

vvvvvvvvvvvvvvvvvvvvvvvvvvvvvvvvvvvvvvvvv

▲ *Match reports for Bronte v Bondi played at Balmain Baths on Wed, 29th Jan 1969 & v Drummoyne played at Drummoyne Baths on Wed, 5th Feb 1969.*

THE SPIRIT OF BRONTE.
by "Morgo".

VERSUS COLLAROY.

Last Wednesday was not a good night for Bronte when we were beaten in 2 out of the 4 grades. Collaroy, despite a scarcity of players, was able to put up a good showing in all grades.

1st Grade.

This was not a very inspiring match. Both teams marked hard and close all night and as a result there was not a great deal of open Polo. Bronte was best served by Don Sarkies, Peter Folden and Gary Cawood.
Bronte 4 (P.Folden 2, W.Parsons 2) bt. Collaroy 2.

2nd Grade.

Seconds just weren't up to their usual selves last Wednesday. They had quite a deal of the ball and yet often threw it away with silly passes and bad play. Maybe they were all still suffering the effects of the trip to Canberra.
Collaroy 2 bt. Bronte 1 (J.Kirkwood).

3rd. Grade.

Thirds started off very slowly and the match was about even until half time. They came good in the last 2 quarters however and eventually ran out 7-3 winners. Bronte's forwards again shone with Bill McCarthy and Ross Selleck scoring the 7 goals between them. In addition Danny Hofbauer and Jack Keane had good games.
Bronte 7 (W.McCarthy 4, R.Selleck 3) bt. Collaroy 3.

4th Grade.

Fourths were outclassed by a surprisingly strong Collaroy side. Lack of penetration again let them down. Steve Kritzler and Lindsey Watson both tried hard.
Collaroy 6 bt. Bronte 0.

OSCAR OF THE WEEK.

To Bill Parsons who this week seems to have the biggest smile in the Bronte club. The reason: he has just announced his engagement to Robyn Campbell. I'm sure everyone in the club joins me in congratulating Robyn and Bill.

SOCIAL HAPPENINGS.

Don't forget the Boat-a-Polo tomorrow -- a day of cruising around the Harbour. Meet at the Halvorsen Wharf at Bobbin Head at 9 a.m.

COMING MATCHES.

Wed 5th March   vs Universities at Balmain.
Wed 12th March vs Western Suburbs at Ashfield.

" THE SPIRIT OF BRONTE."
by Morgo.

VERSUS UNIVERSITIES.

1st Grade.

This was a really hard and close game which could have gone either way. I suppose a draw was the best result, but it must be remembered that Bronte scored two field goals to Uni's one. This tends to show that Bronte were a little unlucky not to win. Perhaps the best feature of each side's play was its defence, with neither side giving an inch all night. Peter Folden and Gary Cawood were the pick of the players in a good team display.
Bronte 2 (P.Folden 2) drew with Universities 2.

2nd Grade.

Second's game was an improvement on last week's, but everyone knows they can play even better. Their play was again marred by foolish passes at critical stages-- something that will have to be rectified. Graham Robinson had a great game and scored all 3 goals, while Phil Bower showed fine form in goals.
Bronte 3 (G.Robinson 3) bt. Universities 2.

3rd Grade.

Third's after a slow start, gradually wore Uni.down and ran out 5-1 winners. They looked impressive at times, and scored some really good goals. Ross Selleck and Chris Simpson played well in the forwards as did Dave Stapleton in the backs.
Bronte 5 (C.Simpson 2, R.Selleck 2, W.McCartny) bt. Universities 1.

4th Grade.

A depleted Fourths were by no means disgraced against Uni., going down 1-3. Bronte's goal was scored by young Geoff Parsons, who banged it into the net just like a veteran. Maybe a certain big brother has been doing a bit of coaching.
Uni. 3 bt. Bronte 1 (G.Parsons.)

OSCAR OF THE WEEK.

To the 7 club members and 3 supporters who attended the Club's Boat-a-Polo at Bobbin Head last Sunday. This was a really great day and it seems a pity that others did not take this opportunity to enjoy themselves.

SOCIAL HAPPENINGS.

Two big social events next weekend.
Friday 14th March.
Another swinging Bronte Harbour Cruise. All those who went to the last one will agree that this must not be missed. Boat leaves Quay Wharf No.2 at 7.15. Tickets available from most club members. Be there!!
Saturday 15th March.
A big party at Bill Parsons, the aim of which is to raise money to send the Colts Team to Brisbane. This is a function that no one must miss.(There will be games of chance for the punters among us.)   Guys-$2.00,   Girls $1.00 and a plate of food. Starts about 8.00p.m.   Be There !!!

COMING MATCHES.

Wed 12th March vs Wests at ~~Ashfield.~~ Drummoyne
Wed 19th March vs Parramatta at Balmain.

▲ Match reports for Bronte v Collaroy played at Manly Baths on Wed, 26th Feb1969 & v Universities played at Balmain Baths on Wed, 5th March 1969.

In Division I, the 3rd Grade finished in second place, but lost to Bondi (2~5) in the final. The 2nd Grade finished second on the ladder as well, and won through to the grand-final, but were narrowly defeated by Balmain (3~4). The 1st Grade also finished the competition in second place with a formidable defensive record, but were trounced by Balmain in the semi-final (3~8), before narrowly losing the final to Universities (8~9).

Billy McCarthy [5]

Billy McCarthy grew up around the 'Five Ways' in Paddington, and on weekends either took the tram to Bondi or walked to Rushcutters Bay Baths for entertainment. He unsuccessfully tried to join Balmain and Drummoyne water polo clubs, before being invited to play water polo with Bronte at Rushie Baths in 1960. John Thornett, who Billy always thought to be a scholar, athlete and gentleman, quickly became his mentor.

Billy began as 3rd Grade goalkeeper in 1960/61, and won a premiership in his inaugural season. But he was dropped by Momie Vadas the next season for refusing to play in goals. Thorn eventually stepped in and sorted out the differences, with Billy later moving into the field for most of the rest of his playing career.

Bronte was a very social club and members would often hang out together. Dick Thornett and Kenny Owens were close mates and were often seen together at the Bondi Rex and Coogee Oceanic. Billy recalls that Dick Thornett was 'the greatest natural athlete' that he had ever struck, despite him often being lazy!

As the new and younger players all came through 3rd

Bill 'Sonny' McCarthy

Grade, Billy mentored many 'recruits' and became known as the 'club developer'. He captain/coached the 3rd Grade side alongside stalwarts Gary Cawood, John Keane and John Solomons for many years, and picked up another 3rd Grade premiership in 1968. He also coached the Bronte Ladies team to a grand-final appearance in 1968.

Billy remembers that an 'unbelievable change' came over the entire club when Graeme Samuel took over as head coach in 1969/70, as he ushered in a completely new attitude across all teams. Fellow West Australian David Neesham also attended training sessions at Rushie in those days and the two of them together, both WA Olympians, ran circles around the rest of us.

Billy was also involved in coaching rugby teams at Scots College and Easts RU, as well as in the USA at Vermont and New Hampshire. He was of the firm opinion that the main reason Bronte fell apart was the lack of juniors coming through. His all time top five players at Bronte were... Dick Thornett, Graeme Samuel, John Thornett, Billy Parsons and Peter Folden, with Donny Sarkies the pick of the goalkeepers.

Always a great club man, it was Billy McCarthy, the club 'developer and mentor', who was also the main driver in organising the successful 2004 Bronte Club Reunion at Easts Rugby Union Club.[5]

" THE SPIRIT OF BRONTE."
by Morgo.

VERSUS WESTERN SUBURBS.

1st Grade.
Firsts were not really impressive in defeating a pretty weak Western Suburbs side 6-0. Bronte scored some good goals, but their overall play was not what it should be. Rolly Flesch and Gary Cawood both had good games.
Bronte 6 (R.Flesch 2, R.See, J.Gahagan, A.Kasco, W.Parsons) bt. Wests 0.

2nd Grade.
Seconds proved much too strong for Wests and were in complete control for the whole game. Seconds seemed to display a lot more teamwork than they have in recent matches and it certainly paid dividends.
Bronte 7 (C.Simpson 3, G.Robinson, P.O'Hara, J.Power, J.Kirkwood) bt. Wests 0.

3rd Grade.
Thirds came up against quite a rugged Bilgola side and had to pull out all stops to win. There was a lack of cohesion due to the absence of regular players, but the team was able to lift their game and ran out winners 3-2. Jack Campbell, Chris Simpson and Danny Hofbauer all played well.
Bronte 3 (C.Simpson 2, W.McCarthy) bt. Bilgola 2.

4th Grade.
Fourths, after leading 2-0 had to be content with a 2-2 draw against Wests. They played well, but a couple of lapses in defence let Wests in. George Glenn scored 2 good goals, while Ernie Kritzler and Alan Webb also played well.
Bronte 2 (G.Glenn 2) drew with Wests 2.

OSCAR OF THE WEEK.
To "ironman" Chris (Kipper) Simpson who on Wednesday night played two full matches against Wests (2nds and 3rds) and as well notched up 5 goals. Well done Chris!

SOCIAL HAPPENINGS.
Don't forget the turn at Bill Parson's tonight. Please note the variation in charges- Guys $1, Girls $1 and a plate of food. It starts about 8p.m. and the address is
8 Goodrich Avenue,
Kingsford.
Be there!!

COMING MATCHES.
Wed 19th March   vs Parramatta at Balmain.
Wed 26th March   vs St.George at Balmain.

ooooooo0000000oooooooo

"THE SPIRIT OF BRONTE."
by Morgo.

VERSUS PARRAMATTA

1st Grade.
Firsts played well only in patches in their 6-1 defeat of Parramatta. Their defence was good, but often, when attacking, there was no one "up front" to take the pass. Quicker breaking seems to be needed. Alex Kasco and Rolly Flesch were the pick of the players.
Bronte 6 (W.Parsons 2, A.Kasco, R.See, J.Gahagan, R.Flesch) bt. Parramatta 1.

2nd Grade.
Seconds completely overwhelmed Parramatta 11-0. They were far too strong in all depart-ments. Despite the weak opposition, however, Seconds are playing much better Polo than they were a month ago and this augers well with the Semis nearly upon us.
Bronte 11 (P.O'Hara 4, C.Simpson 3, J.Kirkwood 3, G.Robinson 1) bt. Parramatta 0.

3rd Grade.
Thirds scored a comfortable 9-2 win over Parramatta and in doing so showed a welcome return to form. The understanding between the forwards is getting better all the time, while the defence was again quite adequate. Ross Selleck scored some great goals, while Danny Hofbauer and Warren Reilly also played well.
Bronte 9 (R.Selleck 5, W.McCarthy 3, W.Reilly 1) bt. Parramatta 2.

4th Grade.
Fourths, after a good start, again tired and were beaten 6-3. The team however was by no means disgraced and the goals scored by George Glenn and Rob Barta were real beauties.
Parramatta 6 bt. Bronte 3 (G.Glenn 2, R.Barta 1)

OSCAR OF THE WEEK.
To the Social Committee for the 2 great functions last weekend. The Harbour Cruise was even bigger and better than the first one, and, although the party at Bill Parson's was not as well attended as would have been liked, everyone who went really had a great time. Well done Social Committee, and thanks to Bill and Mr. and Mrs. Parsons for the use of their home.

COMING MATCHES.
Wed. 26th March   vs.   St.George at Balmain.

xxxxxxxxxxxxxxxxxxxx

▲ Match reports for Bronte v Western Suburbs played at Drummoyne Baths on Wed, 12th March 1969 & v Parramatta played at Balmain Baths on Wed, 19th March 1969.

Graeme

Graeme Samuel was born in Nedlands, in Perth WA. As a youngster he enjoyed swimming at both Nedlands and Claremont Baths on the Swan River and first began playing water polo with the 'Dolphins' under 12's squad at Crawley Baths. Under mentors Frank Sturgeon and Alan Charleston, 'Sammy' developed into a determined and tactical water polo player, and alongside teammates Stan Hammond, Bruce Nicholas and Doug Chant, he was a member of the Dolphins 1st Grade premiership teams of 1963, 64 and 68. His representative career began in 1962, and he remained a valuable member of the WA State team until 1968, although he opted out in 1966 while playing for 'Rote Erde Hamm' in the German League alongside Tom Hoad.

Graeme Samuel was first selected in the Australian team after West Australia won the Australian Championships in Sydney in 1964, and so he competed at the Tokyo Olympic Games under coach Alex Kosegi. He was also a member of the Australian teams for the 1965 World Tour under Nino Sydney, and for the 1967 World Tour under Alex Kosegi. 'Sammy' was also selected in the 1968 Australian team for the Mexico Olympic Games, but this side was tragically denied participation by the Australian Olympic Committee.

Returning to Sydney, Sammy was invited by David Woods to stay at the Woods family home for a few days. However, his 3 day stint turned into 3 months when he joined the Balmain club. Despite being ineligible to compete for NSW due to transfer rules, he greatly contributed to Balmain's 1969 1st

Samuel

Grade premiership that season.

Ten days previously, following Bronte's defeat in the semi-final, and during a post-game celebration at a Balmain pub, Sammy was asked by Don Sarkies, Les Kay, Graeme Robinson and Chris Simpson whether he might be interested in taking on the coaching role at Bronte? Although not really aware of Bronte's pedigree at that stage, the challenge appealed to him and just like that, Bronte had a new head player/coach with international and Olympic experience. Sammy joined the club a few months later and went on to gain another six representative caps with the NSW team until 1975, giving him a total of 12 appearances in the national championships.

Graeme Samuel immediately helped turn the Bronte club around over the next few years, with the 1st Grade being runners-up in 1970, premiers in 1971, and finalists in 1972. Graeme Samuel's outstanding contribution and untiring efforts both as a player and head coach, and his devotion to Bronte Water Polo Club deserve heartfelt congratulations and great admiration across his six seasons with the club. [6]

Graeme Samuel (aka 'Sammy') transferred to Bronte after a short stint with Balmain, but was originally from the Dolphins Water Polo Club of Perth, Western Australia. By 1969 'Sammy' had been on four Australian team tours, including two Olympic tournaments... in all a contribution of 114 caps for Australia, and he was ideally suited to take over from Momie Vadas as head coach at Bronte. LEFT PAGE: Australia v Essen, with Sammy 5th from the left (26th May 1965); Sammy in the 1964 Tokyo Olympic team (back row, 3rd from left); Sammy with Dolphins and Olympic teammate Stan Hammond in 1964. RIGHT PAGE: Sammy in the 1967 Australian team (seated, 2nd from right); Sammy in the ill-fated 1968 Mexico Olympic team.

1968/69 NSWAWPA RESULTS

Division 1, 1st Grade—

	Played	W.	D.	L.	Goals For	Goals Against	Pts.	Pos.
Balmain	18	17	1		106	32	53	1
Bronte	18	14	2	2	75	33	48	2
Universities	18	13	3	2	97	33	47	3
Bondi	18	11	2	5	52	41	42	4
Collaroy	18	8	1	9	54	65	35	5
St. George	18	6	4	8	42	68	34	6
Parramatta	18	4	4	10	24	69	30	7
Drummoyne	18	3	3	12	21	73	27	8
Western Suburbs	18	3	2	13	34	91	26	9

1st Semi-final: Universities 8 def. Bondi 5.
2nd Semi-final: Balmain 8 def. Bronte 3.
Final: Universities 9 def. Bronte 8.
Grand Final: Balmain 2 def. Universities 1.

Division 1, 2nd Grade—

	Played	W.	D.	L.	Forf. or Disq.	Goals For	Goals Against	Pts.	Pos.
Balmain	18	14	3	1	—	70	25	49	1
Bronte	18	15	—	3	—	87	25	48	2
St. George	18	13	1	3	1	66	33	44	3
Universities	18	11	1	6	—	58	40	41	4
Collaroy	18	10	2	6	—	54	46	40	5
Bondi	18	9	2	5	2	44	36	36	6
Parramatta	18	4	2	12	—	28	73	28	7
Western Suburbs	18	4	1	13	—	16	68	27	8
Drummoyne	18	3	—	14	1	16	93	23	9

1st Semi-final: Universities 7 def. St. George 5.
2nd Semi-final: Bronte 4 def. Balmain 2.
Final: Balmain 2 def. Universities 1.
Grand Final: Balmain 4 def. Bronte 3.

Division 1, 3rd Grade—

	Played	W.	D.	L.	Forf. or Disq.	Goals For	Goals Against	Pts.	Pos.
Balmain	18	14	1	3	—	84	24	47	1
Bronte	18	14	1	3	—	83	44	47	2
St. George	18	13	2	2	1	84	33	45	3
Bondi	18	12	2	2	2	55	26	42	4
Universities	18	11	—	7	—	57	42	40	5
Collaroy	18	9	—	9	—	47	46	36	6
Bilgola	18	6	—	12	—	27	92	30	7
Drummoyne	18	4	—	14	—	24	98	26	8
Parramatta	18	4	—	14	—	16	72	26	9

1st Semi-final: Bondi 6 def. St. George 1.
2nd Semi-final: Balmain 3 def. Bronte 2.
Final: Bondi 5 def. Bronte 2.
Grand Final: Bondi 3 def. Balmain 2.

Division 1, 4th Grade—

	Played	W.	D.	L.	Forf. or Disq.	Goals For	Goals Against	Pts.	Pos.
St. George	18	15	1	1	1	83	21	50	1
Balmain	18	14	1	3	—	53	25	47	2
Collaroy	18	11	2	4	1	43	30	41	3
Bondi	18	11	2	2	3	42	20	39	4
Parramatta	18	10	1	7	—	40	41	39	5
Drummoyne	18	8	1	9	—	38	43	35	6
Western Suburbs	18	7	2	9	—	35	50	34	7
Bronte	18	4	2	11	1	29	57	27	8
Universities	18	3	—	15	—	13	89	24	9

1st Semi-final: Bondi 3 def. Collaroy 2.
2nd Semi-final: Balmain 9 def. St. George 7.
Final: St. George 4 def. Bondi 3.
Grand Final: Balmain 6 def. St. George 5.

Division 2, 1st Grade—

	Played	W.	D.	L.	Forf. or Disq.	Goals For	Goals Against	Pts.	Pos.
Maroubra	18	15	1	2	—	101	52	49	1
Balmain	18	13	3	2	—	92	42	47	2
North Sydney	18	12	—	6	—	85	41	42	3
Canterbury	18	11	1	6	—	56	46	41	4
Penrith	18	9	1	8	—	61	56	37	5
Collaroy	18	8	1	8	1	78	74	34	6
Liverpool	18	7	1	9	—	57	54	32	7
Bronte	18	6	—	10	2	43	76	28	8
Northbridge	18	2	—	15	1	34	96	21	9
Illawarra	18	2	—	14	2	43	120	20	10

1st Semi-final: Canterbury 3 def. North Sydney 1.
2nd Semi-final: Balmain 8 def. Maroubra 2.
Final: Maroubra 8 def. Canterbury 2.
Grand Final: Balmain 10 def. Maroubra 1.

1969-70

1969/70 NSWAWPA OFFICIALS: H.K. Porter (Patron); V. Chalwin (President); H.J. Bund (Past President); F. Falson (Chairman); **R. Vadas (Registrar)**; W. Gooley (Secretary); L. Papps (A/Secretary); M. Withers (Comp. Secretary); A. Sparkes (Country Secretary); O. Bogg (Treasurer).

The major sponsors of the Association this season were W.D. & H.O. Wills, the Speedo Knitting Mills for the Pre-Season competition, the Cascade Brewery for the inaugural State Team selection competition, the Shell Company of Australia for the State Junior Championships and Cottee's for the Country Championships.

Special Coaching Tours

Rothmans Sports Foundation again assisted the Association by sponsoring two coaching tours to improve the standard of water polo. NSW captain/coach, Mr. David Woods toured Tasmania lecturing and coaching Tasmanian teams, and he also assisted the Tasmanian team at the Australian Championships. Alex Kosegi again visited Duntroon Military College to coach the College teams.

At this time, a significant source of talent was coming from closer links that had been established with the New South Wales Combined High Schools Sports Association (NSWCHS). School-based water polo competitions were becoming much more popular and interest in the game was bringing many young players into the sport, particularly through the annual NSWCHS knockout tournaments.

By season 1969/70 the St. George-Sutherland District AWPA had grown so strong that they were administering their own competitions and had grown to an involvement of some 41 teams. Matches were played at Gunnamatta Bay (1 & 2) and Carss Park, with admission charges to pools at that time being 20c for Over 16s, and 10c for Under16s!

The Baths & Clubs

The NSWAWPA 1969/70 season again witnessed a number of new developments. A new State team selection competition was inaugurated and sponsored by the Cascade Brewery. As well as the traditional Open Men's team, representative teams were selected for the NSW Country, NSW Ladies and NSW Colts teams. In addition, two new Junior competitions were inaugurated, the first being sponsored by the Shell Company for an U/16 competition and the second was the inaugural 'Col Smee' Memorial Trophy for the Colts.

Following the Pre-Season Cup and the Cascade Cup warm-up competitions, which most players made use of in order to develop their fitness, the summer premiership commenced. The metropolitan competitions were again conducted with Division I consisting of four grades, with two grades each in Divisions II and III, which came mostly from the nine largest and most powerful water polo clubs.

No new clubs joined the NSWAPWA competitions in 1969/70. The following clubs lapsed: Bilgola, Blacktown, Hawkesbury, HMAS Nirimba, Illawarra and University of NSW. The number of entries received in the men's metropolitan competitions dropped to 60 teams from just 21 clubs, which was a substantial decrease.[7]

Representatives in NSW Teams

Such was the dominance of Victoria throughout the 1960's, that by 1969 the NSW Mens State team had only claimed one national title since 1957, so drastic changes were required. The bulk of the team was retained including Bronte's Peter Folden, however four of the five new caps from 1969 were dropped, while two ex-Olympians in Mick Withers (Balmain) and Nick Barnes (Universities) were recalled. The

1969/70 Season Statistics N.S.W.A.W.P.A.

Clubs in the Mens Water Polo Competitions.

Clubs	1	2	3	4	2¹	2²	3ᴱ	3ᵂ	Total
Balmain	●	●	●	●	●	●	●		7
Bondi	●	●	●	●					4
Bronte	●	●	●	●					4
Canterbury						●		●	2
Clovelly						●			1
Collaroy Devils	●	●	●	●					4
Drummoyne	●	●	●	●					4
Judean							●		1
Liverpool							2		2
Maroubra						●			1
Nth Palm Beach						●			1
Nth Sydney						●	●	●	3
Northbridge						●			1
Parramatta	●	●	●	●					4
Parramatta Memorial							2		2
Penrith						●	●	●	3
St. George/Sutherland	●	●	●	●					4
Sth Sydney Police BC							●		1
Sydney University						●	●	●	3
Universities	●	●	●	●					4
Western Suburbs	●	●	●	●					4
	9	9	9	9	8	6	5	5	60

Results of the Mens Water Polo Competitions.

Grade	Premier	Runner-Up
1st	Bondi & Balmain	Pre-Season Comp
1st	Bronte	Cascade Cup Comp
1st	Balmain~4 d. 3~Bronte	
2nd	Bronte~4 d. 3~Balmain	
3rd	Balmain~3 d. 2~St. George/S'land	
4th	Balmain~7 d. 6~St. George/S'land	
Club Champions	BALMAIN	
D2¹ˢᵗ	Penrith~6 d. 5~Balmain	
D2²ⁿᵈ	Nth Sydney~4 d. 3~Penrith	
D3ᴾˡᵃʸᵒff	Liverpool A~6 d. 1~Sth Sydney Police BC	
D3ᴱˢᵗ	Sth Sydney Police BC~3 d. 2~Balmain	
D3ᵂˢᵗ	Liverpool A~5 d. 3~P'matta Memorial A	

NEW SOUTH WALES
AMATEUR WATER POLO ASSOCIATION

**METROPOLITAN
COMPETITION DRAW
1969 - 1970**

BOX A81
P.O. SYDNEY SOUTH
N.S.W. 2000

PRICE 10 CENTS

▲ *1968/69 NSWAWPA Metropolitan Water Polo Draw.*

"Graeme Samuel joined Bronte from Balmain as captain/coach in October 1969 and I finally got the 1st Grade goalkeeping spot from Don. Two years later I was told they were blooding a young goal keeper in Jeff Stubbs from Newtown, and I would have to share games. At 21 I thought I was still young, I also saw that there were people in the Club who wanted to move in different directions, so at the end of 1971/72, I transferred to Balmain."

Phil Bower, 29 Jan 2019

game changer however, was that NSW was bolstered by two West Australians now playing on the East Coast... they were ex-Melville player David Neesham (ACT), and Bronte's new recruit in Graeme Samuel from the Dolphins club in Perth.

The revamped side made all the difference with NSW winning all ten of their matches in a dominant and undefeated display. Victoria was relegated into third place by WA.

Colts Interstate Series

In this season, invitations were extended to the NSW Colts teams from two different States to contest a series of interstate matches. New South Wales selected two Colts teams with the State Colts I making a tour of Tasmania where they were undefeated in all five matches.

1970 NSWAWPA COLTS I: John Stapleton (c, Balmain), Peter Kerr (v/c, St. George), Richie Semmens (Balmain), Joe Falzon (Balmain), Randall Goff (St. George), Warwick Syphers (St. George), Graham Facey (St. George), Ken Brandon (Bondi), Steve Quill (Drummoyne), Ian Baguley (Penrith), Paul Dunford (Coach/Manager, Balmain).

1970 NSWAWPA COLTS II: Brett Gooley (c, St George), Terry Senior (Balmain), Terry Jansen (Balmain), Tony Falson (St. George), Bob Lumb (g, St. George), **Peter O'Hara (Bronte)**, Doug Grevitt (Bondi), Ian Williams (Western Suburbs), Les Morrison (Balmain), Jack Gerrie (Balmain), Les Papps (Coach/Manager, Parramatta).

The NSW State Colts II team, which included Peter O'Hara (Bronte), travelled to Brisbane where they played against various Brisbane club teams and the Queensland State team, but still managed to win three of their four matches.

The Premierships

The pre-season competition, which was conducted on a points basis, was won jointly by both Bondi and Balmain, and the inaugural 'Cascade Cup' competition was won by Bronte.

In the 1st Grade play-offs, Parramatta pioneered their initial 1st Grade semi-final, but were unluckily defeated by Universities

▶ Clash of Simpsons . . . Peter Simpson, left, of Brisbane, moves in quickly to block the pass by Chris Simpson, of Bronte. They were competing in the State waterpolo trials at the Valley Pool today.

NEW SOUTH WALES MENS TEAM
1970 - National Champions - Sydney
From left: David Woods (c/Coach, Balmain), Mick Withers (g, Balmain), Nick Barnes (Universities), David Neesham (ACT), **Graeme Samuel (Bronte)**, Peter Montgomery (Universities), **Peter Folden (Bronte)**, Ian McLauchlain (Balmain), Max May (Balmain), John Harrison (g, Universities), Ken Laws (Balmain). Photo - NSWAWPA Annual Report 1969/70.

(5~6) in the minor semi, and Bronte walloped the minor premiers Balmain (9~3) in the major semi-final. Balmain then narrowly defeated Universities (5~4) to set up a re-match against Bronte in the competition finale.

Going into the grand-final, Balmain's form had been poor, but with perseverance and great resolve, they narrowly overcame a wily and talented Bronte outfit (4~3) to retain their 1st Grade premiership. In this season, Balmain attained the remarkable feat of contesting six grand-finals out of seven competitions, and subsequently celebrated premierships in the 1st, 3rd and 4th Grades in Division I.

With such results, it was little wonder that the Balmain Club also took home the Club Championship. Bronte was however, successful in annexing the 2nd Grade premiership.

BALMAIN AWPC
1969/70 - NSWAWPA Men's 1st Grade Premiers
David Woods (c), John Stapleton, John Waddington, Ian McLauchlain, John McFarlane, Michael Withers (g), Phil Kidd, Eric Fitzgerald, Max May, Ken Laws.

Junior Competitions

The U/16 Shell Shield

The Shell Shield was donated by the oil company of the same name to promote the Under 16's Junior Water Polo tournament, which was conducted on the 14th and 15th March. The series was organised and hosted by the Goulburn Water Polo Club. Nine clubs competed and the eventual winner was

THE AMATEUR SWIMMING UNION
OF AUSTRALIA PRESENTS

THE NATIONAL
WATER POLO
CHAMPIONSHIP

ASHFIELD POOL ASHFIELD, N.S.W.
19th FEBRUARY TO 1st MARCH, 1970

PROGRAMME 20c

▲ *TOP: Program for the 1970 National Championships in Sydney. ABOVE: Les Kay joined up with Bronte at the start of the 1970s, although he didn't coach any teams until 1973/74 , when he took over as coach of the Bronte Ladies team.*

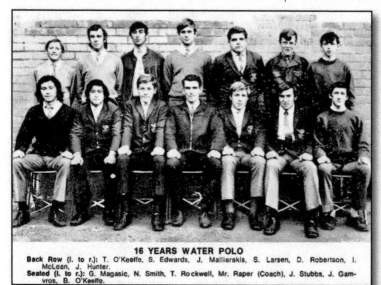

16 YEARS WATER POLO
Back Row (l. to r.): T. O'Keeffe, S. Edwards, J. Malliarakis, S. Larsen, D. Robertson, I. McLean, J. Hunter.
Seated (l. to r.): G. Magasic, N. Smith, T. Rockwell, Mr. Raper (Coach), J. Stubbs, J. Gamvros, B. O'Keeffe.

▲A number of future Bronte recruits came from Enmore BHS. ▼Robbie Vadas was a loyal stalwart for the Bronte Club, seen here graduating from Sydney University.

1st Grade Water Polo Results

Drummoyne Pool:
Drummoyne 4 (T. Smith 2, D. Hendricks, S. Quill) d. West Subs 2 (G. Wulf, I. Phillips).

Gunnamatta Bay Baths:
Universities 8 (W. Phillips 4, P. Montgomery 2, R. Greenaway, D. Cohen) d. St George-Sutherland 2 (T. Falson, B. Falson).

Dawn Fraser Pool: Bronte 6 (P. Folden 3, G. Samuel 2, C. Simpson) d. Parramatta City 1 (C. Cop).

Northbridge Baths:
Bondi 12 (T. Baldock 5, R. Mendels 3, R. de Groot 3, H. Merkur) d. Collaroy Devils 5 (B. Hutchings 3, F. Mayer, P. Sherwood).

Sydney Morning Herald, 5th March 1970.

Drummoyne, coached by their Hon. Secretary, Mr. Roger Wilkinson.

The Colts 'Col Smee' Memorial Trophy

The Bondi Club were applauded for developing an inaugural Colts Championship for Under 18's, to be known as the 'Col Smee Memorial Trophy' in honour of a great Bondi player following his tragic death by snakebite. This competition was an all day event conducted at Rushcutter's Bay Baths with some excellent water polo being played. The draw was seeded to produce a Bondi v St. George final and this proved to be the case, but only after some spirited opposition from Bronte, Balmain and Drummoyne. The eventual champions were St. George who succeeded in winning the Col Smee Trophy in its inaugural year.[7]

Bronte AWPC

"I started out with Bronte in October 1969 at Rushcutters Bay Baths, where after training on Monday nights, the 1st Grade were usually invited to Jack & Joyce Campbells house at Randwick for dinner... and with most of us being bachelors... it was terrific!"

Graeme Samuel, Oct 2020

Now fielding four teams in Division I, Bronte had another outstanding season in 1969/70. The 4th Grade qualified for the play-offs, but lost in the semi-final to Bondi (1~3). The 3rd Grade were undefeated on the year, but lost to Balmain in the final (1~5). Bronte 2nd Grade played brilliantly to finish top of the table, and took the premiership by defeating Balmain in the grand-final (4~3), allowing only 28 goals into their net in the entire season. With Graeme Samuel in the water and at the helm, the 1st Grade finished second on the ladder with the best defensive record, but unfortunately lost the grand-final to Balmain by the odd goal (3~4).

At the end of this season, Bronte AWPC had to make a decision to either pay more for their hiring of the baths at Rushcutters Bay or move on. They decided on the latter and found Watsons Bay Baths to be a good alternative, although nowhere near as convenient.

SYDNEY BOYS HIGH SCHOOL
1970 - NSWCHS Open Knockout Champions
Back row (from left): Glen Gilsenen, Steve Vidal, Ernie Kritzler, Lloyd Byram, Randy Vanderweide. Front row: Paul Connell, Lindsay Cotterill (c), Mr. J. Fraser (Coach), Wayne Turnbull, Steve Cody. (The Record - SBHS Yearbook, 1970).

"I was recruited from Sydney Boys High School for the Bronte club by Robbie Vadas, probably in 4th or 5th form (Year 10/11), without a joining fee. The High team used to train at the old Domain Baths in that not so salubrious harbour water, which probably only got slightly better at Dunc's Rushcutter's Bay Baths. Strangely that was the Bronte home pool, although far-from-home, as we

1969/70 Results

WATER POLO
SYDNEY DIVISION 1
1ST GRADE MATCHES
At Gunnamatta Bay Baths: Parramatta City 3 (C Cop 2 G Hannon) bt St George-Sutherland 2 (B Gooley B Falson). At Ashfield Pool: Universities 11 (P Montgomery 5 W Lamb 2 N Barnes D Cohen J Bennett Greenaway) bt Collaroy Devils 3 (P Drake G Meakin B Hutchings). At Drummoyne Pool: Balmain 2 (M Best K Laws) bt Drummoyne 0 (D Bogg). At Dawn Fraser Pool: Bronte 14 (W Parsons 3 P Folden 3 C Simpson 3 G Samuel 2 J Gahagan 2 P O'Hara) bt Western Suburbs 0.

SMH, 8th Jan, 1970

WATER POLO
SYDNEY FIRST DIVISION
MATCHES
At Drummoyne.—Universities 9 (P Montgomery 3 D Cohen 3 M Phillips) bt Drummoyne 3. At Ashfield.—St. George-Sutherland 5 (T Falson 2 B Gooley 2 K Mackinder) bt Collaroy Devils 1. At Parramatta.—Balmain 6 bt Parramatta City 1. At Dawn Fraser Pool.—Bronte 11 bt Bondi 6. Western Suburbs bye.

SMH, 26th Feb, 1970

WATER POLO
First Division Matches
DRUMMOYNE POOL. — 1st grade: Drummoyne 4 (T Smith 2 D Hendricks S Quill) bt Western Suburbs 2 (G Wull I Phillips). GUNNAMATTA BAY BATHS.—1st grade: Universities 8 (W Phillips 4 P Montgomery 2 R Greenaway D Cohen) bt St George-Sutherland 2 (T Falson B Falson). DAWN FRASER POOL.—1st grade: Bronte 6 (P Folden 3 G Samuel 2 C Simpson) bt Parramatta City 1 (C Cop). NORTHBRIDGE BATHS.—1st grade: Bondi 12 (T Baldock 5 R Mendies 3 R De Groot 3 H Mercur) bt Collaroy Devils 5 (B Hutchings 3 F Mayer P Sherwood).

SMH, 5th Mar, 1970

WATER POLO
In Wellington, N.Z.
Collaroy Devils (N.S.W.) beaten by Hutt Valley 2-4.
SYDNEY FIRST GRADE COMPETITION
At Dawn Fraser Pool: Universities 2 drew with Bronte 2. At Gunnamatta Bay Baths: Bondi 4 bt St George-Sutherland 2. At Drummoyne Pool: Parramatta City 4 bt Drummoyne 3. At Ashfield Pool: Balmain 6 bt Western Suburbs 1. Collaroy Devils bye.

SMH, 12th Feb, 1970

WATER POLO
AT ASHFIELD POOL.—A Div 1 First Grade: St George-Sutherland 7 (K MacKinder 3 B Falson 2 B Gooley P Kerr) bt Western Suburbs 1 (R Groves).
AT DRUMMOYNE POOL.—First Grade: Universities 4 (R Greenaway P Montgomery W Phillips) bt Bondi 2 (E Baldock P Waterman).
AT DAWN FRASER POOL.—First Grade: Bronte 5 (P Folden 3 W Parsons G Samuel) bt Balmain 4.
AT PARRAMATTA POOL.—First Grade: Parramatta City 4 (C Cop 3 F Dalglish) bt Collaroy Devils 1 (F Mayer).

SMH, 5th Feb, 1970

WATER POLO
1st Grade. — At Drummoyne.: Bronte 7 (W Parsons 3 C Simpson 2 P Folden R Flesch) bt Western Suburbs 1 (P Clay). At Parramatta: Parramatta City 7 (C Cop 4 G Hannan 2 R Sarson) bt St George-Sutherland 6 (D Kerr 2 C Williams 2 K Mackinder B Falson). At Dawn Fraser Pool: Balmain 7 (K Laws 2 M May 2 J Stapleton I McLauchlain D Woods) bt Drummoyne 3 (P Smith R Williams S Quill). At Northbridge: Universities 12 (P Montgomery 5 R Greenaway 3 W Phillips 2 D Cohen 2) bt Collaroy Devils 0. Bondi Bye in all four grades.

—SMH, 12th Mar, 1970

WATER POLO: Major competitionals, at Dawn Fraser Pool.—1st grade: Bronte 0 (P Folden 4 W Parsons C Simpson G Samuel D Barkitt) bt Balmain 3 (Fitzgerald M May McLaughlain). 2nd grade: Bronte 8 (J Power O'Hara T Folden J Thornett Kirkwood) bt Balmain 1 (M Best J Waddington R Pearce). 3rd grade: St George-Sutherland 2 (L Kerr 2 M Hunt 2 J Arnold Love) bt Bronte 1 (W McCarthy). 4th grade: St George-Sutherland 7 (M Dunn 3 S Vidal G Ponder C Mollz B Robinson C Love) bt Balmain (Bruce Battin E G Laughtin).

SMH, 30th Mar, 1970

WATER POLO
GRAND FINALS.
At Dawn Fraser Pool.
Ladies: St George (A) 8 (M Lanier 3 R Hardingham 3 A Turnbull 2) bt Bondi (A) 6 (L Saunders 2 C Taylor M Myers S Waddington). Div 2 1st grade: Penrith 6 (R Selleck 3 I Baguley 2 R Taylor) bt Balmain 5 (P Dunford 3 G Wormleaton 2). 2nd grade: North Sydney 4 (S McBurnie 4) bt Penrith 3 (J Murray 2 L Anderson). Div 3 Intersone Grand Final: Liverpool 6 (R West 2 R Brehmann 2 G Payne I Tyrell) bt South Sydney PBC 1 (W Cobbin).

SMH, 1st Apr, 1970

WATER POLO
At Dawn Fraser Pool
1st DIV FINALS.—1st grade: Balmain 5 (D Woods 2 K Laws 2 J Stapleton) bt Universities 4 (P Montgomery 2 W Lamb W Phillips). 2nd grade: Balmain 7 (R Semmens 3 E Matzen 2 J Waddington R Pearce) bt St George-Sutherland 5 (N Frost 2 G Dews R Hahne R Mandelson). 3rd grade: Balmain 5 (Brian Battin 2 T Laws B Moroney I Janson) bt Bronte 1 (W McCarthy). 4th grade: Balmain 5 (G Loughton 2 P Large Bruce Battin G Starling) bt Bondi 2 (P Jager J Cotterill).

SMH, 2nd Apr, 1970

WATER POLO
SYDNEY COMPETITION.—GRAND FINALS.—At Drummoyne Olympic Pool.
1st div 1st grade: Balmain 4 (D Woods K Laws J Stapleton I McLauchlain) bt Bronte 3 (I Folden 2 C Simpson). 2nd grade: Bronte 4 (P O'Hara 2 J Kirkwood Vadas) bt Balmain 3 (K Best R Pender I Waddington). 3rd grade: Balmain 3 (T Laws 2 Brian Battin) bt St George 2 (J Crisp 2). 4th grade: Balmain 7 (G Laughton 4 P Larg 2 S Smith) bt St George 6 (G Ponder 2 M Dunn 2 P Garling D Schmidt).
COMBINED HIGH SCHOOLS OF NSW v VICTORIAN SCHOOLBOYS.—At Parramatta Olympic Pool: NSW 3 (L Cotterill M Eather R Goff) bt Victoria 2 (S McBean 2). Series results: NSW 2 wins 1 draw beat Victoria 1 draw.

SMH, 6th Apr, 1970

BONDI AWPC - The 1969/70 season saw the winding down of one of Sydney's greatest water polo clubs in Bondi AWPC. Although the club struggled on for a few more seasons as Bondi Dolphins, East Sydney, Bondolphins, and another Bondi emerged for a couple of years in Division 3, the great club dissolved altogether after season 1974/75.

1969/70 NSWAWPA RESULTS

FIRST DIVISION
First Grade

	Win	Draw	Loss	Disq.	Goals For	Agst.	Points
BALMAIN	15	1	2	—	97	47	49
BRONTE	14	2	2	—	101	36	48
UNIVERSITIES	14	—	2	1	84	47	46
PARRAMATTA CITY	13	—	5	—	69	48	44
BONDI	11	—	7	—	81	69	40
DRUMMOYNE	7	1	10	—	27	68	33
ST. GEO.-SUTHERLAND	6	—	12	—	47	64	30
COLLAROY DEVILS	5	1	12	—	45	83	29
WESTERN SUBURBS	2	—	16	—	24	114	22

First Semi-Final: Universities 6 defeated Parramatta 5.
Second Semi-Final: Bronte 9 defeated Balmain 3.
Final: Balmain 5 defeated Universities 4.
Grand Final: Balmain 4 defeated Bronte 3.

FIRST DIVISION FIRST GRADE PREMIERS: BALMAIN.

Second Grade

	Win	Draw	Loss	Disq.	Goals For	Agst.	Points
BRONTE	15	—	3	—	67	22	48
BALMAIN	16	—	—	2	70	33	48
ST. GEO.-SUTHERLAND	13	1	4	—	41	28	45
BONDI	11	1	6	—	56	34	41
UNIVERSITIES	10	—	8	—	41	32	38
PARRAMATTA CITY	6	2	10	—	37	62	32
COLLAROY DEVILS	6	1	11	—	35	62	31
DRUMMOYNE	4	4	10	—	16	46	30
WESTERN SUBURBS	2	5	11	—	18	72	27

First Semi-Final: St. George-Sutherland defeated Bondi (disqualified).
Second Semi-Final: Bronte 5 defeated Balmain 3.
Final: Balmain 7 defeated St. George-Sutherland 5.
Grand Final: Bronte 4 defeated Balmain 3.

FIRST DIVISION SECOND GRADE PREMIERS: BRONTE.

Third Grade

	Win	Draw	Loss	Disq.	Goals For	Agst.	Points
Bronte	16	1	1	—	49	17	51
ST. GEO.-SUTHERLAND	16	—	2	—	86	11	50
BALMAIN	13	2	3	—	52	23	46
PARRAMATTA CITY	10	3	5	—	30	35	41
COLLAROY DEVILS	6	3	9	—	31	45	33
UNIVERSITIES	7	1	9	1	36	45	32
WESTERN SUBURBS	6	2	10	—	27	59	32
BONDI	5	2	11	—	16	48	30
DRUMMOYNE	3	2	13	—	18	61	26

First Semi-Final: Balmain 8 defeated Parramatta City 1.
Second Semi-Final: St. George-Sutherland 6 defeated Bronte 1.
Final: Balmain 5 defeated Bronte 1.
Grand Final: Balmain 3 defeated St. George-Sutherland 2.

FIRST DIVISION THIRD GRADE PREMIERS: BALMAIN.

Fourth Grade

	Win	Draw	Loss	Disq.	Goals For	Agst.	Points
ST. GEO.-SUTHERLAND	17	—	1	—	79	11	52
BALMAIN	16	—	2	—	82	9	50
BONDI	14	—	4	—	54	18	46
BRONTE	9	—	9	—	39	42	36
COLLAROY DEVILS	10	—	6	2	43	51	36
WESTERN SUBURBS	9	—	9	—	31	44	36
PARRAMATTA CITY	6	—	10	2	20	68	28
UNIVERSITIES	5	1	8	4	28	68	25
DRUMMOYNE	3	—	14	1—	15	76	25

First Semi-Final: Bondi 3 defeated Bronte 1.
Second Semi-Final: St. George-Sutherland 7 defeated Balmain 3.
Final: Balmain 5 defeated Bondi 2.
Grand Final: Balmain 7 defeated St. George-Sutherland 6.

FIRST DIVISION FOURTH GRADE PREMIERS: BALMAIN.

"After arriving in Sydney at the end of 1968, I picked up a job with Phillip Morris, but I joined Balmain through fellow Olympian, Dave Woods and was a member of their 1969 premiership 1st Grade team. But I already knew Les Kay and Don Sarkies, so during a post game drink at a Balmain pub, I agreed to coach Bronte for the 1969/70 season. Bronte were a top bunch of guys, but needed more knowledge, skills and training... so thats what I gave them! Sadly, the club ended in 1975 when I moved to Maroubra Seals for a season before retiring."

Graeme Samuel, Oct 2020

were like permanent expats. All those harbour training sessions must have done wonders for my immune system.

I soon discovered this Bronte coterie of 'reffo' (mainly Hungarian) water polo masters were quite happy to teach me the game and a few tricks, particularly under Bert's benevolent eye. In the 2nd Grade team I recall a good mixture of veterans, young guys and a few pups like me, with a great team spirit of solid backs and our goalie Phil Bower defending, with mobile forwards in attack like John Thornett, Jon Kirkwood , Tom Folden, Robbo, John Power, and Robbie Vadas et al.

As a junior member I always felt valued and taken care of. John Wardrop would often give me a lift to games in his rapid Mini of the day, and I also remember getting squeezed into Vic McGrath's MK VII Jag for a weekend away to Tamworth and doing the ton up the New England highway!

And of course, assisted by all was my introduction to under-age drinking in a variety of post-game pubs around Sydney, which served me well for my later life at Uni.

My memories of particular matches is vague, but I do recall some rough interactions with our arch-nemesis the Balmain club, who played in the old style and had a few nasty grapplers.

In my final year at school I managed to be selected for the NSW Combined High Schools team, along with future luminaries like Peter Montgomery, and we defeated the Victorian Schoolboys team 4 to 2 in the final, which was no doubt the highlight of my water polo career with my two goal contribution.

After my University studies a few years later, I took off to see the world as a flight steward with QANTAS, but unfortunately that was the end of my water polo career. However, those formative years playing for Bronte Water Polo Club, and with the greatest bunch of guys you'll ever meet holds very fond memories.

Vale Bronte WPC, and long live its surviving members.

Peter O'Hara, 23 October 2020

1970-71

1970/71 NSWAWPA OFFICIALS: H.K. Porter (Patron), V. Chalwin (President), F. Falson (Chairman), **R. Vadas (Registrar)**, W. Gooley (Secretary), L. Papps (A/Secretary); P. Jones (Comp. Secretary), R. Wilkinson (Country Secretary), O. Bogg (Treasurer).

The new season got underway with the 41st NSWAWPA Annual General Meeting in Sydney.

The Baths & Clubs

During this season competition games were contested at Ashfield, Balmain, Drummoyne, Gunnamatta Bay, Parramatta and Northbridge Baths.

Five new clubs joined the NSWAPWA competition in 1970/71 in Avalon-Bilgola, Manly-Warringah, Newtown and Ryde, while Cronulla-Sutherland changed their name from St George. Unfortunately Maroubra, Northbridge and South Sydney Police Boys clubs lapsed, with Collaroy morphing into Manly-Warringah. The number of entries received in the men's metropolitan competitions remained the same as the previous season with 60 teams entering the various competitions from 21 clubs.

There were seven grade premierships conducted across two Divisions throughout the 1970/71 NSWAWPA men's competitions, as well as one grade in the women's competition.[8]

Representatives in NSW Teams

The NSW Men's State team retained eight of its 1970 championship winning team this season, including both Peter Folden and Graeme Samuel of Bronte. Three Balmain players in Ken Laws, Max May and Micky Withers made way for Con Copp and goalkeeper Ben Schmidt (Parramatta), while Bill Phillips Jr. (Universities) returned after a two year hiatus.

> "My recollection of the move to Watson's Bay was that there was conflict with the proprietor of Rushcutters Bay Baths and training times were limited as the pool was shared with Wests. I think that increases in the pool hiring fees also had something to do with it."
>
> *Phil Bower, 29 Jan 2019*

> "Training was two nights a week at Rushie and Saturday afternoon. Rolly Flesch and Peter Folden were there, but even before Watson's Bay,...what concerned me was, we weren't getting any new talent and couldn't seem to recruit anyone at Watson's Bay, so I made a number of appeals for new members over three years."
>
> *Billy McCarthy, Feb 2019*

1970/71 Season Statistics
N.S.W.A.W.P.A.

Clubs in the Mens Water Polo Competitions.

Clubs	1	2	3	4	2¹	2²	2³	Total
Avalon/Bilgola						●		1
Balmain	●	●	●	●	●	2	2	9
Bondi Dolphins	●	●	●	●				4
Bronte	●	●	●	●				4
Canterbury					●		●	2
Clovelly					●		●	2
Cronulla/Sutherland	●	●	●	●	●			5
Drummoyne							●	1
Judean					●		●	2
Liverpool					●		●	2
Manly/Warringah	●	●	●	●				4
Newtown						●		1
Nth Palm Beach							●	1
Nth Sydney					●		●	3
Parramatta City	●	●	●	●				4
Parramatta Memorial							●	1
Penrith					●		●	3
Ryde							●	1
Sydney University					●		●	2
Universities	●	●	●	●				4
Western Suburbs	●	●	●	●				4
	8	8	8	8	8	10	10	60

Results of the Mens Water Polo Competitions.

Grade	Premier	Runner-Up
1st	Balmain	Pre-Season Comp
1st	Bronte	Cascade Cup Comp
1st	Bronte~4	d. 3~Universities
2nd	Balmain~4	d. 3~Bronte
3rd	Cronulla/Sutherland~3	d. 2~Balmain
4th	Cronulla/Sutherland~5	d. 3~Balmain
	Club Champions	BALMAIN
D2 1st	Clovelly~8	d. 6~Penrith
D2 2nd	Balmain A~4	d. 3~Liverpool
D2 3rd	Balmain A~8	d. 7~Balmain B

N.S.W. WATER POLO TEAMS—HOBART, 1971.

Men's Team—Australian Champions (undefeated for the second successive year), Western Australia 2nd, Victoria 3rd.

Women's Team—Third to South Australia (1st) and Victoria (2nd).

Standing—Men: Kon Cop, Mr. Les Papps (Coach, Women's Team), John Harrison, Peter Folden, Ben Schmitz, David Woods (Captain-Coach, Men's Team), Ian McLauchlain, Peter Montgomery, Graeme Samuel, David Neesham (V/Captain), Nick Barnes, Bill Phillips.

Standing—Women: Cathie Taylor, Virginia Turnbull, Marilyn Mitchell, Julie Girdler, Mrs. Nola Goddard (Chaperone, Women's Team), Carolyn Keats.

Seated:—Mr. Bill Gooley (Manager, N.S.W. Combined Team), Ruth Hardingham, Vicki White, Adrienne Turnbull (V/Capt.), Marilyn Myers (Captain, Women's Team), Diane McDougall, Jenny Dunn, Mr. Viv. Chalwin (President, N.S.W.A.W.P.A.).

▲ *Graeme Samuel of the Bronte club, who was never known for his 'legs', in action for NSW against Queensland, at the 1971 Australian Championships in Hobart. LEFT: Peter Folden was regularly the top scorer for Bronte, and was an essential member of the NSW State from 1967 until 1975.*
RIGHT: Official Program for the 1971 National Championships in Hobart, Tasmania.

Once again, NSW was dominant throughout the national championships, and proved to be a formidable side in playing through the week-long competition to remain undefeated in the tournament, with Victoria finishing third behind Western Australia. At these 24th Australian Championships in Hobart, Bronte's Peter Folden was generally acknowledged as the best player of the tournament.

"My father, gave up virtually any involvement in water polo about 1970… and after Graeme Samuel took over. I was originally nervous about Sammys coaching methods, but he was a terrific player and coach. His training was revolutionary, with less emphasis on improving skills… and much more attention to attack, in & out. He brought a completely new style that he tried to get Bronte to play. It was so unorthodox… being a swimming game and to keep the ball moving!"

Robbie Vadas, March 2019

NEW SOUTH WALES COLTS TEAM
1971 - New Zealand Tour
Back row (from left): **Brett Gooley (Bronte)**, Craig Jennings (g, Western Suburbs), **Phil Bower (g, Bronte)**, Joe Falzon (Balmain), Andrew Kerr (Cronulla), Tony Falson (v/c, Cronulla), Terry Jansen (Balmain), Richie Semmens (Balmain), Paul Dunford (Coach, Balmain). Front row: Peter Kerr (c, Cronulla), John Waddington (Balmain), Owen Bogg (Manager), Bruce Falson (Cronulla). Photo - NSWAWPA Annual Report 1970/71.

NSW Colts Tour of New Zealand

An invitation from the New Zealand Amateur Water Polo Board took the NSW Colt's Team on a very successsful nine day tour of New Zealand in January 1971. The talented young team remained undefeated for all of their 13 games, scoring 156 goals and conceded only 42, with the top goal scorers on tour being John Waddington-26; Richie Semmens-24; and Brett Gooley-23.

The Premierships

The men's 1st Grade consisted of the premiers from Balmain, and also Bondi, Bronte, Manly-Warringah, Parramatta, Universities, Western Suburbs and a talented young side from Cronulla-Sutherland, who by season's end had played well enough

Two wins to ACT team

An ACT water polo team won two of its four matches played in Sydney during the weekend.

Chris Lord played very well in goal and the forwards Hugh Crawford and Neville de Mestro improved considerably over the four games.

In the two matches lost, the opposing teams each had NSW and Australian representative players playing for them.

The ACT team was defeated 6-1 by Universities and 3-7 by Bronte and won 8-0 from Bronte Colts and 6-2 from Cronulla-Sutherland.

Canberra Times, 30th Nov 1970

to qualify for their inaugural appearance in the competition play-offs.

Led by their experienced ex-West Australian captain/coach, Graham Samuel, Bronte went into the 1971 grand-final as underdogs. But the resurgent Bronte side, which featured no less than six current or ex-State representatives, battled hard for the 1971 NSWAWPA Men's 1st Grade premiership with their unique style and combination. In the semi-finals, third placed Bronte eliminated Cronulla (7~4) in the minor semi-final and Balmain were narrowly defeated by Universities (2~3) in the major semi-final. Bronte then played above themselves in a very close encounter to defeat the title-holders Balmain (5~4), and thereby qualify for the competition decider.

Using superior tactics throughout, the Bronte 1st Grade team played brilliant water polo thanks to their experienced current and ex members of the NSW State team, to narrowly overcome a talented Universities (4~3) and gain a fifth 1st Grade premiership for their club. Rolly Flesch played an outstanding role in scoring two great goals, while Billy Parsons and Peter Folden added the extras. The win vindicated the new coaching style and strategy of Graeme Samuel, and once again placed Bronte at the very top of water polo in New South Wales, and probably across the country. The grand-final results were published in the Sun-Herald, confirming the Bronte 1st Grade as NSW premiers, with 2nd Grade as runners-up.

Balmain defeated Bronte (4~3) in the 2nd Grade, while Cronulla/Sutherland won both the 3rd Grade (3~2) and 4th Grades (5~3) by defeating Balmain in both grand-finals. In the NSWAWPA women's competition, the Ladies from Sydney's south dominated the season

"Both Brett Gooley and myself were selected in the NSW Colts team that toured NZ, I think in 1971. I came home with pneumonia and was dropped for the 1st Grade grand-final, which if I remember correctly we lost to Balmain."

Phil Bower, 29 Jan 2019

▼ BELOW: Water polo training at Watsons Bay Baths, where Bronte had relocated by 1970/71. BOTTOM: Phil Bower in goal at Watsons Bay, training venue for Bronte AWPC from 1971. - Photos by Phil Bower.

1970/71 NSWAWPA RESULTS

SPEEDO PRE-SEASON

Final Positions: Balmain (8 points) 1, Bronte (7) 2, Cronulla-Sutherland (6) 3, Manly-Warringah (6) 4, Universities (5) 5, Parramatta City (4) 6, Western Suburbs (2) 7, North Sydney (2) 8, Bondi (0) 9, Drummoyne (0) 10.
SPEEDO CUP WINNERS: BALMAIN.

CASCADE CUP

Division 1	Points	Division 2	Points
UNIVERSITIES	8	BRONTE	8
BALMAIN	6	Manly-Warringah	6
CRON.-SUTHERLAND	4	COLTS	4
BONDI	2	PENRITH	2
WESTERN SUBURBS	0	PARRAMATTA CITY	0

Final: Bronte 4 defeated Universities 1.
CASCADE CUP WINNERS: BRONTE.

FIRST DIVISION RESULTS
First Grade

	P.	W.	D.	L.	Forf. or Disq.	Goals F.	A.	Pts.	Place
BALMAIN	14	11	3	—	—	85	35	39	1
UNIVERSITIES	14	11	1	2	—	78	39	37	2
BRONTE	14	7	4	2	1	78	46	31	3
CRONULLA-SUTHERLAND	14	8	1	5	—	75	47	31	4
BONDI	14	8	—	6	—	69	63	30	5
MANLY-WARRINGAH	14	3	—	11	—	42	88	20	6
PARRAMATTA CITY	14	2	—	11	1	30	76	17	7
WESTERN SUBURBS	14	1	1	12	—	26	99	17	8

First Semi-Final: Bronte 7 defeated Cronulla-Sutherland 4.
Second Semi-Final: Universities 3 defeated Balmain 2.
Final: Bronte 5 defeated Balmain 4.
Grand Final: Bronte 4 defeated Universities 3.

Second Grade

	P.	W.	D.	L.	Forf. or Disq.	Goals F.	A.	Pts.	Place
BALMAIN	14	12	1	1	—	99	29	39	1
UNIVERSITIES	14	9	4	—	1	74	39	35	2
BRONTE	14	9	2	3	—	75	33	34	3
CRONULLA-SUTHERLAND	14	9	—	5	—	84	36	32	4
BONDI	14	6	2	6	—	44	54	28	5
WESTERN SUBURBS	14	3	2	9	—	32	56	22	6
MANLY-WARRINGAH	14	1	1	12	—	33	94	17	7
PARRAMATTA CITY	14	1	—	11	2	15	105	14	8

First Semi-Final: Bronte 6 defeated Cronulla-Sutherland 2.
Second Semi-Final: Balmain 2 defeated Universities 1.
Final: Bronte 6 defeated Universities 3.
Grand Final: Balmain 4 defeated Bronte 3.

Third Grade

	P.	W.	D.	L.	Forf. or Disq.	Goals F.	A.	Pts.	Place
CRONULLA-SUTHERLAND	14	13	—	1	—	81	20	40	1
BALMAIN	14	12	1	—	1	83	18	38	2
BRONTE	14	7	1	6	—	49	39	29	3
BONDI	14	6	2	5	1	34	50	27	4
UNIVERSITIES	14	5	2	7	—	42	55	26	5
PARRAMATTA CITY	14	5	1	8	—	28	52	25	6
WESTERN SUBURBS	14	4	1	9	—	24	38	23	7
MANLY-WARRINGAH	14	—	—	14	—	22	92	14	8

First Semi-Final: Bronte 11 defeated Bondi 4.
Second Semi-Final: Cronulla-Sutherland 6 defeated Balmain 3.
Final: Balmain 9 defeated Bronte 8.
Grand Final: Cronulla-Sutherland 3 defeated Balmain 2.

Fourth Grade

	P.	W.	D.	L.	Forf. or Disq.	Goals F.	A.	Pts.	Place
BALMAIN	14	14	—	—	—	80	13	42	1
CRONULLA-SUTHERLAND	14	12	—	2	—	84	14	38	2
WESTERN SUBURBS	14	8	2	4	—	38	40	32	3
BRONTE	14	6	1	5	2	28	36	25	4
BONDI	14	5	1	8	—	25	45	25	5
MANLY-WARRINGAH	14	3	1	10	—	30	51	21	6
UNIVERSITIES	14	3	—	11	—	17	56	20	7
PARRAMATTA CITY	14	2	1	11	—	15	62	19	8

First Semi-Final: Bronte 6 defeated Western Suburbs 5.
Second Semi-Final: Cronulla-Sutherland 5 defeated Balmain 1.
Final: Balmain 10 defeated Bronte 0.
Grand Final: Cronulla-Sutherland 5 defeated Balmain 3.

"Bronte won another 1st Grade grand final in 1970/71... with a whole new team and great players like Billy Parsons, Chris Simpson, Rolly Flesch, Peter Folden and with Graeme Samuel as our coach. I was the only one left from the 1962 team."

Don Sarkies, 27 Jan 2015

with Cronulla-Sutherland 'A' defeating Cronulla-Sutherland 'B' (4~2) in the season grand-final. The Club Championship this year was won by Balmain. [8]

Bronte AWPC

The AGM of Bronte AWPC was held at the Bronte Splashers Clubhouse, Bronte Beach on 20th May 1971 at 7.30pm, where report was made of a very successful season.

Of the four Division I competitions this season, Bronte battled through to contest two grand-finals and 1st Grade also took out the inaugural 'Cascade Cup' competition.

In 4th Grade, Bronte finished fourth and won their semi-final, but were thrashed by a stacked Balmain outfit in the final (0~10). The 3rd Grade fared better in finishing in third place, but narrowly lost the final to Balmain (8~9). The Bronte 2nd Grade also finished in third place, then managed to win their semi-final and final, before losing to Balmain (3~4), by the slightest of margins in the grand-final.

However, it was the 1st Grade under Sammy's leadership that triumphed. Employing deft tactics, the talented side finished in third position for the season, before eliminating Cronulla-Sutherland (7~4) and Balmain (5~4) in the play-offs. They then faced a powerful Universities in the grand-final, but grabbed victory after a torrid match to take a fifth 1st Grade premiership for the club (4~3).

Brett Gooley, who had moved from the Shire to Kensington to complete his Medical School studies and had temporarily transferred to Bronte

1971 - 1ST GRADE PREMIERS

BRONTE AMATEUR WATER POLO CLUB
1970/71 - Mens 1st Grade Premiers - NSWAWPA
Top row (from left): Graeme Samuel (c/pl, Coach, WA, NSW & Aust Rep), Rolly Flesch (NSW Rep), Don Sarkies (g, NSW Rep). Second row: Peter Folden (NSW Rep), Chris Simpson, Phil Bower. Third row: Bill Parsons (NSW Rep), John Power, Tom Folden. Bottom row: Brett Gooley, Dick See (NSW Rep), NSWAWPA Premiership Pewter.

AWPC, was fortunate to find himself in a 1st Grade premiership winning team. Regrettably, Bronte lost a top player at the end of this season when John Gahagan, who at years' end oddly played in the 2nd Grade grand-final, then left the club to join East Sydney.

The loss of John Gahagan affected the fragile balance of depth that the club had otherwise

NEWTOWN ASC

WATER POLO TEAM
Division II, 2nd Grade
1970/71

Wayne Jones (c)	Steven Hunter
Graham Mundy	Harry Klouzal
Jeff Stubbs (g)	Dave Habler
Lance Kerr	Peter Primo
Tracy Rockwell	(Coach)

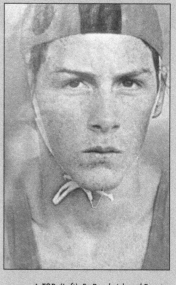

1970/71

Second Grade

	W.	D.	L.	Forf. or Disq.	Goals F.	A.	Pts.	Place
LIVERPOOL	14	3	1	—	114	31	49	1
NORTH SYDNEY	12	5	1	—	89	35	47	2
NEWTOWN	11	3	4	—	87	40	43	3
BALMAIN "A"	9	5	4	—	79	50	41	4
CLOVELLY	8	5	4	1	76	50	38	5
PENRITH	8	3	7	—	62	39	37	6
BALMAIN "B"	7	1	10	—	47	83	33	7
CANTERBURY	6	1	11	—	43	81	31	8
SYDNEY UNIVERSITY	3	—	15	—	33	99	24	9
AVALON-BILGOLA	—	—	18	—	18	140	18	10

First Semi-Final: Balmain "A" 5 defeated Newtown 3.
Second Semi-Final: Liverpool 7 defeated North Sydney 2.
Final: Balmain "A" 10 defeated North Sydney 3.
Grand Final: Balmain "A" 4 defeated Liverpool 3.
SECOND DIVISION SECOND GRADE PREMIERS: BALMAIN "A".

▲ TOP: (Left): Ex-Randwick and Bronte member Peter Primo, coach of Newtown ASC. (Mid): Team roster for Newtown ASC water polo team, a number of whom joined Bronte for season 1971/72. (Right): New Bronte recruit Tracy Rockwell, was also a member of the champion Coogee Junior R&R team, coached by Len Harris (Photo - Time Magazine, May 1971). ◄ The performance of Newtown ASC water polo team during season 1970/71.

1970/71 Results

WATER POLO
AT DAWN FRASER POOL.
[newspaper clipping text]
SMH, 12th Nov, 1970

WATER POLO
CASCADE STATE SELECTION GAMES at Dawn Fraser Pool
[newspaper clipping text]
SMH, 16th Nov, 1970

WATER POLO
CASCADE STATE SELECTION GAMES
At Dawn Fraser Pool
[newspaper clipping text]
SMH, 23rd Nov, 1970

WATER POLO
[newspaper clipping text]
SMH, 26th Nov, 1970

WATER POLO
CASCADE STATE SELECTION GAMES
[newspaper clipping text]
SMH, 30th Nov, 1970

WATER POLO
[newspaper clipping text]
SMH, 4th Dec, 1970

retained. But just as Billy McCarthy had been requesting for the previous couple of seasons, what the club desperately required was an injection of talented youth.

It just so happened that such a lifeline came from an old friend and ex-club member, Peter 'Eyes' Primo, who had taken up the coaching duties for a young team of swimmers from Newtown ASC during the 1970/71 season. At the end of their season the dilemma for 'Eyes' was that despite the boys wanting to continue playing as a team, he was unable to continue coaching. But a solution was found by introducing the young team to Bronte AWPC at the start of the 1971/72 season, providing a much needed boost for Bronte.

However, only around five of the young Newtown players signed on, and as the training commitments were beefed up, and the distance to Watson's Bay was considerable, not all of those stayed on. The four that remained for a season or more were Steven Hunter, Lance Kerr, Tracy Rockwell and promising goalkeeper Jeff Stubbs.

"Billy McCarthy was captain and coach of Bronte 3rd Grade for 13 consecutive years and was highly respected in the game. The members of water polo clubs today barely speak with each other and go home straight after games, or play on their phones... they're certainly missing a lot!"

Brian Ellison, Oct 2018

BRONTE AMATEUR WATER POLO CLUB
1970/71 Annual Report

Ladies & Gentlemen,

On behalf of the committee I submit for your consideration and adoption the Annual Report and Balance Sheet for the 1970/1971 Season.

The old adage of "always a bridesmaid but never a bride" which has dogged Bronte for nine long years, was this season proved wrong by your First Grade side, under the leadership of Graeme Samuel. For the first time in nine years, when the "Vadas inspired side" took out the N.S.W.A.W.P.A. First Grade Premiership, Bronte scraped in the back door of the semis, but went on to win the Premiership.

For the second successive year, Bronte were victorious in capturing the Cascade Shield Sunday State Selection Competition.

"Sam's" job was not an easy one as not only did he have to contend with very bad training facilities, lacksadasical approach to training by some members, State Colts' and Senior Teams' training and trips, but his own self discipline in a role new to him. The fact that all these obstacles proved surmountable is a credit to all concerned.

Members of the winning squad were:

G. Samuel (Capt./Coach)	P. Bower	R. Flesch
P. Folden	T. Folden	B. Gooley	W. Parsons
J. Power	D. Sarkies	R. See	C. Simpson

The experienced Second Grade side, led by "Innkeeper" Ken Owens, made the Grand Final but went down to a determined Balmain side in a game which could not really be termed as one of their better efforts, after some of the excellent games they played throughout the season.

Bill McCarthy's Third Grade "Babes" were a side who never knew when they were beaten and turned in some performances well in advance of their years. The loss of Dave Stapleton and Chris Hickman midway through the season in no way aided their attempt to win the Premiership. However, those who witnessed their valiant fight back in the final against Balmain, when the extra times seemed longer and longer, will no doubt join me in saying 'well played, hard luck, next year is another year". I feel special mention should be made of "Mother" McCarthy's efforts in training this youthful side and bringing them as far as he did.

PRESIDENT'S REPORT:

Even though some members may not agree with me, I feel that the 1970-1971 season was quite a successful year for Bronte.

Look at the final results; our girls, ably captained by Margaret Wilby, and coached by Australian Referee, Bob Vadas, B.Sc.(Hons.), B.A., B.O., etc., reached the semi-finals; and the four mens' teams reaching the finals; the 1st and 2nd grade reaching the grand finals, with the 1st grade winning it.

A special congratulations to our 6th grade (the magnificent six) who won their semi-finals after playing for most of the game with six men only.

Our 3rds were again led and coached this year by that old war (waterpolo) horse, Bill McCarthy, and had some good promising players.

To Captain Coach Ken Owens and my second grade side, better known as the team of oldies and non-swimmers, bad luck in the grand final, next time better.

At last, after a drought of nine years, we won 1st grade (oops, sorry Sam "A" Grade) again. We should have won it last year but unfortunately we didn't.

This year after finishing in 4th position we did it the hard way and finally got there.

Congratulations to our Australian, West Australian and New South Wales representative and Captain Coach of our first grade team, Graham Samuel. A great effort after only being with our club for two years.

Let's hope all grades will get there next season!

DON SARKIES.

BRONTE LADIES TEAMS
(1964 - 1975)

A photograph of play during the 1970 Ladies Interstate Water Polo Series in Sydney.

Throughout the 1962/63 season in New South Wales, requests had been received concerning the possibility of conducting a women's water polo competition. A vast amount of planning, organisation and publicity was required to launch the competition, which had to be achieved in a short space of time. Fred Lamb (immediate past President of the NSWAWPA), put a great deal of effort into the early development of the women's competition in NSW, and was coach of the Balmoral women's team from its inception. Gordon Woods (NSWAWPA President) was also wholeheartedly behind the new initiative.

▼ BELOW (From left): The captain of the Bronte Women's Water polo team, Miss Barbara Bond; captain of the Birchgrove/Balmain team, Miss Pat Woods; and Miss Sandra Primo, who formed the Randwick/Coogee team (Sun-Herald, 27 Feb 1964). BOTTOM: Birchgrove were the inaugural winners of the 1963/64 NSWAWPA women's premiership. Back row (from left): Colleen Miranda, Carol Waddington, Christine Trimble, Flo Scott. Middle row: Julie Cochrane, Joan Dowling, Wendy Pascoe, Lorraine Swindale, Gail Miranda. Front row: Terry Lynch, Sue Stone, Pat Woods (c), Stephanie Dunford. Absent: Allan Stringer (Coach). Photo - Balmain AWPC.

First NSW Women's Water Polo Competition

After much hard work, the inaugural Ladies' Water Polo competition attracted six teams from three existing water polo clubs; Bondi, Bronte and Balmoral, and three brand new clubs formed in Birchgrove, Randwick and Victoria Park. The teams were far from even in strength, but they never lost their spirit and the Association felt there was a tremendous future for the Ladies' competition, and subsequently extended every encouragement to those concerned.

The first official NSW Ladies' water polo competition commenced in November 1963, and although the women were initially looked upon with some element of ridicule by the men, in time they grew to influence the game in a profound way. The

commencement of women's water polo also helped to dispel the image of water polo players as beer swilling, grappling yobbos who were more intent on wrestling, biffing the opposition and spending more time in the pub than in the pool. The entry of the ladies' teams created great interest and emphasis on the technical and faster elements of the game, which had always been there, but were not often recognised.

1963-64 Ladies

All the ladies' teams in the inaugural competition were novices, but they were mostly coached by fellow male club members. The first NSWAWPA Ladies' competition was gathered together from an open invitation to all NSW Swimming Clubs by the NSWASA, with six clubs responding. The very first Ladies' Water Polo premiership was conducted over one round of five matches. The final was contested between the first and second leaders on the points table, and led to an upset win when Birchgrove defeated Balmoral (4~3), who were otherwise undefeated throughout the fledgling competition.[1]

Bronte AWPC

Primarily through the efforts of their inaugural captain Barbara Bond, Bronte Amateur Swimming Club very proudly managed to gather together a team of ladies for the inaugural 1963/64 NSWAWPA competition. Sadly however, the Bronte girls couldn't handle the roughness and firepower of the other sides and didn't manage to win any games at all, finishing bottom of the table with five straight losses from their five matches. They allowed 38 goals through their

> **1963/64 BRONTE ASC Ladies Team**
> Barbara Bond (c)
> Debbie Moyes
> Robyn Croll & Others...
> John Thornett (Coach)

1963/64 Season Statistics N.S.W.A.W.P.A.

Clubs in the Ladies Water Polo Competition.

Clubs	Total
Balmoral	1
Birchgrove	1
Bondi	1
Bronte	1
Randwick	1
Victoria Park	1
	6

Results of the Ladies Water Polo Competitions.

Grade	Premier	Runner-Up
	Birchgrove~4 d. 3~Balmain	

1963/64 NSWAWPA RESULTS

Ladies—	Games Played	Won	Lost	Goals For	Against	Points	Pos.
Balmoral	5	5	—	25	11	15	1
Birchgrove	5	4	1	35	15	13	2
Randwick	5	3	2	25	16	11	3
Bondi	5	2	3	26	18	9	4
Victoria Park	5	1	4	4	26	7	5
Bronte	5	—	5	9	38	5	6

Grand Final: Birchgrove 4 def Balmoral 3.
Metropolitan Ladies' Premiers — BIRCHGROVE.

net, and finished in sixth position on the season. However, their proud achievement was that they would forever be known as one of the pioneer teams in the history of Ladies' water polo in NSW.

Today's sport

WATER POLO.—Metropolitan Premiership: Ashfield B v Balmain B, 7 p.m.; Bronte Ladies v Bondi A, 7.35 p.m.; Possibles v Probables, 8.10 p.m.; Liverpool v Roseville, 9 p.m.

(SMH, 10th Jan 1965)

1964/65 Season Statistics
N.S.W.A.W.P.A.

Clubs in the Ladies Water Polo Competition.

Clubs	Total
Balmoral	1
Birchgrove	2
Bondi	2
Bronte	1
Parramatta	1
Randwick	2
Victoria Park	1
	10

Results of the Ladies Water Polo Competitions.

Grade	Premier	Runner-Up
	Balmoral~4 d. 3~Birchgrove A	

1964/65 NSWAWPA RESULTS

	Played	W.	L.	Forf. or Disq.	Goals For	Against	Pts.	Pos.
Birchgrove A	9	9	0	—	56	9	27	1
Balmoral	9	8	1	—	50	17	25	2
Randwick A	9	7	2	—	44	19	23	3
Bondi A	9	6	3	—	38	23	21	4
Randwick B	9	3	5	1	25	35	14	5
Parramatta	9	3	5	1	37	34	14	6
Birchgrove B	9	3	4	2	16	35	13	7
Bondi B	9	2	6	1	22	49	12	8
Victoria Park	9	3	2	4	17	32	11	9
Bronte	9	1	6	2	7	55	9	10

1st Semi-final: Randwick A 8 def. Bondi A 5.
2nd Semi-final: Balmoral A 6 def. Birchgrove A 3.
Final: Birchgrove A 3 def. Randwick A 1.
Grand Final: Balmoral A 4 def. Birchgrove A 3.

LADIES' METROPOLITAN PREMIERS — BALMORAL A

1964-65 Ladies

Given the success of the previous season, there was increased enthusiasm for the competition with added pressure for country tours, and these initiatives gave women's water polo a significant boost. The Competition Committee also hoped to introduce a B Grade competition in time, for women's teams of lesser standard.

For the 1964/65 season, Parramatta joined the Ladies' competition, while Birchgrove, Bondi and Randwick all fielded two teams each. There being no other changes, this increased the number of competing teams for the second championship to an admirable ten.

The Premiership

In the play-offs Randwick A defeated Bondi A (8~5), and Balmoral A disposed of Birchgrove A (6~3). Birchgrove A' then fought back to defeat Randwick A in the final (3~1). The 1965 Ladies' premiership saw an exact reversal of positions from the previous year. Despite their undefeated season record, Balmoral played intelligent water polo to confirm their dominance over Birchgrove A (4~3).

Bronte AWPC

Despite finishing last on the table for the second year running, the Bronte girls trained and competed with the very best of intentions.

▲ Photo of the Randwick Ladies water polo team of 1965 from left: Sandra Primo, Rhonda Flower, Liz Wilby, Kerrie Hellier, Kathy Wintle, Barbara Shea, Liz Andrews and Marilyn Howard. Photo - Liz Wilby.

However, the girls were totally outclassed by the other sides and could only manage to win one of their nine matches, and forfeited two others. With 55 goals against and scoring just seven of their own, they once again finished last. No one wants to play in a losing team and so these results no doubt had an impact on enthusiasm.

1965-66 Ladies

Unfortunately, the Ladies struggled to maintain a competition in the 1965/66 season and lost teams from Birchgrove B, Bronte, Victoria Park and Randwick B, with no new teams entering the competition. Regrettably, and only in its third year of competition the number of Ladies' teams was going backwards, and this season dropped to a bare minimum of just six teams.

The Premiership

In the play-offs, Parramatta forfeited to Balmain and Bondi B defeated Balmoral. Balmoral then recovered to defeat Balmain in

1965/66 Season Statistics
N.S.W.A.W.P.A.

Clubs in the Ladies Water Polo Competition.

Clubs	Total
Balmoral	1
Birchgrove	1
Bondi	2
Parramatta	1
Randwick	1
	6

Results of the Ladies Water Polo Competitions.

Grade	Premier	Runner-Up
	Bondi B~4 d. 3~Balmoral	

Bondi Women Win Water Polo Title

Bondi lady "Bluebottles" last Sunday won the Metropolitan waterpolo premiership trophy by defeating Balmoral 4-3.

Balmoral went to an early 1-0 lead, but the score was soon levelled with a magnificent sitting shot by Joy Cannot. In the second quarter Joy followed up with two more goals from exact passes by Robyn Carroll.

In the third quarter our goalkeeper, Carrol Scandred, saved several extremely hard shots. The score then was Bondi led 3-2.

The fourth and final quarter saw some good manoeuvres from both sides, with one goal each being scored. Bondi scorer was Colleen O'Leary with a pass shot directly in front of goal. The win made our "Bluebottles" premiers for season 1965-66.

Our side consisted of Carrol Scandred (goal), Pam Hedger and Marilyn Myers (backs), Loraine Cronk and Colleen O'Leary (halves), Robyn Carroll and Joy Cannot (forwards) with Cathy Taylor reserve.

(The Bondi Weekly, 31st March 1966)

▲ *TOP: The 1965/66 Randwick Ladies team, most of whom transferred to Bondi, then to Bronte Ladies for the 1967/68 season. From left: Marilyn Howard, Sandra Primo, Joy Cannot, Kerri Helier, ???, Liz Andrews, ???, Lorraine Grills, Carol Scandrett (maybe) with Liz Wilby not in the photograph. Photo - Margaret Wilby. ABOVE: Players from the Bondi Ladies Water Polo Club of 1965/66, from a Royal Life Saving Club photograph. From left: Robyn Carroll, Sue Flaus, Marilyn Myers, Lorraine Cronk, Lyn Saunders, Pam Hedger, Sharne Aldridge, Cathy Taylor and Dorothy Flaus. Photo - Pam Flesch (Hedger).*

1965/66 BONDI 'A' STINGRAYS
Pam O'Reilly
Lyn Shaw
K. Tyler
Judy O'Reilly
Lyn Saunders
Lee Stokes
Sharne Aldridge
Graham Gairns (Coach)

the final (3~2). This year Graham Gairns was coaching both of Bondi's teams and with some considerable success. In the grand-final Bondi B played brilliantly to defeat the reigning premiers Balmoral in a thrilling encounter, to capture the premiership (4~3). Shortly afterwards, two metropolitan Ladies' teams brightened up the Country Championships in Wagga Wagga when three sides travelled there to keenly contest exhibition matches.[3]

BONDI 'B' Bluebottles
1965/66 - NSWAWPA Ladies Premiers
Carol Scandrett (g), Pam Hedger, Marilyn Myers (backs), Lorraine Cronk, Colleen O'Leary (halves), Robyn Carroll and Joy Cannot (forwards), Graham Gairns (Coach).

Bronte AWPC

Given the disappointing performances of the past two seasons and the 'rough' play they experienced, Bronte did not field a ladies' team for the 1965/66 competition.

1966-67 Ladies

Entering its fourth year, the NSW Ladies' water polo competition was on its knees when only two clubs initially entered teams. Balmoral, Parramatta and Randwick had all dropped out, but fortunately both Birchgrove, who had morphed into Balmain, and Bondi were able to muster two teams each. Then at the last minute, new teams entered from Collaroy and Western Suburbs, which brought the number of competing teams up to an acceptable total of six. However, everyone recognised that more teams were needed to sustain a viable Ladies' competition in the future. On a brighter note, supporters of the women's game were sufficiently impressed to call for the scheduling of a Ladies' Interstate Series as soon as possible.

1966/67 Season Statistics
N.S.W.A.W.P.A.

Clubs in the Ladies Water Polo Competition.

Clubs	Total
Balmain	2
Bondi	2
Collaroy	1
Western Suburbs	1
	6

Results of the Ladies Water Polo Competitions.

Grade	Premier	Runner-Up
	Bondi A~4 d.	3~Bondi B

The Premiership

In the play-offs, Balmain A defeated Collaroy while Bondi A disposed of Bondi B (3~1). Surprisingly, Bondi B then reorganised themselves and

1966/67 BONDI 'B' BLUEBOTTLES
Sue Flaus
Dorothy Flaus
Cathy Taylor
Colleen O'Leary
Carol Scandrett
Sharne Aldridge
Pam Hedger
Lorraine Cronk
Joy Cannot
Graham Gairns (Coach)

defeated Balmain A in a very close final (2~1). The Bondi B win, set up a 'civil war' like battle for the Ladies' premiership, now being an all Bondi affair. Although many supported the underdogs, Bondi B were only just defeated by their big sister team Bondi A (4~3) in what turned out to be a cracker of a grand-final.[4]

BONDI 'A'
1966/67 - NSWAWPA Ladies Premiers
Lyn Shaw, Robyn Carroll, Pam O'Reilly, Lyn Saunders, K. Tyler, Marilyn Myers, Joanne Maxwell, Christine Whillier, Linda Brady, Graham Gairns (Coach).

Bronte AWPC

Once again, Bronte did not field a team in the NSWAWPA Ladies competition this season.

1967-68 Ladies

At the start of the 1967/68 season, there was a discussion among NSWAWPA officials about abandoning the fledgling Ladies' water polo competition. The main difficulty being the lack of teams, but the Association equally didn't want one single club like Balmain or Bondi to dominate the competition by fielding two teams. Apparently a compromise was reached when a majority of the Bondi B team decided they would play under the banner of the Bronte Water Polo Club, and so the competition went ahead.

Regrettably, this year's competition was again limited to only six teams from five clubs, and more clubs were desperately needed to sustain an operable Ladies' water polo competition in the years ahead. This season, the teams from Balmain B and Western Suburbs dropped out, but Bronte, which had been a foundation club in the first Ladies' competition, re-joined along with the up and coming Universities club, thereby maintaining the number of competing teams at six.

1967/68 Season Statistics
N.S.W.A.W.P.A.

Clubs in the Ladies Water Polo Competition.

Clubs	Total
Balmain	1
Bondi	2
Bronte	1
Collaroy	1
Universities	1
	6

Results of the Ladies Water Polo Competitions.

Grade	Premier	Runner-Up
	Bondi A~4 d. 3~Bronte	

NSW Representatives

Following similar developments in both Victoria and South Australia, this year marked the selection of the inaugural NSW Ladies' Water Polo Team. Trials were held and a representative team was chosen to contest an Interstate Series, with a Victorian team travelling to Sydney on the 23rd March 1968, to play two matches. The first at Rushcutters Bay Baths was won by NSW (6~3), while the return match at Balmain Baths was won by Victoria (3~2). Bronte's Lorraine Grills was selected in that very first team and achieved the honour of being Bronte's first ever Ladies' State team representative.

The Premiership

The Ladies competition rounds were normally played on Sunday nights. In the play-offs, Balmain defeated Collaroy (5~3) in the minor semi, while Bondi A disposed of Bronte (3~1) in the major semi-final. Bronte then defeated Balmain in the final (4~2) to secure their place in the competition decider. In the grand-final, the Ladies' premiership was again won by the Bondi Club, who this time defeated Bronte in a very entertaining match (4~3). The impressive win for the Bondi team racked up their third successive premiership.[5]

NEW SOUTH WALES LADIES TEAM
Interstate Series
Sydney, 1968
Sue Waddington (Balmain)
T. Lynch (Balmain)
L. Trimble (Balmain)
Lyn Saunders (Bondi)
Pam O'Reilly (Bondi)
Robyn Carroll (vc, Bondi)
Lyn Shaw (c, Bondi)
K. Tyler (Bondi)
Lorraine Grills (Bronte)
C. Watson (Collaroy)
L. Watson (Collaroy)
Alex Kosegi (Coach),
Herb Bund & Gordon Woods (Managers).

1967/68 BRONTE LADIES TEAM
Carol Scandrett (Bunton, g)
Joy Cannot (Habler)
Pam Hedger (Flesch)
Lorraine Cronk
Rhonda Flower
Liz Wilby (Moses)
Lorraine Grills
Laurel Cannot (Fisher)
Margaret Wilby
Irene Murray
Billy McCarthy (Coach)

▼ The Bronte girls made Irwin Vegg's stay a memorable one. Back row: ???, Lorraine Powel (Sheppard), ???, ??? Front row: Pam Hedger, Irwin Vegg, Rhonda Flower, taken at Rushcutters Bay Baths.

▲Fraternisation between Bronte women and men was a popular pastime, as shown in these photographs of Bronte Water Polo Club members during the Summer of 1968. TOP (Left): Carol Scandrett, Billy Parsons, Dennis Morgan & Pam Hedger. (Right): Peter Folden & Pam Hedger. ABOVE (Left): Lorraine Cronk, Peter Folden & Pam Hedger. (Right): Pam Hedger & Danny Hoffbauer.

1967/68 NSWAWPA RESULTS

LADIES COMPETITION

	Played	Won	Drawn	Lost	Points
Bondi "A"	10	7	2	1	26
Bronte	10	7	1	2	25
Balmain	10	6	1	3	23
Collaroy	10	5	1	4	21
Universities	10	1	1	8	13
Bondi "B"	10	1	—	8	11

1st SEMI	Balmain, 5, defeated Collaroy, 3
2nd SEMI	Bondi "A", 3, defeated Bronte, 1
FINAL	Bronte, 4, defeated Balmain, 2
GRAND FINAL	Bondi "A", 4, defeated Bronte, 3

Bronte AWPC

The team that re-entered the NSWAWPA Ladies' competition this season wasn't really a Bronte initiative, as much as a group of girls that had been moved across from Bondi B, to play under the Bronte colours. But they were warmly welcomed by the Bronte club, and played from the outset with great enthusiasm. Under coach Billy McCarthy, there was a definite purpose in their approach and under the master coach, their results spoke for themselves in only losing two matches in the entire regular season.

Bronte lost to Bondi A in the semi-final (1~3), but won a place in their inaugural grand-final by defeating Balmain (4~2) in the final. The decider was very close throughout, with Bondi just pulled away to take the premiership by the single goal (4~3).

> "When we travelled to Tamworth to play... I was just 15 and not very worldly... and the older boys were trying to get me drunk. I had never had alcohol before and rarely since, but I recall emptying my drinks into one of the boys shoes... but I must have consumed some as I vomited out the car window."
> *Jenny Miley, Sep 2020*

1968-69 Ladies

Now in its fifth season, the Ladies' competition was looking to consolidate their profile and encouraged clubs from Sydney's southern districts for possibly more water polo teams to join the competition. They found the rapidly expanding St. George club willing to contribute two sides, thereby increasing the number of competing teams to eight.

Representatives in NSW Teams

Lorraine Grills (Bronte) lost her place in the 1969 NSW Ladies' team, which experienced a large turnover in personnel for the 1969 Interstate Series in Melbourne. Only five of

NSWAWPA

1968/69 Season Statistics
N.S.W.A.W.P.A.

Clubs in the Ladies Water Polo Competition.

Clubs	Total
Balmain	1
Bondi	2
Bronte	1
Collaroy	1
St George	2
Universities	1
	8

Results of the Ladies Water Polo Competitions.

Grade	Premier	Runner-Up
	St George A~8 d. 4~Bondi A	

NSW LADIES TEAM
1969 - 3rd Place - Interstate Championships - Melbourne
Back row (from left): Cathy Taylor (r, Universities), Lyn Saunders (Bondi), Virginia Turnbull (g, St George), Adrienne Turnbull (St George), Pam O'Reilly (Bondi), Robyn Carroll (vc, Bondi). Middle row: Gail Miranda (Balmain), Vicky White (r, Cronulla)), Lyn Shaw (c, Bondi), Julie Girdler (St George). Front row: Marilyn Myers (Bondi), Jenny Dunn (St George), Sue Waddington (Bondi). Absent: Les Papps (Coach), Pat Jones (Manager). Photo - NSWAPWA Annual Report 1968/69.

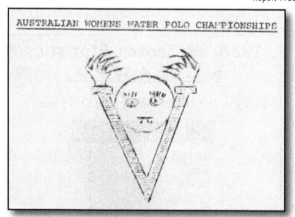

▼ *Unrecognised by the Australian Swimming Association, the 1969 Ladies Interstate Water Polo Championships went ahead at the end of January in Melbourne, as evidenced by the cover of the Program- just love the fingernails and eyelashes!*

the 1968 team were retained, with six new caps forcing their way into the side. The newcomers included G. Miranda (Balmain), Marilyn Myers (Bondi), Julie Girdler, Jenny Dunn and sisters Adrienne and Virginia Turnbull (St. George). The NSW girls finished third behind Victoria and South Australia.

The Premiership

In the Ladies' metropolitan play-offs, Collaroy defeated Balmain (5~3) in the minor semi and an undefeated St. George A disposed of Bondi A (5~4) in the major semi-final. Bondi A then dispatched Collaroy in the final (4~3) to secure a berth in the competition decider. Seeking their fourth consecutive premiership Bondi

A matched up against St. George A, who had only this season entered the competition. Everyone knew the game would be close as during the preliminary rounds these two teams had recorded a draw in their round match.

The St. George team however, were far too strong in the premiership game, winning by a four goal margin (8~4), which capped off an undefeated season in their inaugural year.[6]

1968/69 NSWAWPA RESULTS

Ladies—

	Played	W.	D.	L.	Forf. or Disq.	Goals For	Against	Pts.	Pos.
St. George 'A'	14	11	2	—	1	69	18	37	1
Bondi 'A'	14	9	3	2	—	65	24	35	2
Balmain	14	9	2	3	—	54	29	34	3
Collaroy	14	7	3	4	—	48	27	31	4
St. George 'B'	14	5	2	7	—	36	36	26	5
Bronte	14	5	1	7	1	40	45	24	6
Bondi 'B'	14	2	—	11	1	12	94	17	7
University	14	1	1	9	3	13	62	14	8

1st Semi-final: Collaroy 5 def. Balmain 3.
2nd Semi-final: St. George 'A' 5 def. Bondi 'A' 4.
Final: Bondi 'A' 4 def. Collaroy 3.
Grand Final: St. George 'A' 8 def. Bondi 'A' 4.

ST. GEORGE 'A'
1968/69 - NSWAWPA Ladies Premiers
Adrienne Turnbull (c), Virginia Turnbull (g), Carol Missingham, C. Riley, Marilyn Mitchell, Jenny Dunn, Vicky White, Julie Girdler, Ruth Hardingham, Meredith Lanser, Peter Kerr (Coach).

Bronte AWPC

The shifting fortunes of the infant NSWAWPA Ladies' competition, combined with changes in personnel saw Bronte drop significantly this season. As a result of winning just five of their 14 matches, they failed to make the play-offs and focused instead on the coming year.

1969-70 Ladies

Like a game of 'snakes and ladders', the NSWAWPA Ladies' competition seemed to be alternating between seasons of sufficient entries, followed the next year by a poor turnout, and sadly it seemed that the Ladies' competition this season was destined for yet another meager assembly. Both Collaroy and University failed to re-enter and the number of entries dropped again to just six competing teams from four clubs.

NSW Representatives

Despite placing third, nine of the previous year's team were

1969/70 Season Statistics N.S.W.A.W.P.A.

Clubs in the Ladies Water Polo Competition.

Clubs	Total
Balmain	1
Bondi	2
Bronte	1
St George	2
	6

Results of the Ladies Water Polo Competitions.

Grade	Premier	Runner-Up
	St George A~8 d. 6~Bondi A	

NSW LADIES TEAM
1970 - 3rd Place - Interstate
Championships - Sydney
Back row (from left): Marilyn Mitchell (St George), Pam O'Reilly (Bondi), Pat Jones (Manager), Virginia Turnbull (g, St George), Robyn Carroll (c, Bondi), Carol Missingham (St George). Middle row: Lyn Saunders (Bondi), Adrienne Turnbull (vc, St George), Sue Waddington (Bondi), Jenny Dunn (St George). Front row: Marilyn Myers (Bondi), Meredith Lanser (St George). Absent: Les Papps (Coach). Photo - NSWAPWA Annual Report 1969/70.

retained for the 1970 Ladies' Interstate Championships in Sydney. The only new caps able to work themselves into the team were Lyn Saunders, Marilyn Mitchell and Carol Missingham from the St. George club. However, the home ground advantage didn't play out for the girls this year, as they again finished in third place behind Victoria and South Australia.

The Premiership

In the NSWAWPA women's competition play-offs, St. George B defeated Balmain (7~3) in the minor semi, while St. George A disposed of Bondi A (3~2) in the major semi-final. Bondi A then defeated St. George B in the final (4~0) to secure their place in the competition decider. In the grand-final, the Ladies' premiership was again won by St. George A over Bondi A in a closely contested

1969/70 NSWAWPA RESULTS

LADIES' COMPETITION					Goals		
	Win	Draw	Loss	Disq.	For	Agst.	Points
BONDI 'A'	13	1	1	—	65	18	42
ST. GEORGE 'A'	12	1	2	—	82	14	40
ST. GEORGE 'B'	9	2	4	—	62	33	35
BALMAIN	5	1	8	1	34	52	25
BRONTE	3	1	9	2	24	55	20
BONDI 'B'	—	—	15	—	9	104	15

First Semi-Final: St. George 'B' 7 defeated Balmain 3.
Second Semi-Final: St. George 'A' 3 defeated Bondi 'A' 2.
Final: Bondi 'A' 4 defeated St. George 'B' 0.
Grand Final: St. George 'A' 8 defeated Bondi 'A' 6.

LADIES' PREMIERS: ST. GEORGE 'A'.

Relaxing after their water polo match at the Tamworth Olympic Pool on Saturday night are (from left) Christine Burgess and Colleen Connery, of Bronte, and Pat Buckley and Sue Bradbery, of Tamworth. Bronte won the match by seven goals to one.

◄ *The Bronte Ladies team defeated Tamworth Ladies by 7~1 during the Bronte Club visit to Tamworth in January 1970 (The Northern Daily Leader, Jan 1970).*

match (8~6). The win gained a second successive premiership for the St. George team in their two years of involvement.[7]

ST. GEORGE 'A'
1969/70 - NSWAWPA Ladies Premiers
Adrienne Turnbull (c), Virginia Turnbull (g), Carol Missingham, C. Riley, Marilyn Mitchell, Jenny Dunn, VickyWhite, Ruth Hardingham, Meredith Lanser, Peter Kerr (Coach).

Bronte AWPC

By this time a number of new girls had joined the club in Jenny Miley, Joanne Maxwell and Colleen Connery, but their sincere efforts couldn't overcome the dominance of Bondi and St George. Consequently, they finshed in fifth place and once again failed to qualify for the play-offs.

1969-70 Results

WATER POLO

WOMEN'S OPEN COMPETITION
At Dawn Fraser Pool

Bondi (A) 2 (S Waddington 2) bt St George-Sutherland (A) 1 (R Hardingham); Bronte 7 (J Maxwell 3 M Wilby 3 C Connery) bt Bondi (B) 1 (D Keegan); St George-Sutherland (B) 3 (M Hanson 2 J Hanson) bt Balmain 2 (C Didd J Fisher).

SMH, 17th Feb, 1970

1970-71 Ladies

For the 1970/71 season the NSWAWPA Ladies competition was once again played with just six teams. Bondi B had dropped out, and St. George morphed into Cronulla-Sutherland, but significantly a young Sydney University team entered the competition, which maintained the number of competing teams at six.

Representatives in NSW Teams

The 4th Women's Interstate Championships were held for the first time in conjunction with the Men's Australian Championships in Hobart. However, only five of the 1970 NSW Ladies team were retained in an attempt to make a lunge at the title. Past State reps Cathy Taylor (Sydney Uni) and Julie Girdler (Cronulla) were recalled, while Carolyn Keats, Ruth Hardingham and Vicky White all of the Cronulla club, along with goalkeeper Diane McDougall (Balmain), were the new caps in the side. But while South Australia played through undefeated in this series, NSW again had to be content with third place behind Victoria.

1970/71 Season Statistics
N.S.W.A.W.P.A.

Clubs in the Ladies Water Polo Competition.

Clubs	Total
Balmain	1
Bondi	1
Bronte	1
Cronulla/Sutherland	2
Sydney Uni	1
	6

Results of the Ladies Water Polo Competitions.

Grade	Premier	Runner-Up
	Cron/Suth A~4 d. 2~Cron/Suth B	

NSW WOMENS TEAM
1971 - 3rd Place - Interstate Championships - Hobart
Back row (from left): Cathy Taylor (Sydney Uni), Marilyn Mitchell (Cron-Suth), Virginia Turnbull (g, Cron-Suth), Adrienne Turnbull (vc,Cron-Suth), Ruth Hardingham (Cron-Suth), Marilyn Myers (c, Bondi), Vicky White (Cron-Suth), Julie Girdler (Cron-Suth), Caroline Keats (Cron-Suth), Jenny Dunn (Cron-Suth), Diane McDougall (Balmain). Absent: Les Papps (Coach), N. Goddard (Manager).

1970-71 Results

WATER POLO

At Dawn Fraser Pool.—Women's 1st grade: Sydney University 1 (S Aldridge) bt Bondi 0; Balmain 1 (C Didd) draw with Bronte 1 (M Wilby). Men's 2nd div 2nd grade: Balmain (A) 7 (G Foggarty 3 B Lyndon 3 I McColm) bt Canterbury 1 (D Brighton). 3rd grade: Balmain (A) 3 (I McColm 2 S Hampton) bt Ryde High School 0. At North Sydney Pool.—2nd grade: North Sydney 11 (W Howes 4 G Watson 3 S McBurnie 3 J Taylor) bt Balmain (B) 3 (R Cameron 2 K Hill). 3rd grade: North Sydney 6 (C Turnbull 3 M Hann 2 P Baines) bt Balmain (B) 0.

SMH, 25th Nov, 1970

WATER POLO

At Dawn Fraser Pool. — First semi-finals women's 1st grade: Sydney University 6 (P Carr-Boyd 3 C Taylor 2 B Glover) bt Bronte 3 (M Wilby 2 C Chamberlain); Men's 2nd div 1st grade: Penrith 5 bt North Sydney 3. 2nd grade: Balmain 5 bt Newtown 3. 3rd grade: Balmain (B) 9 bt North Palm Beach 8.

SMH, 17th March 1971

The Premiership

Cronulla-Sutherland steamrolled everyone this year and were undefeated by the end of the season. In the Ladies' competition play-offs, Sydney University defeated Bronte (6~3) in the minor semi, while Cronulla-Sutherland A romped over their comrades Cronulla-Sutherland B (11~2) in the major semi. Surprisingly, and showing their great depth, Cronulla-Sutherland B then reorganised themselves and defeated Sydney University by a whisker in the final (6~5). For the second time in the history of the Ladies' water polo competition, the Cronulla-Sutherland B win had set up a title fight between two teams from the same club. But Cronulla-Sutherland B were far from disgraced in narrowly losing to their big sister team, Cronulla-Sutherland A (4~2) in what turned out to be an entertaining conclusion to the season. The Cronulla-Sutherland A team capped off their undefeated year by capturing the W.D. & H. O. Wills Shield in their inaugural year, an amazing achievement.[8]

Bronte AWPC

Under their new coach Robbie Vadas, and led by the likes of Cathy Chamberlain and Margaret Wilby, the hard work of the Bronte Ladies' team paid off this season. They managed to win six and draw two of their matches, which was just enough to place them fourth on the ladder, and gain a play-off berth. But their finals experience was short-lived when they were defeated by Sydney Uni (3~6), and eliminated in the first semi-final. Nevertheless, Bronte had a nibble of success and were determined to make a better showing in the next season.

1970/71 NSWAWPA RESULTS

LADIES

	W.	D.	L.	Forf. or Disq.	Goals F.	Goals A.	Pts.	Place
CRONULLA-SUTHERLAND "A"	13	—	—	2	92	25	39	1
CRONULLA-SUTHERLAND "B"	10	—	3	2	53	40	33	2
SYDNEY UNIVERSITY	8	1	6	—	54	62	32	3
BRONTE	6	2	6	1	47	54	28	4
BONDI	5	—	9	1	34	47	24	5
BALMAIN		1	9	5	16	68	11	6

First Semi-Final: Sydney University 6 defeated Bronte 3.
Second Semi-Final: Cronulla-Sutherland "A" 11 def. Cronulla-Sutherland "B" 2.
Final: Cronulla-Sutherland "B" 6 defeated Sydney University 5.
Grand Final: Cronulla-Sutherland "A" 4 defeated Cronulla-Sutherland "B" 2.

LADIES' PREMIERS: CRONULLA-SUTHERLAND "A".

1971-72 Ladies

Entries for the 1971/72 Ladies water polo competition almost doubled from the previous year, and the faith and persistence applied to this competition, by the NSWAPWA, finally seemed to have paid off. Surprisingly, the reigning premiers, Cronulla-Sutherland dropped out, but were replaced by teams from Carss Park and Port Hacking, while Parramatta Memorial, Drummoyne and Northbridge entered teams. Both Bondi and Sydney University clubs fielded B teams, which brought the total number up to a very healthy 11 teams from nine different clubs. After eight years, the NSW Ladies' water polo competition finally seemed to be on it's way, and there was no turning back.

Representatives in NSW Teams

1971/72 Season Statistics N.S.W.A.W.P.A.

Clubs in the Ladies Water Polo Competition.

Clubs	Total
Balmain	1
Bondi	2
Bronte	1
Carss Park	1
Drummoyne	1
Northbridge	1
Parramatta Mem	1
Port Hacking	1
Sydney Uni	2
	11

Results of the Ladies Water Polo Competitions.

Grade	Premier	Runner-Up
1st	Carss Park~3	d. 0~Port Hacking
1st	Bronte	Winter Comp

NSW WOMENS TEAM
1972 - 3rd Place - Interstate Championships - Brisbane
From left: Alex Kosegi (Coach, Bondi), Marilyn Myers (vc, Bondi), Adrienne Turnbull (Carss Park), Caroline Keats (Port Hacking), Ruth Hardingham (Port Hacking), Vicky White (Port Hacking), Barbara Glover (Sydney Uni), Virginia Turnbull (g, (Carss Park), Robyn Carroll (c, Bondi), Sue Eather (Carss Park), Mandy Jones (Port Hacking), Meredith Lanser (Port Hacking), Joyce Campbell (Manager, Bronte).

"The past season was probably the most successful since Ladies' water polo commenced in NSW some eight years ago. A record number of twelve teams competed in the competitions, which meant for the first time, both 1st and 2nd Grade competitions were conducted."

NSWAWPA, 1972-73 Annual Report

After three unsuccessful years under Les Papps, the Association appointed Alex Kosegi (Bondi) to take on the coaching reins. Kosegi retained six players from the previous year, and both Robyn Carroll (Bondi) and Meredith Lanser (Cronulla) were recalled, while Barbara Glover (Sydney Uni), Mandy Jones (Port Hacking) and Sue Eather (Carss Park) were the three new caps in the team. But Kosegi's approach still wasn't enough to rescue the Blues, and they finished in third place once again from champions Victoria and South Australia.

1971/72 NSWAWPA RESULTS

LADIES

	Played	W.	D.	L.	Forf.	Goals F.	A.	Points	Position
CARSS PARK	22	21	1	—	—	165	52	65	1
PORT HACKING DOLPHINS	22	18	1	2	1	174	29	58	2
BONDI 'A'	22	15	1	6	—	137	36	53	3
SYDNEY UNIVERSITY "A"	22	15	—	7	—	99	45	52	4
BRONTE	22	12	3	7	—	110	57	49	5
PARRAMATTA MEMORIAL	.	12	2	8	—	89	79	48	6
BALMAIN	22	9	6	7	—	78	65	46	7
SYDNEY UNIVERSITY "B"	22	9	1	12	—	70	129	41	8
DRUMMOYNE	22	5	1	15	1	35	161	32	9
BONDI "B"	22	4	2	16	—	37	169	32	10
NORTHBRIDGE	22	2	—	18	2	14	196	24	11

First Semi-Final:
Second Semi-Final: Port Hacking Dolphins 6 defeated Carss Park 4.
Final:
Grand Final: Carss P . . defeated Port Hacking.
LADIES' PREMIERS. CARSS PARK.

The Premiership
This season saw the NSWAWPA assemble their biggest field of Ladies' teams to date, and the competition between the 11 sides was intense. Despite the upheaval and club switches in the Shire, the southern teams remained dominant this season.

In the NSWAWPA Ladies competition play-offs, Bondi A defeated Sydney University A in the minor semi, while Port Hacking Dolphins disposed of Carss Park (6~4) in an upset, as the latter team had finished the season as undefeated minor premiers. Carss Park then recovered to defeat Bondi A in the final and secured their place in the competition decider. In the grand-final, Carss Park reversed their loss of the major semi-final and defeated Port Hacking (3~0), becoming the fourth club to win the NSWAWPA Ladies' water polo premiership in their first year of competition.[9]

CARSS PARK
1971/72 - NSWAWPA Women's Premiers
Virginia Turnbull (g), Adrienne Turnbull, Marilyn Mitchell, Jenny Dunn, Carol Missingham, Julie Girdler, Sue Price, Sue Eather, Margaret Paul, Jackie Lampe.

Bronte AWPC

Bronte performed admirably and scored 110 goals in the season, but in finishing fifth on the points table, they just failed to qualify for the play-offs. After their hard work, it was a dissappointing finish, but they were determined to come back stronger in the next year.

Remaining defiant, the Bronte women got another chance when they entered and won the inaugural 1972 Winter competition outright.

1972-73 Ladies

By the 1972/73 season the NSWAWPA Ladies' competition had been steadily improving, but this season was probably the most successful since Ladies' water polo had commenced in NSW. Receiving a record number of 12 teams entering the competition this year required the launching of a second grade.

Interestingly, the Ladies' competition was now at the same stage the Men's competition had been, some 70 years previously ie. roughly a dozen dedicated teams competing across two grades. Although Port Hacking had dropped

1972/73 Season Statistics N.S.W.A.W.P.A.

Clubs in the Ladies Water Polo Competitions.

| Clubs | Grades | | Total |
	1st	2nd	
Balmain	●		1
Bondi	●	●	2
Bronte	●	●	2
Carss Park	●		1
Cronulla/Sutherland	●		1
Drummoyne		●	1
Granville RSL		●	1
Northbridge		●	1
Parramatta Mem.	●		1
Sydney Uni	●		1
	7	5	12

Results of the Ladies Water Polo Competitions.

Grade	Premier		Runner-Up
1st	Balmain~4	d.	3~Bronte
2nd	Bondi~4	d.	3~Drummoyne
	Club Champions		BRONTE
1st		Bondi	Winter Comp

out, a new club made their first appearance in Granville RSL. The 'splitting up' of the teams into two grades made the competitions keener and with only a few exceptions, most games were very close. The completion of Sydney University Swimming Pool, which was heated also allowed for a Winter competition to commence for the first time.

Representatives in NSW Teams

The NSWAWPA took drastic steps this year in an attempt to capture the Ladies' Interstate Series, and appointed their third Ladies' coach in three years, in ex-Bronte member Phil Bower (now Balmain). Five players were retained from the 1972 side, while Diane McDougall (Balmain), Marilyn Mitchell and Julie Girdler (Carss Park) were recalled, the latter being her third time. The new caps in the team were Rhonda Laws (Balmain), Tracy Jones (Cronulla), and a strong player from Sydney's east in Lyn Trewhella (Bronte). However, not for any

NSW WOMENS TEAM
1973 - 3rd Place - Interstate Championships - Adelaide
Back row (from left): **Yvette Barta (r,g, Bronte),** Diane McDougall (g, Balmain), Tracey Jones (Cronulla), Adrienne Turnbull (vc, Carss Park), Julie Girdler (Carss Park), **Lyn Trewhella (Bronte)**, Ruth Hardingham (Cronulla), Rhonda Laws (Balmain). Front row: Robin Carroll (c, Bondi), Carolyn Keats (Cronulla), Marilyn Mitchell (Carss Park), Virginia Turnbull (g, Carss Park), Phil Bower (Coach, Balmain). Missing: **Joyce Campbell (Manager, Bronte)**.

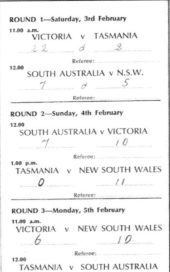

The South Australian Amateur
Water Polo Association

welcomes you to

1973 LADIES

AUSTRALIAN INTERSTATE

WATER POLO SERIES

Competing teams from:

NEW SOUTH WALES
SOUTH AUSTRALIA
TASMANIA
VICTORIA

Venue:

HENLEY & GRANGE COMMUNITY POOL

Note—All matches will commence at advertised starting time.

Carnival Director:

ALLAN DOWLING.

ROUND 1—Saturday, 3rd February

11.00 a.m.
VICTORIA v TASMANIA
22   *2*

Referee:

12.00
SOUTH AUSTRALIA v N.S.W.
7   *5*

Referee:

ROUND 2—Sunday, 4th February

12.00
SOUTH AUSTRALIA v VICTORIA
7   *10*

Referee:

1.00 p.m.
TASMANIA v NEW SOUTH WALES
0   *11*

Referee:

ROUND 3—Monday, 5th February

11.00 a.m.
VICTORIA v NEW SOUTH WALES
6   *10*

Referee:

12.00
TASMANIA v SOUTH AUSTRALIA
0   *19*

Referee:

ROUND 4—Tuesday, 6th February

1.00 p.m.
N.S.W. v SOUTH AUSTRALIA
2   *7*

Referee:

2.00 p.m.
TASMANIA v VICTORIA
2   *16*

Referee:

ROUND 5—Wednesday, 7th February

8.00 a.m.
NEW SOUTH WALES v TASMANIA
11   *3*

Referee:

9.00 a.m.
VICTORIA v SOUTH AUSTRALIA
1   *2*

Referee:

ROUND 6—Thursday, 8th February

1.00 p.m.
SOUTH AUSTRALIA v TASMANIA
13   *2*

Referee:

2.00 p.m.
NEW SOUTH WALES v VICTORIA
4   *4*

Referee:

NEW SOUTH WALES

1 Diane MacDougal
2 Robyn Carroll (capt)
3 Marilyn Mitchell
4 Lynette Trewhella
5 Ruth Hardingham
6 Carolyn Keats
7 Adrienne Turnbull (v/capt)
8 Julie Girdler
9 Tracey Jones
10 Rhonda Laws
11 Virginia Turnbull

Coach: Phillip Bower

Manageress: Joyce Campbell

VICTORIA

1 Heather Millar
2 Maryan Hopkins
3 Carol Ahyee (capt)
4 Sandra Muhleman (v/capt)
5 Gail Williams
6 Kaye Hanlon
7 Janis Crowl
8 Wendy Rooney
9 Julie Giffin
10 Sandra Hinkley
11 Rhonda Dewsnap

Coach: B. Dalvene

Manageress: Elsa Thompson

SOUTH AUSTRALIA

1 Leoni King
2 Kay Stewart
3 Debbie Niblock
4 Frances Killmier
5 Mary Kentish
6 Jill Errington (capt)
7 Jo Courtney
8 Julie Lamont
9 Jo Chartier
10 Julie Keast
11 Margo Clements

Coach: Ray Marshall

Manageress: Iris Marshall

TASMANIA

1 Ludmilla Chudackova
2 Karen Riley
3 Leeanne Adcock
4 Annette De Jong
5 Jenny Leedham
6 Debbie Ricketts
7 Dilys Millhouse (capt)
8 Karen Burdon
9 Clarissa Young
10 Rosylin Case
11 Helen Shields

Coach: P. Bird

Manageress: Dilys Millhouse

lack in trying, the NSW girls just couldn't match the physical prowess of the eventual winners Victoria, and they were once again beaten into third place by South Australia.

▲ *Official Program of the 1973 Ladies Interstate Water Polo Series, although not recognised by the ASA, was conducted by the SAAWPA.*

The Premierships

After a slow start, the Balmain team improved throughout this season and by the the semi-finals found themselves in second position behind Bronte. In the play-offs, Bondi defeated Cronulla (8~5) in the minor semi, while Bronte, who had lost only

"As the leading goal scorers by far, Bronte Ladies had been the most consistent team throughout the 1972/73 season... as exhibited in their goal average... 62 for and only 17 against. But the grand-final provided somewhat of an upset, with Balmain defeating Bronte by 4 goals to 3."
NSWAWPA, 1972-73 Annual Report

one game and appeared to have a mortgage on the title, easily disposed of Balmain (5~2) in the major semi-final. But Balmain pulled themselves together and defeated Bondi in the final (4~3) to secure their place in the competition finale.

Both teams had been consistent semi-finalists over the years and were equally intent on capturing their first Ladies' premiership. The young Balmain team closely followed their coach's instructions, employed superior tactics to defeat Bronte in an upset (4~3), and take their inaugural Ladies' water polo

◀Photographs of the 1973 NSW Ladies water polo team in practice (from top): Adrienne Turnbull gets away from Bronte's Lyn Trewhella; Virginia Turnbull lunges at a shot. ▼Julie Girdler & Lyn Trewhella; and Julie Girdler lets go a shot.

premiership. The Bondi Club was successful in winning the inaugural 2nd Grade premiership with a victory over Drummoyne (4~3), who it might be added had led the competition throughout the season. [10]

Bronte AWPC

At the beginning of this season the Bronte men and women were travelling in opposite directions. While the men were losing strength with club members defecting elsewhere, the women had just won the inaugural Winter

▶Photographs of the 1973 NSW Ladies water polo team in practice (from top): Virginia Turnbull is beaten in goal; Lyn Trewhella (Bronte) throws a lob shot; ▼NSW coach, Phil Bower speaking with his team in a game at Henley Baths, Adelaide.

1972/73 NSWAWPA RESULTS

GRADE I

	Won	Lost	Disq. or Dr. Forf.		Goals for	ag.	Points
BRONTE	9	1	2	—	62	17	31
BALMAIN	8	1	3	—	46	18	29
CRONULLA	9	—	1	2	39	28	28
BONDI	7	—	5	—	39	32	26
PARRAMATTA-MEMORIAL	3	1	8	—	35	55	19
CARSS PARK	4	—	4	4	34	42	16
SYDNEY UNIVERSITY	—	1	9	2	15	78	11

GRADE II

	Won	Lost	Disq. or Dr. Forf.		Goals for	ag.	Points
DRUMMOYNE	8	1	3	—	67	29	29
BONDI	7	2	3	—	53	25	28
BRONTE	6	3	2	1	59	31	26
NORTHBRIDGE	5	2	5	—	42	42	24
GRANVILLE R.S.L.	—	—	—	12	4	98	0

1st SEMI-FINAL: Grade 1, Bondi 8 — Cronulla 5; Grade 2, Bronte 7 — Northbridge 2.
2nd SEMI-FINAL: Grade 1, Bronte 5 — Balmain 2; Grade 2, Bondi 6 — Drummoyne 5.
FINAL: Grade 1, Balmain 4 — Bondi 3; Grade 2, Drummoyne 5 — Bronte 0 (Forfeited).
GRAND FINAL: Balmain 4 — Bronte 3; Grade 2, Bondi 4 — Drummoyne 3.

▲ Photograph of the Trewhella sisters, Lyn and Karen practicing at Watsons Bay Baths.
◄ Loueen Winters, a member of Bronte Ladies 2nd Grade, with Tracy Rockwell in 1973. They shared rides to training in Lulu's mini moke, affectionately called 'Claude.'

competition and were on the ascendancy. Coach Tom Folden, had been successful in recruiting more talent in the off season and there were now a sufficient number of players to field two Bronte women's teams. Infact, Bronte joined Bondi this year as the only two clubs in the competition to field a team in both grades. As the season got underway, it was clear that the Bronte women were a powerful outfit, and had their second State representative selected in top goal scorer, Lyn Trewhella.

By season's end, the Bronte ladies had only lost two of their nine matches, and finished the regular season as minor premiers. In the play-offs Bondi eliminated Cronulla (8~5) in the first semi-final, while Bronte defeated Balmain (5~2) in the major semi-final to qualify for their second grand-final appearance. But problems brewed in the Bronte ranks, which upset the players enough to give Balmain an opening, and they lost by the one goal (3~4) in an upset finish. The saving grace was that the inaugural Ladies' Club Championship was won by Bronte.

1973-74 Ladies

The NSWAWPA witnessed another successful season for Ladies' water polo in 1973/74, with 11 teams from 10 different clubs contesting the two grades of the competition. A record 166 ladies registered for the Winter and new Pre-Season competitions, as well as the regular Summer premiership. Unfortunately, Granville RSL dropped out this year, but they were replaced by a new club from Macquarie University.

Representatives in NSW Teams

Despite third place finishes over the previous five Interstate Championships, the Association stuck with Phil Bower as coach, who held onto the bulk of his 1973 team. What the side needed was strength and speed, which they found in Cathy Hawkins (Sydney Uni), Margaret Wilby and Maree Robinson (Bronte), while Diane Semmens (Balmain) was chosen in the goals. The Bronte girls were on top of the Sydney women's competition this season, and Maree Robinson had four years earlier won the gold medal for 200m butterfly, at the 1970 Commonwealth Games in Edinburgh, Scotland.

The new faces made all the difference as NSW, led by captain Adrienne Turnbull, only dropped one game on their way to their first Interstate Ladies' Water Polo Championship. They had finally relegated Victoria and South Australia to second and third place.

The Premierships

The 1973 Winter competition had been won by Bondi from Sydney University. But jumping out early, the new 'Speedo' Pre-Season competition was captured by the Bronte team, who defeated Bondi (5~1). It was visible to many devotees of the sport in 1973/74 that Bronte, who were coached by

1973/74 Season Statistics N.S.W.A.W.P.A.

Clubs in the Ladies Water Polo Competitions.

Clubs	Grades 1st	2nd	Total
Balmain	●		1
Bondi	●	●	2
Bronte	●		1
Carss Park	●		1
Cronulla/Sutherland	●		1
Drummoyne		●	1
Macquarie Uni		●	1
Northbridge		●	1
Parramatta Mem.	●		1
Sydney Uni		●	1
	6	5	11

Results of the Ladies Water Polo Competitions.

Grade	Premier		Runner-Up
Pre-season	Bronte~5	d.	1~Bondi
1st	Bronte~8	d.	4~Cronulla/Suth
2nd	Sydney Uni~8	d.	7~Drummoyne
	Club Champions		BONDI
1st	Bronte		Winter Comp

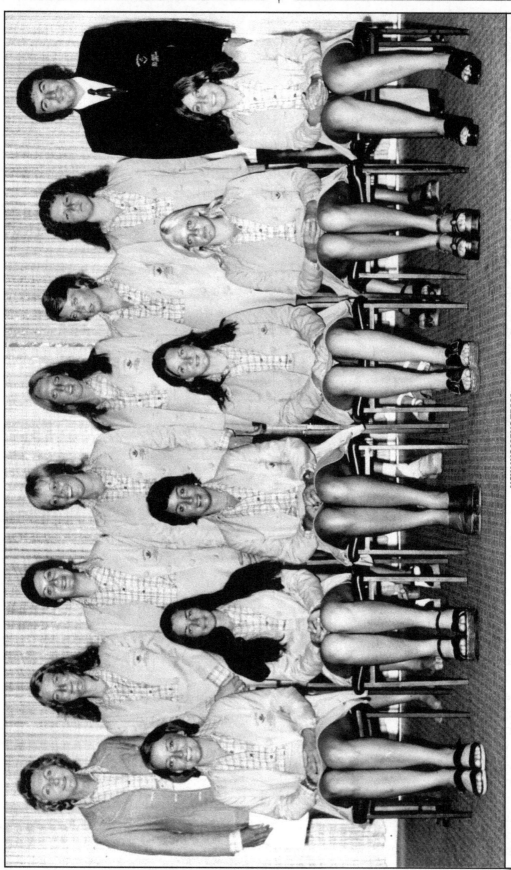

NSW WOMENS TEAM
1974 - Interstate Co-Champions - Melbourne

Back row (from left): Pat Jones (Manager, Cronulla), Marilyn Mitchell (Carss Park), Ruth Hardingham (Cronulla), Caroline Keats (r, Cronulla), **Margaret Wilby (Bronte)**, Debbie McDougall (Balmain), Phil Bower (Coach, Balmain), **Lyn Trewhella (Bronte)**. Front row: Virginia Turnbull (g,Carss Park), Cathy Hawkins (Sydney Uni), **Maree Robinson (Bronte)**, Adrienne Turnbull (c,Carss Park), Diane Semmens (Balmain), Rhonda Laws (Balmain). Photo - Pat Jones.

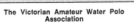

The Victorian Amateur Water Polo Association

welcomes you to

AUSTRALIAN WOMEN'S

1974 WATER POLO CHAMPIONSHIPS

Competing teams from:

NEW SOUTH WALES
SOUTH AUSTRALIA
TASMANIA
VICTORIA
QUEENSLAND

Venue:

NORTHCOTE SWIMMING COMPLEX

NOTE—All matches will commence at advertised starting time.

Carnival Director:
KEVIN McBEAN.

NAMES AND CAP NUMBER OF EACH TEAM

QUEENSLAND

No. 1 Jane Mathewson
2 Sue Raeburn
3 Kathy Beer
4 Carol Hudson (Capt.)
5 Leith Goebel
6 Robyn Dimmock
7 Allison Larkin
8 Nea Scott (V/Capt.)
9 Rainee Skinner
10 Vicki McKain
11 Debbie Handley

Coach: Mr. T. Kean

Manageress: Mrs. G. Domjahn

SOUTH AUSTRALIA

No. 1 Leonie King
2 Sue Turner
3 Frances Killmier
4 Julie Lamont
5 Joanne Chartier
6 Jill Errington (Capt.)
7 Jo Anne Courtney
8 Debbie Niblock
9 Kay Turner
10 Julie Keast (V/Capt.)
11 Vickie Niblock

Coach: Mr. R. Marshall

Manageress: Mrs. I. Marshall

TASMANIA

No. 1 Jan Chipman (V/Capt.)
2 Helen Sheil
3 Leeanne Adcock
4 Jane Langford
5 Jenny Leedham
6 Debbie Ricketts
7 Karen Purdon (Capt.)
8 Anita Wilson
9 Clarissa Young
10 Roslyn Case
11 Keren Dean

Coach: Dilys Millhouse

Manageress: Jan Chipman

NEW SOUTH WALES

No. 1 Virginia Turnbull
2 Adrienne Turnbull (Capt.)
3 Marilyn Mitchell
4 Lynette Trewella
5 Ruth Hardingham
6 Carolyn Keats
7 Rhonda Laws
8 Margaret Wilby
9 Maree Robinson
10 Kathy Hawkins
11 Dianne Semmens (V/Capt.)

Coach: Mr. P. Bower

Manageress: Mrs. P. Jones

VICTORIA

No. 1 Heather Millar
2 Rhonda Dewsnap
3 Carol Angland (Capt.)
4 Judy Toms (V/Capt.)
5 Gail Williams
6 Kaye Hanlon
7 Sue Ferguson
8 Betty Gawthorne
9 Kaylene Roberts
10 Faye Grant
11 Maryanne Hopkins

Coach: Mr. B. Dalvene

Manageress: Mrs. E. Thompson

Hon. Secretary:
K. McBEAN, 46 3492

▲ABOVE: Official Program of the 1974 Australian Womens Water Polo Championships, at Northcote Swimming Complex, Melbourne. MID: Two photographs of the 1974 NSW Ladies Water Polo Team, casual and formal. ▶Official VAWPA Pass for the 1974 Australian Womens Water Polo Championships.

Les Kay, had developed into a formidable team. They had only lost one game during the season and entered the semi-finals with the highest goal average.

In the NSWAWPA Women's competition play-offs, Carss Park defeated the 1973 premiers from Balmain (9~8) in the minor semi, and in an upset in the major semi-final, Cronulla-Sutherland disposed of minor premiers Bronte (5~4). Bronte recovered however, to defeat Carss Park (5~2) in the final to secure a berth in the competition decider. The grand-final saw Bronte reverse their

1973/74 NSWAWPA RESULTS

LADIES

GRADE I

	Won	Dr.	Lost	Goals For	Ag.	Points
BRONTE	10	4	1	64	29	24
CRONULLA	9	1	5	72	38	19
BALMAIN	6	5	4	52	37	17
CARRS PARK	7	1	7	57	47	15
BONDI	5	3	7	51	45	13
PARRAMATTA-MEMORIAL	1	0	14	9	99	2

GRADE II

	Won	Dr.	Lost	Goals For	Ag.	Points
SYDNEY UNIVERSITY	10	0	2	67	12	20
DRUMMOYNE	9	1	2	65	23	19
BONDI	6	0	6	32	30	12
NORTHBRIDGE	4	1	7	31	53	9
MACQUARIE UNIVERSITY	0	0	12	0	77	0

1st SEMI-FINAL: Grade I, Cronulla 5 — Bronte 4; Grade II, Bondi 9 — Northbridge 5.
2nd SEMI-FINAL: Grade I, Carrs Park 9 — Balmain 8; Grade II, Sydney University 7 — Drummoyne 5.
FINAL: Grade I, Bronte 5 — Carss Park 2, Grade II, Drummoyne 4 — Bondi 3.
GRAND FINAL: Grade I, Bronte 8 — Cronulla 4; Grade II, Sydney University 8 — Drummoyne 7.

LADIES' WINTER COMPETITION, 1974

	W.	D.	L.	Goals For.	A.	P.
BRONTE	7	—	3	65	10	14
DRUMMOYNE	6	—	4	32	30	12
BLACKTOWN	5	—	5	18	46	10
UNIVERSITY OF SYDNEY	4	—	6	45	27	8
BONDI	4	—	6	38	15	8
MACQUARIE UNIVERSITY	4	—	6	3	76	8

Premiers: Bronte

loss in the play-offs, to comprehensively defeat Cronulla-Sutherland (8~4), to capture the NSWAWPA Ladies 1st Grade water polo premiership after their third grand-final appearance. Sydney University defeated Drummoyne (8~7) to take out the 2nd Grade premiership.

The 1974 Women's Winter competition was won again by Bronte from Drummoyne.[11]

Bronte AWPC

Right from the outset, the Bronte girls had worked hard and captured the 'Speedo' Pre-Season competition by defeating Bondi (5~1). As the season got underway, three Bronte players were selected in this year's State team, and the side only lost one game in the whole year, entering the semi-finals as minor-premiers with the highest goal average.

However, Bronte faltered in the play-offs, losing to Cronulla (4~5) in the first semi-final, while Carss Park defeated Balmain (9~8). But the Bronte girls stormed back in the final to defeat Carss Park (5~2) and gain a grand-final berth. The following week, the 1974 NSWAWPA Ladies' 1st Grade was decided with Bronte comprehensively defeating Cronulla (8~4) in the grand-final. It was Bronte's first ever Ladies championship, and delivered a sixth 1st Grade premiership for the club. The Bronte women later confirmed their skills and talent by also capturing the 1974 Winter competition outright.

▲ Celebrating the 1st Grade premiership in 1974 were: Mrs Gloria Trewhella, Les Kay (Coach) and captain Margaret Wilby.

1974 - 1ST GRADE PREMIERS

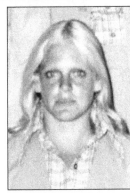

BRONTE AMATEUR WATER POLO CLUB
1973/74 - Womens 1st Grade Premiers - NSWAWPA
TOP (From left): Margaret Wilby (c), Lyn Trewhella, Maree Robinson, Karen Trewhella (g). BOTTOM: Laurel Cannot, Rhonda Thompson, Debbie Graham & Les Kay (Coach). Missing: Lee Davis, Karen Pearce.

▲Most of the winning Bronte Ladies 1st Grade team of 1973/74. From left: Laurel Cannot (g), Debbie Graham, Lyn Trewhella, Karen Trewhella, Cathy Chamberlain?, Lee Davis, Karen Pearce, Rhonda Thompson, Margaret Wilby. (Missing - Maree Robinson). Photo - Karen Copas (nee Trewhella).

1974-75 Ladies

The 1974/75 season was yet again a record year for the NSWAWPA Women's competition with 13 teams entering across two grades for the Summer competition, and just as many teams again in the Winter and Pre-Season contests combined. Unfortunately, the 1972 premiers Carss Park dropped out, but were replaced by two new clubs in Blacktown and the University of NSW.

Representatives in NSW Teams

The ASU finally recognised the Ladies' Interstate Series as a true Australian Championship this year, so there was a lot at stake. Retirements saw Caroline Keats, Ruth Hardingham (Cronulla) and Bronte's Maree Robinson leave the team, along with captain Adrienne Turnbull (Carss Park) after six consecutive seasons, and as captain of the side.

By this stage, places in the NSW Ladies' team were becoming much harder to obtain, with eight encumbents holding onto their positions. Tracy Jones (Cronulla) was recalled, while the two new team caps were Jenny Cameron (Cronulla) and Bronte's goalkeeper Karen Trewhella. Sticking with the tried and tested combination paid off this season, when NSW retained the title by defeating Victoria (4~3) in the final, with Queensland finishing in third place.

The Premierships

The 1974/75 Pre-Season competition was captured by the Bondi team this season, who defeated a very talented team from Blacktown A (2~1).

The Women's Summer competition was however, very hotly contested with Bronte claiming the minor premiership for the third consecutive season. In the play-offs, Balmain romped home over Bondi (7~0) in the minor semi,

1974/75 Season Statistics
N.S.W.A.W.P.A.

Clubs in the Ladies Water Polo Competitions.

Clubs	Grades 1st	2nd	Total
Balmain	●		1
Blacktown	●	●	2
Bondi	●		1
Bronte	●		1
Cronulla/Sutherland	●		1
Drummoyne	●		1
Macquarie Uni		●	1
Northbridge		●	1
Parramatta		●	1
Sydney Uni	●	●	2
Uni of NSW		●	1
	7	6	13

Results of the Ladies Water Polo Competitions.

Grade	Premier		Runner-Up
Pre-season	Bondi~2	d.	1~Blacktown A
1st	Cronulla~3	d.	2~Bronte
2nd	Sydney Uni~5	d.	2~Parramatta
	Club Champions		SYDNEY UNI
1st	Drummoyne		Winter Comp

NSW WOMENS TEAM
1975 - National Champions - Perth
Back row (from left): **Mrs G. Trewhella (Manager, Bronte)**, Jenny Cameron (Cronulla), **Lyn Trewhella (Bronte)**, Tracey Jones (Cronulla), **Margaret Wilby (Bronte)**, Virginia Turnbull (c,g,Balmain), Phil Bower (Coach, Balmain). Front row: **Karen Trewhella (g,Bronte)**, Cathy Hawkins (Sydney Uni), Diane Semmens (vc, Balmain), Debbie McDougall (Balmain), Rhonda Laws (Balmain), Marilyn Mitchell (Balmain). Photo - NSWAWPA 1974/75 Annual Report.

▲MID (Left): Members of the 1975 NSW Womens team soak up the sun at Somerset Pool in Perth. (Right): Karen Trewhella, Diane Semmens, Paul Dunford (NSW U/18s Men's Coach), Margaret Wilby and Lyn Trewhella, enjoying a day out in Perth, 1975. ABOVE: Members of the NSW Womens team celebrate their 4~3 victory over Victoria in the 1975 Australian Championships in Perth.

BRONTE AMATEUR WATER POLO CLUB
1974/75 - Womens 1st Grade Runners-Up - NSWAWPA
From left: ???, Maree Robinson, Lyn Trewhella, Karen Trewhella (g), Margaret Wilby (c, in front), Laurel Cannot, Cathy Chamberlain, Lee Davis. Missing: Rhonda Thompson & Les Kay (Coach).

while Cronulla-Sutherland disposed of Bronte (6~4) in an upset. Bronte then recovered, but had to scramble to barely defeat Balmain (6~5) in the final for a place in the competition decider.

In the 1st Grade grand-final, favourites Bronte did all they could to reverse their loss in the major semi, but in the end, they were narrowly defeated by Cronulla-Sutherland (3~2), in one of the finest games of women's water polo yet witnessed since the competition had commenced. Cronulla seized the Women's 1st Grade premiership, adding a second title to their 1971 victory. In the 2nd Grade competition, Sydney University defeated Parramatta (5~2) to capture the premiership for the second successive year. [12]

1974/75 NSWAWPA RESULTS

LADIES' METROPOLITAN, 1974/75

1st GRADE

	W.	D.	L.	F/D	Goals For	A.	Pts.
BRONTE	12	1	1	—	58	20	25
CRONULLA	10	1	3	—	39	26	21
BONDI	8	1	5	—	40	29	17
BALMAIN	8	1	5	—	43	37	17
SYDNEY UNIVERSITY	8	1	5	—	44	34	17
DRUMMOYNE	3	1	10	—	13	61	7
BLACKTOWN	4	—	10	—	20	44	8

First Semi Final: Bronte 4, Cronulla 6

Second Semi Final: Bondi 0, Balmain 7

Final: Bronte 6, Balmain 5

Grand Final: Cronulla 3, Bronte 2

Premiers: Cronulla

CRONULLA
1974/75 - NSWAWPA Women's 1st Grade Premiers
Margaret Hanson, Michelle Brazier, Carolyn Keats, Leanne Stapleton, Lauren Stapleton, Sharyn Stapleton, Kay Touhill, Jenny Cameron, Tracy Jones, Cheryl Nixon, Jack Keen (Coach).

Bronte AWPC

As the 1974/75 season opened, Bronte ladies were riding high, having won the Pre-Season, Summer and Winter competitions during the 1973/74 season. However, not enough girls turned out to field two teams this year, so Bronte dropped back to only contest the 1st Grade, with slightly less depth.

Bronte lost the Pre-Season competition to Bondi, but once the regular season got underway, Bronte again led from the front, and only dropped one game from their two rounds of the competition. This was the third consecutive year that the Bronte ladies concluded the regular season as minor premiers.

In the play-offs, Bronte faltered in losing to Cronulla (4~6) in the first semi-final, but managed to defeat Balmain in the final (6~5), which placed them into their third consecutive Ladies 1st Grade grand-final. With Bronte having the best defensive statistics, the premiership game developed into a defensive struggle, although Bronte could only manage two goals, which allowed Cronulla to narrowly snatch victory (3~2).

With a number of the girls taking a break through the off-season, the 1975 Winter competition fell to Drummoyne.

1975-76 Ladies

The 1975/76 season was another record year for the NSWAWPA Women's competition with 17 teams from 13 clubs entering across two grades for the Summer competition. Unfortunately, Bronte (1974 premiers) morphed into the Maroubra Seals this year, while the new clubs were from Padstow and Ryde.

Representatives in NSW Teams

Once again under coach Phil Bower and playing at home in Sydney, there were great hopes that the NSW Women would claim their third consecutive national title this

1975/76 Season Statistics N.S.W.A.W.P.A.

Clubs in the Ladies Water Polo Competitions.

Clubs	Grades 1st	Grades 2nd	Total
Balmain	●		1
Blacktown	●	●	2
Bondi	●		1
Cronulla/Sutherland	●		1
Drummoyne	●		1
Macquarie Uni		●	1
Northbridge		●	1
Maroubra Seals	●	●	2
Parramatta	●		1
Padstow		●	1
Ryde	2		2
Sydney Uni	●	●	2
Uni of NSW		●	1
	8	9	17

Results of the Ladies Water Polo Competitions.

Grade	Premier	Runner-Up
1st	Sydney Uni B	Pre-season Comp
1st	Sydney Uni~7 d.	6~Maroubra Seals
2nd	Sydney Uni~7 d.	6~Blacktown
Club Champions		SYDNEY UNI
1st	Sydney Uni	Winter Comp

NSW WOMENS TEAM
1976 - 5th Place - Sydney
Back row (from left): Phil Bower (Coach, Balmain), Caroline Keats (Cronulla), Diane Semmens (Balmain), Cathy Hawkins (Sydney Uni), Debbie McDougall (Balmain), Tracey Jones (Cronulla), Margery Keeble (Manager). Front row: Jenny Howell (Sydney Uni), Rhonda Laws (Balmain), Ruth Hardingham (Cronulla), Virginia Turnbull (c,g, Balmain), **Margaret Wilby (vc, Maroubra Seals)**, Julie Barnard (Balmain). Photo - NSWAWPA 1975/76 Annual Report.

year. Places were tight, but the two new caps were Julie Barnard (Balmain) and Jenny Howell (Sydney Uni), while Carolyn Keats and Ruth Hardingham (Cronulla) were recalled, and seven players retained their spot from the 1975 championship team.

But NSW just couldn't put it together and only managed to win one game in the entire tournament, suffering in the process their worst ever national championship performance and finishing in fifth place. The placings went to Victoria (1st), Queensland (2nd) and South Australia (3rd).

The Premierships

The 1st Grade premiership in this season saw Sydney University narrowly defeat the ex-Bronte team, playing as Maroubra Seals (7~6) in the grand-final.[13]

SYDNEY UNIVERSITY
1975/76 - NSWAWPA Women's 1st Grade Premiers
Cathy Turner (c), Heather Bryant, Lee Dunbar, Jenny Howell, Cathy Hawkins, Fran Nethery, Diane Allison etc...

No one knew it back then, but the 1976 NSWAWPA women's competition heralded a new era of water polo domination that phenomenally extended

Sydney Uni's reign over the title for the next 14 consecutive seasons.

Maroubra Seals AWPC

Just like their male club counterparts, the ex-Bronte women changed over to become Maroubra Seals this season. However, as they did not fragment like the men, the name change had little effect on the performance of the Ladies, and this team had a couple of successful years.

The Maroubra Seals ladies team began the year in superb form, being undefeated in their half of the Pre-Season draw, but losing by a single goal to Sydney Uni B in the play-off (4~5). In the regular season too, the ex-Bronte girls played brilliantly to claim their fourth consecutive minor premiership. They then managed to defeat Sydney Uni in the semi-final (3~2), but couldn't hold off the students in the grand-final, and lost by a whisker in the decider (6~7). The Maroubra Seals ladies team played on throughout the 1976 Winter competition, recording just two losses, but they finished third behind Sydney Uni and Cronulla.

For the 1976/77 season the Maroubra Seals dropped to 2nd Grade, where they finished second in the Pre-Season, but again won through to the grand-final of the Summer competition, where they lost by a goal to Parramatta Memorial ASC (2~3). They also qualified for the final of the Winter competition, but lost to Bondi (1~2).

In 1977/78 the ladies finished second in the 2nd Grade Pre-Season competition, but were re-graded to 1st Grade, where they ended the year in seventh position. After that the team gradually drifted away.

1975/76 NSWAWPA RESULTS

FIRST GRADE

	P.	W.	L.	D.	F/D	Goals For	A.	Pts.
Balmain	14	7	6	1	–	37	28	29
Blacktown	14	4	9	1	–	31	57	23
Bondi	14	6	7	–	–/1	46	43	25
Cronulla	14	7	1	–	3/3	39	41	22
Drummoyne	14	5	7	1	–/1	38	54	24
Maroubra Seals	14	11	3	–	–	49	21	36
Parramatta	14	–	6	–	–/8	8	70	6
Sydney University	14	13	–	1	–	73	7	41

1st Semi Final: Balmain 13, Bondi 2
2nd Semi Final: Maroubra Seals 3, Sydney University 2
Final: Sydney University 4, Balmain 2
Grand Final: Sydney University 7, Maroubra Seals 6
Premiers: Sydney University.

SECOND GRADE

	P.	W.	L.	D.	F/D	Goals For	A.	Pts.
Blacktown	16	10	3	1	1/1	87	30	35
Macquarie University	16	5	3	2	–/6	35	54	22
Maroubra Seals	16	4	11	–	–/2	26	106	25
Northbridge	16	8	6	–	–/2	61	51	30
Padstow	16	1	11	–	–/4	14	138	14
Ryde "A"	16	11	4	1	–	79	36	39
Ryde "B"	16	4	9	1	–/2	29	86	23
Sydney University	16	11	3	2	–	116	26	40
University of N.S.W.	16	12	1	2	–/1	99	19	41

1st Semi Final: Blacktown 7, Ryde "A" 2
2nd Semi Final: Sydney University 10, University of N.S.W. 9
Final: Blacktown 3, University of N.S.W. 2
Grand Final: Sydney University 7, Blacktown 6
Premiers: Sydney University.

A number of matches were played between Bronte, Tamworth and other country clubs during the Southgate Inn Tournament and development visit in Nov 1972.

THE weakened ACT representative water polo team, although losing three of four games in Sydney last week, performed much better than expected and gave John Cording the chance to cement his claim to the goal - keeping post left vacant this season by the non-availability of Chris Lord.

The team, without Pat Armstrong, Bevan Liebke, Roger Martin and Laurie Jackson played the three leading Sydney competition teams, Bronte, Sydney University and East Sydney, for 6-10, 2-7 and 5-8 losses respectively, but won 10-4 against Bronte seconds.

It played best against Sydney University which has five State representatives in its team and it was in this game that Cording particularly showed his ability. Others to play well were Paul Jones and Hugh Crawley.

The ACT coach, Neville de Mestre, hopes a full team will be available for the NSW Country event in Canberra in two weeks. Entries are in from Wagga and Cootamundra, and are expected from Goulburn and Leeton.

Bronte Water Polo Club visit the ACT (The Canberra Times, 25 Nov, 1971, p30).

Going into the 1971/72 season, Bronte AWPC had procured a further five premierships from nine grand-final appearances by its grades, over the previous five seasons. But principally, Bronte were once again the premier club in Sydney, and New South Wales... and being the current premiers, they arguably had the best 1st Grade side in the nation.

However, despite switching to Watson's Bay, a lack of vision was lurking in the background, and a number of successive hurdles for Bronte became critical in the unfortunate series of events that were soon to affect the club and its members.

1971-72

1971/72 NSWAWPA OFFICIALS: Dr. H.K. Porter (Patron); V. Chalwin (President); H.J. Bund (Past President); R. Traynor (Chairman); **R. Vadas (Registrar)**; W.M. Gooley (Secretary); Miss C. Taylor (Comp. Secretary); O. Bogg (Treasurer). **J. Campbell (Asst. Secretary)**.

By the 1971/72 season the NSWAWPA had ten grades competing across three divisions in the men's water polo contests, as well as one grade for the women's competition.

The Competition Committee capably organised the competitions, which were conducted across three divisions with the playing of two rounds.

This year NSWAWPA matches were played at Ashfield, Balmain, Drummoyne, Gunnamatta Bay, Manly, North Sydney, Parramatta and a brand new swimming complex at Sydney University, which was a 50m indoor heated facility.

NSW Combined High Schools
1972 - 1st XI Water Polo Team
From left: ???, Lee Miranda, Damien Gooley, **Lance Kerr, Gary Grant**, Glen Gilsenen, Michael Dunn, Don Cameron (g), Buddy Portier, Kevin Stapleton, Andrew Kerr (c), Ray Mullins (Manager).

In regard to new clubs, Balgowlah, Homebush and Northbridge all joined the competition. Unfortunately, Canterbury and Newtown ASC lapsed, while Judean morphed into the Maccabi Club.

The new Sydney University Swimming Complex provided for the first time, the capability to schedule winter matches, and so 1972 saw the NSWAWPA begin their annual Winter Championships.

Representatives in NSW Teams

NSW Open Mens Team

The NSW Men's team again retained the bulk of their 1970 championship winning team, which included both Peter Folden and Graeme Samuel of Bronte. Bill Phillips Jr. was replaced by his Universities teammate Jim Shekdah, while goalkeeper Ben Schmidt (Parramatta) made way for Micky Withers (Balmain), who was trying out for his fourth Olympic Games. David Neesham returned to bolster his native Western Australia, but was replaced by the highly skilled Rolly Flesch, who after a fabulous premiership winning season with Bronte in 1971, was recalled for a third time.

However, under their Australian coach Ron Wooten, Victoria bounced back to add a 13th national title, with NSW finishing a disappointing third to Western Australia. South Australia performed brilliantly in this tournament with the assistance of their new stars, Charles and Michael Turner. Oddly however, Victoria and Western Australia only had three players each selected in the Olympic team, with five being chosen from third placed NSW. Both Charles Turner and Bronte's Peter Folden, who were the form players of the tournament, were overlooked.

1971/72 Season Statistics N.S.W.A.W.P.A.

Clubs in the Mens Water Polo Competitions.

Clubs	1	2	3	4	2¹	2²	2³	3¹	3²	3³	Total
Avalon/Bilgola									●	●	2
Balgowlah									●		1
Balmain	●	●	●	●	2	●	●	●	●	2	12
Bondi Dolphins						●	●	●			3
Bronte	●	●	●	●	●						5
Clovelly Eskimos						●	●				2
Cronulla-Sutherland	●	●	●	●	●	●					6
Drummoyne							●		●		2
East Sydney	●	●	●	●							4
Homebush							●	●			2
Liverpool							●	●			2
Manly/Warringah	●	●	●	●	●						5
Maccabi (Judean)					●	●	●				3
Nth Palm Beach								●			1
Nth Sydney								●	●	●	3
Northbridge								●	●		2
P'matta Memorial									●	●	2
Penrith								●	●	●	3
Ryde									●		1
Sydney University								●	●		2
Universities	●	●	●	●							4
Western Suburbs	●	●	●	●							4
	7	7	7	7	9	8	7	6	7	6	71

Results of the Mens Water Polo Competitions.

Grade	Premier	Runner-Up
1st	Universities	Pre-Season Comp
1st	Balmain	Cascade Cup Comp
1st	Universities~4 d. 3~Balmain	
2nd	Cronulla-Sutherland~6 d. 5~Balmain	
3rd	Cronulla-Sutherland~7 d. 4~Balmain	
4th	Balmain~6 d. 5~Cronulla-Sutherland	
	Club Champions	BALMAIN
D2 1st	NSW Maccabi~5 d. 3~Drummoyne	
D2 2nd	Liverpool~8 d. 4~Balmain B	
D2 3rd	Drummoyne~4 d. 2~North Sydney	
D3 1st	Balmain D~8 d. 7~Manly/Warringah	
D3 2nd	P'matta Memorial~6 d. 4~Cronulla-Sutherland	
D3 3rd	P'matta Memorial~8 d. 7~Balgowlah	
1st	Bronte & Liverpool	Winter Comp

"I joined Bronte at the start of the 1971/72 season, aged 16. Myself and a whole team of players came across from Newtown ASC water polo team, which was basically a one off amalgamation of swimmers from Newtown ASC and Enmore BHS. We had reached the play-offs in 2nd Grade of Division II, under Peter Primo (Randwick Rugby & Coogee SLSC), but as he couldn't continue as coach, 'Eyes' took us en masse across to Bronte, who had by then moved their training to Watson's Bay."

Tracy Rockwell, Oct 2018

NEW SOUTH WALES TEAM
1972 - Adelaide National Championships - 3rd Place

Back row (from left): John Harrison (g, Universities), Jim Shekdah (Universities), Con Cope (Universities), **Rolly Flesch (Bronte)**, Peter Montgomery (Universities), **Graeme Samuel (Bronte)**, Michael Withers (g, Balmain). Front row: Nick Barnes (Universities), **Peter Folden (Bronte)**, David Woods (c/Coach, Balmain), Bill Gooley (Manager, Cronulla), Ian MacLauchlain (Balmain).
Photo - NSWAWPA Annual Report 1972/73.

NSW Junior Mens Team

This season saw the inaugural U/18 Junior Men's National Championship, which was held in conjunction with the Open Men's Championship in Brisbane. Bronte did not have a representative in this team, however NSW played through undefeated to take out the inaugural title.

The 1972 Olympic Team

The 1972 Australian team played an undefeated warm-up series in New Zealand, and then embarked on a lengthy European tour, where they won more than 50% of their games. However, at the Munich Olympic Games they only managed to win two of their eight matches and finished the competition in 12th place.

The Premierships

In the semi-finals of the men's 1st Grade, third placed Bronte eliminated a strong Cronulla-Sutherland (8~7) in the minor semi-final and Balmain narrowly defeated Universities (5~4) in the major semi-final. Universities then just barely defeated the reigning premiers, Bronte (4~3) to qualify for the competition decider. Assisted by the experience of ex-Hungarian Olympian Oscar Charles as coach, Universities then overcame Balmain (4~3) in the grand-final to win their second 1st Grade premiership. Cronulla defeated Balmain (6~?) in 2nd Grade, and repeated the dose to beat Balmain in 3rd Grade (7~4), while Balmain reversed the trend to defeat Cronulla in 4th Grade (6~5). The Annual Club Championship was won by Balmain.

Following the regular summer season, a Winter competition was inagurated thanks to completion of the new Sydney University Pool, which was heated. The competition was run in both an outright and handicap format. Bronte and Liverpool finished equal premiers for the outright

▲TOP (Left): Official Program for the 1972 National Championships and Olympic Games Trials in Brisbane, Queensland. (Right): Phil Bower joined Balmain in 1973, which was a big loss for Bronte. Phil went on to win a phenomenol 13 Australian Championships for NSW in a coaching career that spanned from 1973 to the present. Phil won nine Australian Championships as coach of the NSW Ladies team, and four Australian Championships as coach of NSW Junior Teams (2 x Junior Mens teams & 2 x Junior Ladies teams). Phil was also appointed Coach of the Australian U/18 Mens team from 1982 to 1985.ABOVE: Competitors and Officials Pass to the 1972 Brisbane National Championships.

"Billy Parsons was normally our go to 'penalty taker' in 1st Grade. But I vividly remember being selected by our captain/coach Graeme Samuel to take a penalty against Balmain, with Olympian Mick Withers facing me in goal. Sammy's reasoning was that Micky hadn't studied my penalty shot, which worked a treat as I scored... but this episode showed what a great asset and tactician Sammy was, to our team and club!"

Chris Simpson, June 2020

Country Trips

Bronte Water Polo Club assumed a tradition of helping develop the great game in the country areas and the club undertook many trips to Canberra, Wagga and Tamworth, where they played at the latter with both men and womens teams in the late 1960's, 1970, 1971 and 1972.

◄ABOVE: Playing in the rain at Tamworth with rainbow included. MID: Identifiable bodies... Vita Folden, Rolly Flesch, Peter Folden (Standing) and Graeme Samuel (behind). ▼BELOW: A Moree player shoots for goal against Cessnock during the 1972 Southgate tournament in Tamworth. BOTTOM: More poolside action at the Tamworth tournament during the 1971 Bronte club trip.

Southgate Inn Tournament

The major final of the Southgate Inn Spring water polo tournament at Tamworth's Scully Park pool on Saturday night was an all Bronte affair with the No 1 team proving too strong for the No 2 side.

Bronte 1 included an Olympic representative, G. Samuel, and was too experienced for the younger No 2 side, winning the final 5-nil.

The game was a fast and interesting one and although the No 2 side tried to breach the defence their efforts were unsuccessful.

The visiting teams at the tournament showed their superiority to the others in the competition.

The minor final was won by Tamworth 2, beating Cessnock 5-1.

For Tamworth Malcolm Dunn netted twice and Paul Hanson, J. Bolden and I. Smith once. Cessnock's lone goal came from J. Schofield.

The females were not left out of the tournament and Tamworth clashed with a Bronte women's team on Saturday afternoon, the game going to the visitors 13-1.

Water polo for women in Tamworth is only just beginning and the inexperienced players tried their hardest but could not stop the flow of Bronte goals.

Tamworth's goal was scored by L. Gaff, who was prominent throughout.

In an under 16 match Tamworth beat Cessnock 4-3. Scorers for the winners were A. Whitehorn with two, S. Fishenden and G. Smith.

Yesterday morning the Bronte No 2 side, which consisted of players under 18 years of age, met a Tamworth High School team. Bronte won the interesting and fast tussle 5-2.

Eleven teams from Bronte, Tamworth, Cessnock and Moree took part in the initial spring tournament.

According to Tamworth water polo officials the tournament was such a success it will become an annual event.

▲Article on the Tamworth Southgate Inn Tournament (The Northern Daily Leader, 27th Nov 1972). ▶ABOVE: Soaking up the 'gamma's' on the Tamworth Pool lawn. MID: Tom and Vita Folden, with Giselle and Robbie Barta. BELOW: Lizards on the lawn... from left: Gary Grant, Lance Kerr, Jeff Stubbs, Tracy Rockwell holding up Margaret Wilby, Robbie Vadas, John Power (pointing) & Robbie Barta (standing).

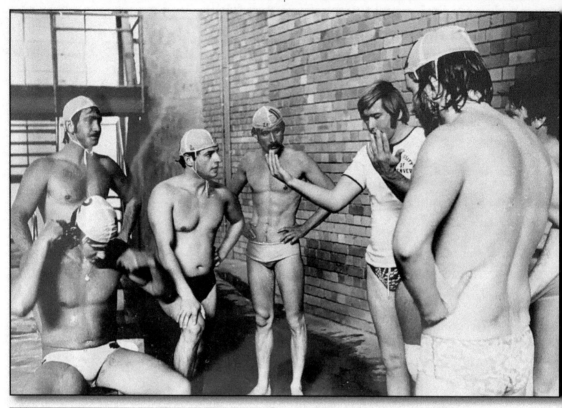

NEW SOUTH WALES AMATEUR WATER POLO ASSOCIATION

address all correspondence to:
The Honorary Secretary,
P.O. Box No. A81.
SYDNEY.SOUTH. 2000.

C I R C U L A R

1) CASCADE CUP FINAL: The Cascade Cup Final is to be held at University Pool on Saturday 16/1/72 Starting 6:45pm.

   PROGRAMME: 6:45 Ladies Possibles V's Probables.
   7:20 Play off for 3rd Pos. in Cascade Cup.
   8:00 State U/18 V's a selected U/21 Team.
   8:45 Final of the Cascade Cup.

   Club secretaries please note that the team listed below is the selected U/21 team to play in this competition.

   TEAM: P. Bower (Bronte), C. Jennings (Wests), A. Falson (Crn), R. Goff (Crn), J. Holt (Crn), W. Syphers (Crn), T. Keen (Crn), P. Lytham (Balmain), W. Farthing (Balmain), L. Lotterill (East Syd), M. Gilsenan (East Syd).

2) AN INVITATION: A meeting of referees and all interested persons is to be held to discuss the new Water Polo Rules and the interpretation of same, with a view of standardising our refereeing. Refreshments will be provided for members attending the meeting. This meeting will be held on 17/1/72 at 8 p.m. at Rugby Union House, 2nd Floor, 10 Crane Place, off Pitt St., Sydney.

3) APPLICATION FOR AUSTRALIAN COACH: Applications for a coach for the Australian Water Polo Team are being called for. Entries close with the A.S.U. of Aust., on the 31-1-72. Intending applicants should enclose statements setting out their qualifications, and these should be in the hands of our Secretary by 12 noon on the 24th January, 1972.

4) NOMINATIONS FOR PUBLICITY OFFICER: Nominations for this position are now being called for, and applications in writing should be forwarded to the Association Secretary

J. CAMPBELL.
Honorary Assistant Secretary.

Saturday 8th January at North Sydney Pool.

ANNOUNCER: K. WHITEHEAD.

TIMEKEEPERS & SECRETARIES: R. VADAS, D. BEATTIE, J. BEATTIE, G. Woods, F. Falson, P. Bower

REFEREE: N. SYDNEY.

GOAL JUDGES: D. HAMILL, P. LARGE.

STATE MANAGER: W. GOOLEY.

T E A M S

THE REST		STATE TEAM.	
D. BULLOCK	(Cronulla)	N. BARNES	
A. FALSON	(Cronulla)	C. COPE	
B. FALSON	(Cronulla - Captain/coach)	R. FLESCH	
J. HOLT	(Cronulla)	P. FOLDEN	
A. KERR	(Cronulla)	J. HARRISON (Vice-Captain)	
P. KERR	(Universities)	I. McLAUGHLIN	
M. MAY	(Balmain)	P. MONTGOMERY	
S. QUILL	(Universities)	G. SAMUEL.	
C. SIMPSON	(Bronte)	J. SHEKHDAH	
		M. WITHERS	
		D. WOODS	(Captain/Coach)

GOALS & LANES to be handled by Mr. John Taylor. North Sydney A.W.P.C.

▲TOP: *Graeme Samuel imparts pre-game instructions to his Bronte 1st Grade at the new Sydney University pool. Players (from left): Tom Folden (standing), Peter Folden (sitting), Robbie Vadas, Chris Simpson, Sammy, John Power (forground) and Ian Leffers. Photo by Phil Bower. ABOVE (Left): NSWAWPA Circular by Joyce Campbell (Bronte AWPC). (Right): Teams for the 1972 NSW selection trials between 'The Rest' and the 'State Team' at North Sydney Pool.*

UNIVERSITIES WPC
1971/72 - NSWAWPA Men's 1st Grade Premiers.
Back row (from left): Peter Kerr, Peter Montgomery, Nick Barnes (c), Brian Randall (g), Alex Urban. Seated: Graham Hannan, Graham Facey, Oscar Charles (Coach), Bill Phillips Jr., Steve Quill, Brian 'God' Elliott.

section and Liverpool also took out handicap honours. [1]

Bronte AWPC

As this summer got underway, it was clear that the slow leak of players to other clubs, probably due to the distance of Watson Bay, had begun to affect the strength of Bronte, and this was particularly felt in the lower grades.

However, Bronte managed to win the 1972 Cascade Cup, which was primarily a pre-season competition to select the NSW State team.

Once again fielding four teams in Division I, Bronte had what might best be called... mixed results for the 1971/72 season. The 4th Grade finished 6th, and 2nd Grade finished 5th, with neither team proceeding to the finals. The 3rd Grade, which had

▲TOP: Pam Hedger with three Bronte greats in Peter Folden, Rolly Flesch and Chris Simpson.

"I transferred to Balmain in 1973 to play in the field, but only once played against Bronte. The next year, all the players who were to represent in the Maccabean Games played for Maccabi in the Sydney 1st Grade competition. By 1975 Bronte changed to Maroubra Seals and I don't believe the club existed again."

Phil Bower, 29 Jan 2019

ST. GEORGE-SUTHERLAND DISTRICT AMATEUR WATER POLO ASSOCIATION — RESULT CARD

Pool: UNIVERSITY   Time: 8.25   Date: 8.3.72
Division: 1   Grade: 1   Round: 1ST SEMI
BRONTE (WHITE) V CRONULLA-SUTH (BLACK)

No.	NAME	SIGNATURE		No.	NAME	SIGNATURE	
1	D. SARKIES			1	D. BULLOCK		
2	G. SAMUEL			2	C. WILLIAMS		
3	W. PARSONS		||	3	W. SYPHERS		||
4	P. FOLDEN			4	T. FALSON		
5	T. FOLDEN			8u	J. HOLT			
6	R. FLESCH			6	A. KERR		||
7	J. POWER				7	M. DUNN		
8	C. SIMPSON		|||	5.	R GOFF		||
9	G. ROBINSON				9	B. FALSON		
10	P. OHARA			10			
11	W. SEE			11			
Captain:		Score (8)		Captain:		Score (7)	
				Referee:			

▲▼ Game cards for Bronte 1st and 3rd Grades in the NSWAWPA semi-finals, held on the 8th March, 1972.

ST. GEORGE-SUTHERLAND DISTRICT AMATEUR WATER POLO ASSOCIATION — RESULT CARD

Pool: UNIVERSITY   Time: 7.15   Date: 8.3.72
Division: 1   Grade: 3   Round: 1ST SEMI
III BRONTE (WHITE) WIN III V UNIVERSITIES (BLACK)

No.	NAME	SIGNATURE		No.	NAME	SIGNATURE	
1	J. STUBBS			1	D. CAMERON		
2	O. SMITH			2	E. TINDALL		
3	S. HUNTER		1	3	I RUSSEL		1
4	G. GRANT		1	4	S. GRANT		1
5	T. ROCKWELL			5	C PHILLIP		
6	P. BELL			6	R WOODHOUSE		
7	R. BARTA			7	J. EBNER		1
8	R. VARAS			8	G DUNN		
9	C. COX			9	R HARRISON		
10				10	W PORTIER		
11	P. BOWER		III	11			
Captain:		Score 4		Captain:		Score 3	
				Referee:		VXXV	

▲ Bronte gold medal, for the inaugural NSWAWPA Winter competition of 1972.

an injection of youth from Newtown ASC finished in third position, but lost to Balmain in the final (4~7). Bronte 1st Grade, who were the reigning premiers played well to finish in third place on the ladder, and defeated Cronulla-Sutherland (8~7) in the semi-final, but they lost in a close contest to Universities in the final (3~4), with Uni's going on to take their second premiership.

After the season ended, Billy Parsons left Bronte when he moved to Brisbane, and goalkeeper Phil Bower, also saw opportunites elsewhere and transferred to Balmain. The loss of these two talented players was to have a big impact on the 1st Grade.

N.S.W. AMATEUR WATER POLO ASSOCIATION — RESULT CARD

Pool: UNI   Time: 8.25   Date: 22.3.72

Division: 1   Grade: 1   Round: FINAL

UNI (WHITE) V BRONTE (BLACK)

No.	NAME	SIGNATURE		No.	NAME	SIGNATURE	
1	B RANDALL	B Randan		1	D. SARKIES		
2	N BARNS	N. Barnes		2	G Samuell		1
3	P. MONTGOMERY	P. Montgomery	11	3	H. PARSONS		1
4	P KERR	P Kerr	1	4	P. FOLDEN	Peter Folden	1
5	C. COPE	C Cope		5	C. SIMPSON		
10	J. SHEKDAR			6	R. FLESCH		
7	S QUILL	S Quill		7	J. POWER	G Power	
8	W. PHILLIPS	W Phillips	1	8	T. FORDEN	Tom Folden	
9	A. URBAN	Urban		9	G Robinson	J Robinson	
10				10	R See	R See	
11				11	JEFF STUBBS	Jeff Stubbs	
Captain:		Score	1	Captain:		Score	3

Referee: R Smee   XXX1

▶▼ *Game cards for Bronte 1st and 3rd Grades in the NSWAWPA Finals on the 22nd March, 1972.*

N.S.W. AMATEUR WATER POLO ASSOCIATION — RESULT CARD

Pool: UNI   Time: 7-15   Date: 22.3.72

Division: 1   Grade: 3   Round: FINAL

BALMAIN (WHITE) V BRONTE (BLACK)

No.	NAME	SIGNATURE		No.	NAME	SIGNATURE	
1	J. McFARLANE			1	Jeff Stubbs	Jeff Stubbs	
2	K. FUNDER		111	2	Greg Smith	Greg Smith	
3	L. MORRISON			3	Steve HUNTER	Steve Hunt	
4	W. FARTHING	W Farthing		4	Craig Grant	G Grant	
5	G. LAUGHTON			5	Tracy Rockwell	Tracy Rockwell	
6	K. GORDON	Ken Gordon	1	6	Bryan Zorta	Bryan Zorta	
7	B. MORONY	B Morony		7	R. SELLECK	Ross Selleck	1.1
8	P. KIDD	Kidd	11	8	P Bell	Pete Bell	
9	R. PIERCE	R Pierce	1	9	G O'KEEFE	Greg O'Keefe	
10	N. LANGE	N Lange		10	R. VADAS	R Vadas	
11	A. STEWART	A Stewart		11	Phil Bower	Phillip Bower	1.1
Captain:	B Morony	Score	7	Captain:	Jeff Stubbs	Score	4

Referee: N. Sydney   XXX1

However, Bronte played creditably to become the inaugural NSWAWPA Winter champions in both the men's and ladie's competitions.

▲ *Magnification of the inscription for NAWAWPA 'Best & Fairest' 1st Grade Player of 1971-72, which went to Rolly Flesch of Bronte AWPC.*

SOCIAL COMMITTEE REPORT:

Dear members, over the past season, socially, we have been quite active (or tough some people might think otherwise) as well as some of our members, who have been active in other ways.

As in past years we had a number of barbecues and for these we must thank Mr. and Mrs. Parsons and Mr. and Mrs. Campbell for our venues.

We tried a few new ideas last season, some were not so financially devastating as others. One such night was a Film Night where, as in many previous cases the members did not attend in great numbers. Another night, much more successfull yet still not attended by all members was a Fashion Parade. This night was assured of success largely through the efforts of one of the Social Committee members Mrs. Myrtle Bell. As usual the Christmas party was quite a night with John Power (alias Santa Clause).

Next year after discussions with the Management Committee apart from the usual social events, some trips away could be organised which were a great boost to the teams morale as well as giving the lower grade members a chance to learn playing with the higher grade players.

I would like to point out to members that the equipment they use would not be available were it not for the money made from these social events; so in future, since you and you alone are the ones who benefit make sure you attend each future function.

Some of our members who I mentioned have been active in other ways are: Gary and Sandra Cawood had a baby girl, Mr. and Mrs. R.See a baby girl, Tom and Vida Folden a baby boy, Ross and Jill Sellick a baby boy; John and Lorraine Power were recently married as were Danny and Robin Hofbauer. Some of you may not know that Robin was the daughter of one of our longest standing and most respected members Jack Campbell. As you can see Bronte is truly a prolific club.

I would like to thank the members of the Social Committee; Phil Bower, Myrtle Bell, Yvette Barta for all the time and effort they put in for our club. Also I must thank the girls from the girl's team for all the work they did.

In ending, some of you may not know that as you are reading this I will be in Southport, Q'land. The past eight years that I have been with the club were some of the best eight years of my life. The fellowship and friends that I gained I will always remember. I hope that all of the younger members will enjoy their future with the club as much as I have. I am sure the club will remain as prominent as ever for there is no other club where you will find a coach with knowledge of waterpolo that Grahame Samuel has. I learnt more in the last two years under Sammy than I did in the previous six.

All I can say further is thank you Bronte Waterpolo Club.

Bill Parsons
Social Secretary

BRONTE AMATEUR WATER POLO CLUB

ANNUAL REPORT

~~BALANCE SHEET~~

1971/1972

PRESIDENT'S REPORT :

The season gone by has unfortunately not been a succesfull one for the club in the sense that we did not win a premiership in any of our grade.

But on the brighter side we had the greatest influx of young talented players joining us in one season in the history of the club.

The influx of new players was also evident in the Ladies Team and they were very unfortunate not to make the semi finals.

This I feel has more than made up for the past season, I think with them in our ranks we undoubtedly will reach the top again and win many more championship.

Don Sarkies
President.

PRESIDENT:
D. SARKIES

HON.SEC.
G. FOLDEN

SECRETARY'S REPORT :

As you all know, due to certain misunderstanding our Club's Secretary resigned during the past season, and I was elected to fill in the position and cope with club duties for the last four months.

I sincerely hope, that the members will be satisfied with the contents of the following report, wich was actually written for me by the members of the Management Committee and the Club's Coaches, I have only stapled them together.

There are no congratulations this year to our teams. Unfortunately we did not win the championship at any grades. Graeme Samuel our coach for First Grade Team is speachless. He just can not find correct words to express his disappointments. He can only hope, that the next season will be successfull and everybody will put more effort in their trainings.

Bill McCarthy coach for the Second Grade Team remarks: " After a complete lack of dedication in the first half of the season, the team knuckled down to win nearly every second round match, missing the semis by a point— A few individuals who trained regularly showed improvement and were the nucleus of the side."

"The Third Grade Team played well during the season making the semi-finals and finishing third in the Competition"— Grahame Robinson the coach reports."All players showed a marked improvement. Team members whom I feel showed particular ability include Jeff Stubbs, Greg Smith, Tracey Rockwell, Gary Grant and the youngest player Greg Cox. The team was also ably captained by Ross Sellick who could only attend the first few matches due to an addition in the family. I hope all players attain further distinction and higher grades in water polo-Looking forward to seeing you at training and at the games in the coming season."

Another disappointed coach for the Fourth Grade Team Eric Folden complained: " The players did not turn up for trainings, as a matter of fact: they did not even turn up for the games. We had 9 losses, 2 wins and 1 forfeit. Very poor show. Fot enough enthusiasm between players. The only player who never missed an opportunity to get into the water deserves a mention: Rayner Barta.— I only hope the next season will be better and the players will give me a chance to coach them."

" The Ladies Team suffured from lack of players which greatly affected their performance last season.— We barely scratched up seven players each week. However, we must congratulate our few experienced players: Margaret Wilby, Rhonda Thompson, Cathy Chamberlain, Laurel Cannot, who with their

1

constant drive and determination pulled a team of inexperienced players though, narrowly knocked out of making the semi-finals. Lee Davis, Yvette Barta, Debbie Grahan and Loueen Winters who played water polo for the first time last season showed excellent improvement."

"I am expecting a great coming season with a few new girls joining us, among them we wellcome Lynn & Karen Trewhella.—Hoping for victory next season. Your coach Tom Folden."

Regular Management Committee Meetings were held through-out the year and attendance records indicate the interest shown by your elected committee, which handled a large volume of business over the past twelve months.

Membership remained rather static in the past few years, but I strongly feel we should increase the membership of teen-age players.

Congratulation to the winners of Best & Fairest Award. They will receive their trophies at the Annual General Meeting.

State Affairs: Congratulation to G.Samuel, P. Folden and R. Flesch for their selection in the State Team.-N.S.W. came third in the Australian Championship this year, held at Brisbane in February.

Congratulation to the five N.S.W. players selected into the Olimpic Team.

Also our congratulation to Joyce Campbell, manageress of the Ladies State Team to her trip to Melbourne.

Our Representatives in the N.S.W. Executive Body: Phil Bower, Don Sarkies, Jack Campbell, Joyce Campbell and Les Kay.

The Club extends thanks to many individuals and organisations, who assisted us financially during the past twelve months.

Also extends thanks to Members and their Families for without their assistance we would be unable to function anywhere near the way, we have been able to.

Our wholehearted thanks go to Joyce Campbell and Phil Bower our Secretary & Treasurer respectively, who have worked so hard over the past year and raised the club to such heights especially financialy for perhaps the first time ever; We are truly sorry to lose them.

Finally my thanks to all the members of the Committee, who helped and supported me during the past few months and assisted the club in every way possible to make the past season a very enjoyable year.

Cisel Folden
Hon.Secretary

2

1971/72 NSWAWPA RESULTS

SPEEDO PRE-SEASON

DIVISION 1:
Universities 20, East Sydney 17, Bronte 16, Cronulla-Sutherland 15, Balmain 15, Manly-Warringah 12, Western Suburbs 10.
Final: Universities 7 defeated East Sydney 1.

CASCADE CUP

Balmain 23, Universities 22, Bronte 20, Cronulla-Sutherland 19, East Sydney 16, Western Suburbs 15, Under-18 14, Manly-Warringah 13, Penrith 3.
First Semi-Final: Balmain 7 defeated Cronulla-Sutherland 2.
Second Semi-Final: Universities 5 defeated Bronte 4.
Final: Universities 6 defeated Balmain 5.

FIRST DIVISION
First Grade

	Played	W.	D.	L.	Goals F.	A.	Points	Position
UNIVERSITIES	14	11	2	1	90	36	38	1
BALMAIN	14	10	2	2	92	52	36	2
BRONTE	14	11	—	3	90	56	36	3
CRONULLA-SUTHERLAND	14	8	1	5	72	52	31	4
EAST SYDNEY	14	5	1	8	50	82	25	5
MANLY-WARRINGAH	14	5	—	9	46	92	24	6
WESTERN SUBURBS	14	2	2	10	31	101	20	7

First Semi-Final: Bronte 8 defeated Cronulla-Sutherland 7.
Second Semi-Final: Balmain 5 defeated Universities 4.
Final: Universities 4 defeated Bronte 3.
Grand Final: Universities 4 defeated Balmain 3.

FIRST DIVISION FIRST GRADE PREMIERS: UNIVERSITIES.

Second Grade

	Played	W.	D.	L.	Goals F.	A.	Points	Position
CRONULLA-SUTHERLAND	14	10	3	1	71	26	37	1
BALMAIN	14	11	—	3	59	41	36	2
EAST SYDNEY	14	9	1	4	53	30	33	3
UNIVERSITIES	14	8	2	4	66	39	32	4
BRONTE	14	7	—	6	46	40	29	5
WESTERN SUBURBS	14	3	—	9	30	86	22	6
MANLY-WARRINGAH	14	2	1	11	20	87	19	7

First Semi-Final: Universities 5 defeated East Sydney 2.
Second Semi-Final: Cronulla-Sutherland 5 defeated Balmain 3.
Final: Balmain 7 defeated Universities 6.
Grand Final: Cronulla-Sutherland 6 defeated Balmain .

FIRST DIVISION SECOND GRADE PREMIERS: CRONULLA-SUTHERLAND.

Third Grade

	Played	W.	D.	L.	Forf.	Goals F.	A.	Points	Position
CRONULLA-SUTHERLAND	14	13	—	1		75	15	40	1
BALMAIN	14	13	—	1		66	17	40	2
BRONTE	14	9	—	5		37	32	32	3
UNIVERSITIES	14	8	1	5		41	35	31	4
WESTERN SUBURBS	14	6	1	7		39	48	27	5
MANLY-WARRINGAH	14	4	—	10		20	76	22	6
EAST SYDNEY	14	2	—	11	1	17	82	17	7

First Semi-Final: Bronte 4 defeated Universities 3.
Second Semi-Final: Cronulla-Sutherland 6 defeated Balmain 4.
Final: Balmain 7 defeated Bronte 4.
Grand Final: Cronulla-Sutherland 7 defeated Balmain 4.

FIRST DIVISION THIRD GRADE PREMIERS: CRONULLA-SUTHERLAND.

Fourth Grade

	Played	W.	D.	L.	Forf.	Goals F.	A.	Points	Position
CRONULLA-SUTHERLAND	14	12	2	—		80	16	40	1
BALMAIN	14	11	1	2	—	65	20	37	2
EAST SYDNEY	14	11	1	2	—	51	27	37	3
MANLY-WARRINGAH	14	6	1	7	—	31	46	27	4
UNIVERSITIES	14	5	2	7	—	24	52	26	5
BRONTE	14	4	—	9	1	19	54	21	6
WESTERN SUBURBS	14	3	1	10	—	19	74	21	7

First Semi-Final: East Sydney 8 defeated Manly-Warringah 3.
Second Semi-Final: Balmain 9 defeated Cronulla-Sutherland 8.
Final: Cronulla-Sutherland 7 defeated East Sydney 0.
Grand Final: Balmain 6 defeated Cronulla-Sutherland 5.

FIRST DIVISION FOURTH GRADE PREMIERS: BALMAIN.

WINTER COMPETITION 1972

	Outright Section					Handicap Section				
	Pl	W	L	Dr	Forf	P	W	L	Dr	Forf	P
LIVERPOOL	9	8	1	—	—	25	8	1	—	—	25
BRONTE	9	8	1	—	—	25	7	2	—	—	23
BALMAIN "C"	9	3	3	1	2	14	5	2	—	2	17
BALGOWLAH "A"	9	3	5	1	—	16	3	6	—	—	15
BONDI DOLPHINS "B"	9	1	6	—	2	9	3	4	—	2	13
EAST SYDNEY	9	5	1	—	3	16	3	3	—	3	12
NORTH SYDNEY	9	2	4	2	1	14	4	4	—	1	16
NORTHBRIDGE	9	1	6	1	1	11	3	5	—	1	14
SYDNEY UNIVERSITY	9	3	4	1	1	15	4	4	—	1	16
UNIVERSITY "B"	9	6	1	—	2	19	3	5	—	1	13

WINNERS OF OUTRIGHT SECTION: Drawn, Liverpool 25; Bronte 25.
WINNER OF HANDICAP SECTION OVERALL: Liverpool, Premiers.

1972-73

1972/73 NSWAWPA OFFICIALS: Dr. H.K. Porter (Patron); V. Chalwin (President); H.J. Bund (Past President); B. Thomson (Chairman); B. Gilbert/K. Connor/K. Cridland/D. Hamill (Registrar); W.M. Gooley (Secretary); **R. Vadas (Comp. Secretary); P. Bower (Treasurer).**

The NSW country clubs were really beginning an involvement in water polo at this stage and Tamworth Water Polo Club held its inaugural Southgate Inn Tournament on 25th November 1972. Entries were received from Cessnock A & B, Tamworth A & B, Gunnedah, Moree and Bronte A & B, with Bronte taking out the title.

The 1973 NSWAWPA 1st Grade grand-final was conducted on the 7th April, and heralded the beginning of a water polo phenomenon in NSW. It brought about the first of 14 grand-final bouts that developed into a great rivalry between Universities and Cronulla over the next 16 seasons.

The Baths & Clubs

The Competition Committee capably organised the competitions, which were again conducted across three divisions and played over two rounds.

This year NSWAWPA matches were scheduled at Ashfield, Balmain, Drummoyne, Gunnamatta Bay, Manly, North Sydney, Parramatta and Sydney University pools, the latter also being used exclusively to run the first ever Winter competition. In regard to new clubs, teams were entered by Carss Park, Manly Rugby, Navy, Padstow and Smithfield, while East Sydney morphed into Bondolphins, while no clubs lapsed.

Representatives in NSW Teams

NSW Open Mens Team

At this time, the Sydney metropolitan competition had witnessed the emergence of an exciting new club from Cronulla, and the composition of the State team reflected this. The new caps were Tony Falson, Randall Goff and Andrew Kerr (Cronulla), goalkeeper Don Cameron and Peter

▼BELOW: The 1973 National Championships was the first occasion that the Mens, Ladies and Junior Mens competitions were conducted simultaneously. BOTTOM: Rosters for the NSW Mens & U/18 Mens State teams of 1973.

"As a club, Bronte organised many trips to help develop the game of water polo in the country areas. I can recall Ken Mills organising a trip to Hobart in the 60's, and a number of trips were made to Canberra, where we played against Duntroon Military College. In fact, the interaction with Canberra resulted in both Robbo and Kipper joining Bronte, when they relocated to Sydney. In 1972 Bronte organised their last country visit to Tamworth, which later developed into a centre of water polo excellence."

Robbie Vadas, March 2019

1972/73 Season Statistics
N.S.W.A.W.P.A.

Clubs in the Mens Water Polo Competitions.

Clubs	1	2	3	4	2^1	2^2	2^3	3^1	3^2	3^3	Total
Avalon/Bilgola								●	●	●	3
Balgowlah									●		1
Balmain	●	●	●	●	●	●	●	●	●	●	10
Bondi										●	1
Bondolphins	●	●	●	●					●	●	6
Bronte	●	●	●	●							4
Carss Park								●			1
Clovelly Eskimos						●		●			2
Cronulla-Sutherland	●	●	●	●		●		●			6
Drummoyne						●	●		●		3
Homebush						●	●				2
Liverpool						●	●	●			3
Manly Rugby								●	●		2
Manly/Warringah	●	●	●	●							4
Navy								●			1
NSW Maccabi					●	●	●				3
Nth Palm Beach									●		1
Nth Sydney						●	●	●			3
Northbridge						●					1
Padstow									●		1
P'matta Memorial								●	●	●	3
Penrith						●	●	●			3
Ryde								●			1
Smithfield									●	●	2
Sydney University						●	●	●			3
Universities	●	●	●	●							4
Western Suburbs	●	●	●	●				●			5
	7	7	7	7	8	8	8	9	9	9	79

Results of the Mens Water Polo Competitions.

Grade	Premier	Runner-Up
1st	Universities	Pre-Season Comp.
1st	Bronte	Cascade Cup Comp.
1st	Universities~6 d. 4~Cronulla-Sutherland	
2nd	Balmain~4 d. 1~Cronulla-Sutherland	
3rd	Cronulla-Sutherland~9 d. 3~Balmain	
4th	Manly/Warringah~11 d. 9~Balmain	
Club Champions	BALMAIN	
D2 1st	NSW Maccabi~8 d. 3~Liverpool	
D2 2nd	Balmain~6 d. 5~Liverpool	
D2 3rd	Liverpool~9 d. 8~Balmain	
D3 1st	Manly/Warringah~4 d. 3~Parramatta	
D3 2nd	Balgowlah~5 d. 4~Balmain	
D3 3rd	Ryde~6 d. 2~Parramatta	
1st	Western Suburbs	Winter Comp.

NEW SOUTH WALES SENIOR	NEW SOUTH WALES U/18
1 D. Cameron	1 Jeff Keane
2 David Woods (capt)	2 Greg Laws (capt)
3 Graham Samuel	3 Bruce Connor
4 Peter Montgomery (v/c)	4 John Cotterill
5 Ian McLauchlain	5 Gary Grant
6 Peter Folden	6 Ken Hill
7 P. Kerr	7 Les Ison
8 A. Kerr	8 Ian Syphers (v/c)
9 A. Falsom	9 Tracey Rockwell
10 R. Goff	10 Mark Turnbull
11 A. Stewart	11 Rayner Barta
Coach: Les Kay	Coach: Paul Dunford
Manager: Mal Hunt	Manager: Dennis Hamill

NEW SOUTH WALES TEAM
1973 - Adelaide National Championships - Champions

Back row (from left): Peter Kerr (Universities), Don Cameron (g, Universities), Tony Falson (Cronulla), Andrew Stewart (g, Balmain), **Peter Folden (Bronte)**, Ian McLauchlain (Balmain), **Graeme Samuel (Bronte)**, Peter Montgomery (vc, Universities). Front row: Andrew Kerr (Cronulla), Mal Hunt (Manager, Cronulla), **Les Kay (Coach, Bronte)**, Randall Goff (Cronulla), David Woods (c, Balmain). Photo - NSWAWPA Annual Report 1972/73.

▲Costume badge for NSWAWPA State team representatives, which operated under auspices of the NSWASA. ▶Letter of appreciation from NSWAWPA for members of the 1973 NSW U/18s team. ▼Official Program for the 1973 National Championships in Adelaide, SA.

Australian Water Polo Championships

Senior & U/18

ADELAIDE — 1973

at

NORTH ADELAIDE SWIMMING CENTRE
HENLEY & GRANGE COMMUNITY POOL

from

SATURDAY 3rd to SUNDAY, 11th FEBRUARY

A.S.U. OFFICIALS:

President: I. F. Howson, O.B.E
Vice-President: A. Stoenbeck
Secretary/Treasurer: S. R. Crange, O.D.E., R.V.O.
Past President: W. Burge Phillips

A.W.P. COMMITTEE:
Hon. Secretary: I. Edge

New South Wales Amateur Water Polo Association

(Affiliated with N.S.W.A.S.A.)

Address all Correspondence to
The Honorary Secretary
P.O. Box No. AM
SYDNEY SOUTH 2000.

Patron:
Dr. H. K. PORTER,
M.B., Ch.M., F.R.C.O.G.

President:
V. J. CHALWIN, Esq.

Chairman:
F. L. FALSON, Esq. 9253917

Dear Tracy

On behalf of the N S W A W P A Executive, and, I am sure, all members of the Association, may I extend warm congratulations to you, as a state representative in Adelaide.

I am proud of our teams' efforts and the results speak for the preparation and trainning which secured them. However, I take even greater pride in the spirit of sportsmanship and teamwork which was shown, both in and out of the water.

Thank you for your contribution to the advancement of water polo, and may you continue your success in our sport:

Yours in sport,

Bruce Thomson 15/2/73

Bruce Thomson

CHAIRMAN.

NEW SOUTH WALES U/18 JUNIOR MENS TEAM
1973 - Adelaide National Championships - Runners-Up

Back row (from left): Dennis Hamill (Manager, Balmain), Paul Dunford (Coach, Balmain), Les Ison (Balmain), **Tracy Rockwell (Bronte)**, **Gary Grant (Bronte)**, Bruce Connor (Liverpool), Ian Syphers (v/c, Cronulla), Mark Turnbull (Bondolphins). Front row: Jeff Keane (g, Cronulla), John Cotterill (Bondolphins), Lee Phillips (r, Manly), Greg Laws (c, Balmain), Ken Hill (Balmain), **Rayner Barta (g, Bronte)**. Photo - John Cotterill

The 1973 Adelaide Nationals
The 1973 Australian Championships were unique for Bronte...

"Bronte Water Polo Club had a very strong contingent at the 1973 national titles in Adelaide. I have great memories of that trip as a member of the U/18 Mens' team. It helped to cement an involvement and passion for our great sport, and many lifelong friendships were forged on this tour. Bronte players Tracy Rockwell, Gary Grant and Raynor Barta were essential members of our team. I also recall being very well attired by Raynor's dad Robbie Barta in NSW

▲ *NSW U/18 State teammates Tracy Rockwell, Jeff Keane (g/k), Mark Turnbull, John Cotterill; NSW v SA at Glenelg Baths;* ◄ *MID: Les Ison, John Cotterill & Mark Turnbull. BELOW: The U/18s practising at Henley Baths.*

knitwear, and we looked quite smart for a motley group of 18 year olds. The Open men and women also had a number of Bronte representives... it was the largest club contingent. We unfortunately lost those championships to WA, with Tracy, our gun player not being well enough, but I congratulate him on this 'History of Bronte Water Polo Club' as well as his very successful 'Water Warriors.' His well written books have brought the fascinating history of Australian Water Polo to light for us all."

John Cotterill
(1973 NSW Jr. Rep)

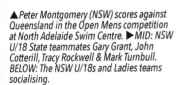

▲Peter Montgomery (NSW) scores against Queensland in the Open Mens competition at North Adelaide Swim Centre. ▶MID: NSW U/18 State teammates Gary Grant, John Cotterill, Tracy Rockwell & Mark Turnbull. BELOW: The NSW U/18s and Ladies teams socialising.

NSW polo rep. in final side

By PETER HOWARD

SATURDAY, JANUARY 20, 1973

Magyars, shooting for three water polo premierships at the Valley Pool tomorrow night, will feature former New South Wales representative Bill Parsons, pictured above.

Parsons, 25, a specialised back, represented New South Wales against Czechoslovakia in 1968 and against the Australian Olympic team last year.

Parsons, who is working on the Gold Coast, was a member of the crack Sydney club Bronte, and played in their A grade winning grand final side in 1970-71.

Magyars will meet Tugun in the A grade grand final at 8.30.

Magyars, who returned to competitive water polo only this season after a three-year absence, also will play in the B and C grade grand finals.

In B grade at 7.30, they will meet University.

In C grade at 6.30 their team, consisting mainly of juniors from the inter-school competition, will meet New Burleigh.

Magyars disbanded three years ago through falling membership.

Yet their three teams have earned favoritism in each grade, by winning the first semi-finals and graduating straight to the grand finals.

Tugun have been premiers for the past three years, and hope to annex their fourth A grade title in a row.

They beat Magyars by one-goal margins at their first meetings this season, but Magyars won 6-0 in return encounter.

● BILL PARSONS

"Robbie Vadas was a very well respected referee. He volunteered a great many hours of his own time as a representative of the Bronte Club, to the NSWAWPA as an official. But he was also a very decent player and reliable club man, playing mostly in 2nd Grade, and even filling in on occasion for the 1st Grade."

Tracy Rockwell, March 2019

▲ *Bronte's Peter Folden was the best player 'not' to be selected in the Australian team, and consistently played well enough to have gained selection, shown here intercepting a pass by Doc Wulf (Wests).*

Kerr (Universities), and goalkeeper Andrew Stewart (Balmain), as well as a new coach in Les Kay (Bronte). Only five players retained their places from the 1972 NSW team, which included both Peter Folden and Graeme Samuel of Bronte, but their talented teammate, Rolly Flesch was omitted.

In 1973 Bronte club established a record in fielding the most number of representatives across the various teams. Bronte's contingent totalled nine, with old boys Phil Bower (Balmain, NSW) and Billy Parsons (Magyars, QLD) also in action.

Peter Folden (NSW Men)
Les Kay (Coach, NSW Men)
Graeme Samuel (NSW Men)
Yvette Barta (r, NSW Women)
Joyce Campbell (Mgr, NSW Women)
Lyn Trewhella (NSW Women)
Rayner Barta (g, U/18 Jr. Men)
Gary Grant (U/18 Jr. Men)
Tracy Rockwell (U/18 Jr. Men)

The 26th Australian Championships were held in Adelaide where NSW played through undefeated to take their 10th national title, over Western Australia and Victoria.

NSW Junior Mens Team

In just the second Under 18's Junior Men's National Championships in Adelaide, Bronte had three of its juniors selected for the team in Tracy Rockwell,

Gary Grant and goalkeeper Raynor Barta. Despite defeating Western Australia in their first match (4~2), they lost the return game (4~7) and the tournament by a single goal on countback.

Australian Team

An Australian team was selected after these championships, which surprisingly only included two members in Peter Montgomery (Universities) and David Woods (Balmain) from the successful NSW team.

The Aussies first played in a series against New Zealand, then engaged themselves in a European tour, which took them for the first time to the island of Malta. After this, the team contested the 1st FINA World Championships in Belgrade, Yugoslavia, where they finished 14th, but they lost only eight of their 27 matches on the tour.

The Premierships

The four NSWAWPA Division I premierships were shared between four different clubs this season with Manly defeating Balmain (11~9) in 4th Grade. Cronulla walloped Balmain (9~3) in the 3rd Grade, while Balmain took revenge on Cronulla in the 2nd Grade (4~1).

In the semi-finals of the men's 1st Grade, fourth placed Bronte was eliminated by Cronulla (7~5) in the minor semi-final, and Universities defeated Balmain (8~4) in the major semi-final. Then

1972/73 NSWAWPA RESULTS

FIRST GRADE

	Won	Lost	Dr.	Disq. or Forf.	Goals for	ag.	Points
BALMAIN	12	1	1	—	89	45	39
UNIVERSITIES	11	2	1	—	87	35	37
CRONULLA-SUTHERLAND	10	2	2	—	76	39	36
BRONTE	8	4	2	—	87	47	32
MANLY-WARRINGAH	4	9	1	—	52	99	23
WESTERN SUBURBS	4	9	1	—	38	95	23
BONDOLPHINS	3	11	—	—	37	106	20

SEMI-FINALS: Cronulla 7 — Bronte 5; Universities 8 — Balmain 4.
FINAL: Cronulla 7 — Balmain 5.
GRAND FINAL: Universities 6 — Cronulla 4.

SECOND GRADE

	Won	Lost	Dr.	Disq. or Forf.	Goals for	ag.	Points
BALMAIN	13	1	—	—	86	26	40
CRONULLA-SUTHERLAND	11	3	—	—	77	37	36
UNIVERSITIES	9	4	1	—	58	32	33
BRONTE	9	5	—	—	65	37	32
MANLY-WARRINGAH	5	7	2	—	35	66	26
WESTERN SUBURBS	4	10	—	—	27	77	22
BONDOLPHINS	3	10	1	—	23	96	21

SEMI-FINALS: Bronte 9 — Universities 6; Balmain 5 — Cronulla 4.
FINAL: Cronulla 9 — Bronte 6.
GRAND FINAL: Balmain 4 — Cronulla 1.

THIRD GRADE

First Division continued

	Won	Lost	Dr.	Disq. or Forf.	Goals for	ag.	Points
BALMAIN	13	—	1	—	63	13	41
CRONULLA-SUTHERLAND	12	2	—	—	73	14	38
UNIVERSITIES	8	5	1	—	40	30	31
BRONTE	8	4	—	2	32	39	28
WESTERN SUBURBS	6	7	1	—	24	37	27
BONDOLPHINS	5	9	—	—	20	60	24
MANLY-WARRINGAH	2	7	1	4	10	69	15

SEMI-FINALS: Universities 8 — Bronte 5; Balmain 4 — Cronulla 3.
FINAL: Cronulla 8 — Universities 2.
GRAND FINAL: Cronulla 9 — Balmain 3.

FOURTH GRADE

	Won	Lost	Dr.	Disq. or Forf.	Goals for	ag.	Points
BALMAIN	13	1	—	—	80	11	40
CRONULLA-SUTHERLAND	12	2	—	—	70	15	38
MANLY-WARRINGAH	10	3	—	1	70	38	33
UNIVERSITIES	8	6	—	—	38	40	30
BRONTE	6	6	1	1	32	57	26
WESTERN SUBURBS	3	9	2	—	18	70	22
BONDOLPHINS	2	11	1	—	11	88	19

SEMI-FINALS: Manly 9 — Universities 3; Balmain 8 — Cronulla 6.
FINAL: Manly ? — Cronulla ?.
GRAND FINAL: Manly 11 — Balmain 9.

WINTER COMPETITION 1973 (Handicap)

FIRST DIVISION

	Won	Lost	Forf.	Goals For	Ag.	Points
WESTERN SUBURBS	7	1	—	51	37½	15
BALMAIN	6	1	1	38½	29½	13
UNIVERSITIES	5	2	1	42	36	12
UNDER-18	4	4	—	57	48½	12
CRONULLA	3	5	—	50½	51½	11
MANLY	4	3	1	45	48½	11
STATE TEAM	2	6	—	63½	68½	10
BRONTE	2	5	1	41½	54	9
BONDOLPHINS	3	3	2	35	51	9

Winners: WESTERN SUBURBS
Runner-up: BALMAIN

SECOND DIVISION

	Played	Won	Lost	Dr.	Forf.	Points
LIVERPOOL	10	7	2	—	1	14
PARRAMATTA	10	6	3	—	1	12
CRONULLA	10	6	4	—	—	12
BRONTE	10	6	4	—	—	12
BALMAIN	10	6	4	—	—	12
C.H.S.	10	5	5	—	—	10
MANLY RU.	10	5	5	—	—	10
SYDNEY UNIVERSITY	10	5	5	—	—	10
NORTH SYDNEY	10	4	4	—	2	8
UNIVERSITYS	10	4	6	—	—	8
BONDOLPHINS	10	3	6	—	1	6
NORTHBRIDGE	10	3	7	—	—	6

Premiers — LIVERPOOL

"Billy Parsons was very accurate when taking 4m penalties... he had an unusual although very effective square shooting style. Rolly Flesch had the best 'bat shot' in the country and I remember the whole crowd at Balmain being stopped in their tracks one night when Rolly once 'kicked' a goal in from 8 metres out! Peter Folden possessed a devastating field shot, which we dubbed the 'snake arm! 'Foldini', as we called him, well deserved, but was denied a place in the Australian team, although I believe he was chosen in an Australian side that played against the Czechoslovakians in 1968."

Tracy Rockwell, Dec 2018

"At Watson's Bay about 1973, there were two 16 year olds and a 14 year old with great potential and they needed nurturing. But Saturday afternoons were difficult for many to get to. We started to play after 6pm when the pool was closed. But we didn't play mixed games and we didn't train for that long, although the Watson's Bay Hotel was a great place to sink a midi or two."

Billy McCarthy, Feb 2019

▼ BELOW: Bronte gold medal, for winning the 'Cascade Cup' Pre-Season Competition of the 1972/73 season. BOTTOM: As a playing captain and coach, Graeme Samuel (aka Sammy), was a hard task master in training and games, but loved to socialise with club mates after 'work'! Photo by Phil Bower.

Cronulla showed their talent in defeating Balmain in the final (7~5) to qualify for their inaugural 1st Grade grand-final. However, after a torrid match, the experience of Universities overcame Cronulla in the grand-final (6~4), to take their third 1st Grade premiership. Balmain once again annexed the NSWAWPA Club Championship.

Following a break after the Summer season concluded, the 1973 Winter competitions got underway. This new event was expanded this year and was conducted across two divisions with Western Suburbs (Division I), and Liverpool (Division II) taking out the respective premierships. [2]

Bronte AWPC

After a 14 year absence from the sport, Dick Thornett (1960 Olympian) staged a return to water polo by playing for a social 5th Grade team for Manly. In spite of the fact that many sports now permitted professionalism, he was once again banned by the NSWAWPA for having played professional rugby league. The decision was a tragedy for our game.

Before this season began, Bronte had lost one of their best players in Billy Parsons, who was quickly snapped up by the Queensland State team, but his absence had a detrimental affect on the firepower of the 1st Grade team.

Bronte qualified for the Division I finals in three of four grades in the 1972/73 season, and it was the season of fourths! The 4th Grade finished fifth and did not qualify for the finals. The 3rd Grade finished in fourth place, but lost to Universities in the semi-final (5~8). The 2nd Grade also finished fourth on the ladder, but were able to win through to the final, where they bowed out to Cronulla (6~9). The 1st Grade also finished in fourth position, but lost to an emerging Cronulla in the semi-final (5~7).

At the end of this season a number of talented and long time Bronte players left the club and joined in with Ernie

Kritzler's band of All Stars. The defections didn't seem to be significant at the time, but results would show that the loss of these players was definitely unfavourable to Bronte's continued viability as an effective water polo club.

Results for Bronte in the Winter Handicap Competition reflected the downturn, where the one team that entered finished second last.

▼ Terry 'Lunky' Clark joined the Magyars Water Polo club when he left Bronte and Sydney for Brisbane about 1967.

MAGYARS WATER POLO CLUB
1972/73 - 1st Grade Premiers - Queensland AWPA
Standing (From left): Ken Swan (c/coach), Jack Lusic (g), **Bill Parsons,** Mike Lusic, Jos Van Opdenbosch Jr., Ross Bauer.
Kneeling: Peter Boyd, Jos van Opdenbosch Sr., John O'Brien.

"I found we were a very close knit club. We used to meet at the Owen's (corner Bronte Rd and Murray St). We were a group of friends and had some great functions (including Scott St). We did a few good trips - we did a trip to Singleton, Wagga a couple of times and Canberra, and to Tasmania in 1965/66.... they were great days."

Don Sarkies, 27 Jan 2015

1973-74

1973/74 NSWAWPA OFFICIALS: Dr. H.K. Porter (Patron); V. Chalwin (President); H.J. Bund (Past President); F.L. Falson (Chairman); B. Gilbert/K. Connor/W. Emanuels-Smith/**R. Barta (Registrar)**;W.M. Gooley (Secretary); **R. Vadas (Comp. Secretary)**; R. Traynor (Treasurer).

1973/74 Season Statistics
N.S.W.A.W.P.A.

Clubs in the Mens Water Polo Competitions.

Clubs	1	2	3	4	2¹	2²	3¹	3²	3³	3⁴	Total
All Stars								●			1
Avalon/Bilgola					●	2					3
Balmain	●	●	●	●	●	●	●	●		●	10
Blacktown								●	●		2
Bondi								●			1
Bondolphins	●	●	●	●					●		5
Bronte	●	●	●	●							4
Carss Park										●	1
Cronulla-Sutherland	●	●	●	2							5
Drummoyne					●	●		●			3
Hawkesbury									●		1
Homebush							●	●			2
Hunters Hill				2							2
Liverpool					●	●		●	●		4
Macquarie Uni.								●			1
Manly/Warringah	●	●	●	●	●			●			7
NSW Maccabi	●	●	●								3
Nth Sydney					●	●		●			3
Northbridge						●					1
Padstow								●			1
Parramatta					●	●	●				3
Penrith					●	●		●	●		4
Revesby									●		1
Ryde					●	●					2
Sydney University					●	●		●			3
Universities	●	●	●	●							4
Western Suburbs	●	●	●	●							4
	8	8	8	8	8	8	7	10	8	8	81

Results of the Mens Water Polo Competitions.

Grade	Premier	Runner-Up
1st	Cronulla-Sutherland	Pre-Season Comp
1st	Universities~4 d.	3~Cronulla-Sutherland
2nd	Cronulla-Sutherland~3 d.	2~Balmain
3rd	Balmain~5 d.	4~Cronulla-Sutherland
4th	Balmain~7 d.	4~Universities
	Club Champions	CRONULLA/S'LAND
D2¹ˢᵗ	Balmain~4 d.	3~Drummoyne
D2²ⁿᵈ	Liverpool~5 d.	3~Balmain
D3¹ˢᵗ	Northbridge~7 d.	6~Blacktown
D3²ⁿᵈ	Balmain~5 d.	3~Blacktown
D3³ʳᵈ	Balmain~7 d.	5~Liverpool
D3⁴ᵗʰ	Bondolphins~9 d.	6~Hawkesbury
1st	Maccabi	Winter Comp

The Baths & Clubs

The Competition Committee capably organised the competitions again this season, which were conducted across three divisions with the playing of two rounds.

Games were conducted for the various NSWAWPA grades at Ashfield, Balmain, Drummoyne, Gunnamatta Bay, Manly, North Sydney, Parramatta and Sydney University, which once again became the venue for the Winter competitions.

The new clubs to field teams this season were Blacktown, Hawkesbury, Hunters Hill, Macquarie University and Revesby. Unfortunately, Balgowlah, Clovelly, Manly Rugby, Navy, North Palm Beach and Smithfield all lapsed, while some of the Bronte players transferred into a new Division 3 team known as the All Stars.

The Maccabi Games

The Judean Water Polo Club had first entered the NSWAWPA competition as far back as the 1956/57 season, but by 1971/72 they had morphed into the Maccabi Club. Many of Maccabi's players were selected in a national team to compete at the 9th Maccabiah Games, which opened on 9th July 1973 and were held in Ramat Gan, Israel. The Games took place just ten months after the 1972 Summer Olympics in Munich, where eleven Israeli athletes and coaches were slain by Palestinian terrorists during the events of the Munich Massacre. Some 60,000 spectators packed

▲ *Bronte's Tom & Vida Folden, Rolly & Pam Flesch & Peter Folden with friend in 1974.*

Ramat Gan Stadium as Golda Meir and Abba Eban paid homage to the murdered athletes.

During these games, the Australian Maccabi water polo team, coached by Olympian Peter Montgomery played very well, but lost two critical matches against Israel and Belgium to finish in fourth position. Although four years away, the players resolved to do better at the next Maccabi Games and thought that playing together as a team in the Sydney competition would be the best way to prepare. This thinking however, was a factor over the following season, and saw the departure of some of Bronte's most talented players.

Representatives in NSW Teams

NSW Open Mens Team

Bronte players Peter Folden, Graeme Samuel and Tracy Rockwell were invited to join the NSW training squad this year, with the former two being successful. At this time, the NSW team was becoming particularly hard to crack with nine players being retained from the championship winning team of 1973. Only the goalkeepers were exchanged with Craig Jennings (Wests) replacing Andrew Stewart (Balmain), while John Harrison was recalled and

"We had some amazingly talented players. At the 1960 Olympics in Rome, Dick Thornett was apparently the only Australian that drew any attention from the other international teams. Otherwise, Rolly was very clever and could play the ball, and score goals with his foot. Sarkies had the quickest reflexes of any goalkeeper in Australia and Peter Folden's shot was envied by many. My top 5 Bronte players of all time, besides my father, would have been... 1st - Dick Thornett; 2nd - Graeme Samuel; 3rd - John Thornett; 4th - Don Sarkies; 5th - Peter Folden & Rolly Flesch."

Robbie Vadas, March 2019

"Northbridge subsequently became a team in the Manly Club and we were quickly and fully absorbed into Manly WP Club. Although initially the home pool was the Harbour Pool at Manly (where the Skiffs Club is now) a very severe storm in 1975 busted the old baths and the Club moved to the Boy Charlton pool near Manly Golf Club. I recall when Dick Thornett returned to play 5th Grade for Manly in 1973, but was banned as a 'professional' under the stupid rules that had kept him out of the game in earlier years."

Jon Kirkwood, June 2018

▲ TOP: Coach of the NSW, Les Kay team feeds the ball to his players during a State team training session in early 1974. ABOVE: Even after moving to Brisbane and joining Magayers in 1973, Billy Parsons remained a formidable player and won a further five caps in the Queensland State team.

replaced Don Cameron, both from the Universities club.

Under coach Les Kay (Bronte), the NSW team again demonstrated their dominance in the national titles with an undefeated record at the 27th Australian Championships in Melbourne.

NSW Junior Mens Team

Bronte did not have any players selected in NSW Junior Men's team for the 3rd U/18 Junior Men's National Championships in Melbourne, although Robbie Barta was the team manager. However, NSW were able to regain the title in the juniors, in an undefeated display from Western Australia and South Australia.

The Premierships

The four NSWAWPA Division I premierships were shared between the three top clubs this season with Balmain defeating Universities (7~4) in 4th Grade. Balmain added another premiership by

NEW SOUTH WALES MENS TEAM
1974 - National Champions - Melbourne

Back row (from left): Ian McLauchlain (Balmain), Peter Kerr (Universities), Tony Falson (Cronulla), **Les Kay (Coach, Bronte)**, John Harrison (g, Universities), **Peter Folden (Bronte)**, **Graham Samuel (Bronte)**. Front row: Craig Jennings (Western Suburbs), Randall Goff (Cronulla), David Woods (c, Balmain), Andrew Kerr (Cronulla), Peter Montgomery (Universities), Mal Hunt (Manager, Cronulla).
Photo - NSWAWPA Annual Report 1973/74.

NEW SOUTH WALES U/18 JUNIOR MENS TEAM
1974 - National Champions - Melbourne
Back row (from left): Michael Vasin (r,???), Wayne Miranda (Balmain), Ralph French (Cronulla), Bruce Jackson (Cronulla), Greg Milham (Cronulla), Mark Penklis (g, Cronulla), Paul Dunford (Coach), **Robbie Barta (Manager, Bronte).** Front row: Ken Hill (Balmain), Andrew Lumb (Cronulla), Jack Keen (c,Cronulla), Chris Robinson (Universities), Lee Burns (Manly), Lee Phillips (Manly). Photo - Chris Robinson.

BRONTE AWPC
1974/75 - 1st Grade Team
Back row (from left): Ted Baldock, Dave Stapleton, John 'Fiji' McLure (g), Tracy Rockwell, Graeme Samuel (c/Coach), Peter Waterman. In front: Greg Bell, Steve Bell.
Missing: Ron De Groot, Chris Simpson. Photo - Tracy Rockwell.

defeating Cronulla (5~4) in the 3rd Grade, while Cronulla reversed the trend to defeat Balmain in the 2nd Grade (3~2).

The 1973/74 NSWAWPA semi-finals of the men's 1st Grade competition saw third placed Balmain eliminate Maccabi (8~6) in the minor semi-final, and Cronulla narrowly defeated Universities (4~3) in the major semi-final. Universities then gained entry to the grand-final by defeating Balmain (5~4) in the preliminary final. After a torrid match, Universities overcame Cronulla (4~3) in the

1974 grand-final to win their third consecutive 1st Grade premiership. The Club Championship was won by Cronulla. [3]

UNIVERSITIES
1973/74 - NSWAWPA Men's 1st Grade Premiers
Nick Barnes (c), Peter Kerr, Peter Montgomery, John Harrison (g), Alex Urban, Graham Hannan, Sandy Grant, Chris Robinson, Oscar Charles (Coach).

Bronte AWPC

The team performances of the 1973/74 season were the worst Bronte Water Polo Club had ever experienced.

The 1st Grade finished in sixth place in the Cascade Cup Pre-Season competition. But much worse was to come, in that not one of the four Division I Bronte teams qualified for the finals, with all of them finishing in sixth place or lower. This was a huge shock for a proud club that had really never seen such poor results. No Bronte team finished with more than five wins on the season from their scheduled 14 matches. The poor performances were an eye opener for the club as well as for other clubs on the Sydney water polo scene.

Having dropped so quickly when they had been 1st Grade premiers just two years previously, was extraordinary. The question on everyone's lips was... could the proud Bronte Water Polo Club recover?

Results for Bronte in the NSWAWPA Winter Competition of 1974, where they finished last on the ladder, were worse again,

1973/74 NSWAWPA RESULTS

CASCADE CUP COMPETITION

	Won	Draw	Lost	Forf.	Goals For	Ag.	Points
STATE TEAM	7	1	—	—	51	9	23
MACCABI	6	1	1	—	44	16	21
CRONULLA	7	—	—	1	48	25	21
UNIVERSITIES	5	2	1	—	44	22	20
BALMAIN	4	—	4	—	43	30	16
BRONTE	4	—	4	—	34	46	16
MANLY	3	—	3	2	32	35	12
UNDER-18	2	—	6	—	26	51	12
WESTERN SUBURBS	0	—	8	—	15	52	8
BONDOLPHINS	0	—	7	1	14	65	7

FINAL: Cronulla defeated Maccabi

FIRST DIVISION — 1973-1974

1ST GRADE

	Won	Dr.	Lost	Goals For	Ag.	Points
CRONULLA	11	2	1	93	50	24
UNIVERSITIES	9	4	1	105	51	22
BALMAIN	10	2	2	99	50	22
MACCABI	8	2	4	85	63	18
MANLY	5	2	7	53	61	12
BRONTE	4	0	10	47	71	8
WESTERN SUBURBS	2	2	10	45	96	6
BONDOLPHINS	0	0	14	21	106	0

SEMI-FINALS: Balmain 8 — Maccabi 6; Cronulla 4 — Universities 3
FINAL: Universities 5 — Balmain 4
GRAND FINAL: Universities 4 — Cronulla 3

2ND GRADE

	Won	Dr.	Lost	Goals For	Ag.	Points
CRONULLA	13	—	1	116	31	26
BALMAIN	11	1.	2	91	29	23
UNIVERSITIES	11	1	2	73	25	23
MANLY	5	2	7	56	45	12
WESTERN SUBURBS	5	2	7	47	62	12
BRONTE	5	—	9	40	69	10
BONDOLPHINS	2	1	11	29	88	5
MACCABI	0	1	13	11	114	1

PLAY-OFF for 4TH   Manly 4 — Wests 0
SEMI-FINALS: Universities 4 — Manly 3; Cronulla 6 — Balmain 2
FINAL: Balmain 5 — Universities 4
GRAND FINAL: Cronulla 3 — Balmain 2

3RD GRADE

	Won	Dr.	Lost	Goals For	Ag.	Points
CRONULLA	13	1	—	105	16	27
BALMAIN	11	2	1	108	21	24
UNIVERSITIES	9	2	3	60	37	20
MANLY	7	2	5	58	40	16
WESTERN SUBURBS	5	0	7	48	77	10
BRONTE	3	1	10	28	59	7
MACCABI	3	0	11	13	91	6
BONDOLPHINS	1	0	13	11	90	2

SEMI-FINALS: Universities 7 — Manly 5; Balmain 8 — Cronulla 6
FINAL: Cronulla 8 — Universities 2
GRAND FINAL: Balmain 5 — Cronulla 4

4TH GRADE

	Won	Dr.	Lost	Goals For	Ag.	Points
BALMAIN	14	—	—	97	20	28
UNIVERSITIES	11	0	3	57	29	22
CRONULLA 'B'	9	2	3	60	26	20
CRONULLA 'A'	8	1	5	65	35	17
MANLY	5	1	8	49	41	11
WESTERN SUBURBS	4	—	10	31	71	8
BRONTE	2	—	12	20	75	4
BONDOLPHINS	1	—	13	9	91	2

SEMI-FINALS: Cronulla 'B' 4 — Cronulla 'A' 2; Balmain 8 — Universities 4
FINAL: Universities 3 — Cronulla 'B' 2
GRAND FINAL: Balmain 7 — Universities 4

CLUB CHAMPIONSHIP

Cronulla 245, Balmain 233, Universities 218, Manly 127, (Maccabi 87, Cronulla 'B' 20) 107, Western Suburbs 88, Bronte 80, Bondolphins 21.

WINTER COMPETITION, 1974

FIRST DIVISION

	Won	Lost	Points
MACCABI	8	1	16
WESTERN SUBURBS	7	2	14
LIVERPOOL	6	3	12
BALMAIN	6	3	12
CRONULLA	6	3	12
BRONTE	6	3	12

Premiers: Maccabi

"Peter 'Wartz' Waterman, John 'Fiji' McLure, Teddy Baldock and Ron de Groot from Bondolphins were all great players and very welcome additions to our dwindling ranks in 1974/75. Had all the Bondi and Bronte members amalgamated back then... we could have been an influential force, but as it was... the two great and historic clubs terminated in the same year."

Tracy Rockwell, Sep 2020

and were a portent of what might be expected in the season ahead.

It was at the end of this season that Bronte experienced another blow to their hopes of saving the situation, with the departure of their stalwarts Rolly Flesch, Peter and Tom Folden, who moved across to the new Masada Club to help that team prepare for the next Maccabi Games. A total absence of new members combined with the departure of experienced players spelled doom for the club unless suitable replacements could be found, and fast.

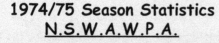

1974/75 Season Statistics
N.S.W.A.W.P.A.

Clubs in the Mens Water Polo Competitions.

Clubs	1	2	3	4	2^1	2^2	2^3	J	3^1	3^2	Total
Army										•	1
Balmain	•	•	•	•	•	•	•	•	•	2	11
Blacktown				•		•		•			3
Blakehurst										•	1
Bondi										•	1
Bondolphins						•	•				2
Bronte	•	•	•								3
Carss Park							•				1
Cronulla-Sutherland	•	•	•	•					•		5
Drummoyne					•	•	•	•			4
Hawkesbury							•				1
Homebush								•	•		2
Liverpool	•	•	•	•					•		5
Macquarie Uni.								•			1
Manly/Warringah	•	•	•	•	•	•	•				7
Masada (Maccabi)	•	•	•	•							4
North Sydney									•	•	2
Northbridge					•						1
Parramatta					•	•	•				3
Penrith					•	•	•	•			4
Ryde							•				1
Sydney University					•	•	•				3
Universities	•	•	•	•							4
University of NSW								•			1
Western Suburbs	•	•	•	•					•		5
	8	8	8	8	7	8	10	7	6	6	76

Results of the Mens Water Polo Competitions.

Grade	Premier		Runner-Up
1st	Cronulla/S'land	.	Pre-Season Comp
1st	Universities~10	d.	6~Balmain
2nd	Cronulla/S'land~11	d.	9~Balmain
3rd	Cronulla/S'land~3	d.	2~Balmain
4th	Balmain~5	d.	2~Cronulla/S'land
Club Champions	BALMAIN		
D2 1st	Drummoyne~9	d.	3~Penrith
D2 2nd	Drummoyne~8	d.	6~Penrith
D2 3rd	Hawkesbury~10	d.	2~Parramatta
J Junior	Cronulla/S'land~8	d.	3~Balmain
D3 1st	Balmain~9	d.	1~North Sydney
D3 2nd	Balmain~9	d.	5~Blakehurst
1st	Cronulla/S'land A		Winter Comp

1974-75

1974/75 NSWAWPA OFFICIALS: Dr. H.K. Porter (Patron); V. Chalwin (President); H.J. Bund (Past President); A. Trevenar (Chairman); K. Connor/W. Copeland/**Mrs G. Trewhella (Registrar)**; Mrs. J. Campbell (Secretary); R. Vadas (Comp. Secretary); R. Traynor (Treasurer).

The Baths & Clubs

Once again the Competition Committee capably organised the season schedule, which was conducted in two rounds across three divisions.

This year NSWAWPA matches were played at Ashfield, Balmain, Drummoyne, Gunnamatta Bay, Manly, North Sydney, Parramatta and Sydney University, which was also used exclusively to run the Winter competition.

In regard to new clubs, teams were entered by Army, Blakehurst and the University of NSW, while the All Stars, Avalon/Bilgola, Hunters Hill, Padstow and Revesby all lapsed.

At the end of season 1969/70 the remnants of the great Bondi Water Polo Club had morphed into Bondolphins, but by 1974 that club had severe problems. Despite their being able to muster four Division I teams during the 1973/74 season, the performance of Bondolphins was abyssmal with every team finishing last on the table. As a result, many of their players looked around for an alternative. Rising Bondolphins star Lindsay Cotterill transferred to Universities, but Bronte benefitted by an influx of excellent Bondolphins players like Teddy Baldock, Ron de Groot, Peter 'Wartz' Waterman and goalkeeper John 'Fiji' McLure.

Representatives in NSW Teams

NSW Open Mens Team

Only Graeme Samuel and Tracy Rockwell were invited to join the NSW State team training squad from Bronte this year, with Sammy gaining his 12th cap in a State team. Peter Folden also held onto his position, but was now representing the Masada club. But slots in the NSW team were being tightly held with nine players again being retained from the championship winning team of 1974. The only changes to the team were goalkeeper Don Cameron (Universities), who was recalled to replace Craig Jennings (Wests), while Iain McLauchlain (Balmain) was replaced by exciting South Australian transfer in Charles Turner (Universities).

> "For three years I gave speeches asking where our new members would come from. We were only at Watson's Bay for a couple of years before the decision was made to transform the club into Maroubra Seals. Sadly, we simply couldn't reform ourselves or attract new talent... and so in 1974 I said... "I'm finished"... and retired."
>
> **Billy McCarthy, Feb 2019**

▼ *Official Program for the 1975 National Championships in Perth, Western Australia.*

NEW SOUTH WALES MENS TEAM
1975 - National Champions - Perth
Back row (from left): Charles Turner (Universities), Peter Montgomery (vc, Universities), Randall Goff (Cronulla), Andrew Kerr (Cronulla), David Woods (c, Balmain), Don Cameron (g, Universities). Front row: Graeme Geldart (r, Cronulla), **Les Kay (Coach, Bronte)**, Brian Gilbert (Manager, Wests), **Peter Folden (Masada)**, Tony Falson (Cronulla), John Harrison (g, Universities), **Graeme Samuel (Bronte)**, Peter Kerr (Universities).
Photo - NSWAWPA 1974/75 Annual Report.

"What happened was... we were struggling from about 1972/1973 to keep teams together, so we put some feelers out to Maroubra Seals Club. They accepted us to play together with their other players so we switched to them in about 1975, but it was very sad to see the end of the great Bronte Water Polo Club. We just couldn't get the numbers... so that was the end of it. Some of us went to play with Northbridge."

Don Sarkies, 27 Jan 2015

WATER POLO CLUB RETIREMENTS

The 1974/75 season also saw the last appearance of another great Sydney water polo club in Bondolphins (ex-Bondi) AWPC.

BONDI AWPC

Bondi ASC was amongst Sydney's earliest swimming clubs, and first entered the water polo competition in 1893/94. They won the first of their 22 1st Grade premierships (from 39 attempts) in 1902/03. Bondi furnished an amazing total of 136 caps for NSW teams:

Name	#NSW Caps	Span
Men's Team (33)		
A.J. Joyce	2 caps	1911-12
A. H. Coulsen	1 cap	1925
T. S. Battersby	1 cap	1925
O. Griffiths	1 cap	1928
T. Meagher	3 caps	1928-30
J. Dempsey*	1 cap	1930
Vic Besomo*	6 caps	1931-40
H. Doerner*(c)	14 caps	1933-51
J. Harrison (g)	1 cap	1933
J. Turnbull*	6 caps	1934-46
P. Gosschalk*	3 caps	1935-38
O. Doerner*(g)	7 caps	1938-51
Clem Walsh	4 caps	1939-47
J. Ferguson*	4 caps	1948-54
L. Ferguson	3 caps	1948-51
K. Erickson	1 cap	1949
A. Hart	2 caps	1949/50
Ray Smee*(c)	7 caps	1950-60
P. Bennett*#1	1 cap	1951
Doug Laing*(g)	6 caps	1952-60
K. Whitehead*(c)	8 caps	1952-60
A. Kosegi	5 caps	1952-56
W. Jones	5 caps	1953-58
R. Sarkies	1 cap	1956
Nino Sydney (c)	6 caps	1957-64
B. Hutchings	4 caps	1959-64
W. Roney	1 cap	1960
A. Langford	3 caps	1961-63
W. Lamb#2	1 cap	1963
P. Waterman (g)	2 caps	1963-67
W. Phillips Jr.#3	1 cap	1964
R. De Groot#4	3 caps	1966-68
R. Langford	1 cap	1968
Ladie's Team (6)		
R. Carroll	5 caps	1968-73
P. O'Reilly	3 caps	1968-70
L. Saunders	3 caps	1968-70
L. Shaw	2 caps	1968-69
K. Tyler	1 cap	1968
M. Myers	4 caps	1969-72

*Olympian or Australian Rep.
#1 1948-58 with VIC State Team (11 caps)
#2 1966-67 with Universities (2 caps)
#3 1962 & 65-71 with Universities (6 caps)
#4 1964 with Parramatta

Under coach Les Kay (Bronte), the NSW team made it three in a row by taking out the 28th Australian Championships in Perth, after defeating Western Australia in the final (6~3), and relegating Queensland to third place.

NSW Junior Mens Team

The cracks were becoming obvious at Bronte, when yet again none of its junior players were selected in NSW Junior Men's team. In this competition, the talented and plucky West Australians equalled the NSW tally of two national titles when they defeated NSW in the final match (4~3).

Australian Team

An Australian team was selected after these championships, which included five players from the successful NSW team. The Aussies played in a New Zealand series, engaged in a World tour, and contested the 2nd FINA World Championships in Cali, Colombia, losing only 13 of their 41 matches in total.

The Premierships

Ominously, Cronulla took out the NSWAWPA 1974/75 Pre-Season Competition. The four NSWAWPA Division I premierships were once again shared between the three top clubs this season with Balmain defeating Cronulla (5~2) in 4th Grade. Cronulla reversed the result in 3rd Grade by defeating Balmain (3~4), while Cronulla repeated their success in defeating Balmain in the 2nd Grade (11~9).

The men's 1st Grade competition saw the inaugural entry of Manly Rugby Union into the play-offs, but they were eliminated by Balmain (6~7) in the minor semi-final, while Universities defeated Cronulla (6~4) in the major semi-final. Balmain then gained entry to the grand-final by narrowly defeating Cronulla (5~4) in the preliminary final. But a talented Universities, assisted by their new South Australian recruit, Charles Turner and Olympian Robert Menzies, easily overcame Balmain (10~6) in the grand-final to win their fourth consecutive 1st Grade premiership.[27] For overall consistency across grades, Balmain won the Club Championship.[4]

UNIVERSITIES AWPC
1974/75 - NSWAWPA Men's 1st Grade Premiers
Peter Montgomery (c/Coach), Peter Kerr, John Holt, Robert Menzies, Warwick Syphers, Don Cameron (g), Graham Hannan, Sandy Grant, Lindsay Cotterill, Chris Robinson, Charles Turner.

Bronte AWPC

The 1974/75 season looked dim for Bronte with a number of their long time greats having transferred to Masada. At this point, Bronte was on the verge of disaster, but unlikely as it was... the club received a rescue of sorts by benefitting from the demise of the Bondolphins Club. Bronte received an influx of experienced ex-Bondolphins players like Teddy Baldock, Ron de Groot, Peter 'Wartz' Waterman and goalkeeper John 'Fiji' McLure.

Despite the new blood, results for Bronte during the NSWAWPA Winter competition of 1974 remained disappointing. The revamped Bronte side managed to secure five draws, but only recorded two wins. Moving into the 1974/75 Summer season... the performances of most of the teams were just as bad if not worse. Also taking its toll upon the situation, and transferring out of Bronte at this time were a number of experienced players that had moved to Northbridge Water Polo Club, a major factor being the travel distance to Watsons Bay.

The defection of players left Bronte unable to field a 4th Grade, although many of its 'old boys' won through to the finals in playing for Northbridge. Despite being bolstered by the few Bondolphins players, Bronte's results by season's end were poor as not one of their three Division I teams qualified for the finals, with all of them finishing in either seventh or eighth place. This was a huge wake-up call for a previously proud and victorious club. Even more galling, was that no team finished with more than four wins from their 21 matches on the season. The substandard

"Don Sarkies was the Bronte 1st Grade goal keeper and also represented NSW on six occasions. Don played for Bronte from 1959 until the club ceased in 1975. After that, Don continued to play polo with Northbridge up until the age of 80, and then took up a support role for his water polo team."

Brian Ellison, Oct 2018

"I had an appendix operation in 1966 that kept me out of the water for a while and I travelled to the UK in 1967. And again in 1971 and 72 when I lived in the UK after marrying Janet over there. I think I began playing with Northbridge when I returned home from the UK in late 1972. A number of Bronte players defected to Northbridge when Bronte closed down... players like Robbo, Kipper Simpson, Dave Malone, Ian Leffers and later of course... the Don."

Jon Kirkwood, June 2018

1974/75 NSWAWPA RESULTS

PRE-SEASON COMPETITION, 1974/75

FIRST DIVISION

All teams played seven games:—

	Points
CRONULLA	12
UNIVERSITIES 'A'	10
BALMAIN	7
MACCABI	7
BONDOLPHINS	5
WESTERN SUBURBS	5
LIVERPOOL	4
UNIVERSITIES 'B'	3
BRONTE	2

Final: Universities 8, Cronulla 4
Premiers: Universities

FIRST GRADE

	P.	W.	D.	L.	F/D	Goals For	A.	Pts.
UNIVERSITIES	21	20	—	1	—	167	51	40
CRONULLA-SUTHERLAND	21	15	3	3	—	133	58	33
BALMAIN	21	15	2	4	—	139	76	32
MANLY R.U.	21	11	2	8	—	68	81	21
MASADA	21	8	3	10	—	89	87	19
LIVERPOOL	21	4	1	16	—	49	142	9
BRONTE	21	4	1	13	3	59	114	9
WESTERN SUBURBS	21	2	1	18	—	52	150	5

1st Semi Final: Balmain 7, Manly 6
2nd Semi Final: Universities 6, Cronulla-Sutherland 4
Final: Balmain 5, Cronulla-Sutherland 4
Grand Final: Universities 10, Balmain 6
Premiers: Universities

2nd GRADE

	P.	W.	D.	L.	F/D	Goals For	A.	Pts.
BALMAIN	21	19	1	1	—	136	40	39
CRONULLA-SUTHERLAND	21	14	3	2	2	94	37	31
UNIVERSITIES	21	13	4	4	—	96	41	30
MANLY	21	11	2	8	—	80	53	24
LIVERPOOL	21	8	2	11	—	59	85	18
WESTERN SUBURBS	21	4	4	13	—	43	109	12
BRONTE	21	3	0	11	7	33	115	6
MASADA	21	2	1	15	3	51	130	5

1st Semi Final: Universities 4, Manly 3
2nd Semi Final: Balmain 4, Cronulla-Sutherland 2
Final: Cronulla-Sutherland 5, Universities 2
Grand Final: Cronulla-Sutherland 11, Balmain 9
Premiers: Cronulla-Sutherland

3rd GRADE

	P.	W.	D.	L.	F/D	Goals For	A.	Pts.
CRONULLA-SUTHERLAND	14	11	2	1	—	73	26	24
BALMAIN	14	11	—	3	—	79	27	22
UNIVERSITIES	14	9	3	2	—	62	24	21
LIVERPOOL	14	9	1	4	—	50	42	19
MANLY	14	7	—	7	—	50	36	14
WESTERN SUBURBS	14	4	—	10	—	29	65	8
MASADA	14	1	—	11	2	17	75	2
BRONTE	14	—	—	13	1	13	95	0

1st Semi Final: Universities 8, Liverpool 3
2nd Semi Final: Cronulla Sutherland 6, Balmain 3
Final: Balmain 8, Universities 2
Grand Final: Cronulla-Sutherland 3, Balmain 2
Premiers: Cronulla-Sutherland

"By 1975... the problem for Bronte was the all weather training venue at Watsons Bay was just too difficult to get to. I was a member of the Club Committee then, but Les Kay was the main motivator in moving us to Maroubra Seals. He pushed the agenda as Maroubra had a pool and facilities. There were a number of people against it, but the majority of the Committee voted for the move. Along with the great Bondi Club, NSW Water Polo lost a lot, when Bronte folded."

Robbie Vadas, March 2019

"I developed a bad knee after retiring, and a Physio told me to swim. So I continued coaching at the Manly pool, which was close to home. In just two weeks the knee was better and I was able to swim and play again. The Manly players were mostly school boys, but all had good skills, so by the 1975/76 season I was coaching and playing again, but with Manly."

Billy McCarthy, Feb 2019

performances brought Bronte to a cross roads, and momentous decisions were required if the club was to survive.

Ominously, feelers were put out for a possible merger with the Maroubra Seals Club by Les Kay. The Seals had a physical clubhouse, a training pool, facilities and funding, but bringing Bronte AWPC to an end wasn't an easy thing to do. Mournfully, the decision to morph the club into Maroubra Seals was the only viable alternative. So with that determination, the great Bronte Water Polo Club perished.

The transition occurred relatively quickly as ex-Bronte members lined up to play in the 1975 Winter competition for Maroubra Seals, and even finished second on the ladder in their half of the 1st Grade event.

The deterioration of Bronte provided clear air for the up and coming Universities and Cronulla-Sutherland clubs, who between them would dominate the Sydney metropolitan water polo competitions for the next quarter of a century.

1975-76

▼ *The 1975/76 season revealed two new Eastern Suburbs water polo clubs in Maroubra Seals and Masada, which had replaced the great Bronte and Bondi clubs. The captains were both ex-Bronte, and many of the opposing players for this match had played together in the past. The sad event provides an example of how club administrators can get it all wrong. Maroubra scraped home by a one goal margin (6~5), and the great Nino Sydney (ex-Bondi) was there to referee.*

1975/76 NSWAWPA OFFICIALS: Dr. H.K. Porter (Patron); V. Chalwin (President); H.J. Bund (Past President); A. Trevenar (Chairman); M. Phillips (Registrar); **Mrs. J. Campbell (Secretary)**; F. Falzon (Comp. Secretary); R. Traynor (Treasurer).

After the decision was taken back in May 1975 to amalgamate with Maroubra Seals, the great Bronte club had ceased to exist, but there remained a number of loyal ex-Bronte members that transferred across. This had the effect of boosting Maroubra Seals immediately into fielding three Division I teams, as well as one Divison 3 team. In addition, the Seals benefitted by welcoming into their ranks the top Ladies' team in Sydney for the coming NSWAWPA competition.

MAROUBRA SEALS (White Caps)	MASADA (Black Caps)
1—JOHN McCLURE	1—DON MURRAY
2—GRAEME SAMUEL (c)	2—PETER FOLDEN (c)
3—PETER WATERMAN	3—RAPHEL MENDELS
4—RON DE GROOT	4—HOWARD ROBY
5—GARY GRANT	5—LINDSAY COTTERILL
6—TED BALDOCK	6—MARK TURNBULL
7—GREG BELL	7—MICK ETHER
8—STEVE BELL	8—WAYNE TURNBULL
9—GRAHAM ROBINSON	9—PETER SWITZER
10—DAVE STAPLETON	10—ROLEY FLESCH
11—DON SARKIES	11—DOUG GREVETT
Referee: NINO SYDNEY	

The Baths & Clubs

This year NSWAWPA matches were played at Ashfield, Balmain, Drummoyne, Gunnamatta Bay, Manly,

North Sydney, Parramatta and Sydney University pools, the latter being used exclusively to run the Winter competition. In regard to new clubs, teams were entered by Eastwood, Navy, Padstow, Roseville and Sutherland, while Army, Blakehurst, Bondi, Bondolphins and Carss Park lapsed, while Bronte morphed into the Maroubra Seals Club.

Representatives in NSW Teams

NSW Open Mens Team

The 1976 Australian Water Polo Championships and Olympic Trials in Sydney set the scene for a tight competition, with the added incentive of 11 Olympic Games berths up for grabs.

Ex-Bronte players Peter Folden (Masada) and Graeme Samuel (Maroubra Seals) having shared 21 national championships between them, were both unavailable, but Tracy Rockwell, now playing with Universities, was finally selected as one of three new caps in the NSW team. Under new coach Robert Menzies (Universities), eight NSW players were retained from the championship winning team of 1975. Graeme Geldart (Cronulla) was the other new cap, while after ten seasons as NSW goalkeeper, John Harrison (Universities) relinquished his place to Michael Turner (Cronulla), another South Australian transferee and Australian representative.

Despite being undefeated throughout the tournament, the star studded NSW team was devastated in the last ten seconds of the final, when Jake Kneebone from the Somerset Club, scored an unlikely backhand from the side of the pool, to capture a fourth national title for Western Australia (4~3). An American infused Queensland team again took out third place.

1975/76 Season Statistics
N.S.W.A.W.P.A.

Clubs in the Mens Water Polo Competitions.

Clubs	1	2	3	4	2¹	2²	2³	J	3¹	3²	Total
Balmain	●	●	●	●	●	●	●	●	●	●	10
Blacktown						●	●			●	3
Cronulla	●	●	●	●				●			5
Drummoyne						●	●	●	●		4
Eastwood									●		1
Hawkesbury								●			1
Homebush									●		1
Liverpool	●	●	●	●				●			5
Macquarie Uni.									●		1
Manly	●	●	●	●							4
Maroubra Seals	●	●	●					●			4
Masada (Maccabi)	●	●	●					●			4
Navy										●	1
North Sydney					●	●	●				3
Northbridge		●									1
Padstow									●		1
Parramatta					●	●	●				3
Penrith					●	●	●	●			4
Roseville									●		1
Ryde					●	●	●				3
Sutherland									●		1
Sydney University					●			●			2
Universities	●	●	●	●				●			5
University of NSW										●	1
Western Suburbs	●	●	●	●		●		●			6
	8	8	8	6	8	8	8	9	6	6	75

Results of the Mens Water Polo Competitions.

Grade	Premier		Runner-Up
1st	Universities		Pre-Season Comp
1st	Cronulla/S'land ~5	d.	4~Universities
2nd	Cronulla/S'land~5	d.	4~Balmain
3rd	Cronulla/S'land~9	d.	8~Balmain
4th	Balmain~8	d.	2~Universities
	Club Champions		BALMAIN
D2 1st	Drummoyne~5	d.	4~Balmain
D2 2nd	Drummoyne~4	d.	6~Balmain
D2 3rd	Balmain~5	d.	4~Parramatta
J junior	Balmain~4	d.	3~Cronulla/S'land
D3 1st	Sutherland~5	d.	0~Hawkesbury
D3 2nd	Eastwood~5	d.	4~Navy
1st	Cronulla/S'land		Winter Comp

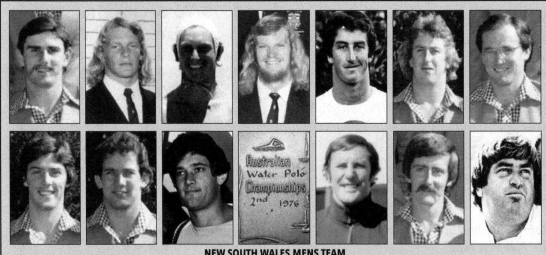

NEW SOUTH WALES MENS TEAM
1976 - Runners-Up - Sydney
Top row (from left): Don Cameron (g, Universities), Tony Falson (Cronulla), Graeme Geldart (Cronulla), Randall Goff (Cronulla), Andrew Kerr (Cronulla), Peter Kerr (Universities), Peter Montgomery (vc, Universities). Bottom row: Tracy Rockwell (Universities), Charles Turner (Universities), Michael Turner (g, Cronulla), David Woods (c, Balmain), Robert Menzies (Coach, Universities), Bruce Falson (Manager, Cronulla). NSWAWPA 1975/76 Annual Report.

Heads rolled in the NSW camp including Robert Menzies, who was otherwise destined for a stellar coaching career. And despite not being given a start in the grand-final, the author was also turfed out of the side the following year by none other than Les Kay when he tookover as coach, which I always attributed as payback for transferring away from Bronte.

NSW Junior Mens Team

No Maroubra Seals juniors were selected in the NSW team for the 5th U/18 Junior Men's National Championships in Sydney. The West Australians raised their tally of national titles to three when they defeated Queensland in the final match (8~4).

The 1976 Olympic Team

The Australian Olympic team was selected after these championships, which included five from NSW, three from the West, two from Victoria and one from Queensland. The Aussies played in a New Zealand series, engaged in a European tour, and contested the 1976 Olympic Games in Montreal, Canada, winning 19 of their 40 matches on tour.

The Premierships

The Manly club once again performed well above expectation this season by qualifying for three of the four Division I play-offs. However, the four NSWAWPA Division I premierships were again mostly fought over between the three top clubs. Balmain defeated Universities (8~5)

The Amateur Swimming Union of Australia
presents

The 1976 Australian
Water Polo Championships
and Olympic Trials

SYDNEY UNIVERSITY SWIMMING POOL

21st February to 29th February

PROGRAMME **50c**

▲MID: *After two seasons in the State training squad, and having transferred to Universities, Tracy Rockwell gained selection in the NSW Men's team in 1976. Sadly Bronte morphed into the Maroubra Seals, and the 'aura' surrounding the once great club evaporated.*
ABOVE: *Official Program for the 1976 National Championships in Sydney.*

in 4th Grade. Cronulla defeated Balmain (9~8) in 3rd Grade, and repeated the dose in 2nd Grade by defeating Balmain (5~4).

The men's 1st Grade competition saw Manly eliminated by Balmain (2~8) in the minor semi-final, while Cronulla defeated Universities (4~2) in the major semi-final. Universities then gained entry to the grand-final by narrowly defeating Balmain (6~5) in the preliminary final. But a talented Cronulla, assisted by their new South Australian recruit, Michael Turner in goals, narrowly overcame Universities (5~4) in the grand-final to win their inaugural 1st Grade premiership. For overall consistency across grades, Balmain took out the Club Championship. The very worst thing of course, was that for the first time in 25 years, there was no Bronte club in the NSWAWPA competition.[5]

Maroubra Seals AWPC

It was with profound regret that the proud Bronte Amateur Water

▶TOP: Peter Folden (left) joined Maroubra Seals for the 1975/76 season, seen here about to shoot against Liverpool. MID: Gary Grant (#5) returned to play for Maroubra Seals v Wests, with Doc Wulf (#2) hanging on, and Craig Jennings in goal. ABOVE: Ted Baldock also continued on with the Maroubra Seals, seen here against Wests in 1976.

1975/76 NSWAWPA RESULTS

FIRST GRADE

	P.	W.	L.	D.	F/D	Goals For	A.	Pts.
Balmain	21	16	4	1	–	149	70	54
Cronulla	21	18	1	–	–/2	131	53	55
Liverpool	21	2	19	–	–	39	134	25
Manly	21	8	10	3	–	71	79	40
Masada	21	3	13	3	–/2	69	143	28
Maroubra Seals	21	7	11	3	–	86	127	38
Universities	21	17	3	1	–	181	57	56
Western Suburbs	21	6	12	3	–	54	117	36

1st Semi Final: Balmain 8, Manly 2
2nd Semi Final: Cronulla 4, Universities 2
Final: Universities 6, Balmain 5
Grand Final: Cronulla 5, Universities 4
Premiers: Cronulla Sutherland.

SECOND GRADE

	P.	W.	L.	D.	F/D	Goals For	A.	Pts.
Balmain	21	14	3	4	–	136	48	53
Cronulla	21	14	3	2	–/2	112	46	49
Liverpool	21	7	14	–	–	56	112	35
Manly	21	14	6	1	–	95	54	50
Masada	21	5	4	–	1/11	33	90	19
Maroubra Seals	21	3	13	–	–/5	29	141	22
Universities	21	17	2	1	–/1	125	46	55
Western Suburbs	21	6	12	–	1/2	46	95	30

1st Semi Final: Cronulla 7, Manly 2
2nd Semi Final: Balmain 4, Universities 3
Final: Cronulla 2, Universities 0
Grand Final: Cronulla 5, Balmain 4
Premiers: Cronulla-Sutherland.

THIRD GRADE

	P.	W.	L.	D.	F/D	Goals For	A.	Pts.
Balmain	14	13	1	–	–	93	13	40
Cronulla	14	9	–	–	–/5	55	26	27
Liverpool	14	2	8	2	–/2	27	59	18
Masada	14	4	7	–	–/3	22	61	19
Maroubra Seals	14	–	7	1	1/5	9	71	9
Universities	14	10	3	–	–/1	48	27	33
Western Suburbs	14	5	7	2	–	34	45	26
Manly	14	9	3	1	–/1	47	33	32

1st Semi Final: Cronulla 6, Manly 2
2nd Semi Final: Balmain 7, Universities 3
Final: Cronulla 11, Universities 2
Grand Final: Cronulla 9, Balmain 8
Premiers: Cronulla-Sutherland

FOURTH GRADE

	P.	W.	L.	D.	F/D	Goals For	A.	Pts.
Balmain	14	11	1	2	–	77	16	38
Cronulla	14	9	1	1	–/3	60	34	30
Liverpool	14	3	5	1	–/5	22	83	16
Manly	14	4	6	1	–/3	39	64	20
Masada	14	3	3	1	1/6	16	43	14
Northbridge	14	7	5	2	–	49	32	30
Universities	14	8	3	2	–/1	56	33	31
Western Suburbs	14	2	8	4	–	34	48	22

1st Semi Final: Cronulla 5, Northbridge 1
2nd Semi Final: Balmain 5, Universities 2
Final: Universities 2, Cronulla 1
Grand Final: Balmain 8, Universities 5
Premiers: Balmain

WINTER COMPETITION, 1976

MEN GRADE 1

	P	W	L	D	F	D	Goals F	A	Pts
Cronulla 'A'	8	7	0	1	0	0	39	13	23
Maroubra Seals	8	6	1	1	0	0	32	14	21
Cronulla 'B'	8	5	2	0	1	0	27	18	17
Western Suburbs	8	4	3	1	0	0	21	15	17
Liverpool	8	3	4	1	0	0	20	24	15
Sydney University	8	3	4	1	0	0	21	27	15
Manly	8	3	5	0	0	0	25	21	14
Universities 'A'	8	2	0	1	1	4	17	26	8
Universities 'B'	8	2	1	0	2	3	14	32	7
Balmain	8	1	3	0	0	4	10	36	6

Polo Club ceased to exist in its own right after the end of the 1974/75 season. However, as had occurred many times in the past through club amalgamations, a deal was struck with Maroubra Seals, which allowed many of the Bronte club members to play on for the Seals.

Maroubra Seals Club actually improved slightly on the results of Bronte's final season, during the Summer competition of 1975/76. They didn't field a 4th Grade team, their 3rd Grade finished last on the ladder without a win, and the 2nd Grade finished in seventh position. However, Maroubra Seals 1st Grade were only narrowly beaten out of fourth position and a semi-final place by Manly. Despite the severe loss of personnel, the Seals managed to win or draw almost half of their 1st Grade matches that year, to finish in fifth position. Commendably, in the 1976 1st Grade Winter competition the Seals only lost one game to finish second behind Cronulla.

By 1976/77, the Seals could only manage ninth, seventh and last across the three grades respectively in the Pre-

Season, although they managed to finish fourth in the 1st Grade Summer competition, losing to Balmain (4~7). Over the coming years the Maroubra Seals experienced some success with a 1977 Winter premiership in 3rd Grade, and a Pre-Season win for 3rd Grade, as well as a 9th Grade premiership in season 1977/78, but a number of club members drifted off after that.

The All Stars

A History of 'Ernie's All Stars' Water Polo Club

" 'Ernie's All Stars' was created by myself and Chris Hickman, as co-owners. Both of us had played for the well-known Bronte Water Polo Club in the 3rd Grade team known as 'McCarthy's Marauders.' The All Stars became the first privately owned sports team in Australia. Over the years some ten ex-Bronte players performed at the highest level for the All Stars.

We established the All Stars back in 1973/74 as a place where fine gentleman could play out their time, but in the 7th Grade. Although experience was not a condition of entry, we were mainly a group of good players who wanted to satisfy the demand of thousands of thrill starved water polo spectators.

The next season we played under the banner of Manly Water Polo, as they needed an extra team. The players were primarily ex-Bronte lower graders, Easts rugby club members and selected friends. That season was hard as they graded us against very tough opposition in 7th Grade, but we finished the competition with four wins, six losses, one draw and a forfeit. Top goal scorers for the season were Chris Hickman (20) and Paul Aisbett (10).

We were on a steep learning curve, but that season saw the beginning of a future sporting empire, and the All Stars were up to the challenge. We never trained in a pool, only at the bar, and consequently had many nights with no reserves, or showed up with insufficient players, but we contested every game in a

WATER POLO CLUB RETIREMENTS

The 1974/75 season saw the last appearance of the great Bronte AWPC.

BRONTE AWPC

Bronte AWPC was a relatively late arrival to Sydney's water polo scene, first entering the water polo competition in 1943/44. They won the first of their six 1st Grade premierships (from 13 attempts) in 1958/59. In its short 25 years of competition, Bronte furnished a total of 55 caps for NSW teams:

Name	#NSW Caps	Span
Men's Team (15)		
J. Thornett	4 caps	1954-60
B. Vadas	4 caps	1954-60
D. See	1 cap	1956
V. McGrath[#1] (c)	6 caps	1957-65
D. Thornett*	4 caps	1958-61
K. Owens	2 caps	1961-62
D Sarkies (g)	6 caps	1961
B Ellison (g)	1 cap	1964
R. Flesch	3 caps	1965-72
P. Folden[#2]	8 caps	1967-75
D. Bullock[#3]	[1 cap]	1968
W. Parsons[#4]	1 cap	1968-78
J. Gahagan	1 cap	1969
G. Samuel*[#5]	6 caps	1970-75
T. Rockwell[#6]	[1 cap]	1976
Ladie's Team (5)		
L. Grills	1 cap	1968
L. Trewhella	3 caps	1973-75
M. Wilby[#7]	2 caps	1974-76
M. Robinson	1 cap	1974
K. Trewhella	1 cap	1975

*Olympian or Australian Rep.
[#1] 1960 Reserve Olympian
[#2] 1975 with Masada WPC
[#3] 1968 with St George WPC
[#4] 1973-78 with QLD State Team (5 caps)
[#5] 1963-68 with WA State Team (6 caps)
[#6] 1976 with Universities WPC
[#7] 1976 with Maroubra Seals WPC

▼ Results for the All Stars in their inaugural season.

THIRD DIVISION — 1973-1974						
FIRST GRADE						
	Played	Won	Lost	Dr.	Dis.	Points
NORTHBRIDGE	12	10	1	1	—	21
BLACKTOWN	12	10	1	1	—	21
AVALON-BILGOLA	12	6	6	0	—	12
BALMAIN	12	5	6	1	—	11
ALL STARS	12	4	7	1	—	9
HOMEBUSH	12	3	9	0	—	6
RYDE	12	1	9	2	—	4

1st SEMI-FINAL: Avalon-Bilgola 3 — Balmain 2
2nd SEMI-FINAL: Northbridge 10 — Blacktown 8
FINAL: Blacktown 12 — Avalon-Bilgola 11
GRAND-FINAL: Northbridge 7 — Blacktown 6

THE ALL STARS
Club Roster

Ernie Kritzler (c)	Bronte WPC
Chris Hickman	Bronte WPC
Billy McCarthy	Bronte WPC
Steve Kritzler	Bronte WPC
Danny Hofbauer	Bronte WPC
Lindsey Watson	Bronte WPC
John Power	Bronte WPC
Gary Cawood	Bronte WPC
Billy Parsons	Bronte WPC
Dennis Morgan	Bronte WPC
Terry 'Lunky' Clark	Bronte WPC
Barney the Bear	Brisbane WPC
Mrs. Judy Buckley	NCR Australia
Paul Jelphs	Easts RLC
Keiran Speed	Easts RUC
Andy Doyle	Easts RUC
Chris Anderson	Easts RUC
Bob Fennell	Easts RUC
Jim King	Easts RUC
Steve Treble	Easts RUC
Ross Field	Easts RUC
Bob Olsen	Easts RUC
Bob Leitch	Bondi WPC
Graham Sellars	Bondi WPC
Chris Butt	Bondi WPC
Ted Baldock	Bondi WPC
Paddo O'Brien	Bondi WPC
Bill Widin	Ex-NSW swimmer
Berliner Swartzenbrot	Loaf of Bread
Mick Nolan	Friend of Hicko
The Black Duck	Friend of Hicko
Wayne Mortimer	Friend of Hicko
Frenchie	Long Bay Gaol (parolled)
Stan Theodore	Friend of Ernie
Ray Allsop	Friend of Ernie
Robert Brooks	Friend of Ernie
Danny the Fireman	Just Showed Up
John Scanlon	Alias for Visitors
Alan Burns	Bondi Beach
Robert Burns	Bondi Beach
John Playfair	Bondi Beach
Mark Meares	Friend of a Friend
Terry the Whale	Friend of Frenchie
Craig Punchy	Friend of Frenchie

Gone to the Great Game in the Sky

Paul Aisbett	Easts RUC
Lloyd Biram	Friend of Ernie
John Aldenhoven	NCR Australia
Frank Squash	Friend of Hicko
'Bill Hickman'	Hicko's dog
'Peter Finch'	Ernie's finch
'Jim Clarke'	Peter Clarke's dog

very relaxed state of mind. Much can be said for our club motto "Kick, punch, bite and scratch, off to the pub and down the hatch." Our motto reflected our play.

The first few seasons weren't that successful, but then came the Jelph's/Kritzler affair. Paul Jelphs was playing in 1st Grade for Easts rugby league, but decided to have a game of water polo with the All Stars to help toughen him up. At a match one night, Paul was sent out for brutality, but refused to front the Judiciary as a professional rugby league player. I went overseas, so as Captain I couldn't front the judiciary either, and as a result we were both handed life bans. Stupidity at the Water Polo Association was rampant in those days. Upon my return from overseas however, I was immediately reinstated.

For the 1976/77 season we tried to enter a new team called "Ernie's All Stars," but that was refused by the Association as being too 'provocative'. Hence we became McKenzie's Bay Water Polo Club, but we were just the All Stars in hoodies.

McKenzie's Bay is a lovely suburb, but at that time no one knew where in Sydney it actually was. That year we also secured the services of the old grey fox, Billy McCarthy. Bill was a living legend and had swum against Boy Charlton at the Domain, and fought Tommy Burns at the old Stadium. We immediately went into intense training at various pubs and places of ill-repute across the Eastern Suburbs. Billy demanded nothing less than a battle-hardened group that was ready to compete.

Private club ownership was progressing. The hard work paid off with a much-improved season and we went into our last game that year as minor premiers. But at poolside, and just ten minutes before our last match of the regular season began, we were informed by the Association that we had missing pieces of registration, and as a result all our season's points were deducted, and dropped from first to last.

The players were incensed and played like men possessed, winning that night by 14~0. The owners of the club reacted immediately, and that night heard the secretary of the Association explain that this was all "bullshit." Our club lawyer and his associate, then went into action. The owners used our accrued funds to threaten a Supreme Court injunction, and all water polo finals were to be stopped by the Court. However, sanity prevailed and we were reinstated by being placed fourth on the ladder. This was the crumbs of a dishonest Association, who took a 'take it or leave it' attitude... there was no justice!

Coach McCarthy was so incensed that he broke with a long standing club tradition, to ban regular training at the pub, and called for long hard training sessions in the water at Watsons Bay, before ending up at the pub.

But our results spoke for themselves... as we defeated Padstow (16~1) in the first semi-final; Roseville (6~3) in the major semi-final; and then Parramatta (7~5) in the grand final. That season we won 15, drew 1 and lost just 3 games, scoring 118 goals with only 36 against. Our top scorers were Chris Hickman (28) and Graham Sellers (22), with 21 different players scoring goals. The owners were overjoyed to win a premiership in only their second season.

Private ownership was working well by 1976, and the All Stars had become legends in their own minds. They were openly called the 'Harlem Globetrotters' of Australian water polo and rightly so. At this time, it was strongly rumored that my parents were linked to Royal Hungarian bloodlines and so a game against the Hungarian national team was being openly discussed.

But we were advised we couldn't tour overseas as Australian water polo players! Immediately the owners responded by informing both the Australian Swimming and Water Polo Associations in writing, that no members of the All Stars would be available for representative honours. Consequently, no All Stars made themselves available for selection in the 1976 Olympic Games.

After this, relations with the Association deteriorated further when they discovered that our secretary, with whom they'd been corresponding with for the past two years was actually Peter Clarke's dog, named 'Jim Clarke'. Being true and honest Australians, we admitted to the error and organised new elections with only Bill Hickman (Chris Hickman's dog) standing for club secretary. We did advise however, that nowhere in the constitution of the Water Polo Association did it state that a dog was not permissible to hold the position of club secretary.

The Association then demanded that Bill step down and be replaced at a new election. So being obliging citizens, we organised another election at which Peter Finch was elected unopposed. Peter was my prized bird of the finch species, but the Association yielded and continued to write to him until 1979.

Following this humiliation, the Association responded by promoting our club upwards by two grades. No team in the history of NSWAWPA had ever been promoted up two grades for winning the previous year. Promotion and

▲ Ex-Bronte club member Chris Hickman, was also co-owner and top goal scorer for the All Stars. Hicko was also a very talented rugby player for Easts Rugby Union Club. ABOVE: The 1976/77 9th Grade premiership trophy and medal for Ernie's All Stars.

SUNDAY, DECEMBER 20, 2015
THE SUN-HERALD

NEWS 3

Scoring a prime spot by the sea

Ern,
If you were shooting from the end at the bottom you would probably knock the top off one of the Opera House's sails! All the best, Bill

Photo: Dallas Kilponen

Sydney Harbour's Campbells Cove was the dramatic backdrop for the launch of Water Polo by the Sea at Circular Quay on Saturday. The event featured two games. Local women's side | Cronulla Sharks took on the Balmain Tigers, pictured. The Sharks triumphed 11-7. Italy, the world's number three team, played the Australian men's team (Aussie Sharks) in the show- | case match ahead of the Australian team's anticipated qualification for the 2016 Olympic Games in Rio de Janeiro, Brazil. The visitors won 14-10.

"Playing one night at Sydney Uni for 'McKenzie's Bay', which had morphed out of the ALL STARS, I really wound up to have a big shot at goal, but it sort of slipped and I smashed the pool clock with a direct hit. The clock was 2 metres above and maybe 3 metres to the left of the goal. Guess you'd call it... a miss!! But it was something that stuck in people's minds as evidenced by the above comment from Billy McCarthy, some 40 years later!"

Ernie Kritzler, July 2020

The "one season club" went for 5 years plus, under a number of club names. Premierships were won. Players were begging to play with the team. Billy McCarthy arrived in our second year and remained until the end. We only ended badly because of that absolute Association dead shit, who disliked Bronte, and what we stood for. He hated the fact that older players could continue playing water polo and really enjoying it playing "the All Star way". But he buckled when we threatened direct legal action against the Association. We were not called the Harlem Globetrotters of Sydney water polo for nothing! We brought life back to water polo in Sydney.

Ernie Kritzler, Sept 2020

relegation were never part of the policy in NSW Water Polo. Only the All Stars received that treatment. We naturally lodged a protest, but it was dismissed.

Yet another controversial year unfolded for the All Stars in 1977, after lodging a formal complaint that no 'independent' referees were being appointed to our games. So... the current leader of the Association, a self-confessed basher of young men in police cells, decided to destroy the club. The season went well with 10 wins from 14 games, 56 goals for and only 21 against, which saw the All Stars march onwards toward the semi-finals. But Association politics were always against us and they resented a true privately owned water polo club.

In the play-offs, we defeated Balmain in the first semi-final (7~5), and Parramatta in the major semi-final (2~1), and then prepared for our second consecutive grand final. The owners were super excited, but unbeknown to us was that a certain Association personality was planning revenge. The team trained diligently at various hotels around the Eastern Suburbs, but our spirits dropped when two mentally disadvantaged Balmain players were appointed as referees for our big game.

In the second minute of the first quarter they sent co-owner, and top goal-scorer Chris Hickman from the pool for 'brutality'. Further ejections continued and during the match, there were times the All Stars were down to just four players, which included the goalie, as our players became cross and more aggressive tactics were employed. The All Stars had to play their opponents as well as the referees, but inevitably lost to North Sydney (3~9).

After the game, the refs were unable to prove the 'brutality' charge. Indeed, no charge was ever laid, and Hicko was never asked to attend the Judiciary. Sent out for brutality... without charge and no Judiciary... that was simply unheard of! As captain, I refused to allow my players to watch the post-game medal presentation, as the club had obviously been cheated. We tried to justify the farce by appealing for a re-match, but were denied.

Surprisingly, the medals for the losers suddenly disappeared, but re-appeared a short time later at our own presentation at the local pub. Sadly the club was later affected when some players broke ranks to start their own club elsewhere. They turned out to be water polo mercenaries... and received upgraded contracts offering free beer. At this point, the club was split, but not broken.

The owners re-grouped and ended McKenzie's Bay, but immediately created Heckenberg Water Polo Club. This became a great secret as the actual location of this suburb was unknown... and so the season passed without dispute. However, the club secured a new patron in Mr. Keith Doyle the MP for Vaucluse.

By 1978 we became Monterey Water Polo Club, although it wasn't the greatest of years, especially when all record of our results was lost in the big Brisbane floods! But we made a major change when the All Stars entertainment division was created and many great functions were held. The biggest and the best was a huge night at Bondi Surf Club when we had two bands playing including 'Mental As Anything'. The idea was to raise money for our junior players, but to our surprise the only player we had under 21 was Frenchie,

▲Newspaper results for McKenzie's Bay Water Polo Club. ▼Ex-Bronte club member, Ernie Kritzler...was a co-Owner and namesake for Ernie's All Stars Water Polo Club, which later became McKenzies Bay Water Polo Club, then Heckenberg Water Polo Club., then Monterey Water Polo Club. Still evading the authorities and now a recluse, Ernie is seen here with mentor Billy McCarthy, ex-Bronte legend.

▲One of the many different T-shirt designs for the All Stars. ▼ Newspaper results for ther All Stars, which morphed into McKenzie's Bay Water Polo Club to avoid detection.

McKenzies Bay WPC Results

Water Polo: McKenzie's Bay All Stars 5 (R. Leach 3, C. Hickman 2), def University of NSW 3.

Water Polo: MacKenzie's Bay All Stars 3 (Bill McCarthy, Robert Brookes, Chris Hickman goals) Vs Roseville 4.

McKenzies Bay All Stars Water Polo: In the first match of the season the club defeated Padstow 6-5 at Balmain. Goals Chris Hickman 3, Wayne Mortimer 2, Ernie Kritzler 1.

Water Polo: McKenzie's Bay All Stars def Balmain "A" 10-1 Scorers for McKenzie's Bay. Graham Sellars 3, Chris Hickman and Robert Brooks 2, Bill Hickman, Jim Thorpe and Keiron Speed 1.

Water polo: McKenzie's Bay All Stars d Balmain 9-0 (E. Kritzler 3, G. Sellars 2, C. Hickman, B. Leitch, R. Field and P. O'Brien 1 each).

Water Polo: McKenzie's Bay All Stars def. Balmain "A" 7-2 Scorers B. Duck 2, D. Hofbauer 1, G. Stein 1, S. Treble 1, P. O'Brien 1, B. Leach 1.

Water Polo: McKenzie's Bay All Stars 6 def. Eastwood 0. All Stars — G Sellars 3, R. Leitch 2, E. Kritzler 1

MacKenzies Bay All Stars Water Polo: MacKenzies Bay d Balmain "B" 5-1 Chris Hickman 4, Ernie Kritzler 1.

Water Polo: McKenzie's Bay All Stars def Parramatta 5-3 Scorers Chris Hickman 3, Ernie Kritzler 1, Lunkley Head 1.

2 (D McGill, W Muir), MacKenzie's Bay 7 (H Wilson, S Dritzler 2, C Brutt, G Selless, D Hovfauer) b Balmain a 2 (L Kelly, C Mara).

who was still in Long Bay Gaol. With so much money and no kids to sponsor, the club took a five star end of year trip to the snow. Frenchie was eventually paroled and played the next season.

During this season, the club played a match at Ashfield Pool and we were leading by four goals, when another NSW Water Polo official decided that our game had to be abandoned, as games were running late. After everyone had travelled such a long way, I went ballistic (to put it mildly) and was accused of 'overly aggressive behaviour' towards this small, petty-minded official. He threatened me with a life suspension at poolside, and I compassionately offered to end my life. The match was abandoned however, and I was handed my second life ban, without even a chance to appear at the Judiciary.

However, I later appealed and was re-instated for the second time. Next, the Association made changes to the constitution and then refused to give clubs copies of the new rules. Therefore, despite all good intentions, it was no surprise that we committed some understandable minor breaches. At that point, the Association came to the realisation that Monterey WPC was actually the All-Stars in drag, so under the new rules the Association began sending us fines. For our part we kept playing, but not paying. Huge fines like $4, $4, $8, $10 and $5 kept pouring in, which came to the colossal total of $31. But the owners remained aloof, and ignored them for the insignificant irrelevant small-minded petty people that they were.

Unfortunately, 1979 saw the start of the end. We recruited well and had won five of our first seven matches. And as per our open-door policy, we welcomed all players who lived by our code of pleasing the thousands of thrill starved spectators, crying out to watch quality water polo. One, amongst many other dark and miserable nights at Balmain... ex-Bronte, NSW and Queensland State team player Billy Parsons, accidentally fell into the pool, and so played for us, as he was already wet... and he just happened to score a few goals in the process!

Sadly, some low life creep, hiding in the shadows at Balmain like a slimy disease on a wall... complained. The Association went into overdrive and banned poor Bill for life, suspended me for three games and fined the club $50. But just four-weeks later, Billy arrived at the Australian Championships and played every game for Queensland. The Association said nothing, so life suspensions were meaningless back then and rarely if ever enforced.

By now, our debt at the Association had climbed to a staggering $81. To make matters worse, club secretary Peter 'Finch' flew the coup, taking all the remaining club funds with him. We regrettably advised the Association that we were unable to pay the fine. Luckily however, club owners Chris Hickman and myself advised that we were going to Japan and promised to track down Peter Finch, but it proved impossible to find Finch in Tokyo.

Then, our pride and long standing tradition of fair play was totally destroyed when on the 23rd April 1979, the Association in their state of total confusion and ineptness, chose to remove all our season points, suspend the club and ban every player for life, due to the outstanding fine.

To summarize, the owners only mission was to play and enjoy water polo. The injustice shown by the Association was just a quest for a power trip and to bully young boys. Their wilful and unjustified behaviour should be a lesson to all future administrators that you need to be dedicated and give support to all players in the competition, not just your favourites. Sadly, we encountered an era when the administration was totally bent, and run by a bunch of miserable paper-pushers. Few were actually human beings!

These Association boffins destroyed the dreams of 27 healthy young water polo players. They managed to ban Andy Doyle twice in one lifetime, and for life at the same time (?). They banned a player who only ever lived under an alias, for life. They banned Mrs. Judy Buckley, an exceptionally talented player, from playing any men's water polo for life. They banned a loaf of bread named 'Berliner Swartzenbrot' for life. And worst of all, despite happily corresponding with two dogs and then a bird for years, and receiving some very confusing messages in return... they banned Mr. Peter Finch (a bird) and

▲ Newspaper results for McKenzie's Bay Water Polo Club. ▼ Letter of support from Keith Doyle (MP), member for Vaucluse, who was Patron of the Monterey Water Polo Club, which was addressed to club secretary, Peter 'Finch'.

PARLIAMENT OF NEW SOUTH WALES
LEGISLATIVE ASSEMBLY

Parliament House, Sydney, 2000
Tel. 230 2111.

14th August, 1978.

Mr. Peter Finch,
Secretary,
Monterey Amateur Water Polo
  Association,
12 Randwick Street,
RANDWICK, N.S.W., 2031.

Dear Mr. Finch,

I was delighted to hear that at the last Annual General Meeting of your Club I was again unanimously elected Patron.

I am aware of the great sense of fair play which pervades your Club. The contribution such clubs as yours make to the life of amateur sport in this State should be appreciated by all sport loving Australians.

Thank you again for the privilege of associating my name with such a fine body of young men as carry the banner of Monterey. I wish you every success in your sporting endeavour this season.

Sincerely,

Keith R. Doyle, M.P.
Member for Vaucluse

- -

PLEASE SEVER HERE

P.S. Should any of your "fine body of young men" incur the wrath of the constabulary, my Parliamentary number if 230 2111.

▲ *The All Stars were masters of psychological warfare, and opponents were immediately demoralised by the site of their front & back T-shirt clad warriors.*

Mr. Jim Clarke (a dog), for life! Bill Hickman, also a dog, was the only member of the club that was spared a life suspension.

The days of Ernie's All Stars playing to the joyous raptures of booked-out crowds were officially over. The dark side had won out, and 27 lives lay shattered. In anger, most of the All Stars retired from playing water polo. Both myself and Chris Hickman were badly scarred by the journey, with Hicko burning his water polo ball in protest. By this stage however, there had been a coup at the Association and the old decrepit network of fools, liars and cheats was deposed. The new administration was a breath of fresh air, but it came just too late to save the All Stars.

On the 27th June 1980, I was again reinstated after my third life suspension and played on until 1985, winning another premiership with Tamarama Water Polo Club. Sadly, injury interrupted my brilliant resurgence and I finally retired from the game a couple of years later."

Such is life.
Ernie Kritzler

Luncheon for Don Sarkies on his 85th Birthday at Randwick in 2018.

From left: Ian Jeffers*, Jon Kirkwood*, Don Sarkies*, Dave Malone*, Phil Brand (behind), Roy Woodhouse, Tracy Rockwell*, John Cason, Rolly Flesch*, Chris Simpson*, Dave Bullock*, Frank O'Brien. [* ex-Members of Bronte WPC]

Northbridge WPC

Northbridge Baths were officially opened on 8th November 1924, and the Northbridge Amateur Swimming Club was formed just over two months later. By season 1926/27 a water polo team entered the NSWASA competition and did so, on and off up until the year 2000.

Following a year off, Northbridge re-joined the NSWAWPA competition with two grades in Division II (2nd Grade and 3rd Grade) for the 1971/72 season, and won a number of premierships. A group of ex-Bronte players later joined Northbridge including... Jon Kirkwood, Ian Leffers, Dave Malone, Ray Mendels, Graham Robinson, Don Sarkies, Chris Simpson and others.

"Northbridge were not associated as a club/team with Manly, other than as a 'retirement village'. Indeed we were arch rivals until at least the late 1970's!"

Phil Brand, Sept 2020

Summary

For all its influence and strength, Bronte never had a clubhouse or a physical home, the club existed for most of its life in the homes and on the kitchen tables of its members. Club records were never continually kept, the club was simply a collection of motivated individuals, who worked together to foster and develop the membership, which in turn produced a truly great club.

When the end came in 1975, no one was really able to put their finger on the cause of Bronte's downfall, as there was no one single reason that brought about the demise of this great club. Rather it was a series of small, seemingly insignificant

▲ *TOP: Painting of Northbridge Baths, training venue for Northbridge Water Polo Club (artist unknown). ABOVE: NSWWPI Championship Medal for Northbridge Water Polo Club.*

NORTHBRIDGE AWPC
1994 - World Masters Games - Brisbane
Back row (from left): David Boylson, Frank O'Brien, Jon Kirkwood, Ian Neilly, Ian Leffers. Seated: Richard Thomas, Don Sarkies, Graham Robinson, Phil Brand, Raphael Mendels, John Pagden. Photo - Don Sarkies.

NORTHBRIDGE AWPC - RESULTS 1971 to 1976

REGISTRAR'S REPORT
SECOND DIVISION 1971-1972

Second Grade

	Win	Lose	Draw	Disq. or Forfeit	For	Against	Points
LIVERPOOL	11	3	—	—	64	30	36
BALMAIN "B"	10	3	1	—	50	29	35
NORTHBRIDGE	8	4	2	—	55	30	32
PENRITH	6	6	2	—	41	32	28
CLOVELLY ESKIMOS	6	5	2	1	41	47	27
N.S.W. MACCABI	5	7	2	—	28	34	26
NORTH SYDNEY	5	9	—	—	28	49	24
BONDI DOLPHINS	—	13	1	—	11	77	15

Semi-Finals: Northbridge v. Penrith.
Liverpool 4 v. Balmain "B" 5.
Final: Liverpool 9 v. Northbridge 5.
Grand Final: Liverpool 8 v. Balmain "B" 4.
Premiers: Liverpool.

SECOND DIVISION

Third Grade

	Win	Lose	Draw	Disq. or Forfeit	For	Against	Points
DRUMMOYNE	9	1	2	—	54	20	32
NORTH SYDNEY	8	4	—	—	45	30	28
BALMAIN "B"	7	3	2	—	44	30	28
NORTHBRIDGE	5	3	4	—	38	29	26
PENRITH	5	6	1	—	37	22	23
BONDI DOLPHINS	2	10	—	—	12	71	16
N.S.W. MACCABI	1	9	1	1	20	48	14

Semi-Finals: Balmain "B" v. Northbridge.
Drummoyne 4 v. North Sydney 3.
Final: North Sydney v.
Grand Final: Drummoyne 4 v. North Sydney 2.
Premiers: Drummoyne.

REGISTRAR'S REPORT
SECOND DIVISION 1972-1973

SECOND GRADE

Second Division

	Played	Won	Lost	Disq. or Dr. Forft.	Goals for	ag.	Points
LIVERPOOL	14	10	1	3	66	23	37
BALMAIN	14	8	1	5	62	26	35
PENRITH	14	8	4	2	56	42	32
DRUMMOYNE	14	6	3	5	53	36	31
SYDNEY UNIVERSITY	14	7	5	2	44	41	30
NORTHBRIDGE	14	4	8	2	43	53	24
NORTH SYDNEY	14	2	11	1	29	68	19
N.S.W. MACCABI	14	—	12	2	20	85	16

SEMI-FINALS: Penrith 9 — Drummoyne 8; Balmain 6 — Liverpool 4.
FINAL: Liverpool 9 — Penrith 3.
GRAND FINAL: Balmain 6 — Liverpool 5.
PREMIERS: Balmain.

THIRD DIVISION — 1973-1974
FIRST GRADE

	Played	Won	Lost	Dr.	Dis.	Points
NORTHBRIDGE	12	10	1	1	—	21
BLACKTOWN	12	10	1	1	—	21
AVALON-BILGOLA	12	6	6	0	—	12
BALMAIN	12	5	6	1	—	11
ALL STARS	12	4	7	1	—	9
HOMEBUSH	12	3	9	0	—	6
RYDE	12	1	9	2	—	4

1st SEMI-FINAL: Avalon-Bilgola 3 — Balmain 2
2nd SEMI-FINAL: Northbridge 10 — Blacktown 8
FINAL: Blacktown 12 — Avalon-Bilgola 11
GRAND-FINAL: Northbridge 7 — Blacktown 6

FIRST DIVISION, 1974/75
4th GRADE

	P.	W.	D.	L.	F/D	Goals For	A.	Pts.
BALMAIN	14	14	—	—	—	68	12	28
CRONULLA-SUTHERLAND	14	11	—	3	—	60	19	22
NORTHBRIDGE	14	9	1	4	—	62	22	19
UNIVERSITIES	14	7	2	5	—	42	27	16
LIVERPOOL	14	4	—	10	—	34	54	8
WESTERN SUBURBS	14	3	2	9	—	19	42	8
MANLY	14	4	—	10	—	33	42	8
MASADA	14	1	1	12	—	7	88	3

1st Semi Final: Universities 6, Northbridge 5
2nd Semi Final: Cronulla-Sutherland 5, Balmain 4
Final: Balmain 8, Universities 1
Grand Final: Balmain 5, Cronulla-Sutherland 2
Premiers: Balmain

METROPOLITAN PREMIERSHIP COMPETITION, 1975/76
"A" DIVISION
FOURTH GRADE

	P.	W.	L.	D.	F/D	Goals For	A.	Pts.
Balmain	14	11	1	2	—	77	16	38
Cronulla	14	9	1	1	–/3	60	34	30
Liverpool	14	5	1	1	–/5	22	83	16
Manly	14	4	6	1	–/3	39	64	20
Masada	14	3	3	1	1/6	16	43	14
Northbridge	14	7	5	2	—	49	32	30
Universities	14	8	3	2	–/1	56	33	31
Western Suburbs	14	2	8	4	—	34	48	22

1st Semi Final: Cronulla 5, Northbridge 1
2nd Semi Final: Balmain 5, Universities 2
Final: Universities 2, Cronulla 1
Grand Final: Balmain 8, Universities 5
Premiers: Balmain

events that combined to deplete its strength, and which in the end sounded the death knell.

Some, but not all of the blows Bronte suffered were... Dick Thornett was banned by NSWASA in 1963; the stalwarts like John Thornett, Dick See etc. began to retire; there was never a clubhouse, a physical link for members to congregate around; the change to Watsons Bay in 1970 was just too far for most members; a series of 1st graders transferred out of the club without replacement; a number of 2nd and 3rd graders transferred to other clubs without replacement; and the lack of new members as foreseen by Billy MacCarthy, didn't fill the team losses. While Graeme Samuels tried his best, without sufficient new and competent players, by 1973/74 the club was doomed.

However, the Bronte diaspora lived on and has had a significant affect on Australian water polo. Phil Bower and Les Kay were responsible for capturing over 35 national titles, Bob Cope was responsible for re-energising the Universities Club and developed water polo at Townsville, Billy Parsons and Lunky heavily influenced the Magyars Club and water polo in Queensland, Alex Kafka developed the Sunshine Coast Club, and even I myself influenced the sport at the University of Oregon in the late 70's and 80's. These and many other Bronte players loved the game so much, and how it brought people together that they felt compelled to spread its character building qualities.

From the founders of this great club right through to those who were there at the end, all felt an immense pride at having been involved with the legendary Bronte Water Polo Club.

▲ Don Sarkies began his water polo career in the late 1950's, and kept goal until 2015, when he was almost 80... a fantastic record.

BRONTE AMATEUR WATI

Back row (*from left*): Frank O'Brien, Chris Hickman, Cheryl Hickman, Danny Hofbauer, Dennis Morgan, Michael Hickman, Wal Northcott, Steve Kritzler, John De Leon, Ernie Kritzler, Peter Bell, Steve Bell, Greg Bell, Jon Kirkwood.

4th row: Lorraine Power (*obscured*), Brian Hallinan, Ross Selleck, Warren Hurt, Dawn Hurt (*front*), Barry Owens, Belinda MacLennan, Jeannie MacLennan, Dawn MacLennan, Pam Flesch (*nee Hedger, obscured*), **Laurel Fisher** (*nee Cannot*), **Margaret Wilby**, Karen Copas (*nee Trewhella*), **Maree Eccleston** (*nee Robinson*), **Liz Moses** (*nee Wilby*), Ian Leffers, Graeme Samuel.

3rd row: John Webber, John Power, Ray Mendels, Lesley MacLennan, Dave Bullock, Peter Newton, Robin Croll, Tom Folden, John Thornett, Peter Folden, Rolly Flesch, Les Kay, Graham Robinson, John Keane, Ron Mendelson, Ray Gallagher, Gus Nicholson.

Chapter 9
THE REUNIONS

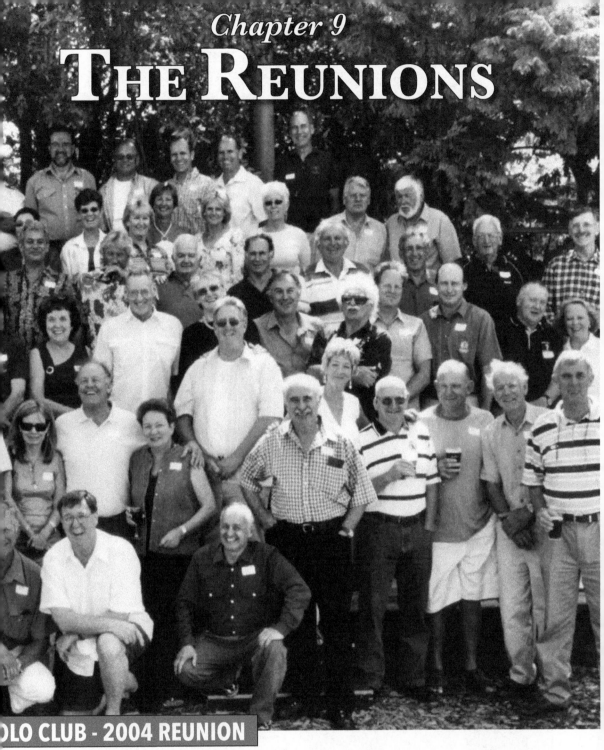

...OLO CLUB - 2004 REUNION

2nd row: Kevin Ashley, Fred Meyer, Pat McGrath (*front*), Dick See, June See, Tracy Rockwell (*front*), Betty Burton, Roy Burton, Jack Brownjohn, Ken Davidson, Don Sarkies, Robin Lehane, Brian Ellison, Margaret Angus, Barry Angus (*front*), Phil Bower, Nino Sydney, Gary Grant, Danny Sydney, David Hallinan, Sue Bell (*nee Keeble*).

Front row: Ken Emerton (*back obscured*), Ann Ellison (*front*), Bob Keyes (*back obscured*), Sue Johnson (*middle obscured*), _____ (*front*), Peter Johnson (*back*), Robyn McGrath (*front*), Julie Keyes, Jan Vesper, Charlie Hitchings, Ray Timewell, Lyn Timewell, Dick Thornett (*back*), Bill Parsons, Louise See, Robert See, Ann Owens, Bill McCarthy, Pauline Walker (*back*), Bill Jones, John Walker, Ken Thornett, Peter Waterman.

Kneeling: Paul Duggan, Warren Riley, Brian Hamill, Terry Clark (*Lunky*), Robbie Vadas.

Present (*not in photo*):   Brian Hutchings, Doug Laing, Shirley Mills, Sue Mills, Eric Fitzgerald, & Viv Thornett.

◀The 2004 Bronte AWPC Reunion. Top: Brian Hallinan, David Hallinan, Terry Clark, Billy McCarthy.

◀Bronte Goalkeepers (Back row): Don Sarkies, Ken Thornett, John Power, Gus Nicholson, Peter Waterman, Brian Ellison. (Front row): John Thornett, Terry Clark, Billy McCarthy, Dave Bullock.

◀One of the originals, Jack Brownjohn & Wally Northcott.

►The 2004
Bronte AWPC
Reunion with Ian
Leffers, Graeme
Samuel, Nino
Sydney.

►Bronte 3rd
Grade (back row):
Chris Hickman,
Danny Hofbauer,
Dennis Morgan;
(front row): John
Keane, Ross
Selleck, Billy
McCarthy, Steve
Kritzler.

►Graeme
Samuel, Billy
Parsons, Graham
Robinson.

BRONTE AMATEUR WATER POLO CLUB - 2004 REUNION

Back row (from left): Frank O'Brien, Chris Hickman, Cheryl Hickman, Danny Hofbauer, Dennis Morgan, Michael Hickman, Wal Northcott, Steve Kritzler, John De Leon, Ernie Kritzler, Peter Bell, Steve Bell, Greg Bell, Jon Kirkwood. **4th row:** Lorraine Power *(obscured)*, Brian Hallinan, Ross Sellick, Warren Hurt, Dawn Hurt *(front)*, Barry Owens, Belinda Maclennan, Jeannie Maclennan, Dawn Maclennan, Pam Flesch *(nee Hedger, obscured)*, Laurel Fisher *(nee Cannot)*, Margaret Wilby, Karen Copas *(nee Trewhella)*, Maree Eccleston *(nee Robinson)*, Liz Moses *(nee Wilby)*, Ian Leffers, Graeme Samuel. **3rd row:** John Weber, John Power, Ray Mendels, Lesley MacLennan, Dave Bullock, Peter Newton, Robin Croll, Tom Folden, Peter Folden, John Thornett, Rolly Flesch, Les Kay, Graham Robinson, John Keane, Ron Mendelson, Ray Gallagher, Gus Nicholson. **2nd row:** Kevin Ashley, Fred Meyer, Pat McGrath *(front)*, Dick See, June See, Tracy Rockwell *(front)*, Betty Burton, Roy Burton, Jack Brownjohn, Ken Davidson, Don Sarkies, Robin Lehane, Brian Ellison, Margaret Angus, Barry Angus *(front)*, Phil Bower, Nino Sydney, Gary Grant, Danny Sydney, David Hallinan, Sue Bell *(nee Keeble)*. **Front row:** Ken Emerton *(back obscured)*, Ann Ellison *(front)*, Bob Keyes *(back obscured)*, Sue Johnson *(middle obscured)*, Barry Angus *(front)*, Peter Johnson *(back)*, Robyn McGrath *(front)*, Julie Keyes, Jan Vesper, Charlie Hitchings, Ray Timewell, Lyn Timewell, Dick Thornett *(back)*, Bill Parsons, Louise See, Robert See, Ann Owens, Bill McCarthy, Pauline Walker *(back)*, Bill Jones, John Walker, Ken Thornett, Peter Waterman. **Kneeling:** Paul Duggan, Warren Riley, Brian Hamill, Terry Clark *(Lunky)*, Robbie Vadas. **Present** *(but not in photo)*: Brian Hutchings, Doug Laing, Shirley Mills, Sue Mills, Eric Fitzgerald, & Viv Thornett.

Don Sarkies – 2018 Book Launch

"Roy Burton worked in maintenance at Sydney University. He played first grade in the mid 50s and would be In his 80s by now. Greg Coulson was a second and third grade fullback at Randwick RFC. I played many games with him. Stan Sparrow was also a first and second grade Randwick player who accompanied Ken Thornett to the UK where Ken switched to League and made his mark. Ken had previously played full back at Randwick and was a great polo goalie who was superseded by Don Sarkies. Mick Downey was an officer in the army who I last saw playing rugby in Townsville. I think he returned to West Australia."

"I started with Bronte in1955 at 13, continuing until about 1960 when I left to start the now prosperous University club. I stopped playing about 55 years later. The most unusual team I played with was the Flounders, a group of University of Michigan male professors, alumni and friends who have played three times a week, Monday, Wednesday and Friday at 12:00 for 30 minutes since 1925 followed by a light lunch, even on holidays. They only wear polo caps but no togs! No one keeps score and the object is to stuff the polo ball into the large gutter whilst the defending team wrestles and pushes the attacking team off the wall. I spent six delightful months there in the late 70s and they continue their unusual polo game today."

Bob Cope, Oct 2020

Candid Photos of Members

▲A collection of NSW State representatives and old Bronte teammates at the memorial service for Les Kay in 2019. From left: Peter Folden, Graeme Samuel, Rolly Flesch, Dave Bullock, Phil Bower and Tracy Rockwell. ◄ABOVE: Old Bronte club mates meet up for a coffee and chat with Tracy Rockwell, Chris Simpson, Don Sarkies and Rolly Flesch. BELOW: Catching up with their Bronte teammates are (from left): Maree Robinson, Rhonda Thompson, Laurel Cannot, Margaret Wilby and Jenny Miley. ▼ The Trewhella sisters, Lyn & Karen unexpectedly met Bob Rockwell in Hong Kong in 1976 and took a photo to prove it!

▲Spanning virtually the entire history of Bronte Water Polo Club between them are ex-NSW reps Tracy Rockwell, Brian Ellison and Rolly Flesch. ▶ABOVE: Catching up at the 'Office', otherwise known as Tamarama Surf Club in 2018 are Rolly Flesch, Tracy Rockwell and Peter O'Hara. BELOW: The Bronte Ladies 1st Grade premiers of 1974 (from left): Jenny Miley, Rhonda Thompson, Laurel Cannot, Margaret Wilby and Maree Robinson. ▼ Photograph of Chris 'Kipper' Simpson, who joined Bronte from Canberra Water Polo Club in 1968.

From top left by column: Peter 'Rocky' Johnson, John Thornett and Ken Thornett in later years. John Cotterill (Bondolphins), John 'Fiji' McLure & Tracy Rockwell at the Biathlon of Sydney, 1989. Ken Thornett and Pauline Walker at the Bronte AWPC 2004 Reunion. The author, Peter 'Yogi' Yaeger of Bondi Club & Rolly Flesch at the 'Office'. Lunky and The Rat shooting the breeze in downtown Woombye in 2020....mates for 73 years and still going strong. Reunion of NSW State Team players... Peter Folden (Bronte), Tracy Rockwell (Bronte & Universities), Chris Robinson (Universities) & Rolly Flesch (Bronte). The author catching with Sarkies at Bondi Junction 2017. The author and John 'Fiji' McLure in 2018.

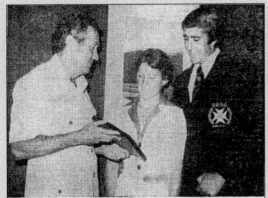

Air New Zealand Queensland sales manager Mr Jack Ward (left), shows Jane Lutvey (centre), captain of the Queensland womens water polo team, and Bill Parson, captain of the mens team, the Air New Zealand Shield for competition between Queensland and New Zealand. Queensland are holders of the shield.

Water polo team leaves

The Queensland men's water polo teams leave Brisbane on Sunday for New Zealand to play a three test series against the New Zealand national team.

Combined with the boys' under 18, and women teams they will compete with the New Zealand national sides for the Air New Zealand Shield won fo

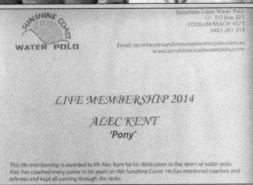

LIFE MEMBERSHIP 2014

ALEC KENT

'Pony'

This life membership is awarded to Mr Alec Kent for his dedication to the sport of water polo. Alec has coached every junior in his years on the Sunshine Coast. He has mentored coaches and referees and kept all coming through the ranks.

From top left by column: Billy Parsons in the news, 1977. The author and Rolly Flesch at the 'Office', 2018. Rolly Flesch and Chris Robinson (Universities) at Tamarama. The Bronte diaspora spread far and wide... with ex-Bronte club man Alex [Kent] Kasco's contribution on the Sunshine Coast being recognised with LIFE MEMBERSHIP in 2014. Dave Malone and Robbo training at Watsons Bay, 1974. The author, Rolly and friends, 2018. The author and long time buddy, Chris Robinson (Universities) at the cricket, 2019. Nothing changes at Bronte, taken 1960!

APPENDIX

Bronte Amateur Water Polo Club Roster 1943-1975

Amer, John
Aisbett, Paul
Anderson, Alan
Ashley, Kevin ✚
Baldock, Ted[J]
Baret, Ken ✚
Barta, Rayner (g)[J]
Barta, Robbie ✚
Barta, Yvette
Bell, Greg
Bell, Peter
Bell, Steve
Boniface, John
Boswarva, Roger
Bower, Phil (g)[J]
Brownjohn, Jack ✚
Bullock, Dave (g)[N]
Burgess, Christine
Burton, Roy
Campbell, Jack ✚
Campbell, Joyce ✚
Cannot, Joy
Cannot, Laurel
Cawood, Gary
Chamberlain, Cathy
Chapman, Karen
Chapman, Rod ✚
Cheeseman, Jenny
Clark, Terry 'Lunky'
Cleland, A.
Copas, John
Cope, Bob
Connery, Colleen
Coulson, Greg
Cox, Greg
Cronk, Lorraine
Davidson, Ken
Davis, Lee
Dawson, R.
De Groot, Ron[N]
De Leon, John
Donohue, John
Doolan, Peter ✚
Downey, Mick
Duggan, Billy

Duggan, Paul
Drewett, Dara
Edwards, Warren
Ellison, Brian (g)[N]
Emerton, Ken
Falson, Roy ✚
FitzPatrick, Brian
FitzPatrick, Kevin
Flesch, Rolly[N]
Flower, Rhonda
Folden, Eric ✚
Folden, Giselle ✚
Folden, Peter[N]
Folden, Tom
Foster, Robert
Gahagan, John[N]
Gilmore, Jack
Glenn, George
Gooley, Bill
Gooley, Brett[J]
Graham, Debbie
Grant, Gary[J]
Grills, Lorraine[N] ✚
Gulyas, George
Hallinan, Brian
Hallinan, Dave
Hamilton-Brown, John
Hanson, Ron ✚
Havas, John
Hedger, Pam
Hickman, Chris
Hickman, Michael
Hillier, Bob
Hitchings, Charles ✚
Hofbauer, Danny
Hunter, Steven
Hurt, Warren
Hutchins, Mo
Jobbins, Mick
Johnson, Peter ✚
Kasco, Alex
Kay, Les[N] ✚
Keane, John
Kerr, Lance
Keyes, Bob

Kirkwood, Jon
Kritzler, Ernie
Kritzler, Steve
Leffers, Ian
Mandelson, Ron
Mason, Pat
Maxwell, Joanne
Mayer, Fred ✚
MacLennan, Dunc ✚
McAdam, Robert
McCarthy, Billy (g)
McFarlane, Col
McGrath, Pat ✚
McGrath, Vic[N] ✚
McLure, John 'Fiji' (g)
Messider, Peter (UK)
Miley, Jenny
Miller, Glenda
Mills, Ken ✚
Morgan, Dennis
Murtagh, Michael
Northcott, Wal
O'Hara, Peter[J]
O'Keefe, Greg
Obey, Arthur ✚
Owens, Barry
Owens, Ken[N] ✚
Parsons, Bill[N]
Parsons, Jeff
Pearce, Karen
Power, John
Prentice, P.
Primo, Peter
Quinlan, Gary
Quinlan, John
Reilly, Wayne
Riley, Warren
Robinson, Graham
Robinson, Maree[N]
Rockwell, Tracy[NJ]
Roden, Jerry
Ryan, Terry
Salt, George
Samuel, Graeme[ON]
Sarkies, Don (g)[N]

Scandrett, Carol
See, Dick[N] ✚
See, Robert
Selleck, Bruce
Selleck, Ross
Simpson, Chris
Smith, Colin
Smith, Greg
Solomon, John
Sparrow, Stan
Stapleton, Dave
Stapleton, John
Steer, Dave
Stubbs, Jeff (g)
Thomas, Dave ✚
Thompson, Rhonda
Thornett, Dick[ON] ✚
Thornett, John[N] ✚
Thornett, Ken (g) ✚
Timewell, Ray
Traynor, Garth
Trewhella, Karen (g)[N]
Trewhella, Lyn[N]
Trewhella, Mrs Gloria
Vadas, Bert 'Momie'[N] ✚
Vadas, Robbie
Vegg, Irwin (USA) ✚
Walker, John
Walker, Kevin ✚
Ward, Joe (g)
Wardrop, John (g)
Waterman, Peter[N]
Watson, Lindsay
Webb, Alan
Webber, John ✚
Wiseman, Don
Wilby, Liz
Wilby, Margaret[N]
Williams, Chris
Winters, Loueen
Zuppan, A.

O *Olympian*
N *NSW Rep*
J *NSW Jr. Rep*
✚ *Passed On*

NB: Apologies to anyone that has been omitted from this roster.

Bronte Amateur Water Polo Club Team Records

Summary of Participation in NSWAPWA Competitions

Grades	# Teams Entered	# Premier-ships	# Runners Up	# Finals	# Semi-Finals	# Teams In Top 4	% Grand-Finals	% Premier-ships	% Years In Top 4
Mens 1st	23	5	4	6	2	17 of 23	39%	22%	74%
Mens 2nd	22	4	6	6	3	19 of 22	45%	18%	86%
Mens 3rd	28	4	3	7	3	17 of 28	25%	14%	61%
Ladies	12	1	3	0	1	5 of 12	42%	8%	42%
Overall	85	14	16	19	9	58 of 85	35%	17%	68%

Annual Results of Entries in NSWAPWA Competitions

Season	NSW Reps Men/Ladies/Jnr	Bronte AWPC Entries in NSWAPWA Competitions	Mens Division I 1st	2nd	3rd	4th	Mens Division II 1st	2nd	3rd	Ladies 1st	2nd
1943/44	No Rep Teams	Inaugural entry...	1								
1944/45	No Rep Teams	Bronte contested...	1								
1945/46	0	Bronte contested... ?	1								
1946/47	0	Bronte contested... ?	1								
1947/48	N/A	No Bronte teams	-								
1948/49	N/A	No Bronte teams	-								
1949/50	N/A	No Bronte teams	-								
1950/51	N/A	No Bronte teams	-								
1951/52	0	Bronte re-entered & contested...			1						
1952/53	0	Bronte contested...		1R		1					
1953/54	2	Bronte contested...	1R	-	1						
1954/55	2	Bronte contested...	1R	1F	2						
1955/56	2	Bronte contested...	2	1	2S						
1956/57	1	Bronte contested...	1S	1	1						
1957/58	2	Bronte contested...	1	-	1						
1958/59	2	NSWAWPA Club Champions	1P	-	2R						
1959/60	4	Bronte contested...	1P	2S	-						
1960/61	4	NSWAWPA Club Champions	1P	1F	1P						
1961/62	2	NSWAWPA Club Champions	1P	1R	2P						
1962/63	2	NSWAWPA Club Champions	1F	2P	1F						
1963/64	4	Bronte contested...	2F	1F	1S					1	
1964/65	3	Bronte contested...	1F	1R	2F					1	
1965/66	1	NSWAWPA Club Champions	1F	1R	1R	Jr					
1966/67	2	Bronte contested...	1	1P	1R						
1967/68	2 / 1 / 0	Bronte contested...	1R	1P	2P				1F	1R	
1968/69	2 / 1 / 0	Bronte contested...	1F	1R	1F	1	1			1	
1969/70	2 / 0 / 1	Bronte contested...	1R	1P	1F	1S				1	
1970/71	2 / 0 / 3	Bronte contested...	1P	1R	1F	1F				1S	
1971/72	3 / 0 / 0	Bronte contested...	1F	1	1F	1			1	1	
1972/73	3 / 2 / 3	Bronte contested...	1S	1F	1S	1				1R	1F
1973/74	3 / 3 / 1	Bronte contested...	1	1	1	1				1P	
1974/75	2 / 4 / 1	Bronte contested...Final entry...	1	1	1					1R	

NOTE: P = Premiers; R = Runners-up; F = Finalists; S = Semi-finalists; and the numbers indicate the number of teams entered in each Grade.

Roll of Honour

Dave Bullock (g)

NSW Rep. - 1969 with St George after leaving Bronte.

Ron De Groot

NSW Rep. - 1965, 1966, 1967, 1968 with Bondi before joining Bronte.

Brian Ellison (g)

NSW Rep. - 1964

Rolly Flesch

NSW Rep. - 1965, 1967 & 1972
NSW 1st Grade Premiership - 1971

Peter Folden

*NSW Rep. - 1967, 68, 69, **70, 71,** 72,*
***73, 74,** and in **1975** with Masada after leaving Bronte.*
5 National Championships
NSW 1st Grade Premiership - 1971

John Gahagan

NSW Rep. - 1969

Lorraine Grills

NSW Ladies Rep. - 1968

Vic McGrath

Olympic Games - 1960 (reserve)
*NSW Rep. - **1957**(w), 58, 60, 61, 63, 64, 65 (c/coach)*
NSW 1st Grade Premierships - 1959, 60, 61 & 62

Ken Owens

*NSW Rep. - 1961 & **1962***
1 National Championship

Bill Parsons

NSW Rep. - 1968
QLD Rep. - 1973, 74, 76, 77, 78
NSW 1st Grade Premiership - 1971
QLD 1st Grade Premiership - 1973

Maree Robinson

*NSW Ladies Rep. - **1974***
1 National Championship
NSW 1st Grade Premiership - 1974

Tracy Rockwell

NSW Rep. - 1976 with Universities after leaving Bronte.
Aust Club Championship -1977
NSW 1st Grade Premiership - 1977

Roll of Honour

Graeme Samuel
Olympic Games - 1964 & 1968
Aust Tours - 1965 & 1967
WA Rep. - 62, 63, 64, 65, 67, 68
NSW Rep. - 70, 71, 72, 73, 74, 75
6 National Championships
WA 1st Grade Premierships - 63, 64, 68
NSW 1st Grade Premiership - 1971

Don Sarkies (g)
NSW Rep. - 61, 62, 63, 64, 65, 66
1 National Championship
NSW 1st Grade Premierships - 1960,
1961, 1962 & 1971

Dick See
NSW Rep. - 1956
NSW 1st Grade Premierships - 1959,
1960, 1962 & 1971

Dick Thornett
Olympic Games - 1960
NSW Rep. -1958, 59, 60, 61
NSW 1st Grade Premierships - 1959,
1960, 1961 & 1962
Triple Australian Representative

John Thornett
NSW Rep. - 1954, 55, 59 & 60
NSW 1st Grade Premierships - 1959,
1960, 1961 & 1962

Karen Trewhella (g)
NSW Ladies Rep. - 1975
1 National Championship
NSW 1st Grade Premiership - 1974

Lyn Trewhella
NSW Ladies Rep. - 1973, 1974, 1975
2 National Championships
NSW 1st Grade Premiership - 1974

Bert Vadas
Played with MTK Budapest
NSW Rep. - 1954, 1955 & 1956
NSW 1st Grade Premierships - 1959,
1960 &1961.

Peter Waterman (g)
NSW Rep. - 1963 & 1967 with Bondi
before joining Bronte.

Margaret Wilby
NSW Ladies Rep. - 1974, 1975 and
in 1976 with Maroubra Seals
2 National Championships
NSW 1st Grade Premiership - 1974

Phil Bower (Coach)
Spending his formative years with
Bronte, Phil went on to successfully coach
numerous NSW State teams.
19 National Championships

Les Kay (Coach)
Spending his formative years with
Bronte, Les went on to successfully
coach numerous NSW State teams.
15 National Championships

Chapter 1

1. *Oz Beaches (2020, August 24). 'Bronte Beach, a locals and tourists favourite in Sydney's eastern suburbs.' Available at... https://www.ozbeaches.com.au/blogs/beaches/bronte-beach-a-favourite-of-locals-and-tourists-in-sydneys-eastern-suburbs.*

2. *Waverley Library, (undated). Bronte Baths: A History [Fact Sheet].*

3. *NSWAWPA, (1941). Annual Report & Balance Sheet 1940/41.*

4. *NSWAWPA, (1942). Annual Report & Balance Sheet 1941/42.*

5. *NSWAWPA, (1943). Annual Report & Balance Sheet 1942/43.*

Chapter 2

1. *NSWAWPA, (1944). Annual Report & Balance Sheet 1943/44.*

2. *NSWAWPA, (1945). Annual Report & Balance Sheet 1944/45.*

3. *NSWAWPA, (1946). Annual Report & Balance Sheet 1945/46.*

4. *NSWAWPA, (1947). Annual Report & Balance Sheet 1946/47.*

5. *NSWAWPA, (1948). Annual Report & Balance Sheet 1947/48.*

6. *NSWAWPA, (1949). Annual Report & Balance Sheet 1948/49.*

7. *NSWAWPA, (1950). Annual Report & Balance Sheet 1949/50.*

8. *NSWAWPA, (1951). Annual Report & Balance Sheet 1950/51.*

9. *Charles, Oscar 1925-2008 (Interviewee), (2007). 'Oscar (Csuvic) Charles interviewed by Tracy Rockwell for Water Polo Australia.' Transcribed on 9 August 2007, at Woollahra, N.S.W.*

10. *Rockwell, Tracy (2009). Water Warriors: Chronicle of Australian Water Polo, Pegasus Publishing, Sydney.*

11. *Vadas, Robbie 1946- (Interviewee), (2019). 'Robbie Vadas interviewed by Tracy Rockwell for Water Polo Australia.' Transcribed on 19 March 2019, at Newtown, N.S.W.*

Chapter 3

1. *Thornett, John, 1935-2019 (Interviewee), (2008). 'John Thornett interviewed by Ian Warden for the Sport oral history project [sound recording].'Recorded on 3 July 2008, in Cowra, N.S.W. [Libraries Australia ID 43253205].*

2. *NSWAWPA, (1952). Annual Report & Balance Sheet 1951/52*

3. *Thornett, Richard, 1940-2011 (Interviewee), (2008). 'Richard 'Dick' Thornett interviewed by Ian Warden for the Sport oral history project [sound recording].'Recorded on 9 August 2008, in Millthorpe, N.S.W. [Libraries Australia ID 45567317].*

4. *NSWAWPA, (1953). Annual Report & Balance Sheet 1952/53*

5. *NSWAWPA, (1954). Annual Report & Balance Sheet 1953/54*

6. *NSWAWPA, (1955). Annual Report & Balance Sheet 1954/55*

7. *NSWAWPA, (1956). Annual Report & Balance Sheet 1955/56*

8. *NSWAWPA, (1957). Annual Report & Balance Sheet 1956/57*

9. *NSWAWPA, (1958). Annual Report & Balance Sheet 1957/58*

Chapter 4

1. *NSWAWPA, (1959). Annual Report & Balance Sheet 1958/59.*

2. *NSWAWPA Annual Report & Balance Sheet 1959/60.*

3. *Woollahra Municipal Council, (2016). Harbour Baths [Local History Facts, B], Dictionary of Sydney, 2016, [https://www.woollahra.nsw.gov.au/library/local_history/local_history_fast_facts/b] ...viewed 09 Feb 2019.*

4. *Thornett, Richard, 1940-2011 (Interviewee), (2008). 'Richard 'Dick' Thornett interviewed by Ian Warden for the Sport oral history project [sound recording].'Recorded on 9 August 2008, in Millthorpe, N.S.W. [Libraries Australia ID 45567317].*

5. *Thornett, Richard, 1940-2011 (Interviewee), (1979). 'Dick Thornett interviewed by Neil Bennetts [sound recording].' Recorded on 12 December 1979, at the Dolphin Hotel, Surry Hills, N.S.W. [nla.obj-222768034].*

6. *Jacobsen, Patricia, Yarranabbe Park, Dictionary of Sydney, 2016, [http://dictionaryofsydney.org/entry/yarranabbe_park]...viewed 09 Feb 2019.*

7. *McLennan, Dunc (2013). Boomerang School [http://mydarlingdarlinghurst.blogspot.com/2013/02/across-border-kings-cross-retailers.html].*

8. *NSWAWPA Annual Report & Balance Sheet 1960/61.*

9. *NSWAWPA Annual Report & Balance Sheet 1961/62.*

10. *Thornett, John (undated) on Wikipedia. Available at https://en.wikipedia.org/wiki/John_Thornett*

11. *Thornett, Ken (undated) on Wikipedia. Available at https://en.wikipedia.org/wiki/Ken_Thornett*

12. *Thornett, Dick (undated) on Wikipedia. Available at https://en.wikipedia.org/wiki/Dick_Thornett.*

13. *Rockwell, Tracy (2009). Water Warriors: Chronicle of Australian Water Polo, Pegasus Publishing, Sydney.*

Chapter 5

1. *Thornett, Richard, 1940-2011 (Interviewee), (2008). 'Richard 'Dick' Thornett interviewed by Ian Warden for the Sport oral history project [sound recording].'Recorded on 9 August 2008, in Millthorpe, N.S.W. [Libraries Australia ID 45567317].*

2. *NSWAWPA (1963). Annual Report & Balance Sheet, 1962/63 Season.*

3. *Johnson, Peter (2020, June 25). In Wikipedia, The Free Encyclopedia. Retrieved 06:59, August 20, 2020, from https://en.wikipedia.org/w/index.php?title=Peter_Johnson_(rugby)&oldid=964372595.*

4. *NSWAWPA (1963). Official Opening of the Springwood Olympic Pool: Water Polo teams in for the Souvenir Program, 27th October 1963, Springwood, NSW.*

5. *NSW Amateur Water Polo Association (1964). Annual Report & Balance Sheet, 1963/64 Season.*

6. *NSW Amateur Water Polo Association (1965). Annual Report & Balance Sheet, 1964/65 Season.*

7. *NSW Amateur Water Polo Association (1966). Annual Report & Balance Sheet, 1965/66 Season.*

Chapter 6
1. *NSWAWPA (1967). Annual Report & Balance Sheet, 1966/67 Season.*

2. *NSWAWPA (1968). Annual Report & Balance Sheet, 1967/68 Season.*

3. *Rockwell, Tracy (2009). Water Warriors: Chronicle of Australian Water Polo, Pegasus Publishing, Sydney.*

4. *NSWAWPA (1969). Annual Report & Balance Sheet, 1968/69 Season.*

5. *McCarthy, Billy (Interviewee), (2020). Billy McCarthy phone interview by Tracy Rockwell for Water Polo Australia.' Transcribed on 30th September 2020, at Woollahra, N.S.W.*

6. *Samuel, Graeme (Interviewee), (2020). Graeme Samuel phone interview by Tracy Rockwell for Water Polo Australia.' Transcribed on 12th October 2020, at Woollahra, N.S.W.*

7. *NSWAWPA (1970). Annual Report & Balance Sheet, 1969/70 Season.*

8. *NSWAWPA (1971). Annual Report & Balance Sheet, 1970/71 Season.*

Caricature of Ken Mills (1966).

Chapter 7
1. *NSWAWPA (1964). Annual Report & Balance Sheet, 1963/64 Season.*

2. *NSWAWPA (1965). Annual Report & Balance Sheet, 1964/65 Season.*

3. *NSWAWPA (1966). Annual Report & Balance Sheet, 1965/66 Season.*

4. *NSWAWPA (1967). Annual Report & Balance Sheet, 1966/67 Season.*

5. *NSWAWPA (1968). Annual Report & Balance Sheet, 1967/68 Season.*

6. *NSWAWPA (1969). Annual Report & Balance Sheet, 1968/69 Season.*

7. *NSWAWPA (1970). Annual Report & Balance Sheet, 1969/70 Season.*

8. *NSWAWPA (1971). Annual Report & Balance Sheet, 1970/71 Season.*

9. *NSWAWPA (1972). Annual Report & Balance Sheet, 1971/72 Season.*

10. *NSWAWPA (1973). Annual Report & Balance Sheet, 1972/73 Season.*

11. *NSWAWPA (1974). Annual Report & Balance Sheet, 1973/74 Season.*

12. *NSWAWPA (1975). Annual Report & Balance Sheet, 1974/75 Season.*

13. *NSWAWPA (1976). Annual Report & Balance Sheet, 1975/76 Season.*

Chapter 8
1. *NSWAWPA (1972). Annual Report & Balance Sheet, 1971/72 Season.*

2. *NSWAWPA (1973). Annual Report & Balance Sheet, 1972/73 Season.*

3. *NSWAWPA (1974). Annual Report & Balance Sheet, 1973/74 Season.*

4. *NSWAWPA (1975). Annual Report & Balance Sheet, 1974/75 Season.*

5. *NSWAWPA (1976). Annual Report & Balance Sheet, 1975/76 Season.*

1943-1975

BRONTE

WATER POLO CLUB